FIVE TO FOUR

A Journey into the Dark Side of the Supreme Court of the United States

Clark Cumings Johnson

Library of Congress Control Number: 2016903791
Published by Clark Cumings Johnson, Birmingham, Michigan

ISBN-10: 0692649328
ISBN-13: 978-0692649329

PREFACE

his book differs from anything you have ever read about the nation and its Supreme Court. I do not write this book from or in promotion of any political or ideological position. I flatly deny having an agenda other than to allow you to enlighten yourself as to why the nation is the way it is today, and the role the Supreme Court has played. Reported opinions based on cases actually heard and ruled upon by the high Court are used as the underlying substance of this work, the exact words of that Court. It is the words of the Court, not mine, upon which I ask you to focus and form your own opinions. I write this book on a foundation and from a perspective of a practicing attorney and professor of law for over forty years while pondering this writing for the past ten, ultimately culminating in this confrontational product dealing with powerful institutions and bring to your attention the matters discussed herein for your thought. As a teacher, my motivation in writing this book is to offer you an opportunity to look into the arcane world of the law, the methodology of the Supreme Court, or more particularly, to present Supreme Court opinions which range from being inconsistent to incoherent and illogical to disingenuous for your review. This book is written for any member of the public, regardless of educational background. I invite you to come on this journey with me.

— Clark Cumings Johnson

TABLE OF CONTENTS

INTRODUCTION TO THE PREMISES

This will not be an easy voyage. Your travels will be fraught with frustration, even consternation, if not anger. This book does not concern itself with my words, which are only intended as a guide, a road map as it were, a light cast upon matters which might justify your attention. Rather, this book concerns itself with the words actually used by the Supreme Court of the United States (SCOTUS), and are presented for your edification and thought. Even if you decide to press on beyond the first several pages, I suspect the likelihood you will finish is probably a toss-up as the challenge will be great. Despite the burden, I assure you the rewards will be worth the effort. Yet added to that, you will have to go beyond these pages to gain a satisfactory understanding of the message intended to be conveyed. You have stepped into a realm where the work never ends. But for now, you will essentially be prodded through what is intended to be the underlying purpose of a legal education, something many lawyers didn't get, and some couldn't. True. You would be surprised. You've had your notice. Get ready and strap yourself in.

The task at hand is enormous. The trail ahead is long and the grade steep. And, it doesn't end here. This will be a lonely ride through a wilderness presenting to you a withering plethora of challenging new and different conceptualizations in an area of human experience called, the law. The "law." Seems simple enough, just a set of rules and regulations the violation of which can lead to some consequential outcomes, right? Actually that is not what "the law" is all about ("law" is more of a verb [loosely] than a noun in our studies here—you will get the idea). There are many lawyers and law students who never come to understand this. Professors? *Comme ci, comme ça.* Most have their own agenda, primarily endogenously driven. Many are spectacular.

Even well-educated and experienced lawyers find, as they should, the experience of reading an appellate court opinion for the first time challenging, in fact, downright work, often a struggle. It is. For students, it borders on the impossible, at least at the outset of their education, if they are getting one. Indeed, several readings will be the order of the day as one sees more and more each time plowing through an opinion. It is a very cerebral experience and a highly intellectual area of thought, formal thought if you are versed in cognitive function. Here you will have the opportunity to have a look into an arcane world few ever have a chance to see. Inadvertently, or advertently, it is kept under wraps, or so one might conclude, arguably simply a by-product of the architecture of the system. On the other hand, writers for public consumption consistently present pap, stories (sometimes with a grain of truth, often not), little snippets of "human interest," often dirt, typically with a mission, or motive, or bent, supposed little secrets of behind-the-scenes truck, substantively meaningless but great for the market, and soaked up by lesser minds, at base what writers think readers want to see. In effect, they are doing the thinking for you. They are telling you what they want you to be told. It's their story. Not here.

Here, it is different. Here you are asked to deal with primary sources upon which this work is based if you want to benefit from what is offered. Original sources are reprinted to provide backdrop for your observation. Others you will have to find online or in the library as referenced in the pages that follow. What is set forth will be sufficient to present the message this work intends to convey. As you proceed you will likely go outside these pages to see what was referenced and form your own conclusions as to why they were suggested, and to continue to do so in the future as new opinions are handed down. This is all about your thoughts, not mine, your thoughts as they are stimulated by the Court's opinions you are reading here. For you to think for a moment the materials are far too complicated, unreadable without long and exhaustive training, or being beyond your intellectual capabilities is utterly false. At first, it will be somewhat of a challenging experience, withering as said. And again, once we really get started many will drop by the wayside. It will not be fun. It is going to get worse. It is apt to begin as an oppressive burden, frustrating, even exasperating, up with which many will not be willing to put. But, I think you will experience some satisfaction as you get into it, and an improved comfort level will emerge for you. Here, someone else won't be doing the work for you as is the standard in the publishing world, the popular press, the best seller claptrap and fouter which requires nothing of you, in fact taking away all of your own independence, initiative, and intellectual integrity. Not here. You will have to strap it on and get ready for the long haul. This is an unusual book. You are going to teach yourself. If you make it, I will be at the same time surprised and elated.

This book is written for citizens of America regardless of background, as well as citizens of any representative Democracy charged with the duty of holding its system of justice, as well as its entire government, accountable to the people. The objective of the founders of this nation was that citizens have an understanding of their government and be able to participate in that government. The intent was that each and every citizen have not only access to its nation's laws but also to how and why they were established, along with their right of participation in their creation.

The approach taken in this book is essentially the presentation of two separate plays, two separate theaters, if you will, of the conduct and development of the United States Supreme Court, and the nation's citizens and their culture, each on their own stages yet inextricably joined in their influence upon one another, all the time leaving to the reader the effect, degree, and beneficence of the relationship. As everyone and every institution seems to have their agendas, we will go backstage (checking political correctness and sensitivities at the door) to observe the unfolding of this symbiotic drama. If at any time you feel "offended," it is time for you get out and spend your time on something else as you have simply missed the point of this exercise, as many will.

Perhaps you are wondering, why bother? Or, more directly, why should I even bother for that matter? I don't expect this writing will change much of anything, although I do harbor some hopes. On the other hand, if there was not so much as a chance, indeed I would not bother. There may be those who will get the idea, but enough to make a difference? Think about the starfish, one among millions washed up onto the shore and tossed back into the sea early one morning by an old fisherman trying to save his world. A passer-by stopped and said: "Old man, why did you bother to throw that starfish back into the sea? There are millions along this shore. You couldn't possibly be so foolish to think that will make any difference,?" Did it make a difference? There will be other questions as we proceed, and as we near the end, answers will emerge.

But what the hey, you have the first seven paragraphs under your belt. Why not try for another? If you made it this far, at least you've distinguished yourself as having joined a minority, and life is not easy for minorities, in this case readers, I mean real readers who from my observations often suffer because of the knowledge they have. Seems paradoxical, doesn't it? They spend much of their lives shaking their heads. Know, however, that for a true reader, this book is red meat. The cut? The very words of the Supreme Court itself. The significance? Virtually no one has read them outside of the arcane fraternity (and even most of them usually don't), and I assure you, you will find much of it painful. Have a nice day.

Ask yourself some questions: Why have our political leaders abandoned statesmanship for becoming purveyors of prevarication to gain and hold on to office? For most, that is their utmost task, is it not? Why? Why are their personal interests more important than those whom they serve, setting aside any notions of a fiduciary duty (yes, you'll need a good law lexicon on the table alongside this book to effectively read it). What happened to "country before self" in the halls of the uptrodden?

Now that the stage has been set, let me introduce you to the players: the Americans…, presumably you.

"Americans" are not, in the connotation, intent, or traditional usage of the term, a "people," a race, a strain, an ethnic stock, or any classification based on genetic markers, or any other some such politically incorrect classification, a concept totally eschewed from our discourse, silent or otherwise. In contrast, and for example, the Chinese are a "people," so too the Germans, the Athabaskans, Arabs, Greeks, and so on. You get the idea. Yet, all kinds of people (or "peoples") are or can be Americans.

Putting it another way, being an American has nothing to do with one's race or "nationality," but rather how we believe the business of life and government ought to be, one's political being, one's national ethos, and not just in terms of freedom and opportunity, but in terms of an overriding philosophy of social order, one's very being within and as a participating member of a collective national community. America was a nation founded upon a way of living and governing in a manner different from the shadows of history, essentially self-government controlled by citizens who ultimately are responsible for their individual and collective fate, as well as their success.

For these new Americans, it was to be by fraternity, imperfect as it may have been, but certainly perfect as intended as a conceptual beginning which was to be improved over time, the political architecture of which was built into the foundational documents. It was a new philosophy begotten of the Enlightenment, a new spirit among people, a constitutional orientation, if you will, establishing fundamental principles of law, the legislative and judicial progeny of which in turn over time was to be reviewed by a supreme court (the heart of what follows) for constitutional compatibility, a process which has re-cast the country into what it is today, including not just the electorate but its elected leaders, the theme and common strand herein. However, the Constitution, as initially charted and chronicled by numerous writings, began to take on a new life in the hands of the Court, the catalyst for this book.

It is not just the concern the American government, if not broken, is breaking up and failing to function in accordance with its principled architecture, but the fact that if you query virtually anyone about the state of the government you will be greeted with a blank stare, no understanding of the question let alone the problem, which is an even greater problem. Much of the citizenry does not have at the minimum a functional education, let alone formal education (degree or not) in the realms of cultural or political literacy. They are effectively a new species of farm animal living on a land of plenty, at least for now. The farm is evident. You live on it, too. The new species? Maybe not quite so much, at least for now.

So, once again, why bother? Likely few will understand, possibly even fewer will agree, and few will actually read this book despite what they say. Just watch. There will be those who try to turn this into a debate. The fact is the book is only an exercise focusing your attention on observable, objective original sources, among the simplest, least contaminated and most effective methods of science, the greatest engine of knowledge and understanding. The only substance put forth as significant will be the exact words of the United States Supreme Court. Those who wish to polemicize miss the point, as this is only a beginning for you. I wish not to be an influencing factor as to your own personal judgments. Suggesting things about which to think? Yes. To that end, I wish only to bring your attention to the arcane world of the third branch of government.

At this point, in this context, the question to be asked is who are the Americans, where are they, or better, what are they?

Is art not the window into the inner soul of culture? The theater, music, the stage, and literature, even television one would have to admit today. To call it burlesque would be a compliment. It is verily a window into the collective psyche—collective in the sense that both actors (performer doesn't seem to be quite the right word) and observers form the objective dyad of the present scene. One needs the other. No wonder Muslims are upset (*U.S. v. [Cassius] Clay* will offer a special treat for you, *infra*). Have you ever thought about this, at least in terms of our permanent assignment, the ever ubiquitous "why"? What is behind all of this? The Muslim radicals are the lunatics, right? Have you ever thought that Americans might be wise to at least observe their message in an attempt to understand where they are coming from? Probably not. Incomprehensible, right? Does anything in this book have to do with Muslims? Absolutely not, although the case could be an eye-opener for some. It is about how I want you to look at and think about things, in this case, the Supreme Court's opinions and the effects they have had on all of us, and hence the nation and its "leaders." I want you to look to see what is behind an opinion and its message, and then generalize that approach to other matters, other pronouncements, as when the Supreme Court (just to pick another hot topic) said abortion is now legal (or, more accurately, excessive restrictions on it are not) and then set out to define parameters (read legislate—constitutionally reserved for the first branch of government). What was the reaction of the populous? Polarization: it was right or it was wrong. That is typically the only focus, and that myopic debate continues to this day nearly half a century later. Does this book have anything to do with abortion, or whether it is right or wrong? Absolutely not, although what you read may also be an epiphany. But again, totally irrelevant here.

The Court said abortion was protected by the Bill of Rights, and if the Court says it is so protected, it is so protected per its powers which it has discovered far beyond its own opinion in the case of *Marbury v. Madison* mentioned *infra.* However, the only question we deal with here is why did the Court make this change to the legal landscape in the country? (Some argued that the landscape had already changed, and if that is true, why? Could it have been a product of previous Supreme Court cases?) Again, the point is not abortion, it is the maps the Court has used in its travels in fashioning opinions. This is not going to be easy. Keep an open mind. There are no hidden missions here, no ulterior agendas. This is not a political book. Politics are superficial. Politicians rarely if ever say anything of substance. It is the "politically" incorrect thing to do. This is an intellectual and analytical work, and I invite you to join in the journey. You should find it to be an exhilarating voyage no matter how you come out. I expect you will also find it to be exhausting. I accept that few will sign on. I will speculate the forests are safe.

II

GETTING STARTED

I have elected to present a series of United States Supreme Court reported opinions which will give you some idea about the nature of thinking of members on that Court. I say that knowing full well much of their thinking is not revealed, or is veiled, or tipped by makeweights (false, even fabricated assumptions), based on assumptions simply not supported by facts or other matters not even considered by the courts below, without any evidence supporting or truth in the decisional equation whatsoever, and even, on occasion, simply concocted to reach a result. Keep your eyes open. You will be able to see these things for yourself. In every case? Far from it. But, there are some surprises in store. The dissenting opinions will often tip you off. Many attorneys glance through them first, especially in SCOTUS cases.

I may make an occasional remark as a prelude to your reading a case in an effort to help draw into focus a matter for your attention, or perhaps to provoke thought. In the process, you will develop perspicacity to see what is actually going on behind the façade of the Court's words, its opinions, its only product (their effect will ultimately be what concerns us). But you are on your own. I wish to add nothing to what the Court has written, nor do I detract from it, nor do I wish to criticize any conclusions of the Court. It is rather the capricious and temperamental manner of reasoning and long-term fallout of the opinions which are brought to your attention. What has been selected are the exact words of the Court. I intend no influence whatsoever, and absolutely nothing personal. Guidance in terms of things you might think about, yes. But I want the cases to speak for themselves. *Res ipsa loquitur* (look it up—now is as good a time as any to reinforce the fact you will need a decent law dictionary—there are cell phone apps which are semi-decent and online lexicon resources—e.g., see footnote 1, page 24, *infra*—I will deal in more depth with the case citation system before the introduction of the first case). The further you push, the more you will not only learn, but you will develop adeptness at understanding the law, its workings, and its intellectual underside, what the "law" really is. You may even develop an appetite for the area. You might be surprised.

Along with these cases will be references to federal appellate court opinions or even state supreme court opinions from which they often have sprung, one of which has also been included here, and with some astonishing results. However, there is no agenda in their selection. As stated, we are to check our politics and sensitivities at the door. The purpose of bringing these cases to your attention is to give you the chance to see how the high court functions, both outwardly and coupled with your insight into its inner workings and psyche. You can do it. You may agree with the Court, or not. Your call. Sometimes a good result is turned right on its head. Sometimes it may look right on the mark. But rightness or wrongness, per se, is not our goal or our mission. Your task will be to determine how the Court ruled as it did, why, the effect of its opinion outside of the case at hand, and whether it should have even heard the matter in the first place. You might even get some answers to the questions posed earlier which were intentionally left open, as well as to those which follow, if you are diligent. In other words, the many "whys" you read earlier (without answers) were merely exercises in getting you ready for what now follows. They were not taunts.

But again, and most importantly, it is the consequences of the cases to which you need to be attuned. Look at the effect the work of this tribunal has had on the country, and on you. The "folks" never see it or think about it. Yet it is there and, for all practical purposes, is seemingly invisible. People are simply oblivious to the real effect the Court has had on their lives. From this arises the catalyst and single purpose of this book, to ask you take a look at and be willing to slog through a foreign land bearing an oppressive load of work and thought along the way. It is your task to think about what you are going to read, and you are the one to contemplate the long-term results, the effects of the Court's work beyond and apart from the Court's opinion on the matter at hand in any given case. Actually, you don't need me, or at least you will not after you get into it.

Just look around. It is all right there in front of you, some would say maybe too close to see, in the theaters, on television, in the literature, in schools and colleges. Sports events, up and down the streets, in your own home, the effects the Court has had upon your own family, on the souls and spirits of your own children, and the children of others, politics, on the sense of service, how we behave, our value sets, on and on *ad nauseam*. Ask yourself the question, were such matters ever taken into consideration at the time this grand legislature of one (in the crucible of a five-to-four opinion) handed down whatever the new "law" (or more accurately *dictum*) was to be? Is the Court truly a thoughtless lot, or does it simply not know what it has done or is doing beyond the politics of the question before it (a genuinely sad indictment if true)? I bend to no one, nor should you. We are citizens. In this country that carries not only rank but responsibility.

I want you to understand the legal world around you, and to have a fair chance to look into the realities of a branch of government which has been kept from you, not necessarily intentionally, but because of the very nature of the beast. Yes it is arcane. It is technical, unfortunately over-technical, it is cerebral, it is complex, but not beyond anyone's capacity who would like to know. The chances are the Justices have absolutely nothing over on you. You would be surprised how mundane, putting it charitably, are most judges and practitioners. And as you proceed, you will become more skilled, the materials will become more understandable and you will see unfold before you a whole new world. This will give you the chance to go over to the other side, but just for a look. Don't let Mephistopheles mislead you into selling your soul.

There will be those among the media who will say I have entered into some sort of premeditated selective process in an attempt to create this or that impression. To quote Alito, that is "not true." There are literally thousands of cases from which to choose; however, I am stuck with being able to offer only a relatively few for your consideration, and even at that, look at how much we will have before us. At the same time, these cases have their own references, as well as references within the references, to countless other cases totally open for your review for whatever purpose you wish or may choose to pursue. But many media types will surely hold forth when in fact most haven't done anything significant on their own. It's not that most are just pathetic fools, it's that they have an audience of pathetic fools ripe for being fooled. Most in the media are uneducated, inexperienced, unaccomplished ne'er-dowells who sit on the sidelines of life and whine, criticizing for the sake of attempting to make themselves, well, look good, look smarter, look powerful. There ought to be a law against it, but oh no, there isn't, they don't have to be correct; in fact, the law is they don't even have to tell the truth. We even have a case on that coming up, falsehoods about "public figures" being protected by the First Amendment. One might think they should have some fiduciary duty of honesty to the public when exercising constitutionally protected free speech. Might one not just assume this is implied in terms of due process, or as Judge Cardozo said referring to fiduciary (acting in the interests of others) duties, "not just honesty alone, but a punctilio of an honor the most sensitive"? (see *Meinhard v. Salmon*, 249 N.Y. 458 [1928]—a case well worth your time reading). It's amazing, the courts and Congress won't let so much as a gram of date-expired food from ever being sold to you under penalty of law, or to allow someone to tear a tag off a mattress, but your minds, and spirits, your very beings, oh no, shove it in. This is a Right we all have. You don't believe me? That's okay. Read on. Let's see what's out there. You are making the judgments. Just remember, be sure to put on your rubbers, unless of course you live in Connecticut (You will understand later).

BIBLIOGRAPHIC METHODOLOGY

point of housekeeping: the cases set out here, known as opinions, are written by appellate courts (we are primarily concerned with SCOTUS cases), and have an identification system which is very simple (as in *Meinhard v. Salmon, supra*). The identifying symbol for the Supreme Court is simply "U.S." or, for example, 381 U.S. 479, which means the 381st volume of the United States Supreme Court's reported opinions with the case in question starting on page 479. This is the "official" citation system for the Supreme Court and best for our purposes here. Other examples will follow. Anyone without legal training, which you are about to acquire, would see this "citation" as being nothing but some numbers and letters. For those with legal training, it would be immediately recognized as a legal citation referring to an opinion handed down by the United States Supreme Court. Among them a few, a very few in fact, would recognize this as the citation to the "landmark" opinion of *Griswold v. Connecticut.*

QUICK NOTES ON SUPREME COURT CASES AS BACKGROUND

Followed by Cassius Clay v. United States

arbury v. Madison, 5 U.S. 137 (1803), was the United States Supreme Court opinion that became the bedrock of what we now know as the power of "judicial review," (or putting it operationally, what does and does not comport with the standards and requirements of the United States Constitution) To put it more directly, the Court took it unto itself in its own interpretation of the Constitution to declare its power to pass on the issue of the constitutionality of an Act of Congress thereby establishing its power of judicial review as itself a constitutional matter. (*Marbury,* and the following note cases, you may wish to read at some future point. It has had lasting impact on every branch of government, at every level, to put it in the mildest of terms, as have the others. For purposes of this exercise, it is not presently necessary as stated principles are sufficient for our purposes here despite being painted with a broad brush.) Noteworthy at this stage, however, is nowhere in that opinion (*Marbury*) did the Court even hint it had legislative powers of any kind, a power which it has exercised time and again since then, and at an accelerating rate, corrupting what had thought to have been the genius of the drafters of the Constitution in its separation of powers architecture.

McCulloch v. Maryland, 17 U.S. 316 (1819), solidified the constitutional supremacy of the federal government over the governments of the states.

Johnson v. M'Intosh, 21 U.S. 543 (1823), is a case worth reading as soon as you are able. It is not included in this book, but is readily available on the internet, at any adequate public or college library, or in any Bar Association, law school, or state library, or at your local courthouse. To read a condensed or "digested" version of it is wholly inadequate. It is a demonstration of the Court stringing out a series of repetitive justifications, rationalizations, and repeated explanations, pitiful actually, none of which make much sense, none of which are particularly relevant to the issue with which the Court was dealing, the Court simply not being able to bring itself to candidly say what had happened to the native "American Indian" and his "land" following the arrival of the European "settlers." In fact, the underlying events were simply acquisition of title to lands by conquest, an event which has played itself out over and over again during the history of mankind. Quite sad, both the events and the opinion. It is not a piece of Marshall's better work (or maybe it is). Its relevancy here is to offer an example of a Supreme Court opinion which many would say simply isn't candid, to put it in the most charitable of terms, with frank disingenuousness being closer to the mark. You need to know the Court has a history of saying what isn't and failing to say what is, at least on occasion, and continues to do so today. Keep your eyes open to the materials which will unfold before you.

Plessy v. Ferguson, 163 U.S. 537 (1896), is a Supreme Court case holding that separate but equal facilities for use by the black and white populations of the country did not offend constitutional principles (despite the fact that both sides of the argument likely knew better). Of course, the purpose of state policies of providing separate and supposedly equal facilities to be used by black and white citizens was to promote and maintain segregation. Life simply tended to be accepted as it was, because, well, that is just the way it was at that time. Few of privilege objected, and those who did…you can probably guess the result. The time had not yet come. For our purposes, the case is not only a good read, but when read along *Brown v. Board of Education*, 347 U.S. 483 (1954), *infra*, the reader here will have a chance to see the Court making an about-face and ultimately doing what even the most pedestrian reading of the Constitution would seem to require (but not so seen at the time).

Lochner v. New York, 198 U.S. 45 (1905), is a case which was later discredited and abandoned as viable precedent, but then began insidiously finding its way back into the Court's "jurisprudence" in later cases such as *Griswold v. Connecticut*, 381 U.S. 479 (1965), one could argue (an opinion previously mentioned and set forth hereinafter). It dealt with a state statute which purported to regulate the maximum hours of employment a laborer could work on a given day or in a given week. The Court found it to be unconstitutional as a state legislative invasion into, *inter alia*, the realm of freedom of contract between individuals (here employer and employee), and being an unwise piece of legislation from the economic perspective. Or, to put it possibly in a more candid light, the Court felt its view of sound economic and social policy was better than that espoused by the state legislature in question without any consideration whatsoever, at least by the majority, regarding the health and welfare of the workers affected (an issue clearly understood to be a state matter under the universally accepted concept of state control over the health, welfare, and morals of the people—or at least that is what we thought). Curiously, the same Court just seven years earlier had ruled in *Plessy* (a case you will never forget after you read it) that it couldn't intervene on any grounds, contrived, constitutional or otherwise, in relation to a state statute which required intra-state railways in Louisiana to provide separate (read separated) seating for whites and blacks, no matter who they were or from where they came, as being an exclusively state matter.

Brown v. Board of Education, 347 U.S. 483 (1954), reversed *Plessy*, becoming the leading school desegregation case in the country, shortly followed by *Brown v. Board of Education*, 349 U.S. 294 (1955), sometimes referred to as "Brown II," which was in effect a piece of vast judicial legislation setting forth the rules and architecture of a school desegregation plan (judicial legislation, although clearly extra-constitutional in nature, yet Congress was not acting, nor were the state legislatures, and something needed to be done). Such *dicta* should not have the force of law, at least according to the stricter of constitutionalists, but does have its validating arguments both ways, a matter we will visit later on, indeed a point raised in the cumulative portions of this work.

Griswold v. Connecticut, 381 U.S. 479 (1965), the case in which the Court (or more accurately, one of the Justices) found a "Right to Privacy" lurking in the shadows (penumbra[1]) of several of the Bill of Rights (being the first ten [some say eight] Amendments to the

---

[1] **Penumbra** – used in legal sense as a metaphor describing implied powers of the federal government or the rights guaranteed by implication in the Constitution. Penumbra doctrine has been used to represent implied powers that arise from a specific rule, and extending the meaning of the rule into its periphery or penumbra. For example, privacy rights without government intervention implied by the First Amendment of the U.S. Constitution (see full history and definition at: http://legal-dictionary.thefreedictionary.com/ penumbra).

United States Constitution found in Appendix II—presumably which you have already read, and if you haven't, do so as it will only take a few minutes and will assist you in these proceedings). This case may not have been a watershed opinion or the fountainhead of the concept, right to privacy, but it did make clear the point the Court had unequivocally arrived at and adopted the conclusion that this concept was now a part of the judicial development of United States Constitutional Law from which has since flowed much "court made law."

One might conclude it is somewhat of a curious opinion when examining it within its own penumbra (you will "get" this later), as it were, and of greater interest is the idea the case may have been accepted for review by the Court with an eye toward doing exactly what a majority of the Court ended up doing, *videlicet*, seeing it as a perfect case and opportunity to do what commentators suggested and the Court arguably did, *sub silentio*, well before the case in fact reached the Court, despite the fact you might think the scrivener went a little wild. Put more plainly, the case could have been decided before the file from the court below even arrived in Washington. Is this not the tripe of town councils vis-à-vis the petitions of its residents? But the Court certainly doesn't do anything of that sort, does it? The Court never makes up its mind before the record is complete and all the arguments and briefs are in, right? The Court doesn't grant *certiorari* (look that up, too) having already made up its mind, or some members having made up their minds, or at least having some preconceived notions of what it is they are going to do once the record formally reaches its offices, does it? But doesn't it have to be true that in cases of *certiorari,* the Court has to know something about the case in order to exercise its discretion as to whether or not to take it up (apart from conflicting decisions between Circuits), and therefore in the exercise of that discretion it has to have an eye toward some purpose particularly in its act of granting *cert.* On the other hand, how could it be any other way in such cases?

Let us prognosticate for a moment: there are likely to be commentators who will say, "Ah ha, there is an agenda with and a mission to promote this or that, liberal versus conservative, or vice versa, and so on and on...." Well, my apologies to the jack-jaws. This case, among several, is suited to begin with in the early stages here because, 1) it is interesting, and 2) if you get started reading it, you will probably finish it, and if you finish it, then 3) you will likely finish the rest of them as they become even more interesting as we progress. If you do get through it, you are assuredly on your way. It will be worth it, I promise.

*

Choosing a limited number of cases because of space issues has been an aggravating task. As alluded to earlier, not everyone would agree with the examples presented as being the best choices for our purposes, and others may well say there are better cases which should have been included. I take issue with neither view. But the *Griswold* case, set out, *infra,* is interesting and *inter alia,* has dramatically contributed to a change in the social, political, and moral landscape of the country on matters ranging far from its subject of contraception, and that's the point. This will become manifest as we proceed. For our purposes, for now however, the case has nothing to do with contraception in Connecticut. It is the process of analysis, the Court's "findings" used in its rationale and logic to justify its conclusions and holding (another legal term which you should look up) with which we are interested, not the subject matter per se, which again is our stance throughout this work. We will not look at the cases from the perspective of right or wrong. Your thoughts on the factual backdrop of any case, its correctness, and related issues are up to you. But for this work, they are irrelevant. I encourage that not be the focus of your attention. Get used to it. We want to observe analysis, methodology, and effect. It is what has happened in the wake of *Griswold* that is our concern, its tangential influences. It isn't easy. You have been "trained" to do just the opposite, learning what you are told, essentially blind acceptance, and focusing on whatever is the issue at hand. In time you may come to understand what the word "law" really means. It is possible. Not everyone gets there. If you follow me, you will. If you finish, you will see why this is important.

Another example is *Roe v. Wade*, 410 U.S. 113 (1973), also included, *infra*, which the media told you legalized abortion, which it didn't, at least in the direct and lawful sense, but bolstered by *dicta* it did in result. It found a Texas statute restricting abortion "unconstitutional" as being overly restrictive in violation of the due process clause or otherwise denying due process as a constitutional matter with issues of privacy, *inter alia,* woven in. Any awkward attempt by the Court gratuitously saying what is legal, and it did, far outside its jurisdiction of judicial review, is only *dicta* (not law), itself being constitutionally infirm and should have no force and effect, at least in theory (it provides only guidance some academics say—but as indicated, more on that later—here that issue is too early).

As a result of *Roe* and its progeny, anyone running for virtually any office is saddled with the perennial question, "Where do *you* stand on abortion?" as being the qualifying factor as to whether or not someone is fit or should hold that office, and often, nothing else. No wonder we are where we are. Single-issue voters fostered by an agenda-driven media all made possible and brought to you by a short-sighted Court in the crafting of non-circumspect opinions (notice the plural form—it will take on meaning as we proceed). We have among such eligible voters, possibly ten million, most likely many more. How did that become such a defining factor in our culture and a political test for qualification? What effect does that have on good government? Think about it. Our work here is not about whether you are for or against it, or whether it is good or bad. Let the lessers wrangle over such issues. I have nothing to say about it. It is not relevant to our work here, but how is it that one issue has come to be the dominant if not the only disqualifying or qualifying standard for so many, if you consider the term "voting" in the full connotation of its meaning. Is there not something jurisprudentially significant here? Was this the foreseen intent of the Court which wrote that opinion? Or did it just stumble its way into this bramble bush even now continuing to struggle with its progeny of countless opinions following it, and surely more yet to come? Did it exercise some sense, or lack of sense, to take on the issue as a constitutional matter, then attempt to legislate upon it, or was its effect and consequences totally unforeseen (which some would say is even more frightening)? Forget about what happened in that case and its effect on its parties. (Ms. Roe's real name was not used in an effort to shield her from aggravation—later it being revealed she wished she had not had the abortion let alone bring the case—which now falls into the realm of common knowledge along with her name—all of which is irrelevant here, but interesting history.) Rather, we are here concerned with the workings of the Court, the logic and justifications it claims to use in crafting an opinion tantamount to legislation, along with the effect this and other cases have had on the nation, its penumbral effects, as it were. That's what this is about. No issue is taken with the outcome of any case or its merits. We are here to look at opinions, using them as an optic into the workings of the Court, its dark side which the public doesn't see as conspicuous as it might be, and to have a chance to think about the effect of the Court's work on the people it is supposed to serve. You will see. You don't need to accept what someone else says, someone else's spin. What you should consider is placed before you. In a sense, you are a modern-day intellectual anthropological archeologist digging through the wreckage and ruins of partisan litigation (and likely to become more so), detritus of social wars as it were, and it is, all flowing from that august body we call the United States Supreme Court.

Then will come *Stenberg v. Carhart,* 530 U.S. 914 (2000), and other jurisprudential progeny (with a string of citations to other cases) affording a general look around the legal landscape. The variety will be evident, as well as their roots, one leading to another. Numerous citation trails will be marked out for you to follow if you wish, here and in other cases themselves. But you need not tarry over this collection. There are other cases dealing with just as fascinating subjects beyond those presented, waiting to be read by you and others in the public (as unlikely as that may be, I feel obligated to initiate the process somewhere), and from which you may continue to form your own opinions and conclusions as jurisprudence evolves. This is at least a start. When going on stage one often doesn't know what works. Sometimes you are surprised what didn't, even disappointed, and sometimes even more surprised as to what did, often unintended! Few perform. But because of those who do, a light is held high so others may have a chance to see what they otherwise might not. Some are called school teachers. All I want you to do is take a look. I may wish I had included other cases or not included something here. Conceivably *Roe* is such a case. We will just have to wait and see. It is explosive and provides a high perch for attacks from many directions. But that's okay. We all enjoy the benefits of the Bill of Rights, don't we (particularly the first Amendment referred to earlier and contained herein—again, be sure to read all of them, and re-read them as we proceed)? This is something which was tested on the eighth grade graduation exam from an earlier time. The education system no longer teaches the substance of these matters. I wonder why?

The People of the United States v. Cassius Clay, reported as *Clay, aka Ali v. United States*, 403 U.S. 698 (1971), (now known to us as Muhammad Ali) will take us on a terpsichorean interlude with the Supreme Court and into the land of the *jihad*, the *Koran*, and why one who was most willing to fight for his own lucre was not willing (required) to fight for his country. That was only some forty plus years ago, and many of you may remember and even be able to add to what was said when we get there. As is standard for the press, none of them got it right and, as with the media in general, nothing of substance in the opinion made it to the light of day, not to mention the public. It was just another field day of attention-getting contrivances all cast in the name of media hype and marketeers. America was just as unenlightened the day after the opinion was handed down as it was the day before, arguably less so, if you get my drift, particularly as it relates to Muslimism and its future here. It's coming, and you should be asking yourself the question, why are not "American Muslims" vocally and publicly objecting to its warring factions? Why? There is an answer.

At the very best, little attention was ever paid to the opinion itself (nothing new). It was widely reported at the time that Muhammad Ali won his claim to "conscientious objector" status relative to his draft into military service, but that is not what happened in SCOTUS. The high court simply reversed on technical grounds the court below which had denied to him that status, despite the fact a specially constituted board of expert members had recommended it be granted to him, nothing more. Put more directly, no court, ever, ruled in Ali's favor on the merits of his claim and case. If Ali could be said to have won, it was only on procedural grounds (something discussed, *infra*) and not on the merits, as it were, but that's not what you were told, and hence one of the reasons for this work encouraging you to read the Court's opinions for yourself and not rely on the take of others, who always have a bent, or more frankly simply don't understand, scripted or not, tripe at best.

And now, stage right, put up your dukes, *Cassius Clay*.

V

CLAY, aka ALI v. UNITED STATES

403 U.S. 698

Certiorari to the United States Court of Appeals for the Fifth Circuit

Per Curiam.

The petitioner was convicted for willful refusal to submit to induction into the Armed Forces. [Citations generally omitted throughout.] [When a citation within a case is used, it is a suggestion to read the case cited.] The judgment of conviction was affirmed by the Court of Appeals for the Fifth Circuit. We granted certiorari, 400 U.S. 990, to consider whether the induction notice was invalid because grounded upon an erroneous denial of the petitioner's claim to be classified as a conscientious objector.

I

The petitioner's application for classification as a conscientious objector was turned down by his local draft board, and he took an administrative appeal. The State Appeal Board tentatively classified him I-A (eligible for unrestricted military service) and referred his file to the Department of Justice for an advisory recommendation.... The FBI then conducted an "inquiry" as required by the statute, interviewing some 35 persons, including members of the petitioner's family and many of his friends, neighbors, and business and religious associates.

There followed a hearing on "the character and good faith of the [petitioner's] objections" before a hearing officer appointed by the Department. The hearing officer, a retired judge of many years' experience, heard testimony from the petitioner's mother and father, from one of his attorneys, from a minister of his religion, and from the petitioner himself. He also had the benefit of a full report from the FBI. On the basis of this record the hearing officer concluded that the registrant was sincere in his objection on religious grounds to participation in war in any form, and he recommended that the conscientious objector claim be sustained.

Notwithstanding this recommendation, the Department of Justice wrote a letter to the Appeal Board, advising it that the petitioner's conscientious objector claim should be denied. Upon receipt of this letter of advice, the Board denied the petitioner's claim without a statement of reasons. After various further proceedings which it is not necessary to recount here, the petitioner was ordered to report for induction. He refused to take the traditional step forward, and this prosecution and conviction followed.

II

In order to qualify for classification as a conscientious objector, a registrant must satisfy three basic tests. He must show that he is conscientiously opposed to war in any form. He must show that this opposition is based upon religious training and belief, as the term has been construed in our decisions. And he must show that this objection is sincere. In applying these tests, the Selective Service System must be concerned with the registrant as an individual, not with its own interpretation of the dogma of the religious sect, if any, to which he may belong.

In asking us to affirm the judgment of conviction, the Government argues that there was a "basis in fact," for holding that the petitioner is not opposed to "war in any form," but is only selectively opposed to certain wars. Counsel for the petitioner, needless to say, takes the opposite position.... [W]e have concluded that even if the Government's position on this question is correct, the conviction before us must still be set aside for another quite independent reason.

III

The petitioner's criminal conviction stemmed from the Selective Service System's denial of his appeal seeking conscientious objector status. That denial, for which no reasons were ever given, was, as we have said, based on a recommendation of the Department of Justice, over-ruling its hearing officer and advising the Appeal Board that it "finds that the registrant's conscientious-objector claim is not sustained and recommends to your Board that he be not [so] classified." This finding was contained in a long letter of explanation, from which it is evident that Selective Service officials were led to believe that the Department had found that the petitioner had failed to satisfy each of the three basic tests for qualification as a conscientious objector.

As to the requirement that a registrant must be opposed to war in any form, the Department letter said that the petitioner's expressed beliefs "do not appear to preclude military service in any form, but rather are limited to military service in the Armed Forces of the United States. . . . These constitute only objections to certain types of war in certain circumstances, rather than a general scruple against participation in war in any form. However, only a general scruple against participation in war in any form can support an exemption as a conscientious objector under the Act...."

As to the requirement that a registrant's opposition must be based upon religious training and belief, the Department letter said: "It seems clear that the teachings of the Nation of Islam preclude fighting for the United States not because of objections to participation in war in any form but rather because of political and racial objections to policies of the United States as interpreted by Elijah Muhammad.... It is therefore our conclusion that registrant's claimed objections to participation in war insofar as they are based upon the teachings of the Nation of Islam, rest on grounds which primarily are political and racial."

As to the requirement that a registrant's opposition to war must be sincere, that part of the letter began by stating that "the registrant has not consistently manifested his conscientious-objector claim. Such a course of overt manifestations is requisite to establishing a subjective state of mind and belief." There followed several paragraphs reciting the timing and circumstances of the petitioner's conscientious objector claim, and a concluding paragraph seeming to state a rule of law – that "a registrant has not shown overt manifestations sufficient to establish his subjective belief where, as here, his conscientious-objector claim was not asserted until military service became imminent."

In this Court the Government has now fully conceded that the petitioner's beliefs *are* based upon "religious training and belief.... There is no dispute that petitioner's professed beliefs were founded on basic tenets of the Muslim religion, as he understood them, and derived in substantial part from his devotion to Allah as the Supreme Being. Thus, under this Court's decision in *United States v. Seeger*, 380 U.S. 163, his claim unquestionably was within the 'religious training and belief' clause of the exemption provision." This concession is clearly correct. For the record shows that the petitioner's beliefs are founded on tenets of the Muslim religion as he understands them. They are surely no less religiously based than those of the three registrants before this Court in *Seeger*.

The Government in this Court has also made clear that it no longer questions the sincerity of the petitioner's beliefs. This concession is also correct. The Department hearing officer – the only person at the administrative appeal level who carefully examined the petitioner and other witnesses in person and who had the benefit of the full FBI file – found "that the registrant is sincere in his objection." The Department of Justice was wrong in advising the Board in terms of a purported rule of law that it should disregard this finding simply because of the circumstances and timing of the petitioner's claim.

Since the Appeal Board gave no reasons for its denial of the petitioner's claim, there is absolutely no way of knowing upon which of the three grounds offered in the Department's letter it relied. Yet the Government now acknowledges that two of those grounds were not valid. And, the Government's concession aside, it is indisputably clear, for the reasons stated, that the Department was simply wrong as a matter of law in advising that the petitioner's beliefs were not religiously based and were not sincerely held.

This case, therefore, falls squarely within the four corners of this Court's decision in *Sicurella v. United States*, 348 U.S. 385. There as here the Court was asked to hold that an error in an advice letter prepared by the Department of Justice did not require reversal of a criminal conviction because there was a ground on which the Appeal Board might properly have denied a conscientious objector classification. This Court refused to consider the proffered alternative ground:

> "[W]e feel that this error of law by the Department, to which the Appeal Board might naturally look for guidance on such questions, must vitiate the entire proceedings at least where it is not clear that the Board relied on some legitimate ground. Here, where it is impossible to determine on exactly which grounds the Appeal Board decided, the integrity of the Selective Service System demands, at least, that the Government not recommend illegal grounds. There is an impressive body of lower court cases taking this position and we believe that they state the correct rule."

The doctrine thus articulated 16 years ago in *Sicurella* was hardly new. It was long ago established as essential to the administration of criminal justice. *Stromberg v. California*, 283 U.S. 359. In *Stromberg* the Court reversed a conviction for violation of a California statute containing three separate clauses, finding one of the three clauses constitutionally invalid. As Chief Justice Hughes put the matter, "[I]t is impossible to say under which clause of the statute the conviction was obtained." Thus, "if any of the clauses in question is invalid under the Federal Constitution, the conviction cannot be upheld."

* * *

The long established rule of law...clearly requires that the judgment before us be reversed.

It is so ordered.

Mr. Justice Marshall took no part in the consideration or decision of this case.

Mr. Justice Douglas, concurring.

I would reverse this judgment of conviction and set the petitioner free.

In *Sicurella v. United States*, 348 U.S. 385, the wars that the applicant would fight were not "carnal" but those "in defense of Kingdom interests." Since it was impossible to determine on exactly which grounds the Appeal Board had based its decision, we reversed the decision sustaining the judgment of conviction. We said: "It is difficult for us to believe that the Congress had in mind this type of activity when it said the thrust of conscientious objection must go to 'participation in war in any form.'"

In the present case there is no line between "carnal" war and "spiritual" or symbolic wars. Those who know the history of the

Mediterranean littoral know that the *jihad* of the Moslem was a bloody war.

* * *

While there are some bits of evidence showing conscientious objection to the Vietnam conflict, the basic objection was based on the teachings of his religion. He testified that he was:

> "sincere in every bit of what the Holy Qur'an and the teachings of the Honorable Elijah Muhammad tell us and it is that we are not to participate in wars on the side of nobody who – on the side of non-believers, and this is a Christian country and this is not a Muslim country, and the Government and the history and the facts shows that every move toward the Honorable Elijah Muhammad is made to distort and is made to ridicule him and is made to condemn him and the Government has admitted that the police of Los Angeles were wrong about attacking and killing our brothers and sisters and they were wrong in Newark, New Jersey, and they were wrong in Louisiana, and the outright, every day oppressors and enemies are the people as a whole, the whites of this nation. So, we are not, according to the Holy Qur'an, to even as much as aid in passing a cup of water to the – even a wounded. I mean, this is in the Holy Qur'an, and as I said earlier, this is not me talking to get the draft board – or to dodge nothing. This is there before I was borned and it will be there when I'm dead but we believe in not only that part of it, but all of it."

At another point he testified: "[T]he Holy Qur'an do teach us that we do not take part of – in any part of war unless declared by Allah himself, or unless it's an Islamic World War, or a Holy War, and it goes as far – the Holy Qur'an is talking still, and saying we are not to even as much as aid the infidels or the nonbelievers in Islam, even to as much as handing them a cup of water during battle."

"So, this is the teachings of the Holy Qur'an before I was born, and the Qur'an, we follow not only that part of it, but every part."

The Koran defines *jihad* as an injunction to the believers to war against nonbelievers:[1] [footnote number as used in opinion]

> "O ye who believe! Shall I guide you to a gainful trade which will save you from painful punishment? Believe in Allah and His Apostle and carry on warfare (*jihad*) in the path of Allah with your possessions and your persons. That is better for you. If ye have knowledge, He will forgive your sins, and will place you in the Gardens beneath which the streams flow, and in fine houses in the Gardens of Eden: that is the great gain."

The Sale edition of the Koran, which first appeared in England in 1734, gives the following translation...:

> "Thus God propoundeth unto men their examples. When ye encounter the unbelievers, strike off their heads, until ye have made a great slaughter among them; and bind them in bonds; and either give them a free dismission afterwards, or exact a ransom; until the war shall have laid down its arms. This shall ye do. Verily if God pleased he could take vengeance on them, without your assistance; but he commandeth you to fight his battles, that he may prove the one of you by the other. And as to those who fight in defence of God's true religion, God will

---

[1] Koran 61:10-13.

"War, then, is here an integral part of the legal system; for in accordance with the doctrine of the *jihad*, which is recognized as 'the peak of religion,' the Islamic commonwealth must be expanding relentlessly, like a caravan continuously on the move, until it becomes coterminous with humanity, at which time war will have been transposed into universal peace." [This footnote and its number are reproduced as they appear in the official opinion.]

not suffer their works to perish: he will guide them and will dispose their heart aright; and he will lead them into paradise, of which he hath told them. O true believers, if ye assist God, by fighting for his religion, he will assist you against your enemies; and will set your feet fast...."

* * *

What Clay's testimony adds up to is that he believes only in war as sanctioned by the Koran, that is to say, a religious war against nonbelievers. All other wars are unjust.

That is a matter of belief, of conscience, or religious principle. Clay..."by reason of religious training and belief" [was] conscientiously opposed to participation in war of the character proscribed by their respective religions. That belief is a matter of conscience protected by the First Amendment which Congress has no power to qualify or dilute as it did in § 6(j) of the Military Selective Service Act of 1967, when it restricted the exemption to those "conscientiously opposed to participation in war in any form." ...Clay [is] in a class honored by the First Amendment, even though those schooled in a different conception of "just" wars may find it quite irrational.

I would reverse the judgment below.

Mr. Justice Harlan, concurring in the result.

I concur in the result on the following ground. The Department of Justice advice letter was at least susceptible of the reading that petitioner's proof of sincerity was insufficient as a matter of law because his conscientious objector claim had not been timely asserted. This would have been erroneous advice had the Department's letter been so read. Since the Appeals Board might have acted on such an interpretation of the letter, reversal is required.

*

Good Morning, America! A new dawn is breaking....

VI

GRISWOLD V. CONNECTICUT

riswold, the next case-in-chief, *infra*, as previously noted, may not be the fountainhead conceptually of the "Right to Privacy" as a constitutionally protected matter. However, it "officially" recognized a new constitutional concept, or certainly solidified it, at least by a "majority" of the Court, in principle if not on grounds. What this case does, *inter alia*, is to set up for all to see (and virtually no one reads these opinions outside of the legal community, and few do even among those within it) how embattled this issue is, a theme which will repeat itself over and over again in later cases, along with the internecine Rolfing of the Court as it wanes and waxes from bench to bench. It will be obvious, and you are apt to be disgusted not with the subject matter of the case(s) (meaningless for us here and never our concern, "silly" according to one justice), but rather the Court's behavior, manner of approach, and analysis. And it sets up for us the opportunity to observe one of the great, if not the greatest, and perennial philosophical divides of the Court often bitterly fought and sometimes cast in terms of the most disparaging and un-courtly kind when taking into account the arcane language of judicial diplomacy otherwise more typically used among the justices in more temperate times.

Douglas wrote the opinion for the Court, such an assignment being one of the responsibilities of the Chief Justice, an opinion in which not one Justice unequivocally joined, but with which a majority did concur in separate opinions, at least with the result, which essentially was, yes Virginia, there really is a "Right to Privacy" guaranteed and protected by the Constitution (where in the Constitution is another matter). As for a general right to privacy apart from an express provision protecting privacy in the Constitution such as the Fourth Amendment (found in Appendix II—re-read it now), the majority of Justices indeed found such a general right but couldn't agree where it was in the document. It was there all right, but where?! For Douglas, that was easy: it's right there in the penumbra (you know, that shadow around a beam of light shining on something, the recesses of the illumination, the luminescent halo that eventually fades out) of the several guaranteed rights along with other express provisions in the Bill of Rights, indeed rights peripheral to those rights specifically granted in those honored and very celebrated Amendments, being "emanations" from those (and other) guarantees which give them life and substance (heavily paraphrased).

I suppose if you are looking for something hard to find, and it is somewhere, you look in the penumbra. And, if you really want to find it, and look hard enough, it will be there, right before your squinting eyes. It isn't going to be in the bright light, of course, as you wouldn't have to be looking for it there, it would be evident, nor would you be able to find it in the dark, so…look in the penumbra. No telling what you will find. I think we are on to something even at the early stage of your education (you will see what I mean later). After *Griswold*'s constitutional machinations (or its attempt to re-write it according to some thought, or amend it without amending it [the Constitution provides for its own amending]), we will read cases on pornography and abortion, for more openers. But don't forget, it's not the subject matter with which we are concerned. We are merely going to witness what the Court is doing, and its effects. I know it is not easy as we are always tempted to get involved in the subject matter of the case at hand. We find it difficult to avoid arguing the merits of the case, its facts, the outcome, who "won," (if there is such a thing in the practice of law) which is the natural temptation. At the same time, we want to think about how a previous case may have influenced a subsequent case dealing with an entirely different subject matter, and the consistency, or lack of consistency the Court manifests in the justifications set forth in its opinions.

Once again, my words are but a suggested guide. There is no mission. There is no crusade. Let the cases speak for themselves. Let the cases speak to you. You decide for yourself what is happening. Most cherish privacy and think it ought to be protected. And, most think the government ought to leave us alone unless we give just cause otherwise, under due process of law, of course. I wish only to alert you to that which you may find informative and interesting.

Again, dissenting opinions are important, in every case. Often they are a prelude to the future. Sometimes not. However, they are typically candid. Politics typically become more evident. Philosophies are brought into contrast. At the same time, both the majority and dissenting opinions set out citations to other cases typically cited for reasons of support, precedent, example, or comparison. They, along with those noted in the text, will lead you on a trail through what has been called the "bramble bush" of the law, giving you access to other relevant and more extensive materials, taking you as far as you might wish to go. This is supposed to be what happens in law school. It is called a legal education. There is no other way to adequately accomplish the mission. And although what is presented here is but a few chips on an enormous mosaic, it is a start. Again, there may be better cases for our purposes, you may find them, and maybe there should be more. Hopefully, others will contribute their thinking and suggestions.

This is going to be a memorable ride, a great adventure. *Clay* was only an appetizer.

Keep in mind that sometimes a word may appear to be nothing but a pedestrian term from the English language. Be careful. Sometimes such words are actually terms of legal art with very technical professional meaning. If you have any doubt as to the meaning of a word in the legal context, that is it may be a common and facially recognizable term, but in the legal context it seems to be unusual, like "standing," look it up in your legal lexicon. There will be times the need is obvious, but not always. Be careful. Be thorough.

At this point I will leave you alone, commenting only, hopefully cogently, as you and the Supreme Court waltz for the next several days. This will be an experience of primarily the Court speaking to you. I'll try to shine a light around for you to see things which could get by, trying to highlight and interweave, as it were, but not to influence. We'll see how it goes. It will be the Court's own words comprising the message. I think you will like it. This can be drudgery, but give it a chance. You will come out the other end a different person.

So, let us continue with a case which highlights as well as any other the "Great Divide" on the Court, the philosophical schism in the realm of sociological jurisprudence which has plagued the Court for decades being nearly wholly unable to find any middle ground, ruling typically on a five-to-four basis causing not only gyrations in the opinions over the years, and from Court to Court as its membership changes, and sways to and fro, but earning the epithet of a "legislature of one" operating often wholly outside of its constitutional privileges let alone duties, and right over the top of a weak-kneed Congress and bar, feckless and civically bankrupt. We shall not let the Court forget for whom it is working, and to whom it ultimately answers.

That about which we need to be mindful in the following case is *not* the Connecticut legislation concerning the availability of contraceptives, but rather a court-generated legal equation and constitutional principle with which the Court could and did work into a variety of unexpected future settings, changing life in America, and in almost every case, by one vote. Its spin-offs are almost unimaginable. Maybe this was the Court's intent, the Connecticut statute simply offering a vehicle. Could that be true? It is kind of an interesting case, some might say, dealing with a "silly" statute according to one Justice, even "asinine" (at page 527 of the official reporter. Page 64, *infra*). However, its significance does not repose in its factual subject matter, birth control among a segment of the citizenry of Connecticut, but rather its legal construct where

SCOTUS found (or at least formally and unequivocally announced discovering) a whole new part of the United States Constitution in the form of "penumbras" or shadows surrounding its many provisions and most especially in the instances of the Bill of Rights, and further seeing spring forth "emanations" of entirely new bodies of law as time passed (From the perspective of some, a court which bases its conclusions on metaphors...penumbras, shadows, and emanations...is a court which is unable to base its findings on rational and real substance, although this is something you will have to decide for yourself). No one is saying that is bad, or good; we are just observing that is what is happening. It is simply how the Court went about doing its business which we observe. If the Court can do this in that case (*Griswold*), it can do it whenever and wherever it so chooses, and it often does. Not so good. Unelected legislators who, on a vote of five to four, can affect not only the lives of everyone in the nation, but the nation itself, is laden with treachery. You will see.

And now, *Griswold v. Connecticut*, from the minds and words of appointed, salaried "civil servants" who sit on the United States Supreme Court (with banners waving and bugles blaring, give us a drum roll please), and by the way, stand back as we roll out the contraceptives; we have a federal constitutional question here! Or do we? I'll see you after the show.

*

GRISWOLD, et al. v. CONNECTICUT
381 U.S. 479

Appeal From The Supreme Court Of Errors Of Connecticut

Mr. Justice Douglas delivered the opinion of the Court.

Appellant Griswold is Executive Director of the Planned Parenthood League of Connecticut. Appellant Buxton is a licensed physician and a professor at the Yale Medical School who served as Medical Director for the League at its Center in New Haven – a center open and operating from November 1 to November 10, 1961, when appellants were arrested.

They gave information, instruction, and medical advice to *married persons* as to the means of preventing conception. They examined the wife and prescribed the best contraceptive device or material for her use. Fees were usually charged, although some couples were serviced free.

The statutes whose constitutionality is involved in this appeal are §§ 53-32 and 54-196 of the General Statutes of Connecticut (1958 rev.). The former provides:

> "Any person who uses any drug, medicinal article or instrument for the purpose of preventing conception shall be fined not less than fifty dollars or imprisoned not less than sixty days nor more than one year or be both fined and imprisoned."

Section 54-196 provides:

> "Any person who assists, abets, counsels, causes, hires or commands another to commit any offense may be prosecuted and punished as if he were the principal offender."

The appellants were found guilty as accessories and fined $100 each, against the claim that the accessory statute as so applied violated the Fourteenth Amendment. The Appellate Division of the Circuit Court affirmed. The Supreme Court of Errors affirmed that judgment....

We think that appellants have standing to raise the constitutional rights of the married people with whom they had a professional relationship.

* * *

Coming to the merits, we are met with a wide range of questions that implicate the Due Process Clause of the Fourteenth Amendment. Overtones of some arguments suggest that *Lochner v. New York*, 198 U.S. 45, should be our guide. But we decline that invitation.... We do not sit as a super-legislature to determine the wisdom, need, and propriety of laws that touch economic problems, business affairs, or social conditions. This law, however, operates directly on an intimate relation of husband and wife and their physician's role in one aspect of that relation.

The association of people is not mentioned in the Constitution nor in the Bill of Rights. The right to educate a child in a school of the parents' choice – whether public or private or parochial – is also not mentioned. Nor is the right to study any particular subject or any foreign language. Yet the First Amendment has been construed to include certain of those rights.

* * *

Without those peripheral rights the specific rights would be less secure.

* * *

In other words, the First Amendment has a penumbra where privacy is protected from governmental intrusion. In like context, we have protected forms of "association" that are not political in the customary sense but pertain to the social, legal, and economic benefit of the members.

* * *

[S]pecific guarantees in the Bill of Rights have penumbras, formed by emanations from those guarantees that help give them life and substance.... Various guarantees create zones of privacy.... The Ninth Amendment provides: "The enumeration in the Constitution, of certain rights, shall not be construed to deny or disparage others retained by the people."

The Fourth and Fifth Amendments were described in *Boyd v. United States*, 116 U.S. 616, 630, as protection against all governmental invasions "of the sanctity of a man's home and the privacies of life." We recently referred in *Mapp v. Ohio*, 367 U.S. 643, 656, to the Fourth Amendment as creating a "right to privacy, no less important than any other right carefully and particularly reserved to the people...."

We have had many controversies over these penumbral rights of "privacy and repose...." These cases bear witness that the right of privacy which presses for recognition here is a legitimate one.

The present case, then, concerns a relationship lying within the zone of privacy created by several fundamental constitutional guarantees. And it concerns a law which, in forbidding the *use* of contraceptives rather than regulating their manufacture or sale, seeks to achieve its goals by means having a maximum destructive impact upon that relationship. Such a law cannot stand in light of the familiar principle, so often applied by this Court, that a "governmental purpose to control or prevent activities constitutionally subject to state regulation may not be achieved by means which sweep unnecessarily broadly and thereby invade the area of protected freedoms." Would we allow the police to search the sacred precincts of marital bedrooms for telltale signs of the use of contraceptives? The very idea is repulsive to the notions of privacy surrounding the marriage relationship.

We deal with a right of privacy older than the Bill of Rights – older than our political parties, older than our school system. Marriage is a coming together for better or for worse, hopefully enduring, and intimate to the degree of being sacred. It is an association that promotes a way of life, not causes; a harmony in living, not political faiths; a bilateral loyalty, not commercial or social projects. Yet it is an association for as noble a purpose as any involved in our prior decisions.

Reversed.

Mr. Justice Goldberg, whom the Chief Justice and Mr. Justice Brennan join, concurring.

I agree with the Court that Connecticut's birth-control law unconstitutionally intrudes upon the right of marital privacy, and I join in its opinion and judgment. Although I have not accepted the view that "due process" as used in the Fourteenth Amendment incorporates all of the first eight Amendments.... I do agree that the concept of liberty protects those personal rights that are fundamental, and is not confined to the specific terms of the Bill of Rights. My conclusion that the concept of liberty is not so restricted and that it embraces the right of marital privacy though that right is not mentioned explicitly in the Constitution is supported both by numerous decisions of this Court, referred to in the Court's opinion, and by the language and history of the Ninth Amendment. In reaching the conclusion that the right of marital privacy is protected, as being within the protected penumbra of specific guarantees of the Bill of Rights, the Court refers to the Ninth Amendment[.] I add these words to emphasize the relevance of that Amendment to the Court's holding.

The Court stated many years ago that the Due Process Clause protects those liberties that are "so rooted in the traditions and conscience of our people as to be ranked as fundamental."

* * *

This Court, in a series of decisions, has held that the Fourteenth Amendment absorbs and applies to the States those specifics of the first eight amendments which express fundamental personal rights. The language and history of the Ninth Amendment reveal that the Framers of the Constitution believed that there are additional fundamental rights, protected from governmental infringement, which exist alongside those fundamental rights specifically mentioned in the first eight constitutional amendments.

The Ninth Amendment reads, "The enumeration in the Constitution, of certain rights, shall not be construed to deny or disparage others retained by the people." The Amendment is almost entirely the work of James Madison. It was introduced in Congress by him and passed the House and Senate with little or no debate and virtually no change in language. It was proffered to quiet expressed fears that a bill of specifically enumerated rights could not be sufficiently broad to cover all essential rights and that the specific mention of certain rights would be interpreted as a denial that others were protected.

* * *

[T]he Framers did not intend that the first eight amendments be construed to exhaust the basic and fundamental rights which the Constitution guaranteed to the people.... To hold that a right so basic and fundamental and so deep-rooted in our society as the right of privacy in marriage may be infringed because that right is not guaranteed in so many words by the first eight amendments to the Constitution is to ignore the Ninth Amendment and to give it no effect whatsoever. Moreover, a judicial construction that this fundamental right is not protected by the Constitution because it is not mentioned in explicit terms by one of the first eight amendments or elsewhere in the Constitution would violate the Ninth Amendment, which specifically states that "[t]he enumeration in the Constitution, of certain rights, shall not be *construed* to deny or disparage others retained by the people."

* * *

Nor am I turning somersaults with history in arguing that the Ninth Amendment is relevant in a case dealing with a *State's* infringement of a fundamental right.... [T]he Ninth Amendment simply lends strong support to the view that the "liberty" protected by the Fifth and Fourteenth Amendments from infringement by the Federal Government or the States is not restricted to rights specifically mentioned in the first eight amendments.

In determining which rights are fundamental, judges are not left at large to decide cases in light of their personal and private notions. Rather, they must look to the "traditions and [collective] conscience of our people" to determine whether a principle is "so rooted [there]...as to be ranked as fundamental." The inquiry is whether a right involved "is of such a character that it cannot be denied without violating those 'fundamental principles of liberty and justice which lie at the base of all our civil and political institutions'...."

* * *

I agree fully with the Court that, applying these tests, the right of privacy is a fundamental personal right, emanating "from the totality of the constitutional scheme under which we live." Mr. Justice Brandeis, dissenting in *Olmstead v. United States*, 277 U.S. 438, 478, comprehensively summarized the principles underlying the Constitution's guarantees of privacy:

> "The protection guaranteed by the [Fourth and Fifth] Amendments is much broader in scope. The makers of our Constitution undertook to secure conditions favorable to the pursuit of happiness. They recognized the significance of man's spiritual nature, of his feelings and of his intellect. They knew that only a part of the pain, pleasure and satisfactions of life are to be found in material things. They sought to protect Americans in their beliefs, their thoughts, their emotions and their sensations. They conferred, as against the Government, the right to be let alone – the most comprehensive of rights and the right most valued by civilized men."

The Connecticut statutes here involved deal with a particularly important and sensitive area of privacy – that of the marital relation and the marital home.

* * *

Although the Constitution does not speak in so many words of the right of privacy in marriage, I cannot believe that it offers these fundamental rights no protection. The fact that no particular provision of the Constitution explicitly forbids the State from disrupting the traditional relation of the family – a relation as old and as fundamental as our entire civilization – surely does not show that the Government was meant to have the power to do so. Rather, as the Ninth Amendment expressly recognizes, there are fundamental personal rights such as this one, which are protected from abridgment by the Government though not specifically mentioned in the Constitution.

My Brother Stewart, while characterizing the Connecticut birth control law as "an uncommonly silly law," would nevertheless let it stand on the ground that it is not for the courts to "'substitute their social and economic beliefs for the judgment of legislative bodies, who are elected to pass laws.'" Elsewhere, I have stated that "[w]hile I quite agree with Mr. Justice Brandeis that...'a...State may...serve as a laboratory; and try novel social and economic experiments,' I do not believe that this includes the power to experiment with the fundamental liberties of citizens...." The vice of the dissenters' views is that it would permit such experimentation by the States in the area of the fundamental personal rights of its citizens.

* * *

Finally, it should be said of the Court's holding today that it in no way interferes with a State's proper regulation of sexual promiscuity or misconduct. As my Brother Harlan so well stated in his dissenting opinion in *Poe v. Ullman, supra,* at 553:

> "Adultery, homosexuality and the like are sexual intimacies which the State forbids...but the intimacy of husband and wife is necessarily an essential and accepted feature of the institution of marriage, an institution which the State not only must allow, but which always and in every age it has fostered and protected. It is one thing when the State exerts its power either to forbid extra-marital sexuality...or to say who may marry, but it is quite another when, having acknowledged a marriage and the intimacies inherent in it, it undertakes to regulate by means of the criminal law the details of that intimacy."

In sum, I believe that the right of privacy in the marital relation is fundamental and basic – a personal right "retained by the people" within the meaning of the Ninth Amendment. Connecticut cannot constitutionally abridge this fundamental right, which is protected by the Fourteenth Amendment from infringement by the States. I agree with the Court that petitioners' convictions must therefore be reversed.

Mr. Justice Harlan, concurring in the judgment.

I fully agree with the judgment of reversal, but find myself unable to join the Court's opinion. The reason is that it seems to me to evince an approach to this case very much like that taken by my Brothers Black and Stewart in dissent, namely: the Due Process Clause of the Fourteenth Amendment does not touch this Connecticut statute unless the enactment is found to violate some right assured by the letter or penumbra of the Bill of Rights.

* * *

In my view, the proper constitutional inquiry in this case is whether this Connecticut statute infringes the Due Process Clause of the Fourteenth Amendment because the enactment violates basic values "implicit in the concept of ordered liberty[.]" I believe that it does. While the relevant inquiry may be aided by resort to one or more of the provisions of the Bill of Rights, it is not dependent on them or any of their radiations. The Due Process Clause of the Fourteenth Amendment stands, in my opinion, on its own bottom.

* * *

While I could not more heartily agree that judicial "self restraint" is an indispensable ingredient of sound constitutional adjudication, I do submit that the formula suggested for achieving it is more hollow than real.

* * *

It will be achieved in this area, as in other constitutional areas, only by continual insistence upon respect for the teachings of history, solid recognition of the basic values that underlie our society, and wise appreciation of the great roles that the doctrines of federalism and separation of powers have played in establishing and preserving American freedoms. Adherence to these principles will not, of course, obviate all constitutional differences of opinion among judges, nor should it. Their continued recognition will, however, go farther toward keeping most judges from roaming at large in the constitutional field than will the interpolation into the Constitution of an artificial and largely illusory restriction on the content of the Due Process Clause.

Mr. Justice White, concurring in the judgment.

In my view this Connecticut law as applied to married couples deprives them of "liberty" without due process of law, as that concept is used in the Fourteenth Amendment. I therefore concur in the judgment of the Court reversing these convictions under Connecticut's aiding and abetting statute.

* * *

Mr. Justice Black, with whom Mr. Justice Stewart joins, dissenting.

I agree with my Brother Stewart's dissenting opinion. And like him I do not to any extent whatever base my view that this Connecticut law is constitutional on a belief that the law is wise or that its policy is a good one. In order that there may be no room at all to doubt why I vote as I do, I feel constrained to add that the law is every bit as offensive to me as it is to my Brethren of the majority and my Brothers Harlan, White and Goldberg who, reciting reasons why it is offensive to them, hold it unconstitutional. There is no single one of the graphic and eloquent strictures and criticisms fired at the policy of this Connecticut law either by the Court's opinion or by those of my concurring Brethren to which I cannot subscribe – except their conclusion that the evil qualities they see in the law make it unconstitutional.

Had the doctor defendant here, or even the nondoctor defendant, been convicted for doing nothing more than expressing opinions to persons coming to the clinic that certain contraceptive devices, medicines or practices would do them good and would be desirable, or for telling people how devices could be used, I can think of no reasons at this time why their expressions of views would not be protected by the First and Fourteenth Amendments, which guarantee freedom of speech. But speech is one thing; conduct and physical activities are quite another.

* * *

One of the most effective ways of diluting or expanding a constitutionally guaranteed right is to substitute for the crucial word or words of a constitutional guarantee another word or words, more or less flexible and more or less restricted in meaning. This fact is well illustrated by the use of the term "right of privacy" as a comprehensive substitute for the Fourth Amendment's guarantee against "unreasonable searches and seizures." "Privacy" is a broad, abstract and ambiguous concept which can easily be shrunken in meaning but which can also, on the other hand, easily be interpreted as a constitutional ban against many things other than searches and seizures. I have expressed the view many times that First Amendment freedoms, for example, have suffered from a failure of the courts to stick to the simple language of the First Amendment in construing it, instead of invoking multitudes of words substituted for those the Framers used. For these reasons I get nowhere in this case by talk about a constitutional "right of privacy" as an emanation from one or more constitutional provisions. I like my privacy as well as the next one, but I am nevertheless compelled to admit that government has a right to invade it unless prohibited by some specific constitutional provision. For these reasons I cannot agree with the Court's judgment and the reasons it gives for holding this Connecticut law unconstitutional.

* * *

The due process argument which my Brothers Harland and White adopt here is based, as their opinions indicate, on the premise that this Court is vested with power to invalidate all state laws that it considers to be arbitrary, capricious, unreasonable, or oppressive, or on this Court's belief that a particular state law under scrutiny has no "rational or justifying" purpose, or is offensive to a "sense of fairness and justice." If these formulas based on "natural justice," or others which mean the same thing, are to prevail, they require judges to determine what is or is not constitutional on the basis of their own appraisal of what laws are unwise or unnecessary. The power to make such decisions is of course that of a legislative body. Surely it has to be admitted that no provision of the Constitution specifically gives such blanket power to courts to exercise such a supervisory veto over the wisdom and value of legislative policies and to hold unconstitutional those laws which they believe unwise or dangerous.... While I completely subscribed to the holding of *Marbury* v. *Madison*, 1 Cranch 137, and subsequent cases, that our Court has constitutional power to strike down statutes, state or federal, that violate commands of the Federal Constitution, I do not believe that we are granted power by the Due Process Clause or any other constitutional provision or provisions to measure constitutionality by our belief that legislation is arbitrary, capricious or unreasonable, or accomplishes no justifiable purpose, or is offensive to our own notions of "civilized standards of conduct." Such an appraisal of the wisdom of legislation is an attribute of the power to make laws, not of the power to interpret them. The use by federal courts of such a formula or doctrine or whatnot to veto federal or state laws simply takes away from Congress and States the power to make laws based on their own judgment of fairness and wisdom and transfers that power to this Court for ultimate determination – a power which was specifically denied to federal courts by the convention that framed the Constitution.

* * *

I repeat so as not to be misunderstood that this Court does have power, which it should exercise, to hold laws unconstitutional where they are forbidden by the Federal Constitution. My point is that there is no provision of the Constitution which either expressly or impliedly vests power in this Court to sit as a supervisory agency over acts of duly constituted legislative bodies and set aside their laws because of the Court's belief that the legislative policies adopted are unreasonable, unwise, arbitrary, capricious or irrational. The adoption of such a loose, flexible, uncontrolled standard for holding laws unconstitutional, if ever it is finally achieved, will amount to a great unconstitutional shift of power to the courts which I believe and am constrained to say will be bad for the courts and worse for the country. Subjecting federal and state laws to such an unrestrained and unrestrainable judicial control as to the wisdom of legislative enactments would, I fear, jeopardize the separation of governmental powers that the Framers set up and at the same time threaten to take away much of the power of States to govern themselves which the Constitution plainly intended them to have.

I realize that many good and able men have eloquently spoken and written, sometimes in rhapsodical strains, about the duty of this Court to keep the Constitution in tune with the times. The idea is that the Constitution must be changed from time to time and that this Court is charged with a duty to make those changes. For myself, I must with all deference reject that philosophy. The Constitution makers knew the need for change and provided for it. Amendment suggested by the people's elected representatives can be submitted to the people or their selected agents for ratification. That method of change was good for our Fathers, and being somewhat old-fashioned I must add it is good enough for me. And so, I cannot rely on the Due Process Clause or the Ninth Amendment or any mysterious and uncertain natural law concept as a reason for striking down this state law. The Due Process Clause with an "arbitrary and capricious" or "shocking to the conscience" formula was liberally used by this Court to strike down economic legislation in the early decades of this century, threatening, many people thought, the tranquility and stability of the Nation. See, *e.g., Lochner* v. *New York,* 198 U.S. 45. That formula, based on subjective considerations of "natural justice," is no less dangerous when used to enforce this Court's views about personal rights than those about economic rights. I had thought that we had laid that formula, as a means for striking down state legislation, to rest once and for all....

In *Ferguson* v. *Skrupa,* 372 U.S. 726, 730, this Court two years ago said in an opinion joined by all the Justices but one that

> "The doctrine that prevailed in *Lochner, Coppage, Adkins, Burns,* and like cases – that due process authorizes courts to hold laws unconstitutional when they believe the legislature has acted unwisely – has long since been discarded. We have returned to the original constitutional proposition that courts do not substitute their social and economic beliefs for the judgment of legislative bodies, who are elected to pass laws."

So far as I am concerned, Connecticut's law as applied here is not forbidden by any provision of the Federal Constitution as that Constitution was written, and I would therefore affirm.

Mr. Justice Stewart, whom Mr. Justice Black joins, dissenting.

Since 1879 Connecticut has had on its books a law which forbids the use of contraceptives by anyone. I think this is an uncommonly silly law. As a practical matter, the law is obviously unenforceable, except in the oblique context of the present case. As a philosophical matter, I believe the use of contraceptives in the relationship of marriage should be left to personal and private choice, based upon each individual's moral, ethical, and religious beliefs. As a matter of social policy, I think professional counsel about methods of birth control should be available to all, so that each individual's choice can be meaningfully made. But we are not asked in this case to say whether we think this law is unwise, or even asinine. We are asked to hold that it violates the United States Constitution. And that I cannot do.

In the course of its opinion the Court refers to no less than six Amendments to the Constitution: the First, the Third, the Fourth, the Fifth, the Ninth, and the Fourteenth. But the Court does not say which of these Amendments, if any, it thinks is infringed by this Connecticut law.

We *are* told that the Due Process Clause of the Fourteenth Amendment is not, as such, the "guide" in this case. With that much I agree. There is no claim that this law, duly enacted by the Connecticut Legislature, is unconstitutionally vague. There is no claim that the appellants were denied any of the elements of procedural due process at their trial, so as to make their convictions constitutionally invalid. And, as the Court says, the day has long passed since the Due Process Clause was regarded as a proper instrument for determining "the wisdom, need, and propriety" of state laws. Compare *Lochner* v. *New York,* 198 U.S. 45, with *Ferguson* v. *Skrupa*, 372 U.S. 726....

As to the First, Third, Fourth, and Fifth Amendment, I can find nothing in any of them to invalidate this Connecticut law, even assuming that all those Amendments are fully applicable against the States. It has not even been argued that this is a law "respecting an establishment of religion, or prohibiting the free exercise thereof." And surely, unless the solemn process of constitutional adjudication is to descend to the level of a play on words, there is not involved here any abridgment of "the freedom of speech, or of the press; or the right of the people peaceably to assemble, and to petition the Government for a redress of grievances." No soldier has been quartered in any house. There has been no search, and no seizure. Nobody has been compelled to be a witness against himself.

The Court also quotes the Ninth Amendment, and my Brother Goldberg's concurring opinion relies heavily upon it. But to say that the Ninth Amendment has anything to do with this case is to turn somersaults with history. The Ninth Amendment, like its companion the Tenth, which this Court held "states but a truism that all is retained which has not been surrendered," *United States* v. *Darby*, 312 U.S. 100, 124, was framed by James Madison and adopted by the States simply to make clear that the adoption of the Bill of Rights did not alter the plan that the *Federal* Government was to be a government of express and limited powers, and that all rights and powers not delegated to it were retained by the people and the individual States. Until today no member of this Court has ever suggested that the Ninth Amendment meant anything else, and the idea that a federal court could ever use the Ninth Amendment to annul a law passed by the elected representatives of the people of the State of Connecticut would have caused James Madison no little wonder.

What provision of the Constitution, then, does make this state law invalid? The Court says it is the right of privacy "created by several fundamental constitutional guarantees." With all deference, I can find no such general right of privacy in the Bill of Rights, in any other part of the Constitution, or in any case ever before decided by this Court.

At the oral argument in this case we were told that the Connecticut law does not "conform to current community standards." But it is not the function of this Court to decide cases on the basis of community standards. We are here to decide cases "agreeably to the

Constitution and laws of the United States." It is the essence of judicial duty to subordinate our own personal views, our own ideas of what legislation is wise and what is not. If, as I should surely hope, the law before us does not reflect the standards of the people of Connecticut, the people of Connecticut can freely exercise their true Ninth and Tenth Amendment rights to persuade their elected representatives to repeal it. That is the constitutional way to take this law off the books.

*

We are back. Are you still here? If you are, welcome to the other side. Reading Supreme Court opinions, especially when one is not used to the task, is far from easy. In fact, it is not easy even for one skilled in the art. One becomes tired of mental gymnastics rather quickly. Incessant pettifogging and biting among members of the Court is both exhausting and depressing. Totally unnecessary. It even raises issues of maturity (not among all) or the ability to think past the "I'm right, you're wrong" mentality that has a tendency to pervade our lives. There is far too often little engagement, rather one judge against another, the heart of the case being neglected and the culture cocked. Look for yourself, you will see it. Amazingly, it only gets worse. One would think the members would have a basic and similar understanding of what the Constitution means along with its historical antecedents and its heavily and extensive chronicled analysis surrounding its creation, as they all have been to law school and read, presumably, the same words and works, and heard from teachers who had fundamentally the same experience...one would think. Yet, for some reason, many feel compelled to spin it in a way which comports with their personal beliefs, curious in that they didn't write it, but instead swore to uphold it.

As you have discovered, there is much to look up, cross references or citations to check, all wrapped up in an arcane style of legal prose. It will get easier, though, and by the time we are well into this work, you will likely be hungry for more with a new-found "bring-it-on" attitude. My guess is (I do not want to become overly enthusiastic or experience any irrational exuberance) it will move many of you on to do more.

Douglas spent his tenure on the Court holding up the left wing, the far left wing (this is not a judgment call, nothing pejorative in any sense, just a fact with which anyone in the business would agree). With his assignment to write the opinion in *Griswold*, his chance for which he had likely been waiting for years had come. At the time his assignment came, he knew he would be writing what was expected to be for the majority (or as it turned out, a majority of sorts).

Now Douglas could set up for all to see not just the philosophical divide, but to bring a new or at least clearly announced jurisprudence to the American people, his philosophy; the general right to privacy as being a frank constitutional matter and protected as such (at least when convenient for the Court to lean upon when necessary to reach a desired result, the practice of which I want you to finely attune your observations). Once that has been done, it wouldn't be easy to change or modify, let alone eliminate, as now being an announced constitutional principle (which we will see play out time and time again), reversals of which are awkward, even intellectually agonizing (which we also get a chance to see). Few would have any difficulty seeing privacy as a fundamental concept of liberty or as an embedded and accepted American tradition from the earliest days, being one of the fundamental precepts not only upon which the nation was formed, but why it was formed. Privacy, as an internality, ranks up with liberty as an externality. Yet, not one other justice in the majority signed on to his thinking, but in separate opinions concurred on "different grounds," as you have seen, along with a howling dissent making for not just a split court, but a divide that would only grow over time. What may have gotten past the dissent (arguably insufficiently addressed) was the idea that Douglas did indeed want to get into matters of regulating personal lives at the federal level, particularly where the states may have been doing things with which he didn't agree (*Lochner?*), as was the case here. Using the Constitution to reach his ends was the perfect tool and theoretical justification. Think about it, if the Supreme Court says the issue is one which concerns the Constitution (remember *Marbury?*) and then proceeds to rule on the issue as a constitutional matter, end of game. Who can argue with that, or more practically speaking, with whom can you argue? To whom do you complain? There is an answer.

Whatever the case, one might consider that Douglas suggested he was invited to use *Lochner* as his guide (the opinion uses the term "our" guide), but "we" decline he says ("we" is interesting remembering no one fully signed on to his thinking anyway), but then apparently proceeded to apply *Lochner*-esque thinking (substituting the Supreme Court's judgment for that of State elected authorities) and to accordingly style his opinion, a point not missed by the dissent. (Had not that formula been laid to rest once and for all? Apparently not.) Why would any judge run this ethical gambit when it could have been left entirely alone, clumsy artifice in exchange for constitutional integrity, or at least consistency? That couldn't be, could it? There must be an answer. He goes on to say that "[w]e do not sit as a super legislature," which is known in professional circles, not law, as an unsolicited denial carrying its own interpretation of fallaciousness. And then he further finds "penumbras" and "peripheral rights" and "emanations" in various guarantees of the Bill of Rights, collectively, apparently, or at least out of the several of which he bothers to reference, taken all together creating "zones of privacy," "radiations," as it were, upon which the case now turns, with an untold number of others to follow in years to come. I'm not sure if it should be referred to as fiction, magic, or alchemy…even creativity might be unfair…or the initiation of a day-to-day constitutional convention. But, what Douglas did, without taking any solidly grounded position in the opinion's holding, is to load the country aboard an unruly horse that would take it into unforeseen and unintended realms. Just watch what happens. You will remember this case (you may find it interesting how you view this case after we have finished with the book, not the subject matter of contraception in Connecticut, but how the scrivener crafted the opinion). At the same time, it is possible that is exactly what he wanted, social regulatory machinery, and get it he did. Just watch as you proceed.

I see in Goldberg's concurring opinion (being nearly twice as long as the "majority" opinion) references to several theoretical if not emotional constructs relating to such matters as privacy being a fundamental concept of liberty reaching beyond the Bill of Rights (speech, religion, being secure against unreasonable search, self-incrimination, etc.) or as being a liberty not just rooted but "deep-rooted" in the traditions of the people so as to be fundamental, indeed part of the collective conscience. Quite a bouquet of legal prose with which most would be hard pressed to disagree, at least *prima facie*. While it seems paradoxical that man as a social animal is also naturally inclined to privacy in the name of, *inter alia*, liberty, there is an explanation. I only point out these thoughts so as to be able to ask you the question, where were these emanations, these concepts, these deeply rooted traditions, the grand collective conscience in later opinions dealing with matters just as sensitive and private, even gut wrenching to some if not most. Since these thoughts are a convenient means here for the plujority, why are they not (since they are constitutional matters) good enough to apply or be binding in other cases down the road? Get yourself ready. It couldn't be that the Court swings its head when it speaks averting the eyes of its own conscience when convenient to do so, or inconvenient not to do so, given the wind, or its own deep-rooted feelings, possibly at the expense of a solid, stable, robust nation with like citizens able to govern themselves through a representative political system? That couldn't be. These honorable servants would not do that, would they? As we get through this, you may develop a schemata of your own.

Anyway, it is not contraception in Connecticut with which we are concerned. As a dissent notes, the issue is too "asinine" for the Court. Yet, most people would see this as the issue in the case and nothing more, the true significance of the case reaching far beyond even most lawyers. But, for us, here, it (contraception) is incidental, merely the canvas upon which the Court stroked its constitutional brush(es). We are interested in something far more important than the outcome of this silly case, or its foray into the world of contraception. We are interested in that which is well beyond the premises of this case. What we see, and will be seeing, is the consequences of the Court's words, without any consideration of contraception, all in relation to the seeming lack of foresight in its drafting. Douglas seized the advantage of finally being a scrivener on such a case and taking a wild swing at attempting to craft something he believed to be good for the country, reaching far beyond sexual devices and the way they do it in Connecticut. Here was an opportunity he likely felt might not come his way again (something you will have to contemplate and decide for yourself—I am only pointing it out for your consideration—I take no position—how could one argue against privacy any more than one could get away with not being for "the children" or "free choice" or "equality"—give it the right name and it is immunized from attack).

At the same time, the case could forcefully be argued as right, or should I say correctly decided, or better yet, its position defensible, lest you get the idea there is any inference I am suggesting it is wrong. It seems, though, one might be concerned with who (or what, constitutionally speaking) decided it and how it was crafted. In the most essential sense, that is what we are about here, the effect the opinion, as written, had *in futuro*, as well as where the justifications it used were not employed in subsequent cases and issues. We are working at a level above taking sides and getting involved in endless and hopeless debate about who or what is right or wrong in terms of this or any other case. This dribbling, carping, and cavil we will leave to members of the burlesque media who even at that are also less than accomplished. We are looking at jurisprudential life in the country and its effects.

Consider this book as a point of departure in your analytical life, not a destination.

VII

ROTH V. UNITED STATES

oth v. United States, 354 U.S. 476 (1957), and the companion case of *Alberts v. California,* are a pair of consolidated cases being appealed from convictions in federal and state courts, respectively, regarding activities under federal and state obscenity statutes, and whether or not they may constitutionally stand under the First Amendment (free speech) so far as the federal conviction is concerned, and the First Amendment as applied to the states under the Fourteenth Amendment so far as the state conviction is concerned. The convictions were upheld, so why present these cases here?

The Court granted *certiorari*, and then proceeded to test whether or not the obscenity statutes under which convictions were obtained in the state and federal courts were constitutional, and it ruled they were. The then Court proceeded to define obscenity in such broad and liberal (not politically speaking) terms…well, you will have to read it for yourself. But just ask yourself the question, what was the majority thinking about when it said only obscenity which is "utterly without redeeming social importance" is not protected by the First Amendment? What does that mean? Think about it.

The Court had on numerous occasions intimated that obscenity was not protected by the freedoms of speech or press. However, as the Court comments at the outset, it was a matter (obscenity) which had never been squarely presented to the Court for such a review. This case did, and may have been selected by the Court for that express purpose, that is to say, for reasons apart from and beyond what happened to the defendants below (at trial). Why now and why this kind of case (factually speaking) is one of those arcane matters shrouded in the secrecy of certain aspects of the Court, an enigma, matters upon which thoughts will be offered later.

Roth was plying his trade by mail, *Alberts* in a bookstore. The question was whether what they were mailing and/or selling in a bookstore was protected constitutionally, as obscene material was not. The jury concluded the statutes were violated. Obscenity had long been considered to not be constitutionally protected. The

Supreme Court found the statutes under which the defendants were convicted passed constitutional muster and did not trammel upon the constitutional safeguards of free speech and expression, or otherwise fail to properly give notice of what was prohibited by the statutes, at least so said some of the justices.

However, the Court went on to discuss what was obscene (essentially utterly without socially redeeming value), or what wasn't. With only a few words, the culture of the country…its spirit, its soul, its value system, inter-gender treatment and behavior, some say…had been changed by a handful of governmental appointees who themselves couldn't agree as to what the standard should be. It's the *dicta* that did it! It tightened the reins on other courts in the land (the trial judges were reined in as to their enforcement of obscenity laws as the boundaries of obscenity now had no discernible borders). Indeed, the Court opened the floodgates of this commodity, and businessmen of every ilk surfed through the sluice. Warren and Harlan voiced their concerns in their opinions. They probably didn't know how correct they were, particularly in terms of concerns over future effects, directly and tangentially. So, it can't be said that Brennan didn't know or wasn't warned. He knew of the concern and ignored it, without any comment, so it can't be a case (among many prior to and after this one) of oops. Foresight? Apparently none. You are the one making the judgment. There are those who would say most of *Roth* is *dicta*. Others would say it is law. When you finish with this, you will be in a position to make that call yourself. In its effect, however, it doesn't really make any difference (it should) because the legislative-like *dicta* carries the weight of law. But the fact is, people in the business—Hollywood and Broadway, Anytown, U.S.A., the foreign importers—latched on to the language and have exploited it either as intended, or unintended. Again, you are on your own. We'll get back together at the end of the case. At this point, do your job.

And now, stage left, *Roth*.

*

ROTH *v.* UNITED STATES

354 U.S. 476

CERTIORARI TO THE UNITED STATES COURT OF APPEALS

FOR THE SECOND CIRCUIT

Mr. Justice Brennan delivered the opinion of the Court.

The constitutionality of a criminal obscenity statute is the question.... [T]he primary constitutional question is whether the federal obscenity statute[1] [the footnote and its text is as it appears in the official reporter] violates the provision of the First Amendment that "Congress shall make no law...abridging the freedom of speech, or of the press...."

* * *

Other constitutional questions are: whether these statutes violate due process, because too vague to support conviction for crime; whether power to punish speech and press offensive to decency and morality is in the States alone, so that the federal obscenity statute violates the Ninth and Tenth Amendments....

Roth conducted a business in New York in the publication and sale of books, photographs and magazines. He used circulars and advertising matter to solicit sales. He was convicted by a jury in the District Court for the Southern District of New York upon 4 counts of a 26-count indictment charging him with mailing obscene circulars and advertising, and an obscene book, in violation of the federal obscenity

---

[1] The federal obscenity statute provided, in pertinent part: "Every obscene, lewd, lascivious, or filthy book, pamphlet, picture, paper, letter, writing, print, or other publication of an indecent character...is declared to be nonmailable matter and shall not be conveyed in the mails or delivered from a post office or by any letter carrier...." [This footnote and its number are reproduced as they appear in the official opinion.]

statute. His conviction was affirmed by the Court of Appeals for the Second Circuit. We granted certiorari.

* * *

The dispositive question is whether obscenity is utterance within the area of protected speech and press. Although this is the first time the question has been squarely presented to this Court, either under the First Amendment or under the Fourteenth Amendment, expressions found in numerous opinions indicate that this Court has always assumed that obscenity is not protected by the freedoms of speech and press. [Several citations omitted.]

The guaranties of freedom of expression in effect in 10 of the 14 States which by 1792 had ratified the Constitution, gave no absolute protection for every utterance.... As early as 1712, Massachusetts made it criminal to publish "any filthy, obscene, or profane song, pamphlet, libel or mock sermon" in imitation or mimicking of religious services....

In light of this history, it is apparent that the unconditional phrasing of the First Amendment was not intended to protect every utterance....

The protection given speech and press was fashioned to assure unfettered interchange of ideas for the bringing about of political and social changes desired by the people. This objective was made explicit as early as 1774 in a letter of the Continental Congress to the inhabitants of Quebec:

> "The last right we shall mention, regards the freedom of the press. The importance of this consists, besides the advancement of the truth, science, morality, and arts in general, in its diffusion of liberal sentiments on the administration of Government, its ready communication of thoughts between subjects, and its consequential promotion of union among them,

whereby oppressive officers are shamed or intimidated, into more honourable and just modes of conducting affairs." 1 Journals of the Continental Congress 108 (1774). [Sometimes citations from the case are provided to afford the reader easy access to the source of this Court's quoted material. In most instances they are omitted. Whether included or omitted carries no message.]

All ideas having even the slightest redeeming social importance – unorthodox ideas, controversial ideas, even ideas hateful to the prevailing climate of opinion – have the full protection of the guaranties, unless excludable because they encroach upon the limited area of more important interests. But implicit in the history of the First Amendment is the rejection of obscenity as utterly without redeeming social importance. This rejection for that reason is mirrored in the universal judgment that obscenity should be restrained, reflected in the international agreement of over 50 nations, in the obscenity laws of all of the 48 States, and in the 20 obscenity laws enacted by the Congress from 1842 to 1956. This is the same judgment expressed by this Court in *Chaplinsky* v. *New Hampshire*, 315 U.S. 568, 571-572:

> "There are certain well-defined and narrowly limited classes of speech, the prevention and punishment of which have never been thought to raise any Constitutional problem. *These include the lewd and obscene.... It has been well observed that such utterances are no essential part of any exposition of ideas, and are of such slight social value as a step to truth that any benefit that may be derived from them is clearly outweighed by the social interest in order and morality....*" [Emphasis added by the Court.]

We hold that obscenity is not within the area of constitutionally protected speech or press.

It is strenuously urged that these obscenity statutes offend the constitutional guaranties because they punish incitation to impure sexual *thoughts,* not shown to be related to any overt antisocial conduct which is or may be incited in the persons stimulated to such *thoughts.* In *Roth,* the trial judge instructed the jury: "The words 'obscene, lewd and lascivious' as used in the law, signify that form of immorality which has relation to sexual impurity and has a tendency to excite lustful *thoughts....* It is insisted that the constitutional guaranties are violated because convictions may be had without proof either that obscene material will perceptibly create a clear and present danger of antisocial conduct, or will probably induce its recipients to such conduct. But, in light of our holding that obscenity is not protected speech, the complete answer to this argument is in the holding of this Court in *Beauharnais* v. *Illinois, supra,* at 266:

> "Libelous utterances not being within the area of constitutionally protected speech, it is unnecessary, either for us or for the State courts, to consider the issues behind the phrase 'clear and present danger.' Certainly no one would contend that obscene speech, for example, may be punished only upon a showing of such circumstances. Libel, as we have seen, is in the same class."

However, sex and obscenity are not synonymous. Obscene material is material which deals with sex in a manner appealing to prurient interest. The portrayal of sex, *e.g.,* in art, literature and scientific works, is not itself sufficient reason to deny material the constitutional protection of freedom of speech and press. Sex, a great and mysterious motive force in human life, has indisputably been a subject of absorbing interest to mankind through the ages; it is one of the vital problems of human interest and public concern. As to all such problems, this Court said in *Thornhill* v. *Alabama,* 310 U.S. 88, 101-102:

"The freedom of speech and of the press guaranteed by the Constitution embraces at the least the liberty to discuss publicly and truthfully *all matters of public concern* without previous restraint or fear of subsequent punishment. The exigencies of the colonial period and the efforts to secure freedom from oppressive administration developed a broadened conception of these liberties as adequate to supply the public need for *information and education with respect to the significant issues of the times*.... Freedom of discussion, if it would fulfill its historic function in this nation, must embrace *all issues about which information is needed or appropriate to enable the members of society to cope with the exigencies of their period.*" [Emphasis added by the Court.]

The fundamental freedoms of speech and press have contributed greatly to the development and well-being of our free society and are indispensable to its continued growth. Ceaseless vigilance is the watchword to prevent their erosion by Congress or by the States. The door barring federal and state intrusion into this area cannot be left ajar; it must be kept tightly closed and opened only the slightest crack necessary to prevent encroachment upon more important interests. It is therefore vital that the standards for judging obscenity safeguard the protection of freedom of speech and press for material which does not treat sex in a manner appealing to prurient interest.

The early leading standard of obscenity allowed material to be judged merely by the effect of an isolated excerpt upon particularly susceptible persons. *Regina* v. *Hicklin*, [1868] L. R. 3 Q. B. 360. Some American courts adopted this standard but later decisions have rejected it and substituted this test: whether to the average person, applying contemporary community standards, the dominant theme of the material taken as a whole appeals to prurient interest. The *Hicklin* test, judging obscenity by the effect of isolated passages upon the most susceptible persons, might well encompass material legitimately treating with sex, and so it must be rejected as unconstitutionally restrictive of the freedoms of speech and press. On the other hand, the substituted standard provides safeguards adequate to withstand the charge of constitutional infirmity.

* * *

[I]n *Roth*, the trial judge instructed the jury as follows:

"...The test is not whether it would arouse sexual desires or sexual impure thoughts in those comprising a particular segment of the community, the young, the immature or the highly prudish or would leave another segment, the scientific or highly educated or the so-called worldly-wise and sophisticated indifferent and unmoved....

"The test in each case is the effect of the book, picture or publication considered as a whole, not upon any particular class, but upon all those whom it is likely to reach. In other words, you determine its impact upon the average person in the community. The books, pictures and circulars must be judged as a whole, in their entire context, and you are not to consider detached or separate portions in reaching a conclusion. You judge the circulars, pictures and publications which have been put in evidence by present-day standards of the community. You may ask yourselves does it offend the common conscience of the community by present-day standards.

* * *

"In this case, ladies and gentlemen of the jury, you and you alone are the exclusive judges of what the common conscience of the community is, and in determining that conscience you are to consider the community as a whole, young and old, educated and uneducated, the religious and the irreligious – men, women and children."

It is argued that the statutes do not provide reasonably ascertainable standards of guilt and therefore violate the constitutional requirements of due process. The federal obscenity statute makes punishable the mailing of material that is "obscene, lewd, lascivious, or filthy…or other publication of an indecent character." …The thrust of the argument is that these words are not sufficiently precise because they do not mean the same thing to all people, all the time, everywhere.

Many decisions have recognized that these terms of obscenity statutes are not precise. This Court, however, has consistently held that lack of precision is not itself offensive to the requirements of due process. "…[T]he Constitution does not require impossible standards"; all that is required is that the language "conveys sufficiently definite warning as to the proscribed conduct when measured by common understanding and practices…." These words, applied according to the proper standard for judging obscenity, already discussed, give adequate warning of the conduct proscribed and mark "…boundaries sufficiently distinct for judges and juries fairly to administer the law…. That there may be marginal cases in which it is difficult to determine the side of the line on which a particular fact situation falls is no sufficient reason to hold the language too ambiguous to define a criminal offense…."

In summary, then, we hold that these statutes, applied according to the proper standard for judging obscenity, do not offend constitutional safeguards against convictions based upon protected material, or fail to give men in acting adequate notice of what is prohibited.

* * *

The judgments are

Affirmed.

Mr. Chief Justice Warren, concurring in the result.

I agree with the result reached by the Court in these cases, but, because we are operating in a field of expression and because broad language used here may eventually be applied to the arts and sciences and freedom of communication generally, I would limit our decision to the facts before us and to the validity of the statutes in question as applied.

* * *

Mr. Justice Harlan, concurring in the result in No. 61, [Roth].

I regret not to be able to join the Court's opinion. I cannot do so because I find lurking beneath its disarming generalizations a number of problems which not only leave me with serious misgivings as to the future effect of today's decisions....

I

My basic difficulties with the Court's opinion are three-fold. First, the opinion paints with such a broad brush that I fear it may result in a loosening of the tight reins which state and federal courts should hold upon the enforcement of obscenity statutes....

In final analysis, the problem presented by these cases is how far, and on what terms, the state and federal governments have power to punish individuals for disseminating books considered to be undesirable because of their nature or supposed deleterious effect upon human conduct....

I do not think that reviewing courts can escape this responsibility by saying that the trier of the facts, be it a jury or a judge, has labeled the questioned matter as "obscene," for, if "obscenity" is to be suppressed, the question whether a particular work is of that character involves not really an issue of fact but a question of constitutional *judgment* of the most sensitive and delicate kind. Many juries might find that Joyce's "Ulysses" or Bocaccio's "Decameron" was obscene, and yet the conviction of a defendant for selling either book would raise, for me, the gravest constitutional problems, for no such verdict could convince me, without more, that these books are "utterly without redeeming social importance." In short, I do not understand how the Court can resolve the constitutional problems now before it without making its own independent judgment upon the character of the material upon which these convictions were based. I am very much afraid that the broad manner in which the Court has decided these cases will tend to obscure the peculiar responsibilities resting on state and federal courts in this field and encourage them to rely on easy labeling and jury verdicts as a substitute for facing up to the tough individual problems of constitutional judgment involved in every obscenity case.

* * *

Mr. Justice Douglas, with whom Mr. Justice Black concurs, dissenting.

When we sustain these convictions, we make the legality of a publication turn on the purity of thought which a book or tract instills in the mind of the reader. I do not think we can approve that standard and be faithful to the command of the First Amendment, which by its terms is a restraint on Congress and which by the Fourteenth is a restraint on the States.

In the *Roth* case the trial judge charged the jury that the statutory words "obscene, lewd and lascivious" describe "that form of immorality which has relation to sexual impurity and has a tendency to excite lustful thoughts." He stated that the term "filthy" in the statute pertains "to that sort of treatment of sexual matters in such a vulgar and indecent way, so that it tends to arouse a feeling of disgust and revulsion." He went on to say that the material "must be calculated to corrupt and debauch the minds and morals" of "the average person in the community," not those of any particular class. "You judge the circulars, pictures and publications which have been put in evidence by present-day standards of the community. You may ask yourselves does it offend the common conscience of the community by present-day standards."

* * *

By these standards punishment is inflicted for thoughts provoked, not for overt acts nor antisocial conduct. This test cannot be squared with our decisions under the First Amendment. Even the ill-starred *Dennis* case conceded that speech to be punishable must have some relation to action which could be penalized by government. *Dennis v. United States*, 341 U.S. 494, 502 511. This issue cannot be avoided by saying that obscenity is not protected by the First Amendment. The question remains, what is the constitutional test of obscenity?

The tests by which these convictions were obtained require only the arousing of sexual thoughts. Yet the arousing of sexual thoughts and desires happens every day in normal life in dozens of ways. Nearly 30 years ago a questionnaire sent to college and normal school women graduates asked what things were most stimulating sexually. Of 409 replies, 9 said "music"; 18 said "pictures"; 29 said "dancing"; 40 said "drama"; 95 said "books"; and 218 said "man."

The test of obscenity the Court endorses today gives the censor free range over a vast domain. To allow the State to step in and punish mere speech or publication that the judge or the jury thinks has an *undesirable* impact on thoughts but that is not shown to be a part of unlawful action is drastically to curtail the First Amendment.

* * *

If we were certain that impurity of sexual thoughts impelled to action, we would be on less dangerous ground in punishing the distributors of this sex literature. But it is by no means clear that obscene literature, as so defined, is a significant factor in influencing substantial deviation from the community standards.

* * *

The absence of dependable information on the effect of obscene literature on human conduct should make us wary. It should put us on the side of protecting society's interest in literature, except and unless it can be said that the particular publication has an impact on action that the government can control.

As noted, the trial judge in the *Roth* case charged the jury in the alternative that the federal obscenity statute outlaws literature dealing with sex which offends "the common conscience of the community." That standard is, in my view, more inimical still to freedom of expression.

The standard of what offends "the common conscience of the community" conflicts, in my judgment, with the command of the First Amendment that "Congress shall make no law...abridging the freedom of speech, or of the press." Certainly that standard would not be an acceptable one if religion, economics, politics or philosophy were involved. How does it become a constitutional standard when literature treating with sex is concerned?

Any test that turns on what is offensive to the community's standards is too loose, too capricious, too destructive of freedom of expression to be squared with the First Amendment. Under that test, juries can censor, suppress, and punish what they don't like, provided the matter relates to "sexual impurity" or has a tendency "to excite lustful thoughts." This is community censorship in one of its worst forms. It creates a regime where in the battle between the literati and the Philistines, the Philistines are certain to win. If experience in this field teaches anything, it is that "censorship of obscenity has almost always been both irrational and indiscriminate."

* * *

I can understand (and at times even sympathize) with programs of civic groups and church groups to protect and defend the existing moral standards of the community. I can understand the motives of the Anthony Comstocks who would impose Victorian standards on the community. When speech alone is involved, I do not think that government, consistently with the First Amendment, can become the sponsor of any of these movements. I do not think that government, consistently with the First Amendment, can throw its weight behind one school or another. Government should be concerned with antisocial conduct, not with utterances. Thus, if the First Amendment guarantee of freedom of speech and press is to mean anything in this field, it must allow protests even against the moral code that the standard of the day sets for the community. In other words, literature should not be suppressed merely because it offends the moral code of the censor.

The legality of a publication in this country should never be allowed to turn either on the purity of thought which it instills in the mind of the reader or on the degree to which it offends the community conscience. By either test the role of the censor is exalted, and society's values in literary freedom are sacrificed.

The Court today suggests a third standard. It defines obscene material as that "which deals with sex in a manner appealing to prurient interest." Like the standards applied by the trial judges below, that standard does not require any nexus between the literature which is prohibited and action which the legislature can regulate or prohibit.

Under the First Amendment, that standard is no more valid than those which the courts below adopted.

I do not think that the problem can be resolved by the Court's statement that "obscenity is not expression protected by the First Amendment." ...[T]here is no special historical evidence that literature dealing with sex was intended to be treated in a special manner by those who drafted the First Amendment. ...I reject too the implication that problems of freedom of speech and of the press are to be resolved by weighing against the values of free expression, the judgment of the Court that a particular form of that expression has "no redeeming social importance." The First Amendment, its prohibition in terms absolute, was designed to preclude courts as well as legislatures from weighing the values of speech against silence. The First Amendment puts free speech in the preferred position.

Freedom of expression can be suppressed if, and to the extent that, it is so closely brigaded with illegal action as to be an inseparable part of it. As a people, we cannot afford to relax that standard. For the test that suppresses a cheap tract today can suppress a literary gem tomorrow. All it need do is to incite a lascivious thought or arouse a lustful desire. The list of books that judges or juries can place in that category is endless.

I would give the broad sweep of the First Amendment full support. I have the same confidence in the ability of our people to reject noxious literature as I have in their capacity to sort out the true from the false in theology, economics, politics, or any other field.

*

The thoughtful, curious, and candid observer may have experienced a mental trace of something like, "why did the Court get involved in this in the manner it did?" Or, why did the Court go so far? Uphold the convictions and give the rationale, fine. What else is there to do? The Court accomplished its constitutional mandate of *Marbury* (ruling on the constitutionality of the statutes at issue), but then somehow now felt a compulsion to go further. The convictions were affirmed and the statutes upon which they were sought could, *sub silentio,* be found to be constitutional (indeed they were), and the defendants had notice of them. What else is there for the justices to do under the claimed constitutional mandate, *viz.,* the power of review? Observe, reader, what their *dictum* hath wrought. Do we know why the case was accepted, or more specifically, do we know why the Court was so gratuitous with its *dictum*? May one assume the subject matter of the defendants' businesses was not protected by the standard enunciated by the Court as their convictions were upheld? If so, I invite you to research and review the materials they were selling (easily available online) and ask yourself the question, would they fail to pass constitutional muster today (I notice they were not set out in the Court's reported opinion)? Or, has our culture changed so much they would be seen as passé? If so, why?

Coming at it differently, ask yourself the question, is it conceivable the case has played a role in the respect we have for one another? As behavior is grounded in our value sets, has it played a role in the lives of our families and children? Has it been embittering? Has it provoked lack of respect or destruction of domestic relations? Has it fostered abuse? At least one of the plujority recognized the problem of the Court painting with too wide a brush, but to which no attention was evidently paid, with another calling for what would amount to a more careful tailoring of the opinion, also ignored, agreeing with the result but cautioning about its future effects (unintended consequences possibly). Was this done purposely notwithstanding the warnings, or simply without perspicacity or sagacity? Why no use of the deep-rooted traditions of a nation or the conscience of the people?

Surely someone must have spoken up during case conferences? Could there have even been at least a clerk among them who might have seen, from even a youthful perspective, something more ahead, or at least voiced a concern there could be an unintended consequence "emanating" from the gratuitous *dicta* incapable of even being known or even knowable, let alone understood. But, oh no, not here, no emanations in this case; in fact, there is not even a penumbra with who knows what might be lurking in its midst. The Court simply forged ahead and attempted to state the legal line defining obscenity, or maybe more accurately, what wasn't, in a way that created a state of affairs where virtually nothing would qualify, an unworkable standard wouldn't you think? Ask it another way: what has the Court found to be unacceptable, and then think about that.

The culture was forever changed. If you ask a young person today (effectively two generations later) about this shift in legal attitude and social standards, they will look at you dumbstruck. Blank faced.

They would have no idea what you are talking about. They have been raised on what was at one time considered obscene, *verboten,* totally unacceptable, but no longer is. It is them. They are now us. And you wonder what has happened to our people? No wonder the invaders are mad. Thank you, Mr. Brennan. Thank you, SCOTUS.

Then along comes our friend from *Griswold*, this time on the other end of the opinion, saying, without emanations in hand, the convictions should be reversed, they cannot constitutionally stand, for the First Amendment means exactly what it says, free speech and free press, period. Everything in the premises here is protected. For Douglas, one can seemingly do no wrong in this area of civil jurisprudence. Nothing exists which can't be constitutionally spoken or written save a communication which in fact is a part of some other criminal act or conspiracy, or a tort, i.e., libel or slander (look them up). Apart from that, he pens, the First Amendment is absolute. I read the last quoted paragraph of his dissent, and set to wondering, did not that essentially happen as a practical matter? Didn't the Court operationally state Douglas' position without being utterly ham-fisted about it? And in the process, wasn't the Court opening the door so wide so as to end all like business coming before it? It has pretty much ended. That couldn't be! Would it do that to the citizens and their country?

We have already noted that a majority of the Court (as apparently has been the case over time) does not feel that all speech is protected, and that within the parameters of even an indefinable limitation, not all speech passes the test. That is to say, not every utterance is protected. Libel (which you now know is a tort) is referenced by the Court as an exception, for example. Or, too, "fighting words" likely to cause a breach of the peace. Statutes calling for such limitations pass constitutional muster if "carefully drawn," "narrowly tailored," and limited to "well-defined" classes of speech reflecting a public interest outweighing free speech. But pornography? Let us now turn to the Court's carefully drawn, narrowly tailored and well-defined conceptualization of obscenity (we leave pornography and its sub-classifications out at this point—it is unnecessarily confusing—or is it all really the same thing, a matter of degree...or the form of the latter in its ultimate utter lack of "value" simply leading to the former...or are we simply talking about sex [in its verb form] published in prurient form as suggested in the majority opinion?).

Obscenity should be rejected from constitutional protection if it is "...utterly without redeeming social importance," it is said. Then the Court goes on to say, seemingly clarifying what it had already said, that "...[t]here are certain well-defined and limited classes of speech, the prevention and punishment of which have never been thought to raise any Constitutional problem. These include the lewd and obscene...." "*It has been well observed that such utterances are no essential part of any exposition of ideas, and are of such slight social value as a step to truth that any benefit that may be derived from them is clearly outweighed by the social interest in order and morality….*" Perfect! So now we know what obscenity is! And then the Court helpfully adds the notion that sex and obscenity are not the same thing, but that which is obscene is that (apparently) which "…deals with sex in a manner appealing to prurient interest." Having read the case, you have already looked up "prurient" and so we don't have to get into that. Oh, what the hey! Come on, it means arousal. If it arouses you it is obscene and therefore illegal, or at least unconstitutional, and utterly without redeeming social importance. Huh? So there you have it, folks. Is that how you read it? I don't know whether or not to just go ahead and turn myself in. And keeping your mouth shut, or your pen in your pocket, just won't do the trick. You have to wear something because dancing around in the nude is speech (see next case please). But the arousal bit seems potentially problematic for I don't know of any day where most anyone isn't, at least if they are paying attention. Maybe just a little bit? Is that okay? But, isn't that the nature of the beast? So, according to the Supremes, we all go to jail. How charming. Maybe thoughts are excepted. Maybe that's because they can't be policed, but arousal can? Oh my God!

Just as an aside, it seems odd that we are not hearing anything in this opinion about metaphysical matters and flowery prosaic bouquets such as "the nation's collective conscience," "embedded American traditions," "fundamental precepts," "deep rooted" and the like. Where are they? Why not here? If they are good enough to justify the finding of privacy on a constitutional basis in Connecticut so we can slide into something a little more comfortable, they certainly ought to be good enough to find some limitation on obscenity as a constitutional matter here, no? I guess what the "average person" feels in the community is going to have to do. But even that didn't last long.

Nice and clear, and if not, the Court takes care of that little matter by saying, "…that lack of precision is not itself offensive to the requirements of due process" (often defined as fair play and fundamental or substantial justice with clear and reasonable notice of that which is permitted and that which is not) or more particularly, I presume, in an area where precision is impossible, or more accurately, doesn't exist. On the other hand, what choice do they have? Once they start, they can't stop. Sounds familiar….

And now, friends, we will observe the Supreme Court dealing with nipples (we all have them – at that moment of creation an equality attack must have erupted…but it pretty much ends there), and for your further reading enjoyment and pleasure, and without any further comment, I lift the curtain on *Barnes v. Glen Theater, Inc.*

VIII

BARNES, PROSECUTING ATTORNEY OF ST. JOSEPH COUNTY,
INDIANA, ET AL. *v.*
GLEN THEATRE, INC., ET AL.
501 U.S. 560
CERTIORARI TO THE UNITED STATES COURT OF APPEALS
FOR THE SEVENTH CIRCUIT

Chief Justice Rehnquist announced the judgment of the Court and delivered an opinion, in which Justice O'Connor and Justice Kennedy join.

Respondents are two establishments in South Bend, Indiana, that wish to provide totally nude dancing as entertainment, and individual dancers who are employed at these establishments. They claim that the First Amendment's guarantee of freedom of expression prevents the State of Indiana from enforcing its public indecency law to prevent this form of dancing. We reject their claim.

The facts appear from the pleadings and findings of the District Court and are uncontested here. The Kitty Kat Lounge, Inc. (Kitty Kat), is located in the city of South Bend. It sells alcoholic beverages and presents "go-go dancing." Its proprietor desires to present "totally nude dancing," but an applicable Indiana statute regulating public nudity requires that the dancers wear "pasties" and "G-strings" when they dance. The dancers are not paid an hourly wage, but work on commission. They receive a 100 percent commission on the first $60 in drink sales during their performances. Darlene Miller, one of the respondents in the action, had worked at the Kitty Kat for about two years at the time this action was brought. Miller wishes to dance nude because she believes she would make more money doing so.

Respondent Glen Theatre, Inc., is an Indiana corporation with a place of business in South Bend. Its primary business is supplying so-called adult entertainment through written and printed materials, movie showings, and live entertainment at an enclosed "bookstore." The live entertainment at the "bookstore" consists of nude and seminude performances and showings of the female body through glass panels. Customers sit in a booth and insert coins into a timing mechanism that permits them to observe the live nude and seminude dancers for a period of time. One of Glen Theatre's dancers, Gayle Ann Marie Sutro, has danced, modeled, and acted professionally for more than 15 years, and in addition to her performances at the Glen Theatre, can be seen in a pornographic movie at a nearby theater.

Respondents sued in the United States District Court for the Northern District of Indiana to enjoin the enforcement of the Indiana public indecency statute, Ind. Code § 35-45-4-1 (1998), asserting that its prohibition against complete nudity in public places violated the First Amendment. The District Court originally granted respondents' prayer for an injunction, finding that the statute was facially overbroad. The Court of Appeals for the Seventh Circuit reversed, deciding that previous litigation with respect to the statute in the Supreme Court of Indiana and this Court precluded the possibility of such a challenge, and remanded to the District Court in order for the plaintiffs to pursue their claim that the statute violated the First Amendment as applied to their dancing. On remand, the District Court concluded that "the type of dancing these plaintiffs wish to perform is not expressive activity protected by the Constitution of the United States," and rendered judgment in favor of the defendants. The case was again appealed to the Seventh Circuit, and a panel of that court reversed the District Court, holding that the nude dancing involved here was expressive conduct protected by the First Amendment. The Court of Appeals then heard the case en banc, and the court rendered a series of comprehensive and thoughtful opinions. The majority concluded that nonobscene nude dancing performed for entertainment is expression protected by the First Amendment, and that the public indecency statute was an improper infringement of that expressive activity because its purpose was to prevent the message of eroticism and sexuality conveyed by the dancers. We granted certiorari, and now hold that the Indiana statutory requirement that the dancers in the establishments involved in this case must wear pasties and G-strings does not violate the First Amendment.

* * *

Indiana, of course, has not banned nude dancing as such, but has proscribed public nudity across the board. The Supreme Court of Indiana has construed the Indiana statute to preclude nudity in what are essentially places of public accommodation such as the Glen Theatre and the Kitty Kat Lounge. In such places, respondents point out, minors are excluded and there are no nonconsenting viewers. Respondents contend that while the State may license establishments such as the ones involved here, and limit the geographical area in which they do business, it may not in any way limit the performance of the dances within them without violating the First Amendment. The petitioners contend, on the other hand, that Indiana's restriction on nude dancing is a valid "time, place, or manner" restriction....

The "time, place, or manner" test was developed for evaluating restrictions on expression taking place on public property which had been dedicated as a "public forum[.]" ...[T]his test has been interpreted to embody much the same standards as those set forth in *United States* v. *O'Brien*, 391 U.S. 367 (1968), and we turn, therefore, to the rule enunciated in *O'Brien*.

O'Brien burned his draft card on the steps of the South Boston Courthouse in the presence of a sizable crowd, and was convicted of violating a statute that prohibited the knowing destruction or mutilation of such a card. He claimed that his conviction was contrary to the First Amendment because his act was "symbolic speech" – expressive conduct. The Court rejected his contention that symbolic speech is entitled to full First Amendment protection, saying:

> "[E]ven on the assumption that the alleged communicative element in O'Brien's conduct is sufficient to bring into play the First Amendment, it does not necessarily follow that the destruction of a registration certificate is constitutionally protected activity. This Court has held that when 'speech' and 'nonspeech' elements are combined in the same course of conduct, a sufficiently important governmental interest in regulating the nonspeech element can justify incidental limitations on First Amendment freedoms. To characterize the quality of the governmental interest which must appear, the Court has employed a variety of descriptive terms: compelling; substantial; subordinating; paramount; cogent; strong. Whatever imprecision inhered in these terms, we think it clear that a government regulation is sufficiently justified if it is within the constitutional power of the Government; if it furthers an important or substantial governmental interest; if the

governmental interest is unrelated to the suppression of free expression; and if the incidental restriction on alleged First Amendment freedoms is no greater than is essential to the furtherance of that interest."

Applying the four-part *O'Brien* test enunciated above, we find that Indiana's public indecency statute is justified despite its incidental limitations on some expressive activity. The public indecency statute is clearly within the constitutional power of the State and furthers substantial governmental interest.... Public indecency statutes such as the one before us reflect moral disapproval of people appearing in the nude among strangers in public places.

* * *

This and other public indecency statutes were designed to protect morals and public order. The traditional police power of the States is defined as the authority to provide for the public health, safety, and morals, and we have upheld such a basis for legislation. In *Paris Adult Theatre I* v. *Slaton*, 413 U.S. 49, 61 (1973), we said:

> "In deciding *Roth* [v. *United States*, 354 U.S. 476 (1957)] this Court implicitly accepted that a legislature could legitimately act on such a conclusion to protect 'the social interest in order and morality.'"

And in *Bowers* v. *Hardwick*, 478 U.S. 186, 196 (1986), we said:

> "The law, however, is constantly based on notions of morality, and if all laws representing essentially moral choices are to be invalidated under the Due Process Clause, the courts will be very busy indeed."

Thus, the public indecency statute furthers a substantial government interest in protecting order and morality.

This interest is unrelated to the suppression of free expression. Some may view restricting nudity on moral grounds as necessarily related to expression. We disagree. It can be argued, of course, that almost limitless types of conduct – including appearing in the nude in public – are "expressive," and in one sense of the word this is true. People who go about in the nude in public may be expressing something about themselves by so doing. But the court rejected this expansive notion of "expressive conduct" in *O'Brien*, saying:

> "We cannot accept the view that an apparently limitless variety of conduct can be labeled 'speech' whenever the person engaging in the conduct intends thereby to express an idea."

* * *

But we do not think that when Indiana applies its statute to the nude dancing in these nightclubs it is proscribing nudity because of the erotic message conveyed by the dancers. Presumably numerous other erotic performances are presented at these establishments and similar clubs without any interference from the State, so long as the performers wear a scant amount of clothing. Likewise, the requirement that the dancers don pasties and G-strings does not deprive the dance of whatever erotic message it conveys; it simply makes the message slightly less graphic. The perceived evil that Indiana seeks to address is not erotic dancing, but public nudity. The appearance of people of all shapes, sizes and ages in the nude at a beach, for example, would convey little if any erotic message, yet the State still seeks to prevent it. Public nudity is the evil the State seeks to prevent, whether or not it is combined with expressive activity.

This conclusion is buttressed by a reference to the facts of *O'Brien*. An Act of Congress provided that anyone who knowingly destroyed a Selective Service registration certificate committed an offense. O'Brien burned his certificate on the steps of the South Boston Courthouse to influence others to adopt his antiwar beliefs. This Court upheld his conviction, reasoning that the continued availability of issued certificates served a legitimate and substantial purpose in the administration of the Selective Service System. O'Brien's deliberate destruction of his certificate frustrated this purpose and "[f]or this noncommunicative impact of his conduct, and for nothing else, he was convicted." 391 U.S., at 382. It was assumed that O'Brien's act in burning the certificate had a communicative element in it sufficient to bring into play the First Amendment, *id.*, at 376, but it was for the noncommunicative element that he was prosecuted. So here with the Indiana statute; while the dancing to which it was applied had a communicative element, it was not the dancing that was prohibited, but simply its being done in the nude.

The fourth part of the *O'Brien* test requires that the incidental restriction on First Amendment freedom be no greater than is essential to the furtherance of the governmental interest. As indicated in the discussion above, the governmental interest served by the text of the prohibition is societal disapproval of nudity in public places and among strangers. The statutory prohibition is not a means to some greater end, but an end in itself. It is without cavil that the public indecency statute is "narrowly tailored"; Indiana's requirement that the dancers wear at least pasties and G-strings is modest, and the bare minimum necessary to achieve the State's purpose.

The judgment of the Court of Appeals accordingly is

Reversed.

Justice Scalia, concurring in the judgment.

I agree that the judgment of the Court of Appeals must be reversed. In my view, however, the challenged regulation must be upheld, not because it survives some lower level of First Amendment scrutiny, but because, as a general law regulating conduct and not specifically directed at expression, it is not subject to First Amendment scrutiny at all.

I

Indiana's public indecency statute provides:

"(a) A person who knowingly or intentionally, in a public place:

"(1) engages in sexual intercourse;

"(2) engages in deviate sexual conduct;

"(3) appears in a state of nudity; or

"(4) fondles the genitals of himself or another person; commits public indecency, a Class A misdemeanor.

"(b) 'Nudity' means the showing of the human male or female genitals, pubic area, or buttocks with less than a fully opaque covering, the showing of the female breast with less than a fully opaque covering of any part of the nipple, or the showing of covered male genitals in a discernibly turgid state."

On its face, this law is not directed at expression in particular. As Judge Easterbrook put it in his dissent below: "Indiana does not regulate dancing. It regulates public nudity.... Almost the entire domain of Indiana's statute is unrelated to expression, unless we view nude beaches and topless hot dog vendors as speech." The intent to convey a "message of eroticism" (or any other message) is not a necessary element of the statutory offense of public indecency; nor does one commit that statutory offense by conveying the most explicit "message of eroticism," so long as he does not commit any of the four specified acts in the process.

Indiana's statute is in the line of a long tradition of laws against public nudity, which have never been thought to run afoul of traditional understanding of "the freedom of speech." ...Were it the case that Indiana *in practice* targeted only expressive nudity, while turning a blind eye to nude beaches and unclothed purveyors of hot dogs and machine tools, it might be said that what posed as a regulation of conduct in general was in reality a regulation of only communicative conduct....

The dissent confidently asserts that the purpose of restricting nudity in public places in general is to protect nonconsenting parties from offense; and argues that since only consenting, admission-paying patrons see respondents dance, that purpose cannot apply and the only remaining purpose must relate to the communicative elements of the performance. Perhaps the dissenters believe that "offense to others" *ought* to be the only reason for restricting nudity in public places generally, but there is no basis for thinking that our society has ever shared that Thoreauvian "you-may-do-what-you-like-so-long-as-it-does-not-injure-someone-else" beau ideal – much less for thinking that it was written into the Constitution. The purpose of Indiana's nudity law would be violated, I think, if 60,000 fully consenting adults crowded into the Hoosier Dome to display their genitals to one another, even if there were not an offended innocent in the crowd. Our society prohibits, and all human societies have prohibited, certain activities not because they harm others but because they are considered, in the traditional phrase, "*contra bonos mores*," *i.e.*, immoral. In American society, such prohibitions have included, for example, sadomasochism, cockfighting, bestiality, suicide, drug use, prostitution, and sodomy. While there may be great diversity of view on whether various of these prohibitions should exist (though I have found few ready to abandon, in principle, all of them), there is no doubt that, absent specific constitutional protection for the conduct involved, the Constitution does not prohibit them simply because they regulate "morality." ...The purpose of the Indiana statute, as both its text and the manner of its enforcement demonstrate, is to enforce the traditional moral belief that people should not expose their private parts indiscriminately, regardless of whether those who see them are disedified. Since that is so, the dissent has no basis for positing that, where only thoroughly edified adults are present, the purpose must be repression of communication.

II

Since the Indiana regulation is a general law not specifically targeted at expressive conduct, its application to such conduct does not in my view implicate the First Amendment.

The First Amendment explicitly protects "the freedom of speech [and] of the press" – oral and written speech – not "expressive conduct." When any law restricts speech, even for a purpose that has nothing to do with the suppression of communication...we insist that it meet the high, First Amendment standard of justification. But virtually *every* law restricts conduct, and virtually *any* prohibited conduct can be performed for an expressive purpose – if only expressive of the fact that the actor disagrees with the prohibition.... It cannot reasonably be demanded, therefore, that every restriction of expression incidentally produced by a general law regulating conduct pass normal First Amendment scrutiny, or even – as some of our cases have suggested, see, *e. g., United States* v. *O'Brien*, 391 U.S. 367, 377 (1968) – that it be justified by an "important or substantial" government interest. Nor do our holdings require such justification: We have never invalidated the application of a general law simply because the conduct that it reached was being engaged in for expressive purposes and the government could not demonstrate a sufficiently important state interest.

This is not to say that the First Amendment affords no protection to expressive conduct. Where the government prohibits conduct *precisely because of its communicative attributes*, we hold the regulation unconstitutional.

* * *

All our holdings (though admittedly not some of our discussion) support the conclusion that "the only First Amendment analysis applicable to laws that do not directly or indirectly impede speech is the threshold inquiry of whether the purpose of the law is to suppress communication. If not, that is the end of the matter so far as First Amendment guarantees are concerned; if so, the court then proceeds to determine whether there is substantial justification for the proscription."

* * *

Indiana may constitutionally enforce its prohibition of public nudity even against those who choose to use public nudity as a means of communication. The State is regulating conduct, not expression, and those who choose to employ conduct as a means of expression must make sure that the conduct they select is not generally forbidden. For these reasons, I agree that the judgment should be reversed.

* * *

Justice White, with whom Justice Marshall, Justice Blackmun, and Justice Stevens join, dissenting.

The first question presented to us in this case is whether nonobscene nude dancing performed as entertainment is expressive conduct protected by the First Amendment. The Court of Appeals held that it is, observing that our prior decisions permit no other conclusion. Not surprisingly, then, the plurality now concedes that "nude dancing of the kind sought to be performed here is expressive conduct within the outer perimeters of the First Amendment...." This is no more than recognizing, as the Seventh Circuit observed, that dancing is an ancient art form and "inherently embodies the expression and communication of ideas and emotions."

* * *

The plurality acknowledges that it is impossible to discern the exact state interests which the Indiana Legislature had in mind when it enacted the Indiana statute, but the plurality nonetheless concludes that it is clear from the statute's text and history that the law's purpose is to protect "societal order and morality." The plurality goes on to conclude that Indiana's statute "was enacted as *a general prohibition*," *ante*, at 568 (emphasis added), on people appearing in the nude among strangers in public places. The plurality then points to cases in which we upheld legislation based on the State's police power, and ultimately concludes that the Indiana statute "furthers a substantial government interest in protecting order and morality." The plurality also holds that the basis for banning nude dancing is unrelated to free expression and that it is narrowly drawn to serve the State's interest.

The plurality's analysis is erroneous in several respects. Both the plurality and Justice Scalia in his opinion concurring in the judgment overlook a fundamental and critical aspect of our cases upholding the States' exercise of their police powers.... [I]n this case Indiana does not suggest that its statute applies to, or could be applied to, nudity wherever it occurs, including the home. We do not understand the plurality or Justice Scalia to be suggesting that Indiana could constitutionally enact such an intrusive prohibition....

We are told by the attorney general of Indiana that the Indiana Supreme Court held that the statute at issue here cannot and does not prohibit nudity as a part of some larger form of expression meriting protection when the communication of ideas is involved. Petitioners also state that the evils sought to be avoided by applying the statute in this case would not obtain in the case of theatrical productions, such as "Salome" or "Hair."

* * *

Thus, the Indiana statute is not a *general* prohibition of the type we have upheld in prior cases. As a result, the plurality and Justice Scalia's simple references to the State's general interest in promoting societal order and morality are not sufficient justification for a statute which concededly reaches a significant amount of protected expressive activity.

* * *

As the State now tells us, and as Justice Souter agrees, the State's goal in applying what it describes as its "content neutral" statute to the nude dancing in this case is "deterrence of prostitution, sexual assaults, criminal activity, degradation of women, and other activities which break down family structure."

* * *

The perceived evil is not erotic dancing but public nudity, which may be prohibited despite any incidental impact on expressive activity. This analysis is transparently erroneous.

In arriving at its conclusion, the plurality concedes that nude dancing conveys an erotic message and concedes that the message would be muted if the dancers wore pasties and G-strings. Indeed, the emotional or erotic impact of the dance is intensified by the nudity of the performers. As Judge Posner argued in his thoughtful concurring opinion in the Court of Appeals, the nudity of the dancer is an integral part of the emotions and thoughts that a nude dancing performance evokes. The sight of a fully clothed, or even a partially clothed, dancer generally will have a far different impact on a spectator than that of a nude dancer, even if the same dance is performed. The nudity is itself an expressive component of the dance, not merely incidental "conduct." We have previously pointed out that "'[n]udity alone' does not place otherwise protected material outside the mantle of the First Amendment."

This being the case, it cannot be that the statutory prohibition is unrelated to expressive conduct. Since the State permits the dancers to perform if they wear pasties and G-strings but forbids nude dancing, it is precisely because of the distinctive, expressive content of the nude dancing performances at issue in this case that the State seeks to apply the statutory prohibition. It is only because nude dancing performances may generate emotions and feelings of eroticism and sensuality among the spectators that the State seeks to regulate such expressive activity, apparently on the assumption that creating or emphasizing such thoughts and ideas in the minds of the spectators may lead to increased prostitution and the degradation of women. But generating thoughts, ideas, and emotions is the essence of communication. The nudity element of nude dancing performances cannot be neatly pigeonholed as mere "conduct" independent of any expressive component of the dance.

* * *

That the performances in the Kitty Kat Lounge may not be high art, to say the least, and may not appeal to the Court, is hardly an excuse for distorting and ignoring settled doctrine. The Court's assessment of the artistic merits of nude dancing performances should not be the determining factor in deciding this case. In the words of Justice Harlan: "[I]t is largely because governmental officials cannot make principled decisions in this area that the Constitution leaves matters of taste and style so largely to the individual." "[W]hile the entertainment afforded by a nude ballet at Lincoln Center to those who can pay the price may differ vastly in content (as viewed by judges) or in quality (as viewed by critics), it may not differ in substance from the dance viewed by the person who...wants some 'entertainment' with his beer or shot of rye." *Salem Inn, Inc.* v. *Frank*, 501 F. 2d 18.

* * *

Accordingly, I would affirm the judgment of the Court of Appeals, and dissent from this Court's judgment.

BOWERS V. HARDWICK

O nly so much can be included in this collection, an unusual book such as it is, with the inclusions here being a challenging process as I commented on earlier (you may have already looked up some references which in your opinion would have been as good if not better than what I have selected—and if all such had been included here, can you imagine what this tome would have become) hopefully with both inclusions and exclusions being at least fairly debatable. Following up on references is a valuable part of this event. Anyway, why not take a look at two cases dealing with sexual preferences, which, you have guessed it, go both ways *and* are both decided on constitutional principles (can you imagine?): *Bowers v. Hardwick, et al.*, 478 U.S.

186 (1986), and *Lawrence, et al., v. Texas*, 539 U.S. 558 (2003), providing an unforgettable ride into the Land of Oz. Again, you are not so much concerned with the subject matter of these cases (as with all the other cases presented—that is a matter for others who would dawdle there) as you are with the process of the Court, its legitimacy, as it were, its fidelity to the Constitution. The first one is another five to four opinion with the second being five to one to three, the one being O'Connor's "concurring in the judgment" of the *Lawrence* court, but going on to say in the second sentence thereof, "I joined *Bowers*, and do not join the Court (in *Lawrence*) in overruling it." In a sense, it is still five to four with O'Connor here trying to ride sidesaddle. We'll leave it there for now. Judge for yourself when you read the cases.

Nevertheless and needless to say, sideliners are going to speculate on why these cases were selected, what motive rests behind their inclusion; is there not something more here than meets, say, the nose? There is. They represent a fairly frank and candid change of position, so to speak, by the Court reversing itself, *albeit* clumsily, explaining (protesting a prior court's view) far too much, one might think, but nevertheless taking into account the *zeitgeist.* That's all. Regardless of what you think about the subject matter of the cases themselves, that which the Court felt it had to do may be commendable. And then again, maybe not. At the same time one should note the Court sported a new membership except for O'Connor, Rehnquist, and Stevens, with O'Connor seemingly taking a split view. She concurred with the result, apparently, but refused to join in its reversal of *Bowers*. Some observers say she sought middle ground, others pointing out she worked mightily in bringing the Court to come together, trying for some kind of consensus, a few holding her up as the perennial deciding factor. Probably little or none of it is true. If anything is perennial, it is these kinds of cases being decided five to four (where anyone can be the deciding vote unless a member is so unstable as to be the one seen as delivering the victory depending on the swing), at least in so many cases in the area of social "jurisprudence." Being in the five doesn't make one the deciding factor. And again, if one had a penchant for wobbling around in philosophy, then one might also be somewhat of a deciding factor, at least for now, but for reasons uncomely, and certainly not a wonderful compliment. You are on your own in deciding, and it deserves thought. Unanimity isn't necessarily the loadstar, as that would eliminate valuable and thought provoking dissents although differing views may also be more wisely reflected in separate and more tailored concurring opinions. On the other hand, keep in mind that writing an opinion and position taking is revealing behavior in the scientific sense, and speaks in its own voice beyond the words pronounced.

Whatever position is taken on these issues, or on which side of *Lochner* doctrine one chooses to stand, is just another illustration of a philosophical break. However, *Lochner* is one of those cases likened to the previously observed unruly horse (or dog) in equity practice (trying to do what is "right"), which unless kept firmly chained is wont to get into places where it ought not be, the business of the States, as some would see it, a matter presumably controlled by the clear meaning of the Tenth Amendment. Once the doctrine was given life, however, the genie is set free, and now what do you do with it? Here the Court seemingly went outside its constitutional authority and again decided to legislate, some would say, or at the very least again opened the door to a legislative career by substituting its judgment for that of an Article One style elected body. And now, in the sodomy cases to follow the Court has again hung out its "Open for Business" shingle. Over the years you will observe it being put up and taken down again and again (sometimes even in the same kind of case). Read again the language in the opening salvos of the *Griswold* opinion (page 53, *supra*) and that which follows: "We do not sit as a super-legislature...." (They are not going to do it; they are going to do it. They didn't; they did.) That was fifty years ago, over a hundred years since *Lochner,* and the battle still rages. Any truth in behavior?

For the Court to put legislation under the constitutional optic for purposes of assessing its fair and even-handed application is one thing. But to re-write it, so as to be a "super-legislature," as one of the members put it, is another. There may be an answer. Why was it that one of the members said, "We do not sit as a super-legislature," and then proceeded to sit as a super-legislature? Why?

There are instances where it is more instructive to look through the eyes of the Court via its reports regarding the subject matter before it while using the vehicle of more than one case, and to seek residence within its intellectual being as revealed in its opinions *seriatim* long enough to observe the contours of its psyche, or its thought processes, its struggles to craft a product, if not a nation. This is not easy work. Sometimes you simply have to wait, for from time to time the brass ring will come back around. While it may be disconcerting, it can provide a revelation into how the Court functions, and maybe even why. It is the only way for a chance to know. It is akin to a psychiatric penetration which the Court is not capable of doing upon itself, or any other body upon itself for that matter. It is not only unable to recognize its inner drives or convictions, collectively or individually, and apparently the panoply of its outward effects, but rather, functions grounded in and bound up within the parameters of the issue before it and how the Constitution ought be employed, and nothing else, locked in the myopic interstitial glue of its own dogma and/or individual philosophical biases. Some would refer to this as scientifically illustrating the limitations of concrete thought. Among the aspects of the Court that can be fatal to its outcome-based success, this is one. In epistemological terms, the Court's inability to anticipate, let alone understand it doesn't know what it cannot or should not do—in simpler terms, to perceive or even recognize (at least five to four) unintended consequences—has been destructive. We will see it time and time again as cases pass before us and we contemplate the effect they have had on the world around us. In effect, the common good and laws which make us truly free envisaged by the drafters are being sacrificed by personal scripts at the side altar (SCOTUS) of the constitutional cathedral (a concept, not a place) instead of taking into consideration what it was intended to do, and not do. A land grab it is. On the other hand, it may be that it, the Court, simply does not bother, or is otherwise beyond the capacity of its clerks' experiences and abilities to process. However, this is not unusual for ultimate institutions or those who fill such roles. This is a phenomenon from which no one is immune. The Captain is the Captain, and the Captain has to decide. The Captain doesn't have an onsite overseer during a storm. If he did, he wouldn't be Captain. So, it becomes the decision which takes stage center with the process taking place behind the curtains of the set with the actors never being aware of the silent artillery set off as a consequence of their actions, the operations on the dark side of the Court. However, there are limiting factors.

History is full of tumultuous blunders, and this is from whence they often come, the inability to see the forest. It is a common mistake for a student to start with the presupposition that whatever a court says is "correct." To the contrary, the opposite would likely be the more successful approach in evaluating and understanding at least some of its sociological jurisprudence, a business out of which it ought to get. Unwarranted? No. There are members of the Court who would candidly say the same thing. Some have. Others have an agenda, something they swore not to promote when they took office. Beyond disgusting.

*

We will now consider some cases on more than an individual basis, an inter-case construct if you will. Are you able to observe the emerging pattern here? *Roe* and *Glucksberg* (as well as *Stenberg, infra,* and the following references to *Gonzales*), or *Roth, Sullivan* and *Snyder,* and much of which lies ahead, *inter alia,* will stand out in this regard. There is a relationship between these cases. Some cases stand alone and speak loudly in their own voice with the character of the Court bursting through without any contrasts being needed to give your work meaning or to otherwise enable you to make an assessment or judgment call on its work product (*Glucksberg*). On occasion, ringing dissents help fill the role (*Roth*). By the way, you probably could have written the dissenting opinions yourself.

We are not concerned with right or wrong, agreeing or disagreeing, or even judgment calls. That is for the media and "teachers" with an agenda. For some, these are matters for classroom debate, hopefully providing an environment for students to discover that indeed there are sides, and just as importantly their effects. For us, it is a matter of observing the work of the Court and the hiatus between it and the needs and quality of life of the people it serves. Seemingly, the

Court could use some non-partisan counsel of its own for it is partisan counsel which in part leads it astray.

For now, however, let us enjoy an intellectual safari. Here, from among many, we have two cases: *Bowers v. Hardwick*, 478 U.S. 186 (1986), and *Lawrence v. Texas*, 539 U.S. 558 (2003). In *Bowers*, the Court reviewed for purposes of constitutionality a Georgia statute criminalizing sodomy, which it upheld five to four. In *Lawrence*, the Court (with five new members) reviewed for purposes of constitutionality a Texas statute criminalizing sodomy between homosexuals, which it struck down, again splitting. Remarkable, you say?

Aside from any issue as to whether or not the Constitution speaks to the issue of sodomy, or whether the drafters intended it to do so, or even whether or not sodomy can be found somewhere in its penumbras, radiations, or emanations, we can understand it does deal with liberty and freedoms. Put another way, is sodomy a federal issue as a constitutional matter?

You have enough in your intellectual arsenal and legal acumen to work through these two cases and recognize not only their nuances, but also what has happened in the world of nine. A couple of thoughts are offered as suggested thinking points. One has already been mentioned: there is what would appear to be a slight variation in the wording of the two statutes, *viz.*, "sodomy" in Georgia and "sodomy between members of the same gender" in Texas. Constitutionally, there is a world of difference, so to speak. At least there is enough difference for the Court to seize upon that opportunity to reverse itself (actually reverse another Court of five members no longer present), while hopefully reversing itself gracefully (which needless to say falls into a less than ideal category of professionalism, constitutionalism, some aspect of *stare decisis*, or even frank politics), whether the earlier Court was said to have "misapprehended" the nature of the issue or not. The fact there are now five new members on the Court at the time of *Lawrence* (homosexual sodomy) is obvious, but how one justice present for both cases straddled both cases deserves at least a passing observation.

Brennan, Burger, Marshall, Powell, and White, *Bowers'* scrivener, are gone the second time around. O'Connor voted to uphold the Georgia sodomy statute, which survived constitutional scrutiny, five to four. Now, thumb ahead and note the first three sentences of her "concurring" opinion in *Lawrence*, dealing with sodomy, this time in Texas. Looks like Justice O'Connor wants it both ways. She can't have it both ways...or maybe she can. Remember, we are looking beyond the opinions. She says she does not join in overturning *Bowers* (sodomy in general) seemingly preserving her position. So, a six to three opinion starts to look like another five to four, this time the other way around. Has sodomy changed or has the Constitution changed? Or, has the Court changed? Or, is it something else?

Whatever the case, sodomy statutes, under the scrutiny of due process and equal protection, did go through a change of fortunes, with O'Connor trying mightily not to change her position, at least overtly. Her problem with the Texas statute is that it was restricted to males, and hence, *sub silentio*, homosexuals, homosexual males that is, and was a denial of equal protection to an entire class of people now openly recognized—sodomists. In other words, a man at the time could sodomize his wife in Texas, but not his boyfriend. This, it is presumed, is a denial of equal protection of the laws. So, O'Connor gets to let the world know how she stands on sodomy in conformance with *Bowers*, but at the same time joins a Court which is about to decriminalize it across the board, again on the footing of due process and privacy, if not equal protection, as it were. Few would doubt she was right as a technical constitutional matter, and why not, the majority was already there anyway, and this way she gets to hit with them, too. Had there only been four votes not counting hers, her concurrence on other grounds (equal protection) would have been the deciding vote, nevertheless resulting in the reversal of *Bowers* (hence sodomy in general) and therefore a fairly dramatic and clear-cut change in the law of the land, to wit: sodomy is constitutional, or at least the statutes against it are not, probably better put.

So, one asks again, what is it that brought about this change? The Court? The Constitution? Maybe it's the *zeitgeist*? The DSM's (Diagnostic and Statistical Manual—a curious title in that no statistics are employed, only data, what there is of it, and there is not much) published by the American Psychiatric Association, now in its fifth edition, were changed over the years by, naturally, a majority vote, eventually taking out homosexuality, per se, as a disorder. Even hysteria got kicked out. Homosexuality is all but gone with any pathologic fleck left only in the overtones of Gender Identity Disorder as a result of the psychiatric board's "split" decision. One year, something is a pathology, the next year, it is not, but something else that wasn't is. Almost sounds like constitutional law. But when the Association invents and dis-invents mental pathologies in this area, it does not use penumbras, emanations, or radiations…it uses down and dirty frank politics…the board simply votes, and membership on the board has changed dramatically over the years. Fascinating, if you think about it. Homosexuality, and its many relatives, hasn't changed much over the millennia. Its practice and prevalence have been quite stable. Its acceptance, however, has varied greatly over time and place. It has been repressed, ignored, accepted, expected, punished, and its social status has run the gamut, much to the surprise of those who may take a dim view. The fact is, as with all sexuality, it is on a curve, a matter dealt with at the end of the book. *Lawrence* (homosexual sodomy), as clumsy a case as it is, does a pretty good job of presenting it in the perspective of the here and now. The opinions almost read like plebiscites. Its observations, however, would not be the way it is seen in many other parts of the world. That's interesting if you think about it. It might not play so well in Rome, Italy, as it might in, say, Rome, New York. Go to parts in the Middle East and one would likely disappear. France? Homosexuality? What's homosexuality?

Again, I will have no further observations following these two cases. You now have plenty with which to work, both endogenously and exogenously. What you will be observing once more is a court reversing itself, an integral part of this exercise.

Now, *Bowers v. Hardwick* and *Lawrence v. Texas.*

*

BOWERS, ATTORNEY GENERAL OF GEORGIA *v.* HARDWICK, ET AL.

478 U.S. 186

CERTIORARI TO THE UNITED STATES COURT OF APPEALS
FOR THE ELEVENTH CIRCUIT

JUSTICE WHITE delivered the opinion of the Court.

In August 1982, respondent Hardwick (hereafter respondent) was charged with violating the Georgia statute criminalizing sodomy by committing that act with another adult male in the bedroom of respondent's home. After a preliminary hearing, the District Attorney decided not to present the matter to the grand jury unless further evidence developed.

Respondent then brought suit in the Federal District Court, challenging the constitutionality of the statute insofar as it criminalized consensual sodomy. He asserted that he was a practicing homosexual, that the Georgia sodomy statute, as administered by the defendants, placed him in imminent danger of arrest, and that the statute for several reasons violates the federal Constitution. The District Court granted the defendants' motion to dismiss for failure to state a claim, relying on *Doe* v. *Commonwealth's Attorney for the City of Richmond*, 403 F. Supp. 1199 (ED Va. 1975), which this Court summarily affirmed, 425 U.S. 901 (1976).

A divided panel of the Court of Appeals for the Eleventh Circuit reversed. 760 F. 2d 1202 (1985). The court first held that, because *Doe* was distinguishable and in any event had been undermined by later decisions, our summary affirmance in that case did not require affirmance of the District Court. Relying on our decisions in *Griswold* v. *Connecticut*, 381 U.S. 479 (1965) [right to privacy re. contraception]; *Eisenstadt* v. *Baird*, 405 U.S. 438 (1972); *Stanley* v. *Georgia*, 394 U.S. 557 (1969); and *Roe* v. *Wade*, 410 U.S. 113 (1973), the court went on to hold that the Georgia statute violated respondent's fundamental rights because his homosexual activity is a private and intimate association that is beyond the reach of state regulation by reason of the Ninth Amendment and the Due Process Clause of the Fourteenth Amendment. The case was remanded for trial, at which, to prevail, the State would have to prove that the statute is supported by a compelling interest and is the most narrowly drawn means of achieving that end.

Because other Courts of Appeals have arrived at judgments contrary to that of the Eleventh Circuit in this case, we granted the Attorney General's petition for certiorari questioning the holding that the sodomy statute violates the fundamental rights of homosexuals. We agree with petitioner that the Court of Appeals erred, and hence reverse its judgment.

This case does not require a judgment on whether laws against sodomy between consenting adults in general, or between homosexuals in particular, are wise or desirable. It raises no question about the right or propriety of state legislative decisions to repeal their laws that criminalize homosexual sodomy, or of state-court decisions invalidating those laws on state constitutional grounds. The issue presented is whether the Federal Constitution confers a fundamental right upon homosexuals to engage in sodomy and hence invalidates the laws of the many States that still make such conduct illegal and have done so for a very long time. The case also calls for some judgment about the limits of the Court's role in carrying out its constitutional mandate.

We first register our disagreement with the Court of Appeals and with respondent that the Court's prior cases have construed the Constitution to confer a right of privacy that extends to homosexual sodomy and for all intents and purposes have decided this case....

Moreover, any claim that these cases nevertheless stand for the proposition that any kind of private sexual conduct between consenting adults is constitutionally insulated from state proscription is unsupportable....

Precedent aside, however, respondent would have us announce, as the Court of Appeals did, a fundamental right to engage in homosexual sodomy. This we are quite unwilling to do. It is true that despite the language of the Due Process Clauses of the Fifth and Fourteenth Amendments, which appears to focus only on the processes by which life, liberty, or property is taken, the cases are legion in which those Clauses have been interpreted to have substantive content, subsuming rights that to a great extent are immune from federal or state regulation or proscription. Among such cases are those recognizing rights that have little or no textual support in the constitutional language....

Striving to assure itself and the public that announcing rights not readily identifiable in the Constitution's text involves much more than the imposition of the Justices' own choice of values on the States and the Federal Government, the Court has sought to identify the nature of the rights qualifying for heightened judicial protection. In *Palko* v. *Connecticut*, 302 U.S. 319, 325, 326 (1937), it was said that this category includes those fundamental liberties that are "implicit in the concept of ordered liberty," such that "neither liberty nor justice would exist if [they] were sacrificed." A different description of fundamental liberties appeared in *Moore* v. *East Cleveland*, 431 U.S. 494, 503 (1977) (opinion of POWELL, J.), where they are characterized as those liberties that are "deeply rooted in this Nation's history and tradition." *Id.*, at 503 (POWELL, J). See also *Griswold* v. *Connecticut*, 381 U.S., at 506 [right to privacy re. contraception].

It is obvious to us that neither of these formulations would extend a fundamental right to homosexuals to engage in acts of consensual sodomy. Proscriptions against that conduct have ancient roots.... Sodomy was a criminal offense at common law and was forbidden by the laws of the original 13 States when they ratified the Bill of Rights. In 1868, when the Fourteenth Amendment was ratified, all but 5 of the 37 States in the Union had criminal sodomy laws. In fact, until 1961, all 50 States outlawed sodomy, and today, 24 States and the District of Columbia continue to provide criminal penalties for sodomy performed in private and between consenting adults.... Against this background, to claim that a right to engage in such conduct is "deeply rooted in this Nation's history and tradition" or "implicit in the concept of ordered liberty" is, at best, facetious.

Nor are we inclined to take a more expansive view of our authority to discover new fundamental rights imbedded in the Due Process Clause. The Court is most vulnerable and comes nearest to illegitimacy when it deals with judge-made constitutional law having little or no cognizable roots in the language or design of the Constitution. That this is so was painfully demonstrated by the face-off between the Executive and the Court in the 1930's, which resulted in the repudiation of much of the substantive gloss that the Court had placed on the Due Process Clauses of the Fifth and Fourteenth Amendments. There should be, therefore, great resistance to expand the substantive reach of those Clauses, particularly if it requires redefining the category of rights deemed to be fundamental. Otherwise, the Judiciary necessarily takes to itself further authority to govern the country without express constitutional authority. The claimed right pressed on us today falls far short of overcoming this resistance.

Respondent, however, asserts that the result should be different where the homosexual conduct occurs in the privacy of the home. He relies on *Stanley* v. *Georgia*, 394 U.S. 557 (1969), where the Court held that the First Amendment prevents conviction for possessing and reading obscene material in the privacy of one's home: "If the First Amendment means anything, it means that a State has no business telling a man, sitting alone in his house, what books he may read or what films he may watch." *Id.*, at 565.

Stanley did protect conduct that would not have been protected outside the home, and it partially prevented the enforcement of state obscenity laws; but the decision was firmly grounded in the First Amendment. The right pressed upon us here has no similar support in the text of the Constitution, and it does not qualify for recognition under the prevailing principles for construing the Fourteenth Amendment. Its limits are also difficult to discern. Plainly enough, otherwise illegal conduct is not always immunized whenever it occurs in the home. Victimless crimes, such as the possession and use of illegal drugs, do not escape the law where they are committed at home. *Stanley* itself recognized that its holding offered no protection for the possession in the home of drugs, firearms, or stolen goods. *Id.*, at 568, n. 11. And if respondent's submission is limited to the voluntary sexual conduct between consenting adults, it would be difficult, except by fiat, to limit the claimed right to homosexual conduct while leaving exposed to prosecution adultery, incest, and other sexual crimes even though they are committed in the home. We are unwilling to start down that road.

Even if the conduct at issue here is not a fundamental right, respondent asserts that there must be a rational basis for the law and that there is none in this case other than the presumed belief of a majority of the electorate in Georgia that homosexual sodomy is immoral and unacceptable. This is said to be an inadequate rationale to support the law. The law, however, is constantly based on notions of morality, and if all laws representing essentially moral choices are to be invalidated under the Due Process Clause, the courts will be very busy indeed. Even respondent makes no such claim, but insists that majority sentiments about the morality of homosexuality should be declared inadequate. We do not agree, and are unpersuaded that the sodomy laws of some 25 States should be invalidated on this basis.

Accordingly, the judgment of the Court of Appeals is

Reversed.

JUSTICE BLACKMUN, with whom JUSTICE BRENNAN, JUSTICE MARSHALL, and JUSTICE STEVENS join, dissenting.

This case is no more about "a fundamental right to engage in homosexual sodomy," as the Court purports to declare, *ante*, at 191, than *Stanley* v. *Georgia*, 394 U.S. 557 (1969), was about a fundamental right to watch obscene movies, or *Katz* v. *United States*, 389 U.S. 347 (1967), was about a fundamental right to place interstate bets from a telephone booth. Rather, this case is about "the most comprehensive of rights and the right most valued by civilized men," namely "the right to be let alone." *Olmstead* v. *United States*, 277 U.S. 438, 478 (1928).

The statute at issue, Ga. Code Ann. § 16-6-2 (1984), denies individuals the right to decide for themselves whether to engage in particular forms of private, consensual sexual activity. The Court concludes that § 16-6-2 is valid essentially because "the laws of...many States...still make such conduct illegal and have done so for a very long time." ...But the fact that the moral judgments expressed by statutes like § 16-6-2 may be "'natural and familiar...ought not to conclude our judgment upon the question whether statutes embodying them conflict with the Constitution of the United States.'" *Roe* v. *Wade*, 410 U.S. 113, 117 (1973), quoting *Lochner* v. *New York*, 198 U.S. 45, 76 (1905).... Like Justice Holmes, I believe that "[i]t is revolting to have no better reason for a rule of law than that so it was laid down in the time of Henry IV. It is still more revolting if the grounds upon which it was laid down have vanished long since, and the rule simply persists from blind imitation of the past." ...I believe we must analyze respondent Hardwick's claim in the light of the values that underlie the constitutional right to privacy. If that right means anything, it means that, before Georgia can prosecute its citizens for making choices about the most intimate aspects of their lives, it must do more than assert that the choice they have made is an "'abominable crime not fit to be named among Christians.'"

* * *

The Court concludes today that none of our prior cases dealing with various decisions that individuals are entitled to make free of governmental interference "bears any resemblance to the claimed constitutional right of homosexuals to engage in acts of sodomy that is asserted in this case." ...While it is true that these cases may be characterized by their connection to protection of the family, see *Roberts* v. *United States Jaycees*, 468 U.S. 609, 619 (1984), the Court's conclusion that they extend no further than this boundary ignores the warning in *Moore* v. *East Cleveland*, 431 U.S. 494, 501 (1977)...against "clos[ing] our eyes to the basic reasons why certain rights associated with the family have been accorded shelter under the Fourteenth Amendment's Due Process Clause." We protect those rights not because they contribute, in some direct and material way, to the general public welfare, but because they form so central a part of an individual's life. "[T]he concept of privacy embodies the 'moral fact that a person belongs to himself and not others nor to society as a whole.'" ...The Court recognized in *Roberts*, 468 U.S., at 619, that the "ability independently to define one's identity that is central to any concept of liberty" cannot truly be exercised in a vacuum; we all depend on the "emotional enrichment from close ties with others."

Only the most willful blindness could obscure the fact that sexual intimacy is "a sensitive, key relationship of human existence, central to family life, community welfare, and the development of human personality[.]" ...The fact that individuals define themselves in a significant way through their intimate sexual relationships with others suggests, in a Nation as diverse as ours, that there may be many "right" ways of conducting those relationships, and that much of the richness of a relationship will come from the freedom an individual has to *choose* the form and nature of these intensely personal bonds....

In a variety of circumstances we have recognized that a necessary corollary of giving individuals freedom to choose how to conduct their lives is acceptance of the fact that different individuals will make different choices. For example, in holding that the clearly important state interest in public education should give way to a competing claim by the Amish to the effect that extended formal schooling threatened their way of life, the Court declared: "There can be no assumption that today's majority is 'right' and the Amish and others like them are 'wrong.' A way of life that is odd or even erratic but interferes with no rights or interest of others is not to be condemned because it is different." ...The Court claims that its decision today merely refuses to recognize a fundamental right to engage in homosexual sodomy; what the Court really has refused to recognize is the fundamental interest all individuals have in controlling the nature of their intimate associations with others.

* * *

The Court's interpretation of the pivotal case of *Stanley* v. *Georgia*, 394 U.S. 557 (1969), is entirely unconvincing. *Stanley* held that Georgia's undoubted power to punish the public distribution of constitutionally unprotected, obscene material did not permit the State to punish the private possession of such material. According to the majority here, *Stanley* relied entirely on the First Amendment, and thus, it is claimed, sheds no light on cases not involving printed materials.... But that is not what *Stanley* said. Rather, the *Stanley* Court anchored its holding in the Fourth Amendment's special protection for the individual in his home:

> "'The makers of our Constitution undertook to secure conditions favorable to the pursuit of happiness. They recognized the significance of man's spiritual nature, of his

feelings and of his intellect. They knew that only a part of the pain, pleasure and satisfactions of life are to be found in material things. They sought to protect Americans in their beliefs, their thoughts, their emotions and their sensations.'

* * *

"These are the rights that appellant is asserting in the case before us. He is asserting the right to read or observe what he pleases – the right to satisfy his intellectual and emotional needs in the privacy of his own home."

* * *

The assertion that "traditional Judeo-Christian values proscribe" the conduct involved...cannot provide an adequate justification for § 16-6-2. That certain, but by no means all, religious groups condemn the behavior at issue gives the State no license to impose their judgments on the entire citizenry. The legitimacy of secular legislation depends instead on whether the State can advance some justification for its law beyond its conformity to religious doctrine.... Thus, far from buttressing his case, petitioner's invocation of Leviticus, Romans, St. Thomas Aquinas, and sodomy's heretical status during the Middle Ages undermines his suggestion that § 16-6-2 represents a legitimate use of secular coercive power. A State can no more punish private behavior because of religious intolerance than it can punish such behavior because of racial animus. "The Constitution cannot control such prejudices, but neither can it tolerate them. Private biases may be outside the reach of the law, but the law cannot, directly or indirectly, give them effect." ...No matter how uncomfortable a certain group may make the majority of this Court, we have held that "[m]ere public intolerance or animosity cannot constitutionally justify the deprivation of a person's physical liberty."

* * *

JUSTICE STEVENS, with whom JUSTICE BRENNAN and JUSTICE MARSHALL join, dissenting.

* * *

Our prior cases make two propositions abundantly clear. First, the fact that the governing majority in a State has traditionally viewed a particular practice as immoral is not a sufficient reason for upholding a law prohibiting the practice; neither history nor tradition could save a law prohibiting miscegenation from constitutional attack. Second, individual decisions by married persons, concerning the intimacies of their physical relationship, even when not intended to produce offspring, are a form of "liberty" protected by the Due Process Clause of the Fourteenth Amendment. *Griswold* v. *Connecticut*, 381 U.S. 479 (1965) [right to privacy re. contraception]. Moreover, this protection extends to intimate choices by unmarried as well as married persons. *Carey* v. *Population Services International*, 431 U.S. 678 (1977); *Eisenstadt* v. *Baird*, 405 U.S. 438 (1972).

* * *

The Court orders the dismissal of respondent's complaint even though the State's statute prohibits all sodomy; even though that prohibition is concededly unconstitutional with respect to heterosexuals; and even though the State's *post hoc* explanations for selective application are belied by the State's own actions. At the very least, I think it clear at this early stage of the litigation that respondent has alleged a constitutional claim sufficient to withstand a motion to dismiss.

I respectfully dissent.

X

LAWRENCE ET AL. *v.* TEXAS
539 U.S. 558
CERTIORARI TO THE COURT OF APPEALS OF TEXAS
FOURTEENTH DISTRICT

JUSTICE KENNEDY delivered the opinion of the Court.

Liberty protects the person from unwarranted government intrusions into a dwelling or other private places. In our tradition the State is not omnipresent in the home. And there are other spheres of our lives and existence outside the home, where the State should not be a dominant presence. Freedom extends beyond spatial bounds. Liberty presumes an autonomy of self that includes freedom of thought, belief, expression, and certain intimate conduct. The instant case involves liberty of the person both in its spatial and in its more transcendent dimensions.

The question before the Court is the validity of a Texas statute making it a crime for two persons of the same sex to engage in certain intimate sexual conduct.

In Houston, Texas, officers of the Harris County Police Department were dispatched to a private residence in response to a reported weapons disturbance. They entered an apartment where one of the petitioners, John Geddes Lawrence, resided. The right of the police to enter does not seem to have been questioned. The officers observed Lawrence and another man, Tyron Garner, engaging in a sexual act. The two petitioners were arrested, held in custody overnight, and charged and convicted before a Justice of the Peace.

* * *

The petitioners exercised their right to a trial *de novo* in Harris County Criminal Court. They challenged the statute as a violation of the Equal Protection Clause of the Fourteenth Amendment and of a like provision of the Texas Constitution.... Those contentions were rejected....

The Court of Appeals for the Texas Fourteenth District considered the petitioners' federal constitutional arguments under both the Equal Protection and Due Process Clauses of the Fourteenth Amendment. After hearing the case en banc the court, in a divided opinion, rejected the constitutional arguments and affirmed the convictions.... The majority opinion indicates that the Court of Appeals considered our decision in *Bowers* v. *Hardwick*, 478 U.S. 186 (1986), to be controlling on the federal due process aspect of the case. *Bowers* then being authoritative, this was proper.

We granted certiorari...to consider three questions:

1.   Whether petitioners' criminal convictions under the Texas "Homosexual Conduct" law – which criminalizes sexual intimacy by same-sex couples, but not identical behavior by different-sex couples – violate the Fourteenth Amendment guarantee of equal protection of the laws.

2. Whether petitioners' criminal convictions for adult consensual sexual intimacy in the home violate their vital interests in liberty and privacy protected by the Due Process Clause of the Fourteenth Amendment.

3. Whether *Bowers* v. *Hardwick, supra*, should be overruled?

The petitioners were adults at the time of the alleged offense. Their conduct was in private and consensual.

We conclude the case should be resolved by determining whether the petitioners were free as adults to engage in the private conduct in the exercise of their liberty under the Due Process Clause of the Fourteenth Amendment to the Constitution. For this inquiry we deem it necessary to reconsider the Court's holding in *Bowers*.

There are broad statements of the substantive reach of liberty under the Due Process Clause in earlier cases, including *Pierce* v. *Society of Sisters*, 268 U.S. 510 (1925), and *Meyer* v. *Nebraska*, 262 U.S. 390 (1923); but the most pertinent beginning point is our decision in *Griswold* v. *Connecticut*, 381 U.S. 479 (1965).

In *Griswold* the Court invalidated a state law prohibiting the use of drugs or devices of contraception and counseling or aiding and abetting the use of contraceptives. The Court described the protected interest as a right to privacy and placed emphasis on the marriage relation and the protected space of the marital bedroom.

After *Griswold* it was established that the right to make certain decisions regarding sexual conduct extends beyond the marital relationship. In *Eisenstadt* v. *Baird*, 405 U.S. 438 1972), the Court invalidated a law prohibiting the distribution of contraceptives to unmarried persons. The case was decided under the Equal Protection Clause, *id.*, at 454; but with respect to unmarried persons, the Court went on to state the fundamental proposition that the law impaired the exercise of their personal rights[.] It quoted from the statement of the Court of

Appeals finding the law to be in conflict with fundamental human rights, and it followed with this statement of its own:

> "It is true that in *Griswold* the right of privacy in question inhered in the marital relationship.... If the right of privacy means anything, it is the right of the *individual*, married or single, to be free from unwarranted governmental intrusion into matters so fundamentally affecting a person as the decision whether to bear or beget a child."

The opinions in *Griswold* and *Eisenstadt* were part of the background for the decision in *Roe* v. *Wade*, 410 U.S. 113 (1973). As is well known, the case involved a challenge to the Texas law prohibiting abortions, but the laws of other States were affected as well. Although the Court held the woman's rights were not absolute, her right to elect an abortion did have real and substantial protection as an exercise of her liberty under the Due Process Clause.

* * *

The facts in *Bowers* had some similarities to the instant case. A police officer, whose right to enter seems not to have been in question, observed Hardwick, in his own bedroom, engaging in intimate sexual conduct with another adult male. The conduct was in violation of a Georgia statute making it a criminal offense to engage in sodomy. One difference between the two cases is that the Georgia statute prohibited the conduct whether or not the participants were of the same sex, while the Texas statute, as we have seen, applies only to participants of the same sex. Hardwick was not prosecuted, but he brought an action in federal court to declare the state statute invalid. He alleged he was a practicing homosexual and that the criminal prohibition violated rights guaranteed to him by the Constitution....

The Court began its substantive discussion in *Bowers* as follows: "The issue presented is whether the Federal Constitution confers a fundamental right upon homosexuals to engage in sodomy and hence invalidates the laws of the many States that still make such conduct illegal and have done so for a very long time." That statement, we now conclude, discloses the Court's own failure to appreciate the extent of the liberty at stake. To say that the issue in *Bowers* was simply the right to engage in certain sexual conduct demeans the claim the individual put forward, just as it would demean a married couple were it to be said marriage is simply about the right to have sexual intercourse. The laws involved in *Bowers* and here are, to be sure, statutes that purport to do no more than prohibit a particular sexual act. Their penalties and purposes, though, have more far-reaching consequences, touching upon the most private human conduct, sexual behavior, and in the most private of places, the home. The statutes do seek to control a personal relationship that, whether or not entitled to formal recognition in the law, is within the liberty of persons to choose without being punished as criminals.

This, as a general rule, should counsel against attempts by the State, or a court, to define the meaning of the relationship or to set its boundaries absent injury to a person or abuse of an institution the law protects. It suffices for us to acknowledge that adults may choose to enter upon this relationship in the confines of their homes and their own private lives and still retain their dignity as free persons. When sexuality finds overt expression in intimate conduct with another person, the conduct can be but one element in a personal bond that is more enduring. The liberty protected by the Constitution allows homosexual persons the right to make this choice.

Having misapprehended the claim of liberty there presented to it, and thus stating the claim to be whether there is a fundamental right to engage in consensual sodomy, the *Bowers* Court said: "Proscriptions against that conduct have ancient roots." ...In academic writings, and in many of the scholarly *amicus* briefs filed to assist the Court in this case, there are fundamental criticisms of the historical premises relied upon by the majority and concurring opinions in *Bowers*.... We need not enter this debate in the attempt to reach a definitive historical judgment, but the following considerations counsel against adopting the definitive conclusions upon which *Bowers* placed such reliance.

* * *

It must be acknowledged, of course, that the Court in *Bowers* was making the broader point that for centuries there have been powerful voices to condemn homosexual conduct as immoral. The condemnation has been shaped by religious beliefs, conceptions of right and acceptable behavior, and respect for the traditional family. For many persons these are not trivial concerns but profound and deep convictions accepted as ethical and moral principles to which they aspire and which thus determine the course of their lives. These considerations do not answer the question before us, however. The issue is whether the majority may use the power of the State to enforce these views on the whole society through operation of the criminal law. "Our obligation is to define the liberty of all, not to mandate our own moral code." *Planned Parenthood of Southeastern Pa.* v. *Casey*, 505 U.S. 833, 850 (1992).

Chief Justice Burger joined the opinion for the Court in *Bowers* and further explained his views as follows: "Decisions of individuals relating to homosexual conduct have been subject to state intervention throughout the history of Western civilization. Condemnation of those practices is firmly rooted in Judeao-Christian moral and ethical standards." 478 U.S., at 196. As with Justice White's assumptions about history, scholarship casts some doubt on the sweeping nature of the statement by Chief Justice Burger as it pertains to private homosexual conduct between consenting adults.... In all events we think that our laws and traditions in the past half century are of most relevance here. These references show an emerging awareness that liberty gives substantial protection to adult persons in deciding how to conduct their private lives in matters pertaining to sex. "[H]istory and tradition are the starting point but not in all cases the ending point of the substantive due process inquiry."

* * *

This emerging recognition should have been apparent when *Bowers* was decided. In 1955 the American Law Institute promulgated the Model Penal Code and made clear that it did not recommend or provide for "criminal penalties for consensual sexual relations conducted in private." ALI, Model Penal Code § 213.2, Comment 2, p. 372 (1980). It justified its decision on three grounds: (1) The prohibitions undermined respect for the law by penalizing conduct many people engaged in; (2) the statutes regulated private conduct not harmful to others; and (3) the laws were arbitrarily enforced and thus invited the danger of blackmail. . . . In 1961 Illinois changed its laws to conform to the Model Penal Code. Other States soon followed....

* * *

The sweeping references by Chief Justice Burger to the history of Western civilization and to Judeo-Christian moral and ethical standards did not take account of other authorities pointing in an opposite direction. A committee advising the British Parliament recommended in 1957 repeal of laws punishing homosexual conduct. ...Parliament enacted the substance of those recommendations 10 years later.

* * *

In our own constitutional system the deficiencies in *Bowers* became even more apparent in the years following its announcement. The 25 States with laws prohibiting the relevant conduct referenced in the *Bowers* decision are reduced now to 13, of which 4 enforce their laws only against homosexual conduct. In those States where sodomy is still proscribed, whether for same-sex or heterosexual conduct, there is a pattern of nonenforcement with respect to consenting adults acting in private. The State of Texas admitted in 1994 that as of that date it had not prosecuted anyone under those circumstances.

* * *

The second post-*Bowers* case of principal relevance is *Romer* v. *Evans*, 517 U.S. 620 (1996). There the Court struck down class-based legislation directed at homosexuals as a violation of the Equal Protection Clause. *Romer* invalidated an amendment to Colorado's Constitution which named as a solitary class persons who were homosexuals, lesbians, or bisexual either by "orientation, conduct, practices or relationships"...and deprived them of protection under state antidiscrimination laws. We concluded that the provision was "born of animosity toward the class of persons affected" and further that it had no rational relation to a legitimate governmental purpose. *Id.*, at 634.

* * *

JUSTICE STEVENS' analysis, in our view, should have been controlling in *Bowers* and should control here.

Bowers was not correct when it was decided, and it is not correct today. It ought not to remain binding precedent. *Bowers* v. *Hardwick* should be and now is overruled.

141

* * *

The judgment of the Court of Appeals for the Texas Fourteenth District is reversed, and the case is remanded for further proceedings not inconsistent with this opinion.

It is so ordered.

JUSTICE O'CONNOR, concurring in the judgment.

The Court today overrules *Bowers* v. *Hardwick*, 478 U.S. 186 (1986). I joined *Bowers*, and do not join the Court in overruling it. Nevertheless, I agree with the Court that Texas' statute banning same-sex sodomy is unconstitutional.... Rather than relying on the substantive component of the Fourteenth Amendment's Due Process Clause, as the Court does, I base my conclusion on the Fourteenth Amendment's Equal Protection Clause.

The Equal Protection Clause of the Fourteenth Amendment "is essentially a direction that all persons similarly situated should be treated alike." ...Under our rational basis standard of review, "legislation is presumed to be valid and will be sustained if the classification drawn by the statute is rationally related to a legitimate state interest."

* * *

We have been most likely to apply rational basis review to hold a law unconstitutional under the Equal Protection Clause where, as here, the challenged legislation inhibits personal relationships....

The statute at issue here makes sodomy a crime only if a person "engages in deviate sexual intercourse with another individual of the same sex." ...Sodomy between opposite-sex partners, however, is not a crime in Texas. That is, Texas treats the same conduct differently based solely on the participants. Those harmed by this law are people who have a same-sex sexual orientation and thus are more likely to engage in behavior prohibited by § 21.06.

The Texas statute makes homosexuals unequal in the eyes of the law by making particular conduct – and only that conduct – subject to criminal sanction....

And the effect of Texas' sodomy law is not just limited to the threat of prosecution or consequence of conviction. Texas' sodomy law brands all homosexuals as criminals, thereby making it more difficult for homosexuals to be treated in the same manner as everyone else. Indeed, Texas itself has previously acknowledged the collateral effects of the law, stipulating in a prior challenge to this action that the law "legally sanctions discrimination against [homosexuals] in a variety of ways unrelated to the criminal law," including in the areas of "employment, family issues, and housing."

* * *

Moral disapproval of a group cannot be a legitimate governmental interest under the Equal Protection Clause because legal classifications must not be "drawn for the purpose of disadvantaging the group burdened by the law." Texas' invocation of moral disapproval as a legitimate state interest proves nothing more than Texas' desire to criminalize homosexual sodomy. But the Equal Protection Clause prevents a State from creating "a classification of persons undertaken for its own sake." And because Texas so rarely enforces its sodomy law as applied to private, consensual acts, the law serves more as a statement of dislike and disapproval against homosexuals than as a tool to stop criminal behavior. The Texas sodomy law "raise[s] the inevitable inference that the disadvantage imposed is born of animosity toward the class of persons affected."

* * *

The Equal Protection Clause "'neither knows nor tolerates classes among citizens.'"

* * *

A State can of course assign certain consequences to a violation of its criminal law. But the State cannot single out one identifiable class of citizens for punishment that does not apply to everyone else, with moral disapproval as the only asserted state interest for the law. The Texas sodomy statute subjects homosexuals to "a lifelong penalty and stigma. A legislative classification that threatens the creation of an underclass...cannot be reconciled with" the Equal Protection Clause....

* * *

A law branding one class of persons as criminal based solely on the State's moral disapproval of that class and the conduct associated with that class runs contrary to the values of the Constitution and the Equal Protection Clause, under any standard of review. I therefore concur in the Court's judgment that Texas' sodomy law banning "deviate sexual intercourse" between consenting adults of the same sex, but not between consenting adults of different sexes, is unconstitutional.

JUSTICE SCALIA, with whom THE CHIEF JUSTICE and JUSTICE THOMAS join, dissenting.

"Liberty finds no refuge in a jurisprudence of doubt." *Planned Parenthood of Southeastern Pa.* v. *Casey*, 505 U.S. 833, 844 (1992). That was the Court's sententious response, barely more than a decade ago, to those seeking to overrule *Roe* v. *Wade*, 410 U.S. 113 (1973). The Court's response today, to those who have engaged in a 17-year crusade to overrule *Bowers* v. *Hardwick*, 478 U.S. 186 (1986), is very different. The need for stability and certainty presents no barrier.

Most of the rest of today's opinion has no relevance to its actual holding – that the Texas statute "furthers no legitimate state interest which can justify" its application to petitioners under rational-basis review. *Ante*, at 578 (overruling *Bowers* to the extent it sustained Georgia's antisodomy statute under the rational-basis test). Though there is discussion of "fundamental proposition[s]," *ante*, at 565, and "fundamental decisions," *ibid.*, nowhere does the Court's opinion declare that homosexual sodomy is a "fundamental right" under the Due Process Clause; nor does it subject the Texas law to the standard of review that would be appropriate (strict scrutiny) if homosexual sodomy *were* a "fundamental right." Thus, while overruling the *outcome* of *Bowers*, the Court leaves strangely untouched its central legal conclusion: "[R]espondent would have us announce...a fundamental right to engage in homosexual sodomy. This we are quite unwilling to do." 478 U.S., at 191. Instead the Court simply describes petitioners' conduct as "an exercise of their liberty" – which it undoubtedly is – and proceeds to apply an unheard-of form of rational-basis review that will have far-reaching implications beyond this case....

I begin with the Court's surprising readiness to reconsider a decision rendered a mere 17 years ago in *Bowers* v. *Hardwick*. I do not myself believe in rigid adherence to *stare decisis* in constitutional cases; but I do believe that we should be consistent rather than manipulative in invoking the doctrine. Today's opinions in support of reversal do not bother to distinguish – or indeed, even bother to mention – the paean to *stare decisis* coauthored by three Members of today's majority in *Planned Parenthood* v. *Casey*. There, when *stare decisis* meant preservation of judicially invented abortion rights, the widespread criticism of *Roe* was strong reason to *reaffirm* it:

"Where, in the performance of its judicial duties, the Court decides a case in such a way as to resolve the sort of intensely divisive controversy reflected in *Roe*[,]...its decision has a dimension that the resolution of the normal case does not carry.... [T]o overrule under fire in the absence of the most compelling reason...would subvert the Court's legitimacy beyond any serious question." 505 U.S., at 866-867.

Today, however, the widespread opposition to *Bowers*, a decision resolving an issue as "intensely divisive" as the issue in *Roe*, is offered as a reason in favor of *overruling* it. See *ante*, at 576-577. Gone, too, is an "enquiry" (of the sort conducted in *Casey*) into whether the decision sought to be overruled has "proven 'unworkable,'" *Casey, supra,* at 855.

Today's approach to *stare decisis* invites us to overrule an erroneously decided precedent (including an "intensely divisive" decision) *if:* (1) its foundations have been "ero[ded]" by subsequent decisions, *ante,* at 576; (2) it has been subject to "substantial and continuing" criticism, *ibid.*; and (3) it has not induced "individual or societal reliance" that counsels against overturning, *ante,* at 577. The problem is that *Roe* itself – which today's majority surely has no disposition to overrule – satisfies these conditions to at least the same degree as *Bowers*.

* * *

Let me be clear that I have nothing against homosexuals, or any other group, promoting their agenda through normal democratic means. Social perceptions of sexual and other morality change over time, and every group has the right to persuade its fellow citizens that its view of such matters is the best. That homosexuals have achieved some success in that enterprise is attested to by the fact that Texas is one of the few remaining States that criminalize private, consensual homosexual acts. But persuading one's fellow citizens is one thing, and imposing one's views in absence of democratic majority will is something else. I would no more *require* a State to criminalize homosexual acts – or, for that matter, display *any* moral disapprobation of them – than I would *forbid* it to do so. What Texas has chosen to do is well within the range of traditional democratic action, and its hand should not be stayed through the invention of a brand-new "constitutional right" by a Court that is impatient of democratic change. It is indeed true that "later generations can see that laws once thought necessary and proper in fact serve only to oppress," *ante*, at 579; and when that happens, later generations can repeal those laws. But it is the premise of our system that those judgments are to be made by the people, and not imposed by a governing caste that knows best.

* * *

The matters appropriate for this Court's resolution are only three: Texas's prohibition of sodomy neither infringes a "fundamental right" (which the Court does not dispute), nor is unsupported by a rational relation to what the Constitution considers a legitimate state interest, nor denies the equal protection of the laws. I dissent.

JUSTICE THOMAS, dissenting.

I join JUSTICE SCALIA's dissenting opinion. I write separately to note that the law before the Court today "is...uncommonly silly." *Griswold* v. *Connecticut*, 381 U.S. 479, 527 (1965) (Stewart, J., dissenting). If I were a member of the Texas Legislature, I would vote to repeal it. Punishing someone for expressing his sexual preference through noncommercial consensual conduct with another adult does not appear to be a worthy way to expend valuable law enforcement resources.

Notwithstanding this, I recognize that as a Member of this Court I am not empowered to help petitioners and others similarly situated. My duty, rather, is to "decide cases 'agreeably to the Constitution and laws of the United States'" *Id.*, at 530. And, just like Justice Stewart, I "can find [neither in the Bill of Rights nor any other part of the Constitution a] general right of privacy," *ibid.*, or as the Court terms it today, the "liberty of the person both in its spatial and more transcendent dimensions," *ante*, at 562.

ROE V. WADE

While we have been observing the Supreme Court busily working on pasties, contraceptives, pornography, and homosexual practices, the upcoming abortion cases provide for us the relief of a little change of scene, it all being emotionally exhausting no matter what side of the fence one might reside.

Roe v. Wade. You know all about it and its progeny, so to speak, right? Actually, very few do. Up until now, you likely only know what you have been told, or what you have heard, the "news." But your sources have always had an agenda, and that agenda may not have even been about abortion, per se. It is often but a front. When you have finished your work here, you will see, or at least you will likely have a take on issues you didn't have before.

This book is not concerned with debate. We stand far back from the opinions, and their sequelae, to examine American jurisprudence and the influence it has had on the nation, notwithstanding what the Constitution may or may not say.

The most salient point of our work is observing that the central issue with which the Court may be dealing typically has little to do with the real matters at hand here, those things with which we are concerned. Rather, it is the impact of what the Court did, or said (particularly in its typical gratuitous *dicta*) in its effort to deal with a given case, the integrity of its reasoning, and how these words have changed the country, possibly for as long as it lasts. Again, right or wrong is not our concern. It is the impact which is significant, the immediate focus of the case itself often fading into obscurity, if not obliquity (see Scalia's dissent in *Stenberg, infra,* without any suggestion as to whether the Justice is right or wrong, but he did see a problem with the business of the Court). It is called the work of the law at the margins, the edges or periphery of what is in fact before the Court, kind of a penumbra sort of thing, if you will, this time emanating from the Court's opinions into other and subsequent matters, and aspects of life in the country. But it is more than that: the Court has put in more time, committed more resources, written more pages of "opinions," concurrences and dissents during its "modern era," suffered more condescension and not just bloody bickering, carrying on a seemingly perpetual constitutional convention on the subject of abortion than likely any other area of activity or class of civil cases in the court of last resort in American jurisprudential history, an American jurisprudential epoch unto itself (bringing back to mind the clog with which divorce has plugged the state trial courts, there often more than all other civil cases combined). Is there a message here? Stop thinking just about abortion, per se. The question is, is there another message here, another issue, something else at work? If so, did the Court miss it? Or, did the Court create it?

A quick visit back to the introduction: as discussed, anyone running for many public offices is saddled with the perennial question, "Where do *you* stand on abortion?" seemingly being the qualifying (or disqualifying) factor as to whether or not someone should (or is fit to) hold office, and often, nothing else for many. Single issue voters. Most are not, but we have millions of them into whose hands the Court has put the nation's future, indirectly the national security. When did that become the defining factor? Think about it. This question is not whether you are for or against it, whether it is good or bad, or whether it serves some other purpose, which *sub silentio* it likely does. Rather, how is it that one issue has become so dominant, the deciding factor for a not insignificant voting bloc of the population, certainly enough to tip results? Was this the foreseen intent of the Court which wrote the seminal opinion on the subject, or was it unforeseen (troubling either way)? Maybe the die was cast in earlier opinions. We are not concerned about the effect the case (or any case) had on the parties. You can read about that and what someone wishes to tell you elsewhere. Rather, we are concerned here with the effect the case and its "progeny" have had both laterally and over time, its consequences as to other cases dealing with the same and other subject matter, as well as for us and those who may follow, respectively.

We are essentially looking at cases as an optic into what happens off the Court's bench, its rationale, the assumptions it makes, and the justifications used in reaching a result. No issue is taken with the result of any case. Put more simply, we are looking at cases as an optic into the workings of the Court, how it goes about its business and creates its product, so as to have a chance to think about the wider cross-cultural and cross-generational effects of its work. We are also concerned with how an opinion may have affected a subsequent opinion, and also how a prior opinion may have affected the one we are examining as well as others in unrelated kinds of cases, at least subject-wise. In other words, seemingly unrelated cases may become very related as they build upon one another forming their own jurisprudential government, their own jurisprudential nation.

Then will come *Stenberg* on partial-birth abortion and citations to other cases affording a general but limited look around this jurisprudential landscape on the subject. Other trails of citations will be marked out, subject after subject, as we proceed. Once again, abortion is not our concern or the subject of any debate here. (See *ante*.)

As far as the next two cases are concerned, and there are many others, you do not need any leading. You have adequate tools and sufficient insight into the "law" to deal with what lies ahead starting with *Roe v. Wade*, 410 U.S. 113 (1973), then followed by the partial-birth abortion case noted. First, *Roe*.

*

ROE ET AL. *v.* WADE, DISTRICT ATTORNEY OF DALLAS
COUNTY

410 U.S. 113

MR. JUSTICE BLACKMUN delivered the opinion of the Court.

This Texas federal appeal and its Georgia companion, *Doe* v. *Bolton, post,* p. 179, present constitutional challenges to state criminal abortion legislation. The Texas statutes under attack here are typical of those that have been in effect in many States for approximately a century. The Georgia statutes, in contrast, have a modern cast and are a legislative product that, to an extent at least, obviously reflects the influences of recent attitudinal change, of advancing medical knowledge and techniques, and of new thinking about an old issue.

We forthwith acknowledge our awareness of the sensitive and emotional nature of the abortion controversy, of the vigorous opposing views, even among physicians, and of the deep and seemingly absolute convictions that the subject inspires. One's philosophy, one's experiences, one's exposure to the raw edges of human existence, one's religious training, one's attitudes toward life and family and their values, and the moral standards one establishes and seeks to observe, are all likely to influence and to color one's thinking and conclusions about abortion.

In addition, population growth, pollution, poverty, and racial overtones tend to complicate and not to simplify the problem.

Our task, of course, is to resolve the issue by constitutional measurement, free of emotion and of predilection. We seek earnestly to do this, and, because we do, we have inquired into, and in this opinion place some emphasis upon, medical and medical-legal history and what that history reveals about man's attitudes toward the abortion procedure over the centuries. We bear in mind, too, Mr. Justice Holmes' admonition in his now-vindicated dissent in *Lochner* v. *New York*, 198 U.S. 45, 76 (1905):

> "[The Constitution] is made for people of fundamentally differing views, and the accident of our finding certain opinions natural and familiar or novel and even shocking ought not to conclude our judgment upon the question whether statutes embodying them conflict with the Constitution of the United States."

I

The Texas statutes that concern us here are Arts. 1191-1194 and 1196 of the State's Penal Code.[1] [The footnote and its text is as it appears in the official reporter.] These make it a crime to "procure an abortion," as therein defined, or to attempt one, except with respect to "an abortion procured or attempted by medical advice for the purpose of saving the life of the mother." Similar statutes are in existence in a majority of the States.

---

[1] "Article 1191. Abortion. If any person shall designedly administer to a pregnant woman or knowingly procure to be administered with her consent any drug or medicine, or shall use towards her any violence or means whatever externally or internally applied, and thereby procure an abortion, he shall be confined in a penitentiary not less than two nor more than five years; if it be done without her consent, the punishment shall be doubled. By 'abortion' is meant that the life of the fetus or embryo shall be destroyed in the woman's womb or that a premature birth thereof be caused."

* * *

"Article 1194. Murder in producing abortion. If the death of the mother is occasioned by an abortion so produced or by an attempt to effect the same it is murder."

"Article 1196. By medical advice. Nothing in this chapter applies to an abortion procured or attempted by medical advice for the purpose of saving the life of the mother." [This footnote and its number are reproduced as they appear in the official opinion.]

Texas first enacted a criminal abortion statute in 1854. Texas Laws 1854, c. 49, § 1, set forth in 3 H. Gammel, Laws of Texas 1502 (1898). This was soon modified into language that has remained substantially unchanged to the present time....

II

Jane Roe, a single woman who was residing in Dallas County, Texas, instituted this federal action in March 1970 against the District Attorney of the county. She sought a declaratory judgment that the Texas criminal abortion statutes were unconstitutional on their face, and an injunction restraining the defendant from enforcing the statutes.

Roe alleged that she was unmarried and pregnant; that she wished to terminate her pregnancy by an abortion "performed by a competent, licensed physician, under safe, clinical conditions"; that she was unable to get a "legal" abortion in Texas because her life did not appear to be threatened by the continuation of her pregnancy; and that she could not afford to travel to another jurisdiction in order to secure a legal abortion under safe conditions. She claimed that the Texas statutes were unconstitutionally vague and that they abridged her right of personal privacy, protected by the First, Fourth, Fifth, Ninth, and Fourteenth Amendments. By an amendment to her complaint Roe purported to sue "on behalf of herself and all other women" similarly situated.

James Hubert Hallford, a licensed physician, sought and was granted leave to intervene in Roe's action. In his complaint he alleged that he had been arrested previously for violations of the Texas abortion statutes and that two such prosecutions were pending against him. He described conditions of patients who came to him seeking abortions, and he claimed that for many cases he, as a physician, was unable to determine whether they fell within or outside the exception recognized by Article 1196. He alleged that, as a consequence, the statutes were vague and uncertain, in violation of the Fourteenth Amendment, and that they violated his own and his patients' rights to privacy in the doctor-patient relationship and his own right to practice medicine, rights he claimed were guaranteed by the First, Fourth, Fifth, Ninth, and Fourteenth Amendments.

* * *

IV

We are next confronted with issues of justiciability, standing, and abstention. Have Roe and the Does established that "personal stake in the outcome of the controversy," *Baker* v. *Carr*, 369 U.S. 186, 204 (1962), that insures that "the dispute sought to be adjudicated will be presented in an adversary context and in a form historically viewed as capable of judicial resolution," *Flast* v. *Cohen*, 392 U.S. 83, 101 (1968), and *Sierra Club* v. *Morton*, 405 U.S. 727, 732 (1972)? And what effect did the pendency of criminal abortion charges against Dr. Hallford in state court have upon the propriety of the federal court's granting relief to him as a plaintiff-intervenor?

A.   *Jane Roe.* Despite the use of the pseudonym, no suggestion is made that Roe is a fictitious person. For purposes of her case, we accept as true, and as established, her existence; her pregnant state, as of the inception of her suit in March 1970 and as late as May 21 of that year when she filed an alias affidavit with the District Court; and her inability to obtain a legal abortion in Texas.

Viewing Roe's case as of the time of its filing and thereafter until as late as May, there can be little dispute that it then presented a case or controversy and that, wholly apart from the class aspects, she, as a pregnant single woman thwarted by the Texas criminal abortion laws, had standing to challenge those statutes....

The appellee notes, however, that the record does not disclose that Roe was pregnant at the time of the District Court hearing on May

22, 1970, or on the following June 17 when the court's opinion and judgment were filed. And he suggests that Roe's case must now be moot because she and all other members of her class are no longer subject to any 1970 pregnancy.

The usual rule in federal cases is that an actual controversy must exist at stages of appellate or certiorari review, and not simply at the date the action is initiated....

But when, as here, pregnancy is a significant fact in the litigation, the normal 266-day human gestation period is so short that the pregnancy will come to term before the usual appellate process is complete. If that termination makes a case moot, pregnancy litigation seldom will survive much beyond the trial stage, and appellate review will be effectively denied. Our law should not be that rigid. Pregnancy often comes more than once to the same woman, and in the general population, if man is to survive, it will always be with us. Pregnancy provides a classic justification for a conclusion of nonmootness. It truly could be "capable of repetition, yet evading review."

* * *

We, therefore, agree with the District Court that Jane Roe had standing to undertake this litigation, that she presented a justiciable controversy, and that the termination of her 1970 pregnancy has not rendered her case moot.

B.   *Dr. Hallford.* The doctor's position is different....

Dr. Hallford is, therefore, in the position of seeking, in a federal court, declaratory and injunctive relief with respect to the same statutes under which he stands charged in criminal prosecutions simultaneously pending in state court. Although he stated that he has been arrested in the past for violating the State's abortion laws, he makes no allegation of any substantial and immediate threat to any federally protected right that cannot be asserted in his defense against the state prosecutions. Neither is there any allegation of harassment or bad-faith prosecution. In order to escape the rule articulated in the cases cited in the next paragraph of this opinion that, absent harassment and bad faith, a defendant in a pending state criminal case cannot affirmatively challenge in federal court the statutes under which the State is prosecuting him, Dr. Hallford seeks to distinguish his status as a present state defendant from his status as a "potential future defendant" and to assert only the latter for standing purposes here.

We see no merit in that distinction....

Dr. Hallford's complaint in intervention, therefore, is to be dismissed. He is remitted to his defenses in the state criminal proceedings against him....

C.   *The Does.* In view of our ruling as to Roe's standing in her case, the issue of the Does' standing in their case has little significance....

Their pleadings present them as a childless married couple, the woman not being pregnant, who have no desire to have children at this time because of their having received medical advice that Mrs. Doe should avoid pregnancy, and for "other highly personal reasons." But they "fear...they may face the prospect of becoming parents." And if pregnancy ensues, they "would want to terminate" it by an abortion. They assert an inability to obtain an abortion legally in Texas and, consequently, the prospect of obtaining an illegal abortion there or of going outside Texas to some place where the procedure could be obtained legally and competently.

* * *

This very phrasing of the Does' position reveals its speculative character. Their alleged injury rests on possible future contraceptive failure, possible future pregnancy, possible future unpreparedness for parenthood, and possible future impairment of health. Any one or more of these several possibilities may not take place and all may not combine. In the Does' estimation, these possibilities might have some real or imagined impact upon their marital happiness. But we are not prepared to say that the bare allegation of so indirect an injury is sufficient to present an actual case or controversy....

The Does therefore are not appropriate plaintiffs in this litigation. Their complaint was properly dismissed by the District Court, and we affirm that dismissal.

V

The principal thrust of appellant's attack on the Texas statutes is that they improperly invade a right, said to be possessed by the pregnant woman, to choose to terminate her pregnancy. Appellant would discover this right in the concept of personal "liberty" embodied in the Fourteenth Amendment's Due Process Clause; or in personal, marital, familial, and sexual privacy said to be protected by the Bill of Rights or its penumbras, see *Griswold* v. *Connecticut*, 381 U.S. 479 (1965)[,]...or among those rights reserved to the people by the Ninth Amendment, *Griswold* v. *Connecticut*, 381 U.S., at 486 (Goldberg, J., concurring). Before addressing this claim, we feel it desirable briefly to survey, in several aspects, the history of abortion, for such insight as that history may afford us, and then to examine the state purposes and interests behind the criminal abortion laws.

VI

It perhaps is not generally appreciated that the restrictive criminal abortion laws in effect in a majority of States today are of relatively recent vintage. Those laws, generally proscribing abortion or its attempt at any time during pregnancy except when necessary to preserve the pregnant woman's life, are not of ancient or even of common-law origin. Instead, they derive from statutory changes effected, for the most part, in the latter half of the 19th century.

1. *Ancient attitudes*. These are not capable of precise determination....

2. *The Hippocratic Oath.* What then of the famous Oath that has stood so long as the ethical guide of the medical profession...? The Oath varies somewhat according to the particular translation, but in any translation the content is clear: "I will give no deadly medicine to anyone if asked, nor suggest any such counsel; and in like manner I will not give to a woman a pessary to produce abortion," or "I will neither give a deadly drug to anybody if asked for it, nor will I make a suggestion to this effect. Similarly, I will not give to a woman an abortive remedy."

Although the Oath is not mentioned in any of the principal briefs in this case of in *Doe* v. *Bolton, post*, p. 179, it represents the apex of the development of strict ethical concepts in medicine, and its influence endures to this day.

* * *

3. *The common law.* It is undisputed that at common law, abortion performed *before* "quickening"—the first recognizable movement of the fetus *in utero*, appearing usually from the 16th to the 18th week of pregnancy"—was not an indictable offense. The absence of a common-law crime for pre-quickening abortion appears to have developed from a confluence of earlier philosophical, theological, and civil and canon law concepts of when life begins. These disciplines variously approached the question in terms of the point at which the embryo or fetus became "formed" or recognizably human, or in terms of when a "person" came into being, that is, infused with a "soul" or "animated." A loose consensus evolved in early English law that these events occurred at some point between conception and live birth. This was "mediate animation." Although Christian theology and the canon

law came to fix the point of animation at 40 days for a male and 80 days for a female, a view that persisted until the 19th century, there was otherwise little agreement about the precise time of formation or animation. There was agreement, however, that prior to this point the fetus was to be regarded as part of the mother, and its destruction, therefore, was not homicide. Due to continued uncertainty about the precise time when animation occurred, to the lack of any empirical basis for the 40-80-day view, and perhaps to Aquinas' definition of movement as one of the two first principles of life, Bracton focused upon quickening as the critical point. The significance of quickening was echoed by later common-law scholars and found its way into the received common law in this country.

Whether abortion of a *quick* fetus was a felony at common law, or even a lesser crime, is still disputed....

4. *The English statutory law.* England's first criminal abortion statute, Lord Ellenborough's Act, 43 Geo. 3, c. 58, came in 1803. It made abortion of a quick fetus, § 1, a capital crime, but in §2 it provided lesser penalties for the felony of abortion before quickening, and thus preserved the "quickening" distinction.

* * *

A seemingly notable development in the English law was the case of *Rex* v. *Bourne*, [1939] 1 K. B. 687. This case apparently answered in the affirmative the question whether an abortion necessary to preserve the life of the pregnant woman was excepted from the criminal penalties of the 1861 Act....

Recently, Parliament enacted a new abortion law. This is the Abortion Act of 1967, 15 & 16 Eliz. 2, c. 87. The Act permits a licensed physician to perform an abortion where two other licensed physicians agree (a) "that the continuance of the pregnancy would involve risk to the life of the pregnant woman, or of injury to the physical or mental health of the pregnant woman or any existing children of her family, greater than if the pregnancy were terminated," or (b) "that there is a substantial risk that if the child were born it would suffer from such physical or mental abnormalities as to be seriously handicapped." The Act also provides that, in making this determination, "account may be taken of the pregnant woman's actual or reasonably foreseeable environment." It also permits a physician, without the concurrence of others, to terminate a pregnancy where he is of the good-faith opinion that the abortion "is immediately necessary to save the life or to prevent grave permanent injury to the physical or mental health of the pregnant woman."

      5.   *The American law.* In this country, the law in effect in all but a few States until mid-19th century was the pre-existing English common law. Connecticut, the first State to enact abortion legislation, adopted in 1821 that part of Lord Ellenborough's Act that related to a woman "quick with child." The death penalty was not imposed. Abortion before quickening was made a crime in that State only in 1860. In 1828, New York enacted legislation that, in two respects, was to serve as a model for early anti-abortion statutes.... By 1840, when Texas had received the common law, only eight American States had statutes dealing with abortion. It was not until after the War Between the States that legislation began generally to replace the common law. Most of these initial statutes dealt severely with abortion after quickening but were lenient with it before quickening. Most punished attempts equally with completed abortions. While many statutes included the exception for an abortion thought by one or more physicians to be necessary to save the mother's life, that provision soon disappeared and the typical law required that the procedure actually be necessary for that purpose.

      Gradually, in the middle and late 19th century the quickening distinction disappeared from the statutory law of most States and the degree of the offense and the penalties were increased. By the end of the

1950's, a large majority of the jurisdictions banned abortion, however and whenever performed, unless done to save or preserve the life of the mother.... In the past several years, however, a trend toward liberalization of abortion statutes has resulted in adoption, by about one-third of the States, of less stringent laws, most of them patterned after the ALI Model Penal Code[.]

* * *

It is thus apparent that at common law, at the time of the adoption of our Constitution, and throughout the major portion of the 19th century, abortion was viewed with less disfavor than under most American statutes currently in effect....

6.   *The position of the American Medical Association.* The anti-abortion mood prevalent in this country in the late 19th century was shared by the medical profession. Indeed, the attitude of the profession may have played a significant role in the enactment of stringent criminal abortion legislation during that period.

* * *

In 1871 a long and vivid report was submitted by the Committee on Criminal Abortion. It ended with the observation, "We had to deal with human life. In a matter of less importance we could entertain no compromise. An honest judge on the bench would call things by their proper names. We could do no less."

* * *

Except for periodic condemnation of the criminal abortionist, no further formal AMA action took place until 1967. In that year, the

Committee on Human Reproduction urged the adoption of a stated policy of opposition to induced abortion, except when there is "documented medical evidence" of a threat to the health or life of the mother, or that the child "may be born with incapacitating physical deformity or mental deficiency," or that a pregnancy "resulting from legally established statutory or forcible rape or incest may constitute a threat to the mental or physical health of the patient," two other physicians "chosen because of their recognized professional competence have examined the patient and have concurred in writing," and the procedure "is performed in a hospital accredited by the Joint Commission on Accreditation of Hospitals."

* * *

In 1970, after the introduction of a variety of proposed resolutions, and of a report from its Board of Trustees, a reference committee noted "polarization of the medical profession on this controversial issue"; division among those who had testified; a difference of opinion among AMA councils and committees; "the remarkable shift in testimony" in six months, felt to be influenced "by the rapid changes in state laws and by the judicial decisions which tend to make abortion more freely available;" and a feeling "that this trend will continue." On June 25, 1970, the House of Delegates adopted preambles and most of the resolutions proposed by the reference committee. The preambles emphasized "the best interests of the patient," "sound clinical judgment," and "informed patient consent," in contrast to "mere acquiescence to the patient's demand." The resolutions asserted that abortion is a medical procedure that should be performed by a licensed physician in an accredited hospital only after consultation with two other physicians and in conformity with state law, and that no party to the procedure should be required to violate personally held moral principles....

7.   *The position of the American Public Health Association.* In October 1970, the Executive Board of the APHA adopted Standards for Abortion Services. These were five in number:

"a. Rapid and simple abortion referral must be readily available through state and local public health departments, medical societies, or other non-profit organizations.

"b. An important function of counseling should be to simplify and expedite the provision of abortion services; it should not delay the obtaining of these services.

"c. Psychiatric consultation should not be mandatory. As in the case of other specialized medical services, psychiatric consultation should be sought for definite indications and not on a routine basis.

"d. A wide range of individuals from appropriately trained, sympathetic volunteers to highly skilled physicians may qualify as abortion counselors.

"e. Contraception and/or sterilization should be discussed with each abortion patient."

* * *

It was said that "a well-equipped hospital" offers more protection "to cope with unforeseen difficulties than an office or clinic without such resources.... The factor of gestational age is of overriding importance." Thus, it was recommended that abortions in the second trimester and early abortions in the presence of existing medical complications be performed in hospitals as inpatient procedures....

8.   *The position of the American Bar Association.* At its meeting in February 1972 the ABA House of Delegates approved, with 17 opposing votes, the Uniform Abortion Act that had been drafted and approved the preceding August by the Conference of commissioners on

Uniform State Laws. 58 A. B. A. J. 380 (1972)....[40] [The footnote and its text is as it appears in the official reporter.]

VII

Three reasons have been advanced to explain historically the enactment of criminal abortion laws in the 19th century and to justify their continued existence.

It has been argued occasionally that these laws were the product of a Victorian social concern to discourage illicit sexual conduct. Texas, however, does not advance this justification in the present case, and it appears that no court or commentator has taken the argument seriously. The appellants and *amici* contend, moreover, that this is not a proper state purpose at all and suggest that, if it were, the Texas statutes are overbroad in protecting it since the law fails to distinguish between married and unwed mothers.

A second reason is concerned with abortion as a medical procedure. When most criminal abortion laws were first enacted, the

---

[40] UNIFORM ABORTION ACT

"Section 1. [*Abortion Defined; When Authorized.*]

"(a) 'Abortion' means the termination of human pregnancy with an intention other than to produce a live birth or to remove a dead fetus.

"(b) An abortion may be performed in this state only if it is performed:

"(1) by a physician licensed to practice medicine [or osteopathy] in this state or by a physician practicing medicine [or osteopathy] in the employ of the government of the United States or of this state, [and the abortion is performed [in the physician's office or in a medical clinic, or] in a hospital approved by the [Department of Health] or operated by the United States, this state, or any department, agency, or political subdivision of either;] or by a female upon herself upon the advice of the physician; and

"(2) within [20] weeks after the commencement of the pregnancy [or after [20] weeks only if the physician has reasonable cause to believe (i) there is a substantial risk that continuance of the pregnancy would endanger the life of the mother, (ii) that the child would be born with grave physical or mental defect, or (iii) that the pregnancy resulted from rape or incest, or illicit intercourse with a girl under the age of 16 years.].... [This footnote and its number are reproduced as they appear in the official opinion.]

procedure was a hazardous one for the woman. This was particularly true prior to the development of antisepsis. Antiseptic techniques, of course, were based on discoveries by Lister, Pasteur, and others first announced in 1867, but were not generally accepted and employed until about the turn of the century. Abortion mortality was high. Even after 1900, and perhaps until as late as the development of antibiotics in the 1940's, standard modern techniques such as dilation and curettage were not nearly so safe as they are today. Thus, it has been argued that a State's real concern in enacting a criminal abortion law was to protect the pregnant woman, that is, to restrain her from submitting to a procedure that placed her life in serious jeopardy.

Modern medical techniques have altered this situation. Appellants and various *amici* refer to medical data indicating that abortion in early pregnancy, that is, prior to the end of the first trimester, although not without its risk, is now relatively safe....

The third reason is the State's interest – some phrase it in terms of duty – in protecting prenatal life. Some of the argument for this justification rests on the theory that a new human life is present from the moment of conception. The State's interest and general obligation to protect life then extends, it is argued, to prenatal life. Only when the life of the pregnant mother herself is at stake, balanced against the life she carries within her, should the interest of the embryo or fetus not prevail. Logically, of course, a legitimate state interest in this area need not stand or fall on acceptance of the belief that life begins at conception or at some other point prior to live birth. In assessing the State's interest, recognition may be given to the less rigid claim that as long as at least *potential* life is involved, the State may assert interests beyond the protection of the pregnant woman alone.

Parties challenging state abortion laws have sharply disputed in some courts the contention that a purpose of these laws, when enacted, was to protect prenatal life. Pointing to the absence of legislative history to support the contention, they claim that most state laws were designed solely to protect the woman. Because medical advances have lessened this concern, at least with respect to abortion in early pregnancy, they argue that with respect to such abortions the laws can no longer be justified by any state interest. There is some scholarly support for this view of original purpose. The few state courts called upon to interpret their laws in the late 19th and early 20th centuries did focus on the State's interest in protecting the woman's health rather than in preserving the embryo and fetus. Proponents of this view point out that in many States, including Texas, by statute or judicial interpretation, the pregnant woman herself could not be prosecuted for self-abortion or for cooperating in an abortion performed upon her by another. They claim that adoption of the "quickening" distinction through received common law and state statutes tacitly recognizes the greater health hazards inherent in late abortion and impliedly repudiates the theory that life begins at conception.

It is with these interests, and the weight to be attached to them, that this case is concerned.

VIII

The Constitution does not explicitly mention any right of privacy. In a line of decisions, however...the Court has recognized that a right of personal privacy, or a guarantee of certain areas or zones of privacy, does exist under the Constitution. In varying contexts, the Court or individual Justices have, indeed, found at least the roots of that right in the First Amendment...in the Fourth and Fifth Amendments...in the penumbras of the Bill of Rights, in the Ninth Amendment, or in the concept of liberty guaranteed by the first section of the Fourteenth Amendment. These decisions make it clear that only personal rights that can be deemed "fundamental" or "implicit in the concept of ordered liberty," are included in this guarantee of personal privacy....

This right of privacy, whether it be founded in the Fourteenth Amendment's concept of personal liberty and restrictions upon state action, as we feel it is, or, as the District Court determined, in the Ninth Amendment's reservation of rights to the people, is broad enough to encompass a woman's decision whether or not to terminate her pregnancy. The detriment that the State would impose upon the pregnant woman by denying this choice altogether is apparent. Specific and direct harm medically diagnosable even in early pregnancy may be involved. Maternity, or additional offspring, may force upon the woman a distressful life and future. Psychological harm may be imminent. Mental and physical health may be taxed by child care. There is also the distress, for all concerned, associated with the unwanted child, and there is the problem of bringing a child into a family already unable, psychologically and otherwise, to care for it. In other cases, as in this one, the additional difficulties and continuing stigma of unwed motherhood may be involved. All these are factors the woman and her responsible physician necessarily will consider in consultation.

On the basis of elements such as these, appellant and some *amici* argue that the woman's right is absolute and that she is entitled to terminate her pregnancy at whatever time, in whatever way, and for whatever reason she alone chooses. With this we do not agree. Appellant's arguments that Texas either has no valid interest at all in regulating the abortion decision, or no interest strong enough to support any limitation upon the woman's sole determination, are unpersuasive. The Court's decisions recognizing a right of privacy also acknowledge that some state regulation in areas protected by that right is appropriate. As noted above, a State may properly assert important interest in safeguarding health, in maintaining medical standards, and in protecting potential life. At some point in pregnancy, these respective interests become sufficiently compelling to sustain regulation of the factors that govern the abortion decision. The privacy right involved, therefore, cannot be said to be absolute. In fact, it is not clear to us that the claim asserted by some *amici* that one has an unlimited right to do with one's body as one pleases bears a close relationship to the right of privacy previously articulated in the Court's decisions....

We, therefore, conclude that the right of personal privacy includes the abortion decision, but that this right is not unqualified and must be considered against important state interests in regulation.

We note that those federal and state courts that have recently considered abortion law challenges have reached the same conclusion. A majority, in addition to the District Court in the present case, have held state laws unconstitutional, at least in part, because of vagueness or because of overbreadth and abridgment of rights....

Others have sustained state statutes....

Although the results are divided, most of these courts have agreed that the right of privacy, however based, is broad enough to cover the abortion decision; that the right, nonetheless, is not absolute and is subject to some limitations; and that at some point the state interests as to protection of health, medical standards, and prenatal life, become dominant. We agree with this approach.

Where certain "fundamental rights" are involved, the Court has held that regulation limiting these rights may be justified only by a "compelling state interest"...and that legislative enactments must be narrowly drawn to express only the legitimate state interests at stake....

* * *

IX

The District Court held that the appellee failed to meet his burden of demonstrating that the Texas statute's infringement upon Roe's rights was necessary to support a compelling state interest, and that, although the appellee presented "several compelling justifications for state presence in the area of abortions," the statutes outstripped these justifications and swept "far beyond any areas of compelling state interest." ...Appellant and appellee both contest that holding. Appellant, as has been indicated, claims an absolute right that bars any state imposition of criminal penalties in the area. Appellee argues that the State's determination to recognize and protect prenatal life from and after conception constitutes a compelling state interest. As noted above, we do not agree fully with either formulation.

A. The appellee and certain *amici* argue that the fetus is a "person" within the language and meaning of the Fourteenth Amendment. In support of this, they outline at length and in detail the well-known facts of fetal development. If this suggestion of personhood is established, the appellant's case, of course, collapses, for the fetus' right to life would then be guaranteed specifically by the Amendment. The appellant conceded as much on reargument. On the other hand, the appellee conceded on reargument that no case could be cited that holds that a fetus is a person within the meaning of the Fourteenth Amendment.

The Constitution does not define "person" in so many words. . . . None indicates, with any assurance, that it has any possible pre-natal application.

All this, together with our observation, *supra*, that throughout the major portion of the 19th century prevailing legal abortion practices were far freer than they are today, persuades us that the word "person," as used in the Fourteenth Amendment, does not include the unborn....

This conclusion, however, does not of itself fully answer the contentions raised by Texas, and we pass on to other considerations.

B. The pregnant woman cannot be isolated in her privacy. She carries an embryo and, later, a fetus, if one accepts the medical definitions of the developing young in the human uterus.... As we have intimated above, it is reasonable and appropriate for a State to decide that at some point in time another interest, that of health of the mother or that of potential human life, becomes significantly involved. The woman's privacy is no longer sole and any right of privacy she possesses must be measured accordingly.

Texas urges that, apart from the Fourteenth Amendment, life begins at conception and is present throughout pregnancy, and that, therefore, the State has a compelling interest in protecting that life from and after conception. We need not resolve the difficult question of when life begins. When those trained in the respective disciplines of medicine, philosophy, and theology are unable to arrive at any consensus, the judiciary, at this point in the development of man's knowledge, is not in a position to speculate as to the answer.

It should be sufficient to note briefly the wide divergence of thinking on this most sensitive and difficult question. There has always been strong support for the view that life does not begin until live birth. This was the belief of the Stoics. It appears to be the predominant, though not the unanimous, attitude of the Jewish faith. It may be taken to represent also the position of a large segment of the Protestant community, insofar as that can be ascertained; organized groups that have taken a formal position on the abortion issue have generally regarded abortion as a matter for the conscience of the individual and her family. As we have noted, the common law found greater significance in quickening. Physicians and their scientific colleagues have regarded that event with less interest and have tended to focus either upon conception, upon live birth, or upon the interim point at which the fetus becomes "viable," that is, potentially able to live outside the mother's womb, albeit with artificial aid. Viability is usually placed at about seven months (28 weeks) but may occur earlier, even at 24 weeks. The Aristotelian theory of "mediate animation," that held sway throughout the Middle Ages and the Renaissance in Europe, continued to be official Roman Catholic dogma until the 19th century, despite opposition to this "ensoulment" theory from those in the Church who would recognize the existence of life from the moment of conception. The latter is now, of course, the official belief of the Catholic Church. As one brief *amicus* discloses, this is a view strongly held by many non-Catholics as well, and by many physicians. Substantial problems for precise definition of this view are posed, however, by new embryological data that purport to indicate that conception is a "process" over time, rather than an event, and by new medical techniques such as menstrual extraction, the "morning-after" pill, implantation of embryos, artificial insemination, and even artificial wombs.

In areas other than criminal abortion, the law has been reluctant to endorse any theory that life, as we recognize it, begins before live birth or to accord legal rights to the unborn except in narrowly defined situations and except when the rights are contingent upon live birth. For example, the traditional rule of tort law denied recovery for prenatal injuries even though the child was born alive. That rule has been changed in almost every jurisdiction. In most States, recovery is said to be permitted only if the fetus was viable, or at least quick, when the injuries were sustained, though few courts have squarely so held. In a recent development, generally opposed by the commentators, some States permit the parents of a stillborn child to maintain an action for wrongful death because of prenatal injuries. Such an action, however, would appear to be one to vindicate the parents' interest and is thus consistent with the view that the fetus, at most, represents only the potentiality of life. Similarly, unborn children have been recognized as acquiring rights or interests by way of inheritance or other devolution of property, and have been represented by guardians *ad litem*. Perfection of the interests involved, again, has generally been contingent upon live birth. In short, the unborn have never been recognized in the law as persons in the whole sense.

X

In view of all this, we do not agree that, by adopting one theory of life, Texas may override the rights of the pregnant woman that are at stake. We repeat, however, that the State does have an important and legitimate interest in preserving and protecting the health of the pregnant woman, whether she be a resident of the State or a nonresident who seeks medical consultation and treatment there, and that it has still *another* important and legitimate interest in protecting the potentiality of human life. These interests are separate and distinct. Each grows in substantiality as the woman approaches term and, at a point during pregnancy, each becomes "compelling."

With respect to the State's important and legitimate interest in the health of the mother, the "compelling" point, in the light of present medical knowledge, is at approximately the end of the first trimester. This is so because of the now-established medical fact, referred to above at 149, that until the end of the first trimester mortality in abortion may be less than mortality in normal childbirth. It follows that, from and after this point, a State may regulate the abortion procedure to the extent that the regulation reasonably relates to the preservation and protection of maternal health. Examples of permissible state regulation in this area are requirements as to the qualifications of the person who is to perform the abortion; as to the licensure of that person; as to the facility in which the procedure is to be performed, that is, whether it must be a hospital or may be a clinic or some other place of less-than-hospital status; as to the licensing of the facility; and the like.

This means, on the other hand, that, for the period of pregnancy prior to this "compelling" point, the attending physician, in consultation with his patient, is free to determine, without regulation by the State, that, in his medical judgment, the patient's pregnancy should be terminated. If that decision is reached, the judgment may be effectuated by an abortion free of interference by the State.

With respect to the State's important and legitimate interest in potential life, the "compelling" point is at viability. This is so because the fetus then presumably has the capability of meaningful life outside the mother's womb. State regulation protective of fetal life after viability thus has both logical and biological justifications. If the State is interested in protecting fetal life after viability, it may go so far as to proscribe abortion during that period, except when it is necessary to preserve the life or health of the mother.

Measured against these standards, Art. 1196 of the Texas Penal Code, in restricting legal abortions to those "procured or attempted by medical advice for the purpose of saving the life of the mother," sweeps too broadly. The statute makes no distinction between abortions performed early in pregnancy and those performed later, and it limits to a single reason, "saving" the mother's life, the legal justification for the procedure. The statute, therefore, cannot survive the constitutional attack made upon it here.

* * *

XI

* * *

This holding, we feel, is consistent with the relative weights of the respective interests involved, with the lessons and examples of medical and legal history, with the lenity of the common law, and with the demands of the profound problems of the present day. The decision leaves the State free to place increasing restrictions on abortion as the period of pregnancy lengthens, so long as those restrictions are tailored to the recognized state interests. The decision vindicates the right of the physician to administer medical treatment according to his professional judgment up to the points where important state interests provide compelling justifications for intervention. Up to those points, the abortion decision in all its aspects is inherently, and primarily, a medical decision, and basic responsibility for it must rest with the physician. If an individual practitioner abuses the privilege of exercising proper medical judgment, the usual remedies, judicial and intra-professional, are available.

XII

Our conclusion that Art. 1196 is unconstitutional means, of course, that the Texas abortion statutes, as a unit, must fall. The exception of Art. 1196 cannot be struck down separately, for the State would be left with a statute proscribing all abortion procedures no matter how medically urgent the case.

Although the District Court granted appellant Roe declaratory relief, it stopped short of issuing an injunction against enforcement of the Texas statutes. The Court has recognized that different considerations enter into a federal court's decision as to declaratory relief, on the one hand, and injunctive relief, on the other.... We are not dealing with a state that, on its face, appears to abridge free expression, an area of particular concern under *Dombrowski* and refined in *Younger* v. *Harris*, 401 U.S., at 50.

* * *

It is so ordered.

MR. JUSTICE STEWART, concurring.

In 1963, this Court, in *Ferguson* v. *Skrupa*, 372 U.S. 726, purported to sound the death knell for the doctrine of substantive due process, a doctrine under which many state laws had in the past been held to violate the Fourteenth Amendment. As Mr. Justice Black's opinion for the Court in *Skrupa* put it: "We have returned to the original constitutional proposition that courts do not substitute their social and economic beliefs for the judgment of legislative bodies, who are elected to pass laws."

Barely two years later, in *Griswold* v. *Connecticut*, 381 U.S. 479, the Court held a Connecticut birth control law unconstitutional. In view of what had been so recently said in *Skrupa*, the Court's opinion in *Griswold* understandably did its best to avoid reliance on the Due Process Clause of the Fourteenth Amendment as the ground for decision. Yet, the Connecticut law did not violate any provision of the Bill of Rights, nor any other specific provision of the Constitution. So it was clear to me then, and it is equally clear to me now, that the *Griswold* decision can be rationally understood only as a holding that the Connecticut statute substantively invaded the "liberty" that is protected by the Due Process Clause of the Fourteenth Amendment. As so understood, *Griswold* stands as one in a long line of pre-*Skrupa* cases decided under the doctrine of substantive due process, and I now accept it as such.

* * *

As Mr. Justice Harlan once wrote: "[T]he full scope of the liberty guaranteed by the Due Process Clause cannot be found in or limited by the precise terms of the specific guarantees elsewhere provided in the Constitution. This 'liberty' is not a series of isolated points pricked out in terms of the taking of property; the freedom of speech, press, and religion; the right to keep and bear arms; the freedom from unreasonable searches and seizures; and so on. It is a rational continuum which, broadly speaking, includes a freedom from all substantial arbitrary impositions and purposeless restraints . . . and which also recognizes, what a reasonable and sensitive judgment must, that certain interests require particularly careful scrutiny of the state needs asserted to justify their abridgment." ...In the words of Mr. Justice Frankfurter, "Great concepts like...'liberty'...were purposely left to gather meaning from experience. For they relate to the whole domain of social and economic fact, and the statesmen who founded this Nation knew too well that only a stagnant society remains unchanged."

* * *

As recently as last Term, in *Eisenstadt* v. *Baird*, 405 U.S. 438, 453, we recognized "the right of the *individual*, married or single, to be free from unwarranted governmental intrusion into matters so fundamentally affecting a person as the decision whether to bear or beget a child." That right necessarily includes the right of a woman to decide whether or not to terminate her pregnancy. "Certainly the interests of a woman in giving of her physical and emotional self during pregnancy and the interests that will be affected throughout her life by the birth and raising of a child are of a far greater degree of significance and personal intimacy than the right to send a child to private school protected in *Pierce* v. *Society of Sisters*, 268 U.S. 510 (1925), or the right to teach a foreign language protected in *Meyer* v. *Nebraska*, 262 U.S. 390 (1923)."

* * *

Clearly, therefore, the Court today is correct in holding that the right asserted by Jane Roe is embraced within the personal liberty protected by the Due Process Clause of the Fourteenth Amendment.

* * *

MR. JUSTICE REHNQUIST, dissenting.

The Court's opinion brings to the decision of this troubling question both extensive historical fact and a wealth of legal scholarship. While the opinion thus commands my respect, I find myself nonetheless in fundamental disagreement with those parts of it that invalidate the Texas statute in question, and therefore dissent.

* * *

II

...I have difficulty in concluding, as the Court does, that the right of "privacy" is involved in this case. Texas, by the statute here challenged, bars the performance of a medical abortion by a licensed physician on a plaintiff such as Roe. A transaction resulting in an operation such as this is not "private" in the ordinary usage of that word. Nor is the "privacy" that the Court finds here even a distant relative of the freedom from searches and seizures protected by the Fourth Amendment to the Constitution, which the Court has referred to as embodying a right to privacy....

If the Court means by the term "privacy" no more than that the claim of a person to be free from unwanted state regulation of consensual transactions may be a form of "liberty" protected by the Fourteenth Amendment, there is no doubt that similar claims have been upheld in our earlier decisions on the basis of that liberty. I agree with the statement of Mr. Justice Stewart in his concurring opinion that the "liberty," against deprivation of which without due process the Fourteenth Amendment protects, embraces more than the rights found in the Bill of Rights. But that liberty is not guaranteed absolutely against deprivation, only against deprivation without due process of law. The test traditionally applied in the area of social and economic legislation is whether or not a law such as that challenged has a rational relation to a valid state objective.... The Due Process Clause of the Fourteenth Amendment undoubtedly does place a limit, albeit a broad one, on legislative power to enact laws such as this. If the Texas statute were to prohibit an abortion even where the mother's life is in jeopardy, I have little doubt that such a statute would lack a rational relation to a valid state objective.... But the Court's sweeping invalidation of any restrictions on abortion during the first trimester is impossible to justify under that standard, and the conscious weighing of competing factors that the Court's opinion apparently substitutes for the established test is far more appropriate to a legislative judgment than to a judicial one.

The Court eschews the history of the Fourteenth Amendment in its reliance on the "compelling state interest" test.... But the Court adds a new wrinkle to this test by transposing it from the legal considerations associated with the Equal Protection Clause of the Fourteenth Amendment to this case arising under the Due Process Clause of the Fourteenth Amendment. Unless I misapprehend the consequences of this transplanting of the "compelling state interest test," the Court's opinion will accomplish the seemingly impossible feat of leaving this area of the law more confused than it found it.

While the Court's opinion quotes from the dissent of Mr. Justice Holmes in *Lochner* v. *New York*, 198 U.S. 45, 74 (1905), the result it reaches is more closely attuned to the majority opinion of Mr. Justice Peckham in that case. As in *Lochner* and similar cases applying substantive due process standards to economic and social welfare legislation, the adoption of the compelling state interest standard will inevitably require this Court to examine the legislative policies and pass on the wisdom of these policies in the very process of deciding whether a particular state interest put forward may or may not be "compelling." The decision here to break pregnancy into three distinct terms and to outline the permissible restrictions the State may impose in each one, for example, partakes more of judicial legislation than it does of a determination of the intent of the drafters of the Fourteenth Amendment.

The fact that a majority of the States reflecting, after all, the majority sentiment in those States, have had restrictions on abortions for at least a century is a strong indication, it seems to me, that the asserted right to an abortion is not "so rooted in the traditions and conscience of our people as to be ranked as fundamental[....]" Even today, when society's views on abortion are changing, the very existence of the debate is evidence that the "right" to an abortion is not so universally accepted as the appellant would have us believe.

To reach its result, the Court necessarily has had to find within the scope of the Fourteenth Amendment a right that was apparently completely unknown to the drafters of the Amendment. As early as 1821, the first state law dealing directly with abortion was enacted by the Connecticut Legislature.... By the time of the adoption of the Fourteenth Amendment in 1868, there were at least 36 laws enacted by state or territorial legislatures limiting abortion. While many States have amended or updated their laws, 21 of the laws on the books in 1868 remain in effect today. Indeed, the Texas statute struck down today was, as the majority notes, first enacted in 1857 and "has remained substantially unchanged to the present time."

There apparently was no question concerning the validity of this provision or of any of the other state statutes when the Fourteenth Amendment was adopted. The only conclusion possible from this history is that the drafters did not intend to have the Fourteenth Amendment withdraw from the States the power to legislate with respect to this matter.

* * *

For all of the foregoing reasons, I respectfully dissent.

*

Consistent with the struggle anyone would experience in attempting to maintain neutrality in a narrative intended only to be a guide through a thicket of diverse materials, the most I care to say in this particularly volatile area, a political minefield, as it were, would simply be to suggest the idea there were forces at work in the backwaters of what seemed to be the observable *zeitgeist*. How did that occur? At the same time, other forces on a broad spectrum basis were never mobilized as there never was really a discernible front. But even with all that aside, the question we work on is the same one from the beginning: what has come of all this, was it foreseen, and where is it going? What does all this bode for the future for everyone totally apart from the issue of abortion, per se?

From some corners, it has been heard that abortion is not a constitutional matter anymore than gender reassignment, sacrificial surgery of a Siamese twin, *therapis terminus*, with a continuing list being seemingly endless, even mothers for hire, or fathers for that matter, while legislation relating to such matters clearly is, since *Marbury*, constitutionally testable and therefore within the jurisdiction of the Court. It's not that there shouldn't be rules which pass constitutional muster, but to make such questions themselves constitutional issues, and then proceed to write laws governing such matters, seems to fly in the face of the separation of powers architecture of the Constitution. If the Court decides such matters on the basis of public policy, then it is legislating far beyond any legitimate judicial function. Legislation is public policy. Arguably, many believe the Court should not try to draft public policy, but rather test legislative responses. What we have observed is the Court taking up a matter and, by the legerdemain of the stroke of a pen, turning it into a constitutional issue beyond the reach of any relief or dissent (sound familiar, M. Justices?). It then proceeds to justify its own legislation on its view of "fundamental concepts of liberty" or "privacy" or rights of "due process," "emanations," "radiations," "fundamental guarantees," "the conscience of a nation," "deep rooted traditions," peeking out at us from underneath penumbras here and there in the Bill of Rights. And finally, selectively applying all of this in a way which will result in a desired outcome, seems to be prodigious judicial alchemy if not outright necromancy. Yet, who is able to effectively argue with that? We will see. For now, to recognize the problem will suffice. Solutions will come. For us, the issue is not abortion, but what the Court does, how it does it, and what the Court will do in the future.

One of the prices to be paid, however, for such judicial behavior, is a loss of respect and credibility at least in the context of a violation of the separation of powers which, take note, is itself a constitutional matter, a genuine constitutional matter. Continually trotting out the Constitution and then torquing its words, coupled with words and phrases such as the "collective consciousness" of the nation, to make it fit something for which it was never designed, let alone contemplated, the morals and welfare of the people (left to the States and the people, constitutionally), produces the kind of results and unintended effects you have already seen in even the earliest stages of your own judicial review.

Americans are not taught law, and to foist upon them this arcane constitutional charade, leaving them helpless to understand or even object, amounts to constituting a frank fraud upon them. They have no way of knowing as a general proposition. They know something may be wrong, but they don't know what it is, or why. They know it certainly doesn't comport with what Adams or Franklin or Jefferson or Madison or Washington would have approved. Pick your model. Here it would not make any difference. To think that matters such as those the Court now takes as raising constitutional issues, and then legislate upon them, would have been laughable, or worse. Today? What happened? You may be surprised.

Courts are intended to make judgments. Judgments should be based upon laws of wise restraint. One could easily conclude that is not what the Court did in virtually any given case. Read the cases and see instead what has happened as a result of them. As suggested in the Introduction, look around, quietly observe.

Then there is the other side which takes a reciprocal course. Without constitutional pronouncements of a legislative character, it is said, there can be no substance, no real meat in the decisions. The Constitution is a living document that grows with every decision of the Court, and with these changes comes about continuing constitutional conventions of sorts, alive and flourishing in its continually updated relevance, revision upon revision, as it marches along with time (giving *Marbury* coats of continually new colors). But one might ask, at what time, what drum, whose bugle, and to what expense? We'll see.

Why did the Court ever get into this swamp in the first place (see dissents in the following case which demonstrate this struggle)? The Court has to wobble, or "tailor," or say it didn't say what it plainly said, or complain that what it said has been misinterpreted ... partially reverse itself, or just flat out reverse itself, with or without candor, leaving itself open to even further ridicule and contempt (usually limited to the more learned in the profession as no one else knows what it is doing because the public doesn't read what you are reading, nor do most lawyers) which in the end will ultimately result in the Court simply losing its influence and power, and its ability to carry out its orders.

At this point, noting the copious citations which load the following case, all of which would take months to read and digest, along with the explanations and re-explanations followed by justification after justification, rationale compounded upon rationale (reminiscent of the pitiful apologia and attempted catharsis of *Johnson, supra*), punctuated with historical points and counterpoints when all taken together add up to nothing more than a cerebral trashing of the truth (or so one might glean from the dissents, and viewed on the basis of mere objective observations, the propriety of the case or cases being entirely left to you to be considered outside our task here). The Court lets you know it is about to set out to write some law governing the availability and timing limitations of abortion. Clothing it in irrelevant academics behind the mask of meaningless discussions, monologues in fact, simply makes it more illegitimate than its being wrapped in constitutional veils. The transparency is callow. Courts are simply not equipped to, nor do they legislate well, being without the machinery and hearings structure common to lawful legislative methodology and process. Again, we are not looking at the outcome of a case or its holding, we are looking at process and methodology, the tactics employed by the Court to get from there (then) to here (now), and their related side-effects.

Now, what about partial-birth abortions? Should they be available or not? Not our concern for purposes of this exercise. Review the initial legislation the Court laid down in *Roe*. Would not partial-birth abortion be a natural follow on? Well, so says the Court in the following opinion, yes. With foresight?

Of course there seemingly should be some limits, and as an illustration of what has evolved following *Roe* and been crafted in that regard, your attention is now directed to *Stenberg v. Carhart*, 530 U.S. 914 (2000). What is apt to follow after that defies imagination, or so one might think; you will see.

XII

STENBERG, ATTORNEY GENERAL OF NEBRASKA, ET AL. v.
CARHART
CERTIORARI TO THE UNITED STATES COURT OF APPEALS
FOR THE EIGHTH CIRCUIT
530 U.S. 914

JUSTICE BREYER delivered the opinion of the Court.

We again consider the right to an abortion. We understand the controversial nature of the problem. Millions of Americans believe that life begins at conception and consequently that an abortion is akin to causing the death of an innocent child; they recoil at the thought of a law that would permit it. Other millions fear that a law that forbids abortion would condemn many American women to lives that lack dignity, depriving them of equal liberty and leading those with least resources to undergo illegal abortions with the attendant risks of death and suffering. Taking account of these virtually irreconcilable points of view, aware that constitutional law must govern a society whose different members sincerely hold directly opposing views, and considering the matter in light of the Constitution's guarantees of fundamental individual liberty, this Court, in the course of a generation, has determined and then redetermined that the Constitution offers basic protection to the woman's right to choose. *Roe* v. *Wade*, 410 U.S. 113 (1973); *Planned Parenthood of Southeastern Pa.* v. *Casey*, 505 U.S. 833 (1992). We shall not revisit those legal principles. Rather, we apply them to the circumstances of this case.

Three established principles determine the issue before us. We shall set them forth in the language of the joint opinion in *Casey*. First, before "viability . . . the woman has a right to choose to terminate her pregnancy." *Id.*, at 870 (plurality opinion).

Second, "a law designed to further the State's interest in fetal life which imposes an undue burden on the woman's decision before fetal viability" is unconstitutional....

Third, "'subsequent to viability, the State in promoting its interest in the potentiality of human life may, if it chooses, regulate, and even proscribe, abortion except where it is necessary, in appropriate medical judgment, for the preservation of the life or health of the mother.'"

* * *

We apply these principles to a Nebraska law banning "partial birth abortion." The statute reads as follows:

"No partial birth abortion shall be performed in this state, unless such procedure is necessary to save the life of the mother whose life is endangered by a physical disorder, physical illness, or physical injury, including a life-endangering physical condition caused by or arising from the pregnancy itself."

* * *

The statute defines "partial birth abortion" as:

> "an abortion procedure in which the person performing the abortion partially delivers vaginally a living unborn child before killing the unborn child and completing the delivery."

It further defines "partially delivers vaginally a living unborn child before killing the unborn child" to mean:

> "deliberately and intentionally delivering into the vagina a living unborn child, or a substantial portion thereof, for the purpose of performing a procedure that the person performing such procedure knows will kill the unborn child and does kill the unborn child."

We hold that this statute violates the Constitution.

I

A

Dr. Leroy Carhart is a Nebraska physician who performs abortions in a clinical setting. He brought this lawsuit in Federal District Court seeking a declaration that the Nebraska statute violates the Federal Constitution, and asking for an injunction forbidding its enforcement. After a trial on the merits, during which both sides presented several expert witnesses, the District Court held the statute unconstitutional. 11 F. Supp. 2d 1099 (Neb. 1998). On appeal, the Eighth Circuit affirmed. 192 F. 3d 1142 (1999); [....] We granted certiorari to consider the matter.

B

Because Nebraska law seeks to ban one method of aborting a pregnancy, we must describe and then discuss several different abortion procedures. Considering the fact that those procedures seek to terminate a potential human life, our discussion may seem clinically cold or callous to some, perhaps horrifying to others. There is no alternative way, however, to acquaint the reader with the technical distinctions among different abortion methods and related factual matters, upon which the outcome of this case depends....

The evidence before the trial court, as supported or supplemented in the literature, indicates the following:

1. About 90% of all abortions performed in the United States take place during the first trimester of pregnancy, before 12 weeks of gestational age.... During the first trimester, the predominant abortion method is "vacuum aspiration," which involves insertion of a vacuum tube (cannula) into the uterus to evacuate the contents. Such an abortion is typically performed on an outpatient basis under local anesthesia.... Vacuum aspiration is considered particularly safe. The procedure's mortality rates for first trimester abortion are, for example, 5 to 10 times lower than those associated with carrying the fetus to term. Complication rates are also low.... As the fetus grows in size, however, the vacuum aspiration method becomes increasingly difficult to use....

2. Approximately 10% of all abortions are performed during the second trimester of pregnancy (12 to 24 weeks). In the early 1970's, inducing labor through the injection of saline into the uterus was the predominant method of second trimester abortion.... Today, however, the medical profession has switched from medical induction of labor to surgical procedures for most second trimester abortions. The most commonly used procedure is called "dilation and evacuation" (D&E). That procedure (together with a modified form of vacuum aspiration used in the early second trimester) accounts for about 95% of all abortions performed from 12 to 20 weeks of gestational age.

3. D&E "refers generically to transcervical procedures performed at 13 weeks gestation or later."

* * *

Between 13 and 15 weeks of gestation:

"D&E is similar to vacuum aspiration except that the cervix must be dilated more widely because surgical instruments are used to remove larger pieces of tissue. Osmotic dilators are usually used. Intravenous fluids and an analgesic or sedative may be administered. A local anesthetic such as a paracervical block may be administered, dilating agents, if used, are removed and instruments are inserted through the cervix into the uterus to remov[e] fetal and placental tissue. Because fetal tissue is friable and easily broken, the fetus may not be removed intact. The walls of the uterus are scraped with a curette to ensure that no tissue remains."

After 15 weeks:

"Because the fetus is larger at this stage of gestation (particularly the head), and because bones are more rigid, dismemberment or other destructive procedures are more likely to be required than at earlier gestational ages to remove fetal and placental tissue."

After 20 weeks:

"Some physicians use intrafetal potassium chloride or digoxin to induce fetal demise prior to a late D&E (after 20 weeks), to facilitate evacuation."

* * *

4. When instrumental disarticulation incident to D&E is necessary, it typically occurs as the doctor pulls a portion of the fetus through the cervix into the birth canal. Dr. Carhart testified at trial as follows:

"Dr. Carhart: ...'The dismemberment occurs between the traction of...my instrument and the countertraction of the internal os of the cervix....

"Counsel: 'So the dismemberment occurs after you pulled a part of the fetus through the cervix, is that correct?

"Dr. Carhart: 'Exactly. Because you're using – The cervix has two strictures or two rings, the internal os and the external os...that's what's actually doing the dismembering....

5. The D&E procedure carries certain risks. The use of instruments within the uterus creates a danger of accidental perforation and damage to neighboring organs. Sharp fetal bone fragments create similar dangers. And fetal tissue accidentally left behind can cause infection and various other complications.... Nonetheless studies show that the risks of mortality and complication that accompany the D&E procedure between the 12th and 20th weeks of gestation are significantly lower than those accompanying induced labor procedures (the next safest midsecond trimester procedures)....

6. At trial, Dr. Carhart and Dr. Stubblefield described a variation of the D&E procedure, which they referred to as an "intact D&E." ...The procedure then involves removing the fetus from the uterus through the cervix "intact," i.e. in one pass, rather than in several passes. *Ibid.* It is used after 16 weeks at the earliest, as vacuum aspiration becomes ineffective and the fetal skull becomes too large to pass through the cervix. The intact D&E proceeds in one of two ways, depending on the presentation of the fetus. If the fetus presents head first (a vertex presentation), the doctor collapses the skull; and the doctor then extracts the entire fetus through the cervix. If the fetus presents feet first (a breech presentation), the doctor pulls the fetal body through the cervix, collapses the skull, and extracts the fetus through the cervix.

* * *

II

The question before us is whether Nebraska's statute, making criminal the performance of a "partial birth abortion," violates the Federal Constitution, as interpreted in *Planned Parenthood of*

Southeastern Pa. v. *Casey*, 505 U.S. 833 (1992), and *Roe* v. *Wade*, 410 U.S. 113 (1973). We conclude that it does for at least two independent reasons. First, the law lacks any exception "'for the preservation of the...health of the mother.'" ...Second, it "imposes an undue burden on a woman's ability" to choose a D&E abortion, thereby unduly burdening the right to choose abortion itself.

A

The *Casey* plurality opinion reiterated what the Court held in *Roe*; that "'subsequent to viability, the State in promoting its interest in the potentiality of human life may, if it chooses, regulate, and even proscribe, abortion *except where it is necessary, in appropriate medical judgment, for the preservation of the life or health of the mother.*'"

* * *

1

Nebraska responds that the law does not require a health exception unless there is a need for such an exception. And here there is no such need, it says. It argues that "safe alternatives remain available" and "a ban on partial-birth abortion/D&X would create no risk to the health of women." ...The problem for Nebraska is that the parties strongly contested this factual question in the trial court below; and the findings and evidence support Dr. Carhart.

* * *

In sum, Nebraska has not convinced us that a health exception is "never necessary to preserve the health of women." ...Rather, a statute that altogether forbids D&X creates a significant health risk. The statute consequently must contain a health exception. ...[W]here substantial medical authority supports the proposition that banning a particular abortion procedure could endanger women's health, *Casey* requires the statute to include a health exception when the procedure is "'necessary, in appropriate medical judgment, for the preservation of the life or health of the mother.'" ...Requiring such an exception in this case is no departure from *Casey*, but simply a straightforward application of its holding.

B

The Eighth Circuit found the Nebraska statute unconstitutional because, in *Casey*'s words, it has the "effect of placing a substantial obstacle in the path of a woman seeking an abortion of a nonviable fetus." ...It thereby places an "undue burden" upon a woman's right to terminate her pregnancy before viability. Nebraska does not deny that the statute imposes an "undue burden" *if* it applies to the more commonly used D&E procedure as well as to D&X. And we agree with the Eighth Circuit that it does so apply.

* * *

In sum, using this law some present prosecutors and future Attorneys General may choose to pursue physicians who use D&E procedures, the most commonly used method for performing previability second trimester abortions. All those who perform abortion procedures using that method must fear prosecution, conviction, and imprisonment. The result is an undue burden upon a woman's right to make an abortion decision. We must consequently find the statute unconstitutional.

The judgment of the Court of Appeals is

Affirmed.

JUSTICE STEVENS, with whom JUSTICE GINSBURG joins, concurring.

Although much ink is spilled today describing the gruesome nature of late-term abortion procedures, that rhetoric does not provide me a *reason* to believe that the procedure Nebraska here claims it seeks to ban is more brutal, more gruesome, or less respectful of "potential life" than the equally gruesome procedure Nebraska claims it still allows. JUSTICE GINSBURG and Judge Posner have, I believe, correctly diagnosed the underlying reason for the enactment of this legislation – a reason that also explains much of the Court's rhetoric directed at an objective that extends well beyond the narrow issue that this case presents. The rhetoric is almost, but not quite, loud enough to obscure the quiet fact that during the past 27 years, the central holding of *Roe* v. *Wade*, 410 U.S. 113 (1973), has been endorsed by all but 4 of the 17 Justices who have addressed the issue. That holding – that the word "liberty" in the Fourteenth Amendment includes a woman's right to make this difficult and extremely personal decision – makes it impossible for me to understand how a State has any legitimate interest in requiring a doctor to follow any procedure other than the one that he or she reasonably believes will best protect the woman in her exercise of this constitutional liberty. But one need not even approach this view today to conclude that Nebraska's law must fall. For the notion that either of these two equally gruesome procedures performed at this late state of gestation is more akin to infanticide than the other, or that the State furthers any legitimate interest by banning one but not the other, is simply irrational....

JUSTICE O'CONNOR, concurring.

The issue of abortion is one of the most contentious and controversial in contemporary American society. It presents extraordinarily difficult questions that, as the Court recognizes, involve "virtually irreconcilable points of view." The specific question we face today is whether Nebraska's attempt to proscribe a particular method of abortion, commonly known as "partial birth abortion," is constitutional. For the reasons stated in the Court's opinion, I agree that Nebraska's statute cannot be reconciled with our decision in *Planned Parenthood of*

Southeastern Pa. v. *Casey*, 505 U.S. 833 (1992), and is therefore unconstitutional. I write separately to emphasize the following points.

First, the Nebraska statute is inconsistent with *Casey* because it lacks an exception for those instances when the banned procedure is necessary to preserve the health of the mother....

* * *

Second, Nebraska's statute is unconstitutional on the alternative and independent ground that it imposes an undue burden on a woman's right to choose to terminate her pregnancy before viability. Nebraska's ban covers not just the dilation and extraction (D&X) procedure, but also the dilation and evacuation (D&E) procedure, "the most commonly used method for performing previability second trimester abortions."

* * *

JUSTICE GINSBURG, with whom JUSTICE STEVENS joins, concurring.

I write separately only to stress that amidst all the emotional uproar caused by an abortion case, we should not lose sight of the character of Nebraska's "partial birth abortion" law. As the Court observes, this law does not save any fetus from destruction, for it targets only "a *method* of performing abortion." Nor does the statute seek to protect the lives or health of pregnant women. Moreover, as JUSTICE STEVENS points out, *ante*, at 946 (concurring opinion), the most common method of performing previability second trimester abortions is no less distressing or susceptible to gruesome description. Seventh Circuit Chief Judge Posner correspondingly observed, regarding similar bans in Wisconsin and Illinois, that the law prohibits the D&X procedure "not because the procedure ills the fetus, not because it risks worse complications for the woman than alternative procedures would do, not because it is a crueler or more painful or more disgusting method of terminating a pregnancy." *Hope Clinic* v. *Ryan*, 195 F. 3d 857, 881 (CA7 1999) (dissenting opinion). Rather, Chief Judge Posner commented, the law prohibits the procedure because the state legislators seek to chip away at the private choice shielded by *Roe* v. *Wade*, 410 U.S. 113 (1973), even as modified by *Planned Parenthood of Southeastern Pa.* v. *Casey*, 505 U.S. 833 (1992).

A state regulation that "has the purpose or effect of placing a substantial obstacle in the path of a woman seeking an abortion of a nonviable fetus" violates the Constitution. Such an obstacle exists if the State stops a woman from choosing the procedure her doctor "reasonably believes will best protect the woman in [the] exercise of [her] constitutional liberty." ...Again as stated by Chief Judge Posner, "if a statute burdens constitutional rights and all that can be said on its behalf is that it is the vehicle that legislators have chosen for expressing their hostility to those rights, the burden is undue."

CHIEF JUSTICE REHNQUIST, dissenting.

I did not join the joint opinion in *Planned Parenthood of Southeastern Pa.* v. *Casey*, 505 U.S. 833 (1992), and continue to believe that case is wrongly decided.... I believe JUSTICE KENNEDY and JUSTICE THOMAS have correctly applied *Casey*'s principles and join their dissenting opinions.

JUSTICE SCALIA, dissenting.

I am optimistic enough to believe that, one day, *Stenberg* v. *Carhart* will be assigned its rightful place in the history of this Court's jurisprudence beside *Korematsu* and *Dred Scott*. The method of killing a human child – one cannot even accurately say an entirely unborn human child – proscribed by this statute is so horrible that the most clinical description of it evokes a shudder of revulsion. And the Court must know (as most state legislatures banning this procedure have concluded) that demanding a "health exception" – which requires the abortionist to assure himself that, in his expert medical judgment, this method is, in the case at hand, marginally safer than others (how can one prove the contrary beyond a reasonable doubt?) – is to give live-birth abortion free rein. The notion that the Constitution of the United States, designed, among other things, "to establish Justice, insure domestic Tranquility...and secure the Blessings of Liberty to ourselves and our Posterity," prohibits the States from simply banning this visibly brutal means of eliminating our half-born posterity is quite simply absurd.

Even so, I had not intended to write separately here until the focus of the other separate writings (including the one I have joined) gave me cause to fear that this case might be taken to stand for an error different from the one that it actually exemplifies. Because of the Court's practice of publishing dissents in the order of the seniority of their authors, this writing will appear in the United States Reports before those others, but the reader will not comprehend what follows unless he reads them first.

* * *

The two lengthy dissents in this case have, appropriately enough, set out to establish that today's result does not follow from this Court's most recent pronouncement on the matter of abortion, *Planned Parenthood of Southeastern Pa.* v. *Casey*, 505 U.S. 833 (1992). It would be unfortunate, however, if those who disagree with the result were induced to regard it as merely a regrettable misapplication of *Casey*. It is not that, but is *Casey*'s logical and entirely predictable consequence. To be sure, the Court's construction of this statute so as to make it include procedures other than live-birth abortion involves not only a disregard of fair meaning, but an abandonment of the principle that even ambiguous statutes should be interpreted in such fashion as to render them valid rather than void. *Casey* does not permit *that* jurisprudential novelty – which must be chalked up to the Court's inclination to bend the rules when any effort to limit abortion, or even to speak in opposition to abortion, is at issue....

But the Court gives a second and independent reason for invalidating this human (not to say antibarbarian) law: That it fails to allow an exception for the situation in which the abortionist believes that this live-birth method of destroying the child might be safer for the woman....

I have joined JUSTICE THOMAS's dissent because I agree that today's decision is an "unprecedented expansio[n]" of our prior cases, *post*, at 1012, "is not mandated" by *Casey*'s "undue-burden" test, *post*, at 1010, and can even be called (though this pushes me to the limit of my belief) "obviously irreconcilable with *Casey*'s explication of what its undue-burden standard requires," *post*, at 983. But I never put much stock in *Casey*'s explication of the inexplicable. In the last analysis, my judgment that *Casey* does not support today's tragic result can be traced to the fact that what I consider to be an "undue burden" is different from what the majority considers to be an "undue burden" – a conclusion that cannot be demonstrated true or false by factual inquiry or legal reasoning. It is a value judgment, dependent upon how much one respects (or believes society ought to respect) the life of a partially delivered fetus, and how much one respects (or believes society ought to respect) the freedom of the woman who gave it life to kill it. Evidently, the five Justices in today's majority value the former less, or the latter more, (or both), than the four of us in dissent. Case closed. There is no cause for anyone who believes in *Casey* to feel betrayed by this outcome. It has been arrived at by precisely the process *Casey* promised – a democratic vote by nine lawyers, not on the question whether the text of the Constitution has anything to say about this subject (it obviously does not); nor even on the question (also appropriate for lawyers) whether the legal traditions of the American people would have sustained such a limitation upon abortion (they obviously would); but upon the pure policy question whether this limitation upon abortion is "undue" – *i.e.*, goes too far.

In my dissent in *Casey*, I wrote that the "undue burden" test made law by the joint opinion created a standard that was "as doubtful in application as it is unprincipled in origin," *Casey*, 505 U.S., at 985; "hopelessly unworkable in practice," *id.*, at 986; "ultimately standardless," *id.*, at 987. Today's decision is the proof. As long as we are debating this issue of necessity for a health-of-the-mother exception on the basis of *Casey*, it is really quite impossible for us dissenters to contend that the majority is *wrong* on the law – any more than it could be said that one is *wrong in law* to support or oppose the death penalty, or to support or oppose mandatory minimum sentences. The most that we can honestly say is that we disagree with the majority on their policy-judgment-couched-as-law. And those who believe that a 5-to-4 vote on a policy matter by unelected lawyers should not overcome the judgment of 30 state legislatures have a problem, not with the *application* of *Casey*, but with its *existence*. *Casey* must be overruled.

While I am in an I-told-you-so mood, I must recall my bemusement, in *Casey*, at the majority opinion's expressed belief that *Roe* v. *Wade*, 410 U.S. 133 (1973), had "call[ed] the contending sides of a national controversy to end their national division by accepting a common mandate rooted in the Constitution," *Casey*, 505 U.S., at 867, and that the decision in *Casey* would ratify that happy truce. It seemed to me, quite to the contrary, that "*Roe* fanned into life an issue that has inflamed our national politics in general, and has obscured with its smoke the selection of Justices to this Court in particular, ever since"; and that, "by keeping us in the abortion-umpiring business, it is the perpetuation of that disruption, rather than of an *Pax Roeana*, that the Court's new majority decrees." *Id.*, at 995-996. Today's decision, that the Constitution of the United States prevents the prohibition of a horrible mode of abortion, will be greeted by a firestorm of criticism – as well it should. I cannot understand why those who *acknowledge* that, in the opening words of JUSTICE O'CONNOR's concurrence, "[t]he issue of abortion is one of the most contentious and controversial in contemporary American society," *ante*, at 947, persist in the belief that this Court, armed with neither constitutional text nor accepted tradition, can resolve that contention and controversy rather than be consumed by it. If only for the sake of its own preservation, the Court should return this matter to the people – where the Constitution, by its silence on the subject, left it – and let *them* decide, State by State, whether this practice should be allowed. *Casey* must be overruled.

JUSTICE KENNEDY, with whom THE CHIEF JUSTICE joins, dissenting.

For close to two decades after *Roe* v. *Wade*, 410 U.S. 113 (1973), the Court gave but slight weight to the interests of the separate States when their legislatures sought to address persisting concerns raised by the existence of a woman's right to elect an abortion in defined circumstances. When the Court reaffirmed the essential holding of *Roe*, a central premise was that the States retain a critical and legitimate role in legislating on the subject of abortion, as limited by the woman's right the Court restated and again guaranteed. *Planned Parenthood of Southeastern Pa.* v. *Casey*, 505 U.S. 833 (1992). The political processes of the state are not to be foreclosed from enacting laws to promote the life of the unborn and to ensure respect for all human life and its potential. The State's constitutional authority is a vital means for citizens to address these grave and serious issues, as they must if we are to progress in knowledge and understanding and in the attainment of some degree of consensus.

The Court's decision today, in my submission, repudiates this understanding by invalidating a statute advancing critical state interests, even though the law denies no woman the right to choose an abortion and places no undue burden upon the right. The legislation is well within the State's competence to enact. Having concluded Nebraska's law survives the scrutiny dictated by a proper understanding of *Casey*, I dissent from the judgment invalidating it.

I

The Court's failure to accord any weight to Nebraska's interest in prohibiting partial birth abortion is erroneous and undermines its discussion and holding. The Court's approach in this regard is revealed by its description of the abortion methods at issue, which the Court is correct to describe as "clinically cold or callous." *Ante*, at 923. The majority views the procedures from the perspective of the abortionist, rather than from the perspective of a society shocked when confronted with a new method of ending human life. Words invoked by the majority, such as "transcervical procedures," "[o]smotic dilators," "instrumental disarticulation," and "paracervical block," may be accurate and are to some extent necessary, *ante*, at 924-925; but for citizens who seeks to know why laws on this subject have been enacted across the Nation, the words are insufficient. Repeated references to sources understandable only to a trained physician may obscure matters for persons not trained in medical terminology. Thus it seems necessary at the outset to set forth what may happen during an abortion.

* * *

As described by Dr. Carhart, the D&E procedure requires the abortionist to use instruments to grasp a portion (such as a foot or hand) of a developed and living fetus and drag the grasped portion out of the uterus into the vagina. . . . Dr. Carhart uses the traction created by the opening between the uterus and vagina to dismember the fetus, tearing the grasped portion away from the remainder of the body. The traction between the uterus and vagina is essential to the procedure because attempting to abort a fetus without using that traction is described by Dr. Carhart as "pulling the cat's tail" or "drag[ging] a string across the floor, you'll just keep dragging it. It's not until something grabs the other end that you are going to develop traction." The fetus, in many cases, dies just as a human adult or child would: It bleeds to death as it is torn limb from limb. The fetus can be alive at the beginning of the dismemberment process and can survive for a time while its limbs are being torn off. Dr. Carhart agreed that "[w]hen you pull out a piece of the fetus, let's say, an arm or a leg and remove that, at the time just prior to removal of the portion of the fetus,...the fetus [is] alive." Dr. Carhart has observed fetal heartbeat via ultrasound with "extensive parts of the fetus removed," and testified that mere dismemberment of a limb does not always cause death because he knows of a physician who removed the arm of a fetus only to have the fetus go on to be born "as a living child with one arm." At the conclusion of a D&E abortion no intact fetus remains. In Dr. Carhart's words, the abortionist is left with "a tray full of pieces."

The other procedure implicated today is called "partial birth abortion" or the D&X. The D&X can be used, as a general matter, after 19 weeks' gestation because the fetus has become so developed that it may survive intact partial delivery from the uterus into the vagina. In the D&X, the abortionist initiates the woman's natural delivery process by causing the cervix of the woman to be dilated, sometimes over a sequence of days. The fetus' arms and legs are delivered outside the uterus while the fetus is alive; witnesses to the procedure report seeing the body of the fetus moving outside the woman's body. At this point, the abortion procedure has the appearance of a live birth. As stated by one group of physicians, "[a]s the physician manually performs breech extraction of the body of a live fetus, excepting the head, she continues in the apparent role of an obstetrician delivering a child." With only the head of the fetus remaining in utero, the abortionist tears open the skull.

According to Dr. Martin Haskell, a leading proponent of the procedure, the appropriate instrument to be used at this stage of the abortion is a pair of scissors.... Witnesses report observing the portion of the fetus outside the woman react to the skull penetration. The abortionist then inserts a suction tube and vacuums out the developing brain and other matter found within the skull. The process of making the size of the fetus' head smaller is given the clinically neutral term "reduction procedure." Brain death does not occur until after the skull invasion, and, according to Dr. Carhart, the heart of the fetus may continue to beat for minutes after the contents of the skull are vacuumed out. The abortionist next completes the delivery of a dead fetus, intact except for the damage to the head and the missing contents of the skull.

* * *

Casey held that cases decided in the wake of *Roe* v. *Wade*, 410 U.S. 113 (1973), had "given [state interests] too little acknowledgment and implementation."

* * *

Casey is premised on the States having an important constitutional role in defining their interests in the abortion debate. It is only with this principle in mind that Nebraska's interests can be given proper weight. The State's brief describes its interests as including concern for the life of the unborn and "for the partially-born," in preserving the integrity of the medical profession, and in "erecting a barrier to infanticide."

* * *

States may take sides in the abortion debate and come down on the side of life, even life in the unborn:

> "Even in the earliest stages of pregnancy, the State may enact rules and regulations designed to encourage [a woman] to know that there are philosophic and social arguments of great weight that can be brought to bear in favor of continuing the pregnancy to full term and that there are procedures and institutions to allow adoption of unwanted children as well as a certain degree of state assistance if the mother chooses to raise the child herself."

States also have an interest in forbidding medical procedures which, in the State's reasonable determination, might cause the medical profession or society as a whole to become insensitive, even disdainful, to life, including life in the human fetus. Abortion, *Casey* held, has consequences beyond the woman and her fetus. The States' interests in regulating are of concomitant extension. *Casey* recognized that abortion is "fraught with consequences for...the persons who perform and assist in the procedure [and for] society which must confront the knowledge that these procedures exist, procedures some deem nothing short of an act of violence against innocent human life."

A State may take measures to ensure the medical profession and its members are viewed as healers, sustained by a compassionate and rigorous ethic and cognizant of the dignity and value of human life, even life which cannot survive without the assistance of others.

Casey demonstrates that the interests asserted by the State are legitimate and recognized by law. It is argued, however, that a ban on the D&X does not further these interests. This is because, the reasoning continues, the D&E method, which Nebraska claims to be beyond its intent to regulate, can still be used to abort a fetus and is no less dehumanizing than the D&X method.... The issue is not whether members of the judiciary can see a difference between the two procedures. It is whether Nebraska can. The Court's refusal to recognize Nebraska's right to declare a moral difference between the procedures is a dispiriting disclosure of the illogic and illegitimacy of the Court's approach to the entire case.

* * *

Witnesses to the procedure relate that the fingers and feet of the fetus are moving prior to the piercing of the skull; when the scissors are inserted in the back of the head, the fetus' body, wholly outside the woman's body and alive, reacts as though startled and goes limp. D&X's stronger resemblance to infanticide means Nebraska could conclude the procedure presents a greater risk of disrespect for life and a consequent greater risk to the profession and society, which depend for their sustenance upon reciprocal recognition of dignity and respect. The Court is without authority to second-guess this conclusion.

* * *

II

Demonstrating a further and basic misunderstanding of *Casey*, the Court holds the ban on the D&X procedure fails because it does not include an exception permitting an abortionist to perform a D&X whenever he believes it will best preserve the health of the woman. Casting aside the views of distinguished physicians and the statements of leading medical organizations, the Court awards each physician a veto power over the State's judgment that the procedures should not be performed. Dr. Carhart has made the medical judgment to use the D&X procedure in every case, regardless of indications, after 15 weeks' gestation. Requiring Nebraska to defer to Dr. Carhart's judgment is no different from forbidding Nebraska from enacting a ban at all; for it is now Dr. Leroy Carhart who sets abortion policy for the State of Nebraska, not the legislature or the people....

I am in full agreement with JUSTICE THOMAS that the appropriate *Casey* inquiry is not, as the Court would have it, whether the State is preventing an abortionist from doing something that, in his medical judgment, he believes to be the most appropriate course of treatment. *Casey* addressed the question "whether the State can resolve...philosophic questions [about abortion] in such a definitive way that a woman lacks all choice in the matter." We decided the issue against the State, holding that a woman cannot be deprived of the opportunity to make reproductive decisions. *Casey* made it quite evident, however, that the State has substantial concerns for childbirth and the life of the unborn and may enact laws "which in no real sense depriv[e] women of the ultimate decision." Laws having the "purpose or effect of placing a substantial obstacle in the path of a woman seeking an abortion of a nonviable fetus" are prohibited. Nebraska's law does not have this purpose or effect.

* * *

Courts are ill-equipped to evaluate the relative worth of particular surgical procedures. The legislatures of the several States have superior factfinding capabilities in this regard. In an earlier case, JUSTICE O'CONNOR had explained that the general rule extends to abortion cases, writing that the Court is not suited to be "the Nation's *ex officio* medical board with powers to approve or disapprove medical and operative practices and standards throughout the United States."

* * *

IV

Ignoring substantial medical and ethical opinion, the Court substitutes its own judgment for the judgment of Nebraska and some 30 other States and sweeps the law away. The Court's holding stems from misunderstanding the record, misinterpretation of *Casey*, outright refusal to respect the law of a State, and statutory construction in conflict with settled rules. The decision nullifies a law expressing the will of the people of Nebraska that medical procedures must be governed by moral principles having their foundation in the intrinsic value of human life, including the life of the unborn. Through their law the people of Nebraska were forthright in confronting an issue of immense moral consequence. The State chose to forbid a procedure many decent and civilized people find so abhorrent as to be among the most serious of crimes against human life, while the State still protected the woman's autonomous right of choice as reaffirmed in *Casey*. The Court closes its eyes to these profound concerns.

From the decision, the reasoning, and the judgment, I dissent.

JUSTICE THOMAS, with whom THE CHIEF JUSTICE and JUSTICE SCALIA join, dissenting.

In 1973, this Court struck down an Act of the Texas Legislature that had been in effect since 1857, thereby rendering unconstitutional abortion statutes in dozens of States. *Roe* v. *Wade*, 410 U.S. 113, 119. As some of my colleagues on the Court, past and present, ably demonstrated, that decision was grievously wrong.... Abortion is a unique act, in which a woman's exercise of control over her own body ends, depending on one's view, human life or potential human life. Nothing in our Federal Constitution deprives the people of this country of the right to determine whether the consequences of abortion to the fetus and to society outweigh the burden of an unwanted pregnancy on the mother. Although a State *may* permit abortion, nothing in the Constitution dictates that a State *must* do so.

In the years following *Roe*, this Court applied, and, worse, extended, that decision to strike down numerous state statutes that purportedly threatened a woman's ability to obtain an abortion. The Court voided parental consent laws...legislation requiring that second-trimester abortions take place in hospitals...and even a requirement that both parents of a minor be notified before their child has an abortion[.] It was only a slight exaggeration when this Court described, in 1976, a right to abortion "without interference from the State." ...The Court's expansive application of *Roe* in this period, even more than *Roe* itself, was fairly described as the "unrestrained imposition of [the Court's] own, extraconstitutional value preferences" on the American people.

* * *

Today, the Court inexplicably holds that the States cannot constitutionally prohibit a method of abortion that millions find hard to distinguish from infanticide and that the Court hesitates even to describe.... In striking down this statute – which expresses a profound and legitimate respect for fetal life and which leaves unimpeded several other safe forms of abortion – the majority opinion gives the lie to the promise of *Casey* that regulations that do no more than "express profound respect for the life of the unborn are permitted, if they are not a substantial obstacle to the woman's exercise of the right to choose" whether or not to have an abortion." ...Today's decision is so obviously irreconcilable with *Casey*'s explication of what its undue-burden standard requires, let alone the Constitution, that it should be seen for what it is, a reinstitution of the pre-*Webster* abortion-on-demand era in which the mere invocation of "abortion rights" trumps any contrary societal interest. If this statute is unconstitutional under *Casey*, then *Casey* meant nothing at all, and the Court should candidly admit it.

* * *

We were reassured repeatedly in *Casey* that not all regulations of abortion are unwarranted and that the States may express profound respect for fetal life. Under *Casey*, the regulation before us today should easily pass constitutional muster. But the Court's abortion jurisprudence is a particularly virulent strain of constitutional exegesis. And so today we are told that 30 States are prohibited from banning one rarely used form of abortion that they believe to border on infanticide. It is clear that the Constitution does not compel this result.

I respectfully dissent.

*

The vote: five to four.

A more recent case on partial-birth abortion decided after *Stenberg* can be read in *Gonzales v. Carhart*, 550 U.S. 124 (2007), again five to four, upholding a federal ban. Cases along the precedential trail dealing with penumbral issues surrounding abortion are exemplified by *Webster v. Reproduction Health Services*, 492 U.S. 490 (1989), and *Planned Parenthood v. Casey*, 505 U.S. 833 (1992). There are several others. Staying away from the emotions of the issues, the history of this segment of American jurisprudence presents a remarkable journey of intellectual gymnastics, the substance of which is virtually unknown to everyone in the country.

XIII

BAREFOOT V. ESTELLE

arefoot v. Estelle, 463 U.S. 880 (1983), is a death penalty case. Ministers of justice tend to do some lumping on occasion as a reductionist strategy of uncomplicating things, and categorizing for purposes of convenience, simplification, and ease of "understanding." When the heavy thinking starts, details are broken out and the game is afoot. Such lumping, or clumping, is seen in the ubiquitous abortion cases, pornography cases, Second Amendment cases, jurisdictional cases, securities cases, an occasional tax case, and oh yes, death penalty cases, nearly all of which bring back into play over and over again, as may be convenient for the Court to reach a desired result, the constitutional pawns of "Due Process," "Equal Protection of the

Law," "Privileges and Immunities" and their little sisters, or better, cousins several times removed (by marriage, divorce, or party), such as "privacy," "penumbras," "our heritage," the "conscience of the people" and other emanations, which is enough to plug the *corpus callosum* of even the best of the slingers. If I were to recite for you the evidentiary facts in *Barefoot*, you would have some choice language. I would expect it. In fact, if you didn't I would be surprised. Instead, let the Court tell you.

Here is a suggestion: as you read the majority and dissenting opinions, observe all the wonderful substantive and procedural niceties of our constitutional jurisprudence, all the marvelous safeguards and requirements providing for and preserving justice (I am fighting with myself to not say the best justice money can buy, or *contra* if one doesn't have it, an issue with which the Court will also deal in *Caperton, infra*), noting how delicate matters of this kind are handled by our highest court sedulously fostering the rights of every individual, be he prince or pauper or an American Indian ("It is better that a thousand guilty men go free...."). Then stage left, as the drama of the case unfolds, out trots Grigson (I cannot bring myself to say Dr. Grigson), who, *inter alia*, works as a prison psychiatrist for the "Corrections Department" of the State of Texas, not exactly the land of milk and honey. But wait a minute, Grigson never trotted out, no one ever saw him! In fact, Grigson, known as "Dr. Death" (quoting the Court) in his world (apparently the original Dr. Death, at least in the "modern" era), never saw Barefoot, not even once, with the exception of sitting in the courtroom during the sentencing phase of his trial. Yet when he testified as to Barefoot's likelihood to commit violence in the future he said there was not just a chance that Barefoot would be violent, but on a scale of one to ten, the chance that Barefoot would strike again was above ten! Yes, that is what he said, and the Court accepted this testimony and ruled accordingly! This is not just an example of the best justice money can buy; this is an example of the State of Texas getting more than its money's worth! Barefoot didn't get the justice money could buy—he didn't have any money. Yes, the State of Texas did allocate $500.00 to Barefoot to retain expert witnesses (in the world of reality such expertise costs tens of thousands of dollars in a case such as this, a capital case). And you thought that couldn't happen? Down the tracks chugs the Toonerville Trolley, next stop, the death house.

You see, in *Estelle v. Smith* coming up and following *Barefoot* here, but decided two years before *Barefoot*, the Court held that a *Miranda* warning had to be given to a defendant about to be interrogated by a psychiatrist for the state where the psychiatric examination was being carried out to determine the prisoner's competency to stand trial, that anything he said could be and here (*Estelle*) was used later at the sentencing phase of his case following the defendant's capital conviction. Result in *Estelle*: case overturned. No Miranda warning: "You have the right to remain silent; anything you say can and will be used against you in a court of law; you have the right to the assistance of counsel; if you cannot afford counsel, the State will provide counsel for you..." in a nutshell.

Oh oh! So now what does Grigson do? Don't bother to see the patient/condemned, naturally. Of course! Problem solved. Fits right in with his *modus*: he says he has seen thirty to forty thousand individuals so far, and doing some simple math, let's see, even if he spent only one half a day with each to examine, evaluate, and write up his findings (keep in mind he is sometimes dealing with people whose lives hang in the balance where testing can require days and analysis months), that would take on the basis of a 250-day working year about 80 years to accomplish (40,000 divided by 2 per day = 20,000 now divided by 250 work days per year = 80) and this doesn't include any other matters to which Dr. Death may have had to attend, administratively or "professionally." Solution? See the condemned in less time..., or how about not at all? Yes. A whole new aura of American jurisprudence. Patient no see; Miranda no give.

This time Grigson trots out at trial, right past Barefoot, whom he had never seen before (Natch. See *Estelle, infra*), and says he is, *inter alia*, a "criminal sociopath"—a diagnosis or diagnostic classification not to be found in the American Psychiatric Association's Diagnostic and Statistical Manual of the day even way back in 1983. Sociopathic Personality Disorder may be found, but the more pejorative and frightening term of "criminal sociopath" can't—and that "there was no known cure for the condition," unless, of course, you live (or commit your crime) in Texas. Whatever the case, Grigson placed upon this soul the kiss of death…without ever having previously seen him. I would be inclined to call that the immaculate misconception. Think about the facts in the case and you decide.

Maybe it would be best if I made no further comment when you have finished the two next cases. I'll think about it. After all, this is now becoming more and more your task—you and the Court.

Read the two following cases: first, *Barefoot*: (To get the full impact of *Barefoot*, you likely will have to read it at least twice. I did.)

*

BAREFOOT *v.* ESTELLE, DIRECTOR, TEXAS DEPARTMENT OF
CORRECTIONS

463 U.S. 880

CERTIORARI TO THE UNITED STATES COURT OF APPEALS
FOR THE FIFTH CIRCUIT

JUSTICE WHITE delivered the opinion of the Court.

* * *

I

On November 14, 1978, petitioner was convicted of the capital murder of a police officer in Bell County, Tex. A separate sentencing hearing before the same jury was then held to determine whether the death penalty should be imposed.... [T]wo special questions were to be submitted to the jury: whether the conduct causing death was "committed deliberately and with reasonable expectation that the death of the deceased or another would result"; and whether "there is a probability that the defendant would commit criminal acts of violence that would constitute a continuing threat to society." ...The jury answered both of the questions put to them in the affirmative, a result which required the imposition of the death penalty.

On appeal to the Texas Court of Criminal Appeals, petitioner urged, among other submissions, that the use of psychiatrists at the punishment hearing to make predictions about petitioner's future conduct was unconstitutional because psychiatrists, individually and as a class, are not competent to predict future dangerousness. Hence, their predictions are so likely to produce erroneous sentences that their use violated the Eighth and Fourteenth Amendments. It was also urged, in any event, that permitting answers to hypothetical questions by psychiatrists who had not personally examined petitioner was constitutional error. The court rejected all of these contentions and affirmed the conviction and sentence.

* * *

III

* * *

A

The suggestion that no psychiatrist's testimony may be presented with respect to a defendant's future dangerousness is somewhat like asking us to disinvent the wheel. In the first place, it is contrary to our cases. If the likelihood of a defendant's committing further crimes is a constitutionally acceptable criterion for imposing the death penalty, which it is...and if it is not impossible for even a lay person sensibly to arrive at that conclusion, it makes little sense, if any, to submit that psychiatrists, out of the entire universe of persons who might have an opinion on the issue, would know so little about the subject that they should not be permitted to testify.

* * *

Acceptance of petitioner's position that expert testimony about future dangerousness is far too unreliable to be admissible would immediately call into question those other contexts in which predictions of future behavior are constantly made. For example, in *O'Connor* v. *Donaldson*, 422 U.S. 563, 576 (1975), we held that a nondangerous mental hospital patient could not be held in confinement against his will.

* * *

In the second place, the rules of evidence generally extant at the federal and state levels anticipate that relevant, unprivileged evidence should be admitted and its weight left to the factfinder, who would have the benefit of cross-examination and contrary evidence by the opposing party. Psychiatric testimony predicting dangerousness may be countered not only as erroneous in a particular case but also as generally so unreliable that it should be ignored. If they jury may make up its mind about future dangerousness unaided by psychiatric testimony, jurors should not be barred from hearing the views of the State's psychiatrists along with opposing views of the defendant's doctors.

Third, petitioner's view mirrors the position expressed in the *amicus* brief of the American Psychiatric Association (APA). As indicated above, however, the same view was presented and rejected in *Estelle* v. *Smith*. We are no more convinced now that the view of the APA should be converted into a constitutional rule barring an entire category of expert testimony. We are not persuaded that such testimony is almost entirely unreliable and that the factfinder and the adversary system will not be competent to uncover, recognize, and take due account of its shortcomings.

The *amicus* does not suggest that there are not other views held by members of the Association or of the profession generally. Indeed, as this case and others indicate, there are those doctors who are quite willing to testify at the sentencing hearing, who think, and will say, that they know what they are talking about, and who expressly disagree with the Association's point of view. Furthermore, their qualifications as experts are regularly accepted by the courts. If they are so obviously wrong and should be discredited, there should be no insuperable problem in doing so by calling members of the Association who are of that view and who confidently assert that opinion in their *amicus* brief. Neither petitioner nor the Association suggests that psychiatrists are always wrong with respect to future dangerousness, only most of the time. Yet the submission is that this category of testimony should be excised entirely from all trials. We are unconvinced, however, at least as of now, that the adversary process cannot be trusted to sort out the reliable from the unreliable evidence and opinion about future dangerousness, particularly when the convicted felon has the opportunity to present his own side of the case.

* * *

B

Whatever the decision may be about the use of psychiatric testimony, in general, on the issue of future dangerousness, petitioner urges that such testimony must be based on personal examination of the defendant and may not be given in response to hypothetical questions. We disagree. Expert testimony, whether in the form of an opinion based on hypothetical questions or otherwise, is commonly admitted as evidence where it might help the factfinder do its assigned job.

* * *

C

As we understand petitioner, he contends that even if the use of hypothetical questions in predicting future dangerousness is acceptable as a general rule, the use made of them in his case violated his right to due process of law. For example, petitioner insists that the doctors should not have been permitted to give an opinion on the ultimate issue before the jury, particularly when the hypothetical questions were phrased in terms of petitioner's own conduct; that the hypothetical questions referred to controverted facts; and that the answers to the questions were so positive as to be assertions of fact and not opinion. These claims of misuse of the hypothetical questions, as well as others, were rejected by the Texas courts, and neither the District Court nor the Court of Appeals found any constitutional infirmity in the application of the Texas Rules of Evidence in this particular case. We agree.

IV

In sum, we affirm the judgment of the District Court. There is no doubt that the psychiatric testimony increased the likelihood that petitioner would be sentenced to death, but this fact does not make that evidence inadmissible, any more than it would with respect to other relevant evidence against any defendant in a criminal case....

The judgment of the District Court is

Affirmed.

* * *

JUSTICE MARSHALL, with whom JUSTICE BRENNAN joins, dissenting.

I cannot subscribe to the Court's conclusion that the procedure followed by the Court of Appeals in this case was "not inconsistent with our cases." Nor can I accept the notion that it would be proper for a court of appeals to adopt special "summary procedures" for capital cases. On the merits, I would vacate petitioner's death sentence.

* * *

IV

Adhering to my view that the death penalty is under all circumstances cruel and unusual punishment prohibited by the Eighth and Fourteenth Amendments, see *Gregg* v. *Georgia*, 428 U.S. 153, 231 (1976) (Marshall, J., dissenting); *Furman* v. *Georgia*, 408 U.S. 238, 358-

369 (1972) (Marshall, J., concurring), I would vacate petitioner's death sentence.

JUSTICE BLACKMUN, with whom JUSTICE BRENNAN and JUSTICE MARSHALL join as to Parts I-IV, dissenting.

...The Court holds that psychiatric testimony about a defendant's future dangerousness is admissible, despite the fact that such testimony is wrong two times out of three. The Court reaches this result – even in a capital case – because, it is said, the testimony is subject to cross-examination and impeachment. In the present state of psychiatric knowledge, this is too much for me. One may accept this in a routine lawsuit for money damages, but when a person's life is at stake – no matter how heinous his offense – a requirement of greater reliability should prevail. In a capital case, the specious testimony of a psychiatrist, colored in the eyes of an impressionable jury by the inevitable untouchability of a medical specialist's words, equates with death itself.

I

To obtain a death sentence in Texas, the State is required to prove beyond a reasonable doubt that "there is a probability that he defendant would commit criminal acts of violence that would constitute a continuing threat to society." ...As a practical matter, this prediction of future dangerousness was the only issue to be decided by Barefoot's sentencing jury.

At the sentencing hearing, the State established that Barefoot had two prior convictions for drug offenses and two prior convictions for unlawful possession of firearms. None of these convictions involved acts of violence. At the guilt stage of the trial, for the limited purpose of establishing that the crime was committed in order to evade police custody...the State had presented evidence that Barefoot had escaped from jail in New Mexico where he was being held on charges of statutory rape and unlawful restraint of a minor child with intent to commit sexual penetration against the child's will. The prosecution also called several character witnesses at the sentencing hearing, from towns in five States. Without mentioning particular examples of Barefoot's conduct, these witnesses testified that Barefoot's reputation for being a peaceable and law-abiding citizen was bad in their respective communities.

Last, the prosecution called Doctors Holbrook and Grigson, whose testimony extended over more than half the hearing. Neither had examined Barefoot or requested the opportunity to examine him. In the presence of the jury, and over defense counsel's objection, each was qualified as an expert psychiatrist witness. Doctor Holbrook detailed at length his training and experience as a psychiatrist, which included a position as chief of psychiatric services at the Texas Department of Corrections. He explained that he had previously performed many "criminal evaluations," and that he subsequently took the post at the Department of Corrections to observe the subjects of these evaluations so that he could "be certain those opinions that [he] had were accurate at the time of trial and pretrial." He then informed the jury that it was "within [his] *capacity as a doctor of psychiatry* to predict the future dangerousness of an individual within a *reasonable medical certainty,"* and that he could give *"an expert medical opinion* that would be *within reasonable psychiatric certainty* as to whether or not that individual would be dangerous to the degree that there would be a probability that that person would commit criminal acts of violence in the future that would constitute a continuing threat to society," (emphasis supplied [by the Court]).

Doctor Grigson also detailed his training and medical experience, which, he said, included examination of "between thirty and forty thousand individuals," including 8,000 charged with felonies, and at least 300 charged with murder. He testified that with enough information he would be able to "give *a medical opinion within reasonable psychiatric certainty* as to the psychological or psychiatric makeup of an individual," (emphasis supplied [by the Court]) and that this skill was "particular to the field of psychiatry and not to the average layman."

Each psychiatrist then was given an extended hypothetical question asking him to assume as true about Barefoot the four prior convictions for nonviolent offenses, the bad reputation for being law-abiding in various communities, the New Mexico escape, the events surrounding the murder for which he was on trial and, in Doctor Grigson's case, the New Mexico arrest. On the basis of the hypothetical question, Doctor Holbrook diagnosed Barefoot "within a reasonable psychiatr[ic] certainty," as a "criminal sociopath." He testified that he knew of no treatment that could change this condition, and that the condition would not change for the better but "may become accelerated" in the next few years. Finally, Doctor Holbrook testified that, "within reasonable psychiatric certainty," there was "a probability that the Thomas A. Barefoot in that hypothetical will commit criminal acts of violence in the future that would constitute a continuing threat to society," and that his opinion would not change if the "society" at issue was that within Texas prisons rather than society outside prison.

Doctor Grigson then testified that, on the basis of the hypothetical question, he could diagnose Barefoot "within reasonable psychiatric certainty" as an individual with "a fairly classical, typical, sociopathic personality disorder." He placed Barefoot in the "most severe category" of sociopaths (on a scale of one to ten, Barefoot was "above ten"), and stated that there was no known cure for the condition. Finally, Doctor Grigson testified that whether Barefoot was in society at large or in a prison society there was a "*one hundred percent and absolute*" chance that Barefoot would commit future acts of criminal violence that would constitute a continuing threat to society (emphasis supplied [by the Court]).

On cross-examination, defense counsel questioned the psychiatrists about studies demonstrating that psychiatrists' predictions of future dangerousness are inherently unreliable. Doctor Holbrook indicated his familiarity with many of these studies but stated that he disagreed with their conclusions. Doctor Grigson stated that he was not familiar with most of these studies, and that their conclusions were accepted by only a "small minority group" of psychiatrists – "[i]t's not the American Psychiatric Association that believes that."

After an hour of deliberation, the jury answered "yes" to the two statutory questions, and Thomas Barefoot was sentenced to death.

II

A

The American Psychiatric Association (APA), participating in this case as *amicus curiae*, informs us that "[t]he unreliability of psychiatric predictions of long-term future dangerousness is by now an established fact within the profession." ...The APA's best estimate is that *two out of three* predictions of long-term future violence made by psychiatrists are wrong. The Court does not dispute this proposition, and indeed it could not do so; the evidence is overwhelming. For example, the APA's Draft Report of the Task Force on the Role of Psychiatry in the Sentencing Process (1983) (Draft Report) states that "[c]onsiderable evidence has been accumulated by now to demonstrate that long-term prediction by psychiatrists of future violence is an extremely inaccurate process." John Monahan, recognized as "the leading thinker on this issue" even by the State's expert witness at Barefoot's federal habeas corpus hearing, concludes that "the 'best' clinical research currently in existence indicates that psychiatrists and psychologists are accurate in no more than one out of three predictions of violent behavior," even among populations of individuals who are mentally ill and have committed violence in the past.... Another study has found it impossible to identify any subclass of offenders "whose members have a greater-than-even chance of engaging again in an assaultive act." ...Yet another commentator observes: "In general, mental health professionals...are more likely to be wrong than right when they predict legally relevant behavior. When predicting violence, dangerousness, and suicide, they are far more likely to be wrong than right." ...Neither the Court nor the State of Texas has cited a single reputable scientific source contradicting the unanimous conclusion of professionals in this field that psychiatric predictions of long-term future violence are wrong more often than they are right.

The APA also concludes, as do researchers that have studied the issue, that psychiatrists simply have no expertise in predicting long-term future dangerousness. A layman with access to relevant statistics can do at least as well and possibly better; psychiatric training is not relevant to the factors that validly can be employed to make such predictions, and psychiatrists consistently err on the side of overpredicting violence. Thus, while Doctors Grigson and Holbrook were presented by the State and by self-proclamation as experts at predicting future dangerousness, the scientific literature makes crystal clear that they had no expertise whatever. Despite their claims that they were able to predict Barefoot's future behavior "within reasonable psychiatric certainty," or to a "one hundred percent and absolute" certainty, there was in fact no more than a one in three chance that they were correct.

B

It is impossible to square admission of this purportedly scientific but actually baseless testimony with the Constitution's paramount concern for reliability in capital sentencing. Death is a permissible punishment in Texas only if the jury finds beyond a reasonable doubt that there is a probability the defendant will commit future acts of criminal violence. The admission of unreliable psychiatric predictions of future violence, offered with unabashed claims of "reasonable medical certainty" or "absolute" professional reliability, creates an intolerable danger that death sentences will be imposed erroneously.

The plurality in *Woodson* v. *North Carolina*, 428 U.S. 280, 305 (1976), stated:

> "Death, in its finality, differs more from life imprisonment than a 100-year prison term differs from one of only a year or two. Because of that qualitative difference, there is a corresponding difference in the need for reliability in the determination that death is the appropriate punishment in a specific case."

The Court does not see fit to mention this principle today, yet it is as firmly established as any in our Eighth Amendment jurisprudence. Only two weeks ago, in *Zant* v. *Stephens*, 462 U.S. 862, 884 (1983), the Court described the need for reliability in the application of the death penalty as one of the basic "themes...reiterated in our opinions discussing the procedures required by the Constitution in capital sentencing determinations." See *Eddings* v. *Oklahoma*, 455 U.S. 104, 110-112 (1982) (capital punishment must be "imposed fairly, and with reasonable consistency, or not at all")....

The danger of an unreliable death sentence created by this testimony cannot be brushed aside on the ground that the "'jury [must] have before it all possible relevant information about the individual defendant whose fate it must determine.'" ...Although committed to allowing a "wide scope of evidence" at presentence hearings...the Court has recognized that "consideration must be given to the quality, as well as the quantity, of the information on which the sentencing [authority] may rely."

* * *

Indeed, unreliable scientific evidence is widely acknowledged to be prejudicial. The reasons for this are manifest. "The major danger of scientific evidence is its potential to mislead the jury; an aura of scientific infallibility may shroud the evidence and thus lead the jury to accept it without critical scrutiny." ...Where the public holds an exaggerated opinion of the accuracy of scientific testimony, the prejudice is likely to be indelible.... There is little question that psychiatrists are perceived by the public as having a special expertise to predict dangerousness, a perception based on psychiatrists' study of mental disease.... It is this perception that the State in Barefoot's case sought to exploit. Yet mental disease is not correlated with violence...and the stark fact is that no such expertise exists. Moreover, psychiatrists, it is said, sometimes attempt to perpetuate this illusion of expertise...and Doctors Grigson and Holbrook – who purported to be able to predict future dangerousness "within reasonable psychiatric certainty," or absolutely – present extremely disturbing examples of this tendency. The problem is not uncommon.

* * *

Psychiatric predictions of future dangerousness *are not accurate*; wrong two times out of three, their probative value, and therefore any possible contribution they might make to the ascertainment of truth, is virtually nonexistent.... Indeed, given a psychiatrist's prediction that an individual will be dangerous, it is more likely than not that the defendant will *not* commit further violence. It is difficult to understand how the admission of such predictions can be justified as advancing the search for truth, particularly in light of their clearly prejudicial effect.

Thus, the Court's remarkable observation that "[n]either petitioner nor the [APA] suggests that psychiatrists are *always wrong* with respect to future dangerousness, *only most of the time*," misses the point completely, and its claim that this testimony was no more problematic than "other relevant evidence against any defendant in a criminal case," is simply incredible. Surely, this Court's commitment to ensuring that death sentences are imposed reliably and reasonably requires that nonprobative and highly prejudicial testimony on the ultimate question of life or death be excluded from a capital sentencing hearing.

III

A

Despite its recognition that the testimony at issue was probably wrong and certainly prejudicial, the Court holds this testimony admissible because the Court is "unconvinced...that the adversary process cannot be trusted to sort out the reliable from the unreliable evidence and opinion about future dangerousness." ...One can only wonder how juries are to separate valid from invalid expert opinions when the "experts" themselves are so obviously unable to do so. Indeed, the evidence suggests that juries are not effective at assessing the validity of scientific evidence....

There can be no question that psychiatric predictions of future violence will have an undue effect on the ultimate verdict. Even judges tend to accept psychiatrists' recommendations about a defendant's dangerousness with little regard for cross-examination or other testimony.... There is every reason to believe that inexperienced jurors will be still less capable of "separate[ing] the wheat from the chaff," despite the Court's blithe assumption to the contrary[.] The American Bar Association has warned repeatedly that sentencing juries are particularly incapable of dealing with information relating to "the likelihood that the defendant will commit other crimes," and similar predictive judgments.... But the Court in this case, in its haste to praise the jury's ability to find the truth, apparently forgets this well-known and worrisome shortcoming.

As if to suggest that petitioner's position that unreliable expert testimony should be excluded is unheard of in the law, the Court relies on the proposition that the rules of evidence generally "anticipate that relevant, unprivileged evidence should be admitted and its weight left to the factfinder, who would have the benefit of cross-examination and contrary evidence by the opposing party." But the Court simply ignores hornbook law that, despite the availability of cross-examination and rebuttal witnesses, "opinion evidence is not admissible if the court believes that the state of the pertinent art or scientific knowledge does not permit a reasonable opinion to be asserted." ...Because it is feared that the jury will overestimate its probative value, polygraph evidence, for example, almost invariably is excluded from trials despite the fact that, at a conservative estimate, an experienced polygraph examiner can detect truth or deception correctly about 80 to 90 percent of the time.... In no area is purportedly "expert" testimony admitted for the jury's consideration where it cannot be demonstrated that it is correct more often than not. "It is inconceivable that a judgment could be considered an 'expert' judgment when it is less accurate than the flip of a coin." The risk that a jury will be incapable of separating "scientific" myth from reality is deemed unacceptably high.

B

The Constitution's mandate of reliability, with the stakes at life or death, precludes reliance on cross-examination and the opportunity to present rebuttal witnesses as an antidote for this distortion of the truth-finding process. Cross-examination is unlikely to reveal the fatuousness of psychiatric predictions because such predictions often rest, as was the case here, on psychiatric categories and intuitive clinical judgments not susceptible to cross-examination and rebuttal.... The APA particularly condemns the use of the diagnosis employed by Doctors Grigson and Holbrook in this case, that of sociopathy:

"In this area confusion reigns. The psychiatrist who is not careful can mislead the judge or jury into believing that a person has a major mental disease simply on the basis of a description of prior criminal behavior. Or a psychiatrist can mislead the court into believing that an individual is devoid of conscience on the basis of a description of criminal acts alone.... The profession of psychiatry has a responsibility to avoid inflicting this confusion upon the courts and to spare the defendant the harm that may result.... Given our uncertainty about the implications of the finding, the diagnosis of sociopathy...should not be used to justify or to support predictions of future conduct. There is no certainty in this area."

It is extremely unlikely that the adversary process will cut through the façade of superior knowledge.

* * *

Nor is the presentation of psychiatric witnesses on behalf of the defense likely to remove the prejudicial taint of misleading testimony by prosecution psychiatrists. No reputable expert would be able to predict with confidence that the defendant will *not* be violent; at best, the witness will be able to give his opinion that all predictions of dangerousness are unreliable. Consequently, the jury will not be presented with the traditional battle of experts with opposing views on the ultimate question. Given a choice between an expert who says that he can predict with certainty that the defendant, whether confined in prison or free in society, will kill again, and an expert who says merely that no such prediction can be made, members of the jury charged by law with making the prediction surely will be tempted to opt for the expert who claims he can help them in performing their duty, and who predicts dire consequences if the defendant is not put to death.

* * *

One searches the Court's opinion in vain for a plausible justification for tolerating the State's creation of this risk of an erroneous death verdict. As one Court of Appeals has observed:

> "A courtroom is not a research laboratory. The fate of a defendant...should not hang on his ability to successfully rebut scientific evidence which bears an 'aura of special reliability and trustworthiness,' although, in reality the witness is testifying on the basis of an unproved hypothesis...which has yet to gain general acceptance in its field." *United States* v. *Brown*, 557 F. 2d 541, 556 (CA6 1977).

Ultimately, when the Court knows full well that psychiatrists' predictions of dangerousness are specious, there can be no excuse for imposing on the defendant, on pain of his life, the heavy burden of convincing a jury of laymen of the fraud.

IV

The Court is simply wrong in claiming that psychiatric testimony respecting future dangerousness is necessarily admissible in light of *Jurek* v. *Texas*, 428 U.S. 262 (1976), or *Estelle* v. *Smith*, 451 U.S. 454 (1981)....

In *Smith*, the psychiatric testimony at issue was given by the same Doctor Grigson who confronts us in this case, and his conclusions were disturbingly similar to those he rendered here. The APA, appearing as *amicus curiae*, argued that all psychiatric predictions of future dangerousness should be excluded from capital sentencing proceedings. The Court did not reach this issue, because it found Smith's death sentence invalid on narrower grounds: Doctor Grigson's testimony had violated Smith's Fifth and Sixth Amendment rights. Contrary to the Court's inexplicable assertion in this case, *Smith* certainly did not reject the APA's position. Rather, the Court made clear that "the holding in *Jurek* was guided by recognition that the inquiry [into dangerousness] mandated by Texas law does *not* require resort to medical experts." If

Jurek and *Smith* held that psychiatric predictions of future dangerousness are admissible in a capital sentencing proceeding as the Court claims, this guiding recognition would have been irrelevant.

* * *

Our constitutional duty is to ensure that the State proves future dangerousness, if at all, in a reliable manner, one that ensures that "any decision to impose the death sentence be, and appear to be, based on reason rather than caprice or emotion." *Gardner* v. *Florida*, 430 U.S., at 358. Texas' choice of substantive factors does not justify loading the factfinding process against the defendant through the presentation of what is, at bottom, false testimony.

V

I would vacate petitioner's death sentence, and remand for further proceedings consistent with these views.

*

Nice, eh? Grigson never saw the patient, I mean condemned. How convenient! Now no need for a Miranda warning which might cause the condemned to clam up, as it were. Little did Grigson ever know the Court, yes SCOTUS, wouldn't even care if he was right (or wrong), or in the Court's own words, just "some of the time." Nice work if you can get it, and you can get it if you try, in this instance, forty thousand times. Almost seems irreverent, doesn't it? However, much truth is spoken in jest, such jest having its own penumbra encompassing far more than the immediate point being made, the immediate case at hand, if you get my drift. One laughs to tears.

Estelle v. Smith, 451 U.S. 454 (1981), may explain, as suggested, why Grigson never met with Barefoot. In *Estelle*, Ernest Smith was charged in a capital murder with malice aforethought case attendant to his participation in an armed robbery of a grocery store in which his accomplice shot a clerk. Grigson was called in by the State of Texas to evaluate Smith's competency to stand trial (essentially a matter of whether Smith understood the charges against him and whether or not he was able to assist his attorney with his defense). Although you probably have this one figured out already, following a 90-minute interview, Grigson did find the defendant competent to stand trial, and tried he was, convicted, and sentenced to death, naturally. During these proceedings, Grigson not only assisted the prosecution in getting the judge to set down the matter for trial, but later in the proceedings assisted the jury in its decision to impose the death sentence. With information gleaned during the 90-minute pretrial competency examination of Smith, Grigson testified at the sentencing hearing, *inter alia*, that the defendant was "a very severe sociopath" who "will only get worse" and for which "there is no treatment, no medicine." Sound familiar? It gets better.

A nice, neat, tidy case of a caught bad guy who is only going to get worse over time, and being disposed of by society according to law. However, there are a couple of little problems. It seems that Grigson's pretrial examination of Smith, who we will refer to as Ernie, was to determine competency, not future dangerousness. At the initiation of that examination, Grigson failed to warn Ernie, who was in the custody of the authorities, that what he said could be used against him in a court of law, that he could remain silent, and that he was entitled to counsel, part of what is now known as the *Miranda* warning aforesaid based on some legislation written by the Supreme Court in *Miranda v. Arizona*, 384 U.S. 436 (1966), a case which would be advantageous for you to read at your first opportunity (Ernesto Miranda's conviction was overturned and he was retried and convicted this time upon the testimony of his estranged wife who he had recently sued for custody of their child, and following his ultimate release from imprisonment was knifed in a Phoenix bar and succumbed to his injuries). Grigson thereafter proceeded to testify at the sentencing stage—and you guessed it: this guy was not only bad news, but the embodiment of worse news coming. Sound familiar? Do you think he ever testified in other cases to the contrary? Maybe a few? Even once?

Now that you have a little idea as to where this case is going, keep in mind that Grigson never met with Barefoot in the preceding case, *supra*. Here, Ernie dodged a bullet, so to speak, as he was resentenced to life on a lesser included offense.

And now, *Estelle*.

XIV

ESTELLE, CORRECTIONS DIRECTOR *v.* SMITH

451 U.S. 454

CERTIORARI TO THE UNITED STATES COURT OF APPEALS

FOR THE FIFTH CIRCUIT

CHIEF JUSTICE BURGER delivered the opinion of the Court.

We granted certiorari to consider whether the prosecution's use of psychiatric testimony at the sentencing phase of respondent's capital murder trial to establish his future dangerousness violated his constitutional rights.

I

A

On December 28, 1973, respondent Ernest Benjamin Smith was indicted for murder arising from his participation in the armed robbery of a grocery store during which a clerk was fatally shot, not by Smith, but by his accomplice.... Texas announced its intention to seek the death penalty. Thereafter, a judge of the 195th Judicial District Court of Dallas County, Texas, informally ordered the State's attorney to arrange a psychiatric examination of Smith by Dr. James P. Grigson to determine Smith's competency to stand trial.

Dr. Grigson, who interviewed Smith in jail for approximately 90 minutes, concluded that he was competent to stand trial....

In Texas, capital cases require bifurcated proceedings – a guilt phase and a penalty phase. If the defendant is found guilty, a separate proceeding before the same jury is held to fix the punishment. At the penalty phase, if the jury affirmatively answers three questions on which the State has the burden of proof beyond a reasonable doubt, the judge must impose the death sentence.... One of the three critical issues to be resolved by the jury is "whether there is a probability that the defendant would commit criminal acts of violence that would constitute a continuing threat to society." In other words, the jury must assess the defendant's future dangerousness.

At the commencement of Smith's sentencing hearing, the State rested "[s]ubject to the right to reopen." Defense counsel called three lay witnesses: Smith's stepmother, his aunt, and the man who owned the gun Smith carried during the robbery. Smith's relatives testified as to his good reputation and character. The owner of the pistol testified as to Smith's knowledge that it would not fire because of a mechanical defect. The State then called Dr. Grigson as a witness.

Defense counsel were aware from the trial court's file of the case that Dr. Grigson had submitted a psychiatric report in the form of a letter advising the court that Smith was competent to stand trial. This report termed Smith "a severe sociopath," but it contained no more specific reference to his future dangerousness. Before trial, defense counsel had obtained an order requiring the State to disclose the witnesses it planned to use both at the guilt stage and, if known, at the penalty stage. Subsequently, the trial court had granted a defense motion to bar the testimony during the State's case in chief of any witness whose name did not appear on that list. Dr. Grigson's name was not on the witness list, and defense counsel objected when he was called to the stand at the penalty phase.

In a hearing outside the presence of the jury, Dr. Grigson stated: (a) that he had not obtained permission from Smith's attorneys to examine him; (b) that he had discussed his conclusions and diagnosis with the State's attorney; and (c) that the prosecutor had requested him to testify and had told him, approximately five days before the sentencing hearing began, that his testimony probably would be needed within the week. The trial judge denied a defense motion to exclude Dr. Grigson's testimony on the ground that his name was not on the State's list of witnesses....

After detailing his professional qualifications by way of foundation, Dr. Grigson testified before the jury on direct examination: (a) that Smith "is a very severe sociopath"; (b) that "he will continue his previous behavior"; (c) that his sociopathic condition will "only get worse"; (d) that he has no regard for another human being's property or for their life, regardless of who it may be"; (e) that "[t]here is no treatment, no medicine...that in any way at all modifies or changes this behavior"; (f) that he "is going to go ahead and commit other similar or same criminal acts if given the opportunity to do so"; and (g) that he "has no remorse or sorrow for what he has done." Dr. Grigson, whose testimony was based on information derived from his 90-minute "mental status examination" of Smith (i.e., the examination ordered to determine Smith's competency to stand trial), was the State's only witness at the sentencing hearing.

The jury answered the three requisite questions in the affirmative, and, thus, under Texas law the death penalty for Smith was mandatory....

B

After unsuccessfully seeking a writ of habeas corpus in the Texas state courts, Smith petitioned for such relief in the United States

District Court for the Northern District of Texas.... The District Court vacated Smith's death sentence because it found constitutional error in the admission of Dr. Grigson's testimony at the penalty phase. The court based its holding on the failure to advise Smith of his right to remain silent at the pretrial psychiatric examination and the failure to notify defense counsel in advance of the penalty phase that Dr. Grigson would testify. The court concluded that the death penalty had been imposed on Smith in violation of his Fifth and Fourteenth Amendment rights to due process and freedom from compelled self-incrimination, his Sixth Amendment right to the effective assistance of counsel, and his Eighth Amendment right to present complete evidence of mitigating circumstances.

* * *

II

A

Of the several constitutional issues addressed by the District Court and the Court of Appeals, we turn first to whether the admission of Dr. Grigson's testimony at the penalty phase violated respondent's Fifth Amendment privilege against compelled self-incrimination because respondent was not advised before the pretrial psychiatric examination that he had a right to remain silent and that any statement he made could be used against him at a sentencing proceeding. Our initial inquiry must be whether the Fifth Amendment privilege is applicable in the circumstances of this case.

(1)

The State argues that respondent was not entitled to the protection of the Fifth Amendment because Dr. Grigson's testimony was used only to determine punishment after conviction, not to establish guilt. In the State's view, "incrimination is complete once guilt has been adjudicated," and, therefore, the Fifth Amendment privilege has no relevance to the penalty phase of a capital murder trial....

The Fifth Amendment, made applicable to the states through the Fourteenth Amendment, commands that "[n]o person...shall be compelled in any criminal case to be a witness against himself." The essence of this basic constitutional principle is "the requirement that the State which proposes to convict *and punish* an individual produce the evidence against him by the independent labor of its officers, not by the simple, cruel expedient of forcing it from his own lips."

* * *

The Court has held that "the availability of the [Fifth Amendment] privilege does not turn upon the type of proceeding in which its protection is invoked, but upon the nature of the statement or admission and the exposure which it invites." In this case, the ultimate penalty of death was a potential consequence of what respondent told the examining psychiatrist. Just as the Fifth Amendment prevents a criminal defendant from being made "'the deluded instrument of his own conviction,'"...it protects him as well from being made the "deluded instrument" of his own execution.

We can discern no basis to distinguish between the guilt and penalty phases of respondent's capital murder trial so far as the protection of the Fifth Amendment privilege is concerned. Given the gravity of the decision to be made at the penalty phase, the State is not relieved of the obligation to observe fundamental constitutional guarantees.... Any effort by the State to compel respondent to testify against his will at the sentencing hearing clearly would contravene the Fifth Amendment. Yet the State's attempt to establish respondent's future dangerousness by relying on the unwarned statements he made to Dr. Grigson similarly infringes Fifth Amendment values.

(2)

* * *

Dr. Grigson's diagnosis, as detailed in his testimony, was not based simply on his observation of respondent. Rather, Dr. Grigson drew his conclusions largely from respondent's account of the crime during their interview, and he placed particular emphasis on what he considered to be respondent's lack of remorse. Dr. Grigson's prognosis as to future dangerousness rested on statements respondent made, and remarks he omitted, in reciting the details of the crime. The Fifth Amendment privilege, therefore, is directly involved here because the State used as evidence against respondent the substance of his disclosures during the pretrial psychiatric examination.

The fact that respondent's statements were uttered in the context of a psychiatric examination does not automatically remove them from the reach of the Fifth Amendment. The state trial judge, *sua sponte*, ordered a psychiatric evaluation of respondent for the limited, neutral purpose of determining his competency to stand trial, but the results of that inquiry were used by the State for a much broader objective that was plainly adverse to respondent. Consequently, the interview with Dr. Grigson cannot be characterized as a routine competency examination restricted to ensuring that respondent understood the charges against him and was capable of assisting in his defense. Indeed, if the application of Dr. Grigson's findings had been confined to serving that function, no Fifth Amendment issue would have arisen.

* * *

To meet its burden, the State used respondent's own statements, unwittingly made without an awareness that he was assisting the State's efforts to obtain the death penalty. In these distinct circumstances, the Court of Appeals correctly concluded that the Fifth Amendment privilege was implicated.

(3)

In *Miranda* v. *Arizona*, 384 U.S. 436, 467 (1966), the Court acknowledged that "the Fifth Amendment privilege is available outside of criminal court proceedings and serves to protect persons in all settings in which their freedom of action is curtailed in any significant way from being compelled to incriminate themselves." *Miranda* held that "the prosecution may not use statements, whether exculpatory or inculpatory, stemming from custodial interrogation of the defendant unless it demonstrates the use of procedural safeguards effective to secure the privilege against self-incrimination." Thus, absent other fully effective procedures, a person in custody must receive certain warnings before any official interrogation, including that he has a "right to remain silent" and that "anything said can and will be used against the individual in court."

* * *

The considerations calling for the accused to be warned prior to custodial interrogation apply with no less force to the pretrial psychiatric examination at issue here.

* * *

These safeguards of the Fifth Amendment privilege were not afforded respondent and, thus, his death sentence cannot stand.

* * *

III

Respondent's Fifth and Sixth Amendment rights were abridged by the State's introduction of Dr. Grigson's testimony at the penalty phase, and, as the Court of Appeals concluded, his death sentence must be vacated. Because respondent's underlying conviction has not been challenged and remains undisturbed, the State is free to conduct further proceedings not inconsistent with this opinion. Accordingly, the judgment of the Court of Appeals is

Affirmed.

JUSTICE BRENNAN.

I join the Court's opinion. I also adhere to my position that the death penalty is in all circumstances unconstitutional.

JUSTICE MARSHALL, concurring in part.

I adhere to my consistent view that the death penalty is under all circumstances cruel and unusual punishment forbidden by the Eighth and Fourteenth Amendments....

JUSTICE STEWART, with whom JUSTICE POWELL joins, concurring in the judgment.

The respondent had been indicted for murder and a lawyer had been appointed to represent him before he was examined by Dr. Grigson at the behest of the State. Yet that examination took place without previous notice to the respondent's counsel. The Sixth and Fourteenth Amendments...made impermissible the introduction of Dr. Grigson's testimony against the respondent at any stage of his trial.

I would for this reason affirm the judgment before us without reaching the other issues discussed by the Court.

JUSTICE REHNQUIST, concurring in the judgment.

I concur in the judgment because...respondent's counsel should have been notified prior to Dr. Grigson's examination of respondent....

Since this is enough to decide the case, I would not go on to consider the Fifth Amendment issues and cannot subscribe to the Court's resolution of them. I am not convinced that any Fifth Amendment rights were implicated by Dr. Grigson's examination of respondent. Although the psychiatrist examined respondent prior to trial, he only testified concerning the examination after respondent stood convicted....

Even if there are Fifth Amendment rights involved in this case, respondent never invoked these rights when confronted with Dr. Grigson's questions. The Fifth Amendment privilege against compulsory self-incrimination is not self-executing.... The *Miranda* requirements were certainly not designed by this Court with psychiatric examinations in mind. Respondent was simply not in the inherently coercive situation considered in *Miranda*. He had already been indicted, and counsel had been appointed to represent him. No claim is raised that respondent's answers to Dr. Grigson's questions were "involuntary" in the normal sense of the word. Unlike the police officers in *Miranda*, Dr. Grigson was not questioning respondent in order to ascertain his guilt or innocence. Particularly since it is not necessary to decide this case, I would not extend the *Miranda* requirements to cover psychiatric examinations such as the one involved here.

*

So, in *Barefoot*, no meeting, presto, no Miranda warning given! Grigson may now testify his heart out about the mental status of the patient (or examinee) who is now about to be condemned to death by the State based, practically speaking, exclusively on his testimony without ever having ever seen him. The Miranda warning unanimously required by *Estelle* is simply bypassed, and *Barefoot's* conviction stands, on a split decision. Again, one laughs to tears. I can't wait for you to read the *Caperton* cases, *infra*, to give you a sense of just how much justice money can buy.

But first, let us turn to truth-in-media: *New York Times Co. v. Sullivan.*

XV

NEW YORK TIMES CO. V. SULLIVAN

oliticians and their political ads are often known to launch attacks on one another to discredit their respective opposition while at the same time currying favor from their own side of the fence without much regard as to the truth of the matter they put forth. Many find it utterly disgusting, repulsive. Much of the "media" is not reticent about jumping on the bandwagon and broadcasting the same material for their candidate of choice in looping presentations to the public during all times of the day, notwithstanding what any journalistic school of thought would consider to be its duty to its audience, the voter, and the best interests of the nation under fought-and-died-for concepts of freedom of the press, presumably a responsible press.

In *New York Times Co. v. Sullivan*, 376 U.S. 254 (1964), the Court held that no liability could be imposed on what would otherwise be libelous speech eligible to be redressed in a civil action (keeping in mind that certain speech may even be criminal in nature, such as conspiracy to commit a crime or to incite a riot) where the target of that speech was essentially a "public figure," regardless of its falsity. Falsity alone is simply not enough. A public figure need not even be an elected official or one running for office. For a declarant to be held liable for money damages, the plaintiff would have to show the statement was not only false, but was made with the knowledge that it in fact was false (or made in reckless disregard of the truth of the matter) and with actual malice aforethought to harm. In other words, this is the stuff you get filled up to here with during the election cycles. If you have wondered why, the answer is about to follow.

In the concurring opinions, it is suggested there are no restraints whatsoever, one of the proponents being Douglas, who dissented in *Roth* contending there are no constitutional limits relative to obscene materials, which visited upon the American people the obscenity doctrine with which you are now familiar, academically, legally, and in real life, saying there were no limits in either case. That is to say, no restraints, no realistic limitations whatsoever, effectively what *Roth* did, should be the standard here. Right or wrong, or whether you like it or not (which may be different matters), that is the result of the opinion, although Douglas would likely have carried it further.

However, *New York Times* does reflect something different, again without any references or implications as to "correctness," in that the opinion seems to demonstrate an attempt to craft something which at least holds a candle up to moderation, or a reach for some kind of restraint as circumstantially grounded with its *malum in se* limits.

New York Times, in a relatively rare unanimous opinion, is offered without further comment; the laws of wise restraint be damned.

*

NEW YORK TIMES CO. *v.* SULLIVAN

376 U.S. 254

CERTIORARI TO THE SUPREME COURT OF ALABAMA

MR. JUSTICE BRENNAN delivered the opinion of the Court.

We are required in this case to determine for the first time the extent to which the constitutional protections for speech and press limit a State's power to award damages in a libel action brought by a public official against critics of his official conduct.

Respondent L. B. Sullivan is one of the three elected Commissioners of the City of Montgomery, Alabama. He testified that he was "Commissioner of Public Affairs and the duties are supervision of the Police Department, Fire Department, Department of Cemetery and Department of Scales." He brought this civil libel action against the four individual petitioners, who are Negroes and Alabama clergymen, and against petitioner the New York Times Company, a New York corporation which publishes the New York Times, a daily newspaper. A jury in the Circuit Court of Montgomery County awarded him damages of $500,000, the full amount claimed, against all the petitioners, and the Supreme Court of Alabama affirmed.

Respondent's complaint alleged that he had been libeled by statements in a full-page advertisement that was carried in the New York Times on March 29, 1960. Entitled "Heed Their Rising Voices," the advertisement began by stating that "As the whole world knows by now, thousands of Southern Negro students are engaged in widespread non-violent demonstrations in positive affirmation of the right to live in human dignity as guaranteed by the U.S. Constitution and the Bill of Rights." It went on to charge that "in their efforts to uphold these guarantees, they are being met by an unprecedented wave of terror by those who would deny and negate that document which the whole world looks upon as setting the pattern for modern freedom...." Succeeding paragraphs purported to illustrate the "wave of terror" by describing certain alleged events.

* * *

Of the 10 paragraphs of text in the advertisement, the third and a portion of the sixth were the basis of respondent's claim of libel. They read as follows:

Third paragraph:

"In Montgomery, Alabama, after students sang 'My Country, 'Tis of Thee' on the state Capitol steps, their leaders were expelled from school, and truckloads of police armed with shotguns and tear-gas ringed the Alabama State College Campus. When the entire student body protested to state authorities by refusing to re-register, their dining hall was padlocked in an attempt to starve them into submission."

Sixth paragraph:

"Again and again the Southern violators have answered Dr. King's peaceful protests with intimidation and violence. They have bombed his home almost killing his wife and child. They have assaulted his person. They have arrested him seven times – for 'speeding,' 'loitering' and similar 'offenses.' And now they have charged him with 'perjury' – a *felony* under which they could imprison him for *ten years*...."

Although neither of these statements mentions respondent by name, he contended that the word "police" in the third paragraph referred to him as the Montgomery Commissioner who supervised the Police Department, so that he was being accused of "ringing" the campus with police. He further claimed that the paragraph would be read as imputing to the police, and hence to him, the padlocking of the dining hall in order to starve the students into submission. As to the sixth paragraph, he contended that since arrests are ordinarily made by the police, the statement "They have arrested [Dr. King] seven times" would be read as referring to him; he further contended that the "They" who did the arresting would be equated with the "They" who committed the other described acts and with the "Southern violators." Thus, he argued, the paragraph would be read as accusing the Montgomery police, and hence him, of answering Dr. King's protests with "intimidation and violence," bombing his home, assaulting his person, and charging him with perjury. Respondent and six other Montgomery residents testified that they read some or all of the statements as referring to him in his capacity as Commissioner.

It is uncontroverted that some of the statements contained in the two paragraphs were not accurate descriptions of events which occurred in Montgomery. Although Negro students staged a demonstration on the State Capitol steps, they sang the National Anthem and not "My Country, 'Tis of Thee." Although nine students were expelled by the State Board of Education, this was not for leading the demonstration at the Capitol, but for demanding service at a lunch counter in the Montgomery County Courthouse on another day. Not the entire student body, but most of it, had protested the expulsion, not by refusing to register, but by boycotting classes on a single day; virtually all the students did register for the ensuing semester. The campus dining hall was not padlocked on any occasion, and the only students who may have been barred from eating there were the few who had neither signed a preregistration application nor requested temporary meal tickets. Although the police were deployed near the campus in large numbers on three occasions, they did not at any time "ring" the campus, and they were not called to the campus in connection with the demonstration on the State Capitol steps, as the third paragraph implied. Dr. King had not been arrested seven times, but only four; and although he claimed to have been assaulted some years earlier in connection with his arrest for loitering outside a courtroom, one of the officers who made the arrest denied that there was such an assault.

On the premise that the charges in the sixth paragraph could be read as referring to him, respondent was allowed to prove that he had not participated in the events described. Although Dr. King's home had in fact been bombed twice when his wife and child were there, both of these occasions antedated respondent's tenure as Commissioner, and the police were not only not implicated in the bombings, but had made every effort to apprehend those who were. Three of Dr. King's four arrests took place before respondent became Commissioner. Although Dr. King had in fact been indicted (he was subsequently acquitted) on two counts of perjury, each of which carried a possible five-year sentence, respondent had nothing to do with procuring the indictment.

* * *

The manager of the Advertising Acceptability Department testified that he had approved the advertisement for publication because he knew nothing to cause him to believe that anything in it was false, and because it bore the endorsement of "a number of people who are well known and whose reputation" he "had no reason to question." Neither he nor anyone else at the Times made an effort to confirm the accuracy of the advertisement, either by checking it against recent Times news stories relating to some of the described events or by any other means.

Alabama law denies a public officer recovery of punitive damages in a libel action brought on account of a publication concerning his official conduct unless he first makes a written demand for a public retraction and the defendant fails or refuses to comply. Respondent served such a demand upon each of the petitioners. None of the individual petitioners responded to the demand, primarily because each took the position that he had not authorized the use of his name on the advertisement and therefore had not published the statements that respondent alleged had libeled him. The Times did not publish a retraction in response to the demand, but wrote respondent a letter stating, among other things, that "we . . . are somewhat puzzled as to how you think the statements in any way reflect on you," and "you might, if you desire, let us know in what respect you claim that the statements in the advertisement reflect on you." Respondent filed this suit a few days later without answering the letter. The Times did, however, subsequently publish a retraction of the advertisement upon the demand of Governor John Patterson of Alabama, who asserted that the publication charged him with "grave misconduct and...improper actions and omissions as Governor of Alabama and Ex-Officio Chairman of the State Board of Education of Alabama."

* * *

The trial judge submitted the case to the jury under instructions that the statements in the advertisement were "libelous per se" and were not privileged, so that petitioners might be held liable if the jury found that they had published the advertisement and that the statements were made "of and concerning" respondent. The jury was instructed that, because the statements were libelous *per se*, "the law...implies legal injury from the bare fact of publication itself," "falsity and malice are presumed," "general damages need not be alleged or proved but are presumed," and "punitive damages may be awarded by the jury even though the amount of actual damages is neither found nor shown." An award of punitive damages – as distinguished from "general" damages, which are compensatory in nature – apparently requires proof of actual malice under Alabama law, and the judge charged that "mere negligence or carelessness is not evidence of actual malice or malice in fact, and does not justify an award of exemplary or punitive damages." He refused to charge, however, that the jury must be "convinced" of malice, in the sense of "actual intent" to harm or "gross negligence and recklessness," to make such an award, and he also refused to require that a verdict for respondent differentiate between compensatory and punitive damages. The judge rejected petitioners' contention that his rulings abridged the freedoms of speech and of the press that are guaranteed by the First and Fourteenth Amendments.

In affirming the judgment, the Supreme Court of Alabama sustained the trial judge's rulings and instructions in all respects. It held that "where the words published tend to injure a person libeled by them in his reputation, profession, trade or business, or charge him with an indictable offense, or tend to bring the individual into public contempt," they are "libelous per se"; that "the matter complained of is, under the above doctrine, libelous per se, if it was published of and concerning the plaintiff"; and that it was actionable without "proof of pecuniary injury...such injury being implied." It approved the trial court's ruling that the jury could find the statements to have been made "of and concerning" respondent, stating: "We think it common knowledge that the average person knows that municipal agents, such as police and firemen, and others, are under the control and direction of the city governing body, and more particularly under the direction and control of a single commissioner. In measuring the performance or deficiencies of such groups, praise or criticism is usually attached to the official in complete control of the body." In sustaining the trial court's determination that the verdict was not excessive, the court said that malice could be inferred from the Times' "irresponsibility" in printing the advertisement while "the Times in its own files had articles already published which would have demonstrated the falsity of the allegations in the advertisement"; from the Times' failure to retract for respondent while retracting for the Governor, whereas the falsity of some of the allegations was then known to the Times and "the matter contained in the advertisement was equally false as to both parties"; and from the testimony of the Times' Secretary that, apart from the statement that the dining hall was padlocked, he thought the two paragraphs were "substantially correct." The court reaffirmed a statement in an earlier opinion that "There is no legal measure of damages in cases of this character." It rejected petitioners' constitutional contentions with the brief statements that "The First Amendment of the U.S. Constitution does not protect libelous publications" and "The Fourteenth Amendment is directed against State action and not private action."

Because of the importance of the constitutional issues involved, we granted the separate petitions for certiorari of the individual petitioners and of the Times. We reverse the judgment. We hold that the rule of law applied by the Alabama courts is constitutionally deficient for failure to provide the safeguards for freedom of speech and of the press that are required by the First and Fourteenth Amendments in a libel action brought by a public official against critics of his official conduct.

* * *

II

* * *

The general proposition that freedom of expression upon public questions is secured by the First Amendment has long been settled by our decisions. The constitutional safeguard, we have said, "was fashioned to assure unfettered interchange of ideas for the bringing about of political and social changes desired by the people." ..."The maintenance of the opportunity for free political discussion to the end that government may be responsive to the will of the people and that changes may be obtained by lawful means, an opportunity essential to the security of the Republic, is a fundamental principle of our constitutional system." ..."[I]t is a prized American privilege to speak one's mind, although not always with perfect good taste, on all public institutions"...and this opportunity is to be afforded for "vigorous advocacy" no less than "abstract discussion."

* * *

The First Amendment, said Judge Learned Hand, "presupposes that right conclusions are more likely to be gathered out of a multitude of tongues, than through any kind of authoritative selection. To many this is, and always will be, folly; but we have staked upon it our all." *United States* v. *Associated Press*, 52 F. Supp. 362, 372 (D. C. S. D. N. Y. 1943). Mr. Justice Brandeis, in his concurring opinion in *Whitney* v. *California*, 274 U.S. 357, 375-376, gave the principle its classic formulation:

> "Those who won our independence believed...that public discussion is a political duty; and that this should be a fundamental principle of the American government. They recognized the risks to which all human institutions are subject. But they knew that order cannot be secured merely through fear of punishment for its infraction; that it is hazardous to discourage thought, hope and imagination; that fear breeds repression; that repression breeds hate; that hate menaces stable government; that the path of safety lies in the opportunity to discuss freely supposed grievances and proposed remedies; and that the fitting remedy for evil counsels is good ones. Believing in the power of reason as applied through public discussion, they eschewed silence coerced by law – the argument of force in its worst form. Recognizing the occasional tyrannies of governing majorities, they amended the Constitution so that free speech and assembly should be guaranteed."

Thus we consider this case against the background of a profound national commitment to the principle that debate on public issues should be uninhibited, robust, and wide-open, and that it may well include vehement, caustic, and sometimes unpleasantly sharp attacks on government and public officials.... The present advertisement, as an expression of grievance and protest on one of the major public issues of our time, would seem clearly to qualify for the constitutional protection. The question is whether it forfeits that protection by the falsity of some of its factual statements and by its alleged defamation of respondent.

Authoritative interpretations of the First Amendment guarantees have consistently refused to recognize an exception for any test of truth – whether administered by judges, juries, or administrative officials – and especially one that puts the burden of proving truth on the speaker.... The constitutional protection does not turn upon "the truth, popularity, or social utility of the ideas and beliefs which are offered." ...As Madison said, "Some degree of abuse is inseparable from the proper use of every thing; and in no instance is this more true than in that of the press." ...That erroneous statement is inevitable in free debate, and that it must be protected if the freedoms of expression are to have the "breathing space" that they "need...to survive[.]"

* * *

Injury to official reputation affords no more warrant for repressing speech that would otherwise be free than does factual error. Where judicial officers are involved, this Court has held that concern for the dignity and reputation of the courts does not justify the punishment as criminal contempt of criticism of the judge or his decision.... This is true even though the utterance contains "half-truths" and "misinformation."...Such repression can be justified, if at all, only by a clear and present danger of the obstruction of justice. ...If judges are to be treated as "men of fortitude, able to thrive in a hardy climate"...surely the same must be true of other government officials, such as elected city commissioners. Criticism of their official conduct does not lose its constitutional protection merely because it is effective criticism and hence diminishes their official reputations.

* * *

The constitutional guarantees require, we think, a federal rule that prohibits a public official from recovering damages for a defamatory falsehood relating to his official conduct unless he proves that the statement was made with "actual malice" – that is, with knowledge that it was false or with reckless disregard of whether it was false or not.

* * *

We conclude that such a privilege is required by the First and Fourteenth Amendments.

III

We hold today that the Constitution delimits a State's power to award damages for libel in actions brought by public officials against critics of their official conduct. Since this is such an action, the rule requiring proof of actual malice is applicable. While Alabama law apparently requires proof of actual malice for an award of punitive damages, where general damages are concerned malice is "presumed." Such a presumption is inconsistent with the federal rule. "The power to create presumptions is not a means of escape from constitutional restrictions"..."the showing of malice required for the forfeiture of the privilege is not presumed but is a matter for proof by the plaintiff...." ...Since the trial judge did not instruct the jury to differentiate between general and punitive damages, it may be that the verdict was wholly an award of one or the other. But it is impossible to know, in view of the general verdict returned. Because of this uncertainty, the judgment must be reversed and the case remanded.

* * *

The judgment of the Supreme Court of Alabama is reversed and the case is remanded to that court for further proceedings not inconsistent with this opinion.

Reversed and remanded.

MR. JUSTICE BLACK, with whom MR. JUSTICE DOUGLAS joins, concurring.

I concur in reversing this half-million-dollar judgment against the New York Times Company and the four individual defendants. In reversing the Court holds that "the Constitution delimits a State's power to award damages for libel in actions brought by public officials against critics of their official conduct." I base my vote to reverse on the belief that the First and Fourteenth Amendments not merely "delimit" a State's power to award damages to "public officials against critics of their official conduct" but completely prohibit a State from exercising such a power. The Court goes on to hold that a State can subject such critics to damages if "actual malice" can be proved against them. "Malice," even as defined by the Court, is an elusive, abstract concept, hard to prove and hard to disprove. The requirement that malice be proved provides at best an evanescent protection for the right critically to discuss public affairs and certainly does not measure up to the sturdy safeguard embodied in the First Amendment. Unlike the Court, therefore, I vote to reverse exclusively on the ground that the Times and the individual defendants had an absolute, unconditional constitutional right to publish in the Times advertisement their criticisms of the Montgomery agencies and officials....

The half-million-dollar verdict does give dramatic proof, however, that state libel laws threaten the very existence of an American press virile enough to publish unpopular views on public affairs and bold enough to criticize the conduct of public officials. The factual background of this case emphasizes the imminence and enormity of that threat. One of the acute and highly emotional issues in this country arises out of efforts of many people, even including some public officials, to continue state-commanded segregation of races in the public schools and other public places, despite our several holdings that such a state practice is forbidden by the Fourteenth Amendment. Montgomery is one of the localities in which widespread hostility to desegregation has been manifested. This hostility has sometimes extended itself to persons who favor desegregation, particularly to so-called "outside agitators," a term which can be made to fit papers like the Times, which is published in New York. The scarcity of testimony to show that Commissioner Sullivan suffered any actual damages at all suggests that these feelings of hostility had at least as much to do with rendition of this half-million-dollar verdict as did an appraisal of damages. Viewed realistically, this record lends support to an inference that instead of being damaged Commissioner Sullivan's political, social, and financial prestige has likely been enhanced by the Times' publication. Moreover, a second half-million-dollar libel verdict against the Times based on the same advertisement has already been awarded to another Commissioner. There a jury again gave the full amount claimed. There is no reason to believe that there are not more such huge verdicts lurking just around the corner for the Times or any other newspaper or broadcaster which might dare to criticize public officials. In fact, briefs before us show that in Alabama there are now pending eleven libel suits by local and state officials against the Times seeking $5,600,000, and five such suits against the Columbia Broadcasting System seeking $1,700,000. Moreover, this technique for harassing and punishing a free press – now that it has been shown to be possible – is by no means limited to cases with racial overtones; it can be used in other fields where public feelings may make local as well as out-of-state newspapers easy prey for libel verdict seekers.

In my opinion the Federal Constitution has dealt with this deadly danger to the press in the only way possible without leaving the free press open to destruction – by granting the press an absolute immunity for criticism of the way public officials do their public duty.

* * *

MR. JUSTICE GOLDBERG, with whom MR. JUSTICE DOUGLAS joins, concurring in the result.

* * *

In my view, the First and Fourteenth Amendments to the Constitution afford to the citizen and to the press an absolute, unconditional privilege to criticize official conduct despite the harm which may flow from excesses and abuses....

XVI

SNYDER V. PHELPS

nyder v. Phelps, 562 U.S. 443 (2011), is a case which presents some interesting judicial issues for thought along with the Court's usual methodologies and intellectual gambits, once again in the arena of free expression (speech). And, again, we are not concerned with the case per se, but rather how the Court dealt with, or didn't deal with (avoided) the problem presented. It is easy to look at the facts and draw conclusions on grounds of common sense, experience, or now, even the Constitution, which is supposed to protect everyone in a balancing of interests. You have more than enough legal acumen to make a reasonable judgment as to how the Court might be expected to act, as contrasted with what it did to reach its result. You also might think about all the great tools available to the Court; a national conscience, deep-rooted traditions, fundamental rights, all in the name of freedom, liberty and privacy along with what the drafters surely would have intended or what they never thought about as being inconceivable; all this in addition to penumbras, emanations, radiations, transcendental dimensions, and mysteries of life which the Court has used, or not used, for whatever the occasion may have called for in hammering the Constitution into what it and its backwaters have become (the Constitution is properly thought of as including its related jurisprudence arising out of case law). You might hear others refer to the facts in the case as "compelling" (put on your waders) or you might be able to make your own decision with ease, even without being compelled, let alone compulsed. If a plebiscite had been taken in this case, the result might be more than lopsided, possibly overwhelming, with only fools and those of the most evil sort finding themselves in a reed-thin minority. Yet, in other settings of a more restricted and defined sample, one might suppose it could fairly go the other way. This case gives another facet of the business of the "law." Let's see what happens here, and your reaction.

The story begins with a young Marine being laid to rest by his family and friends during which time members of an unaffiliated (irrelevant but mentioned by the Court) Baptist church with a membership of what is believed to be fewer than ten (also irrelevant) chose to demonstrate and picket in the vicinity of the funeral announcing their stance, apparently, on such matters as the military, sexual orientation, Catholic priests, and other concerns selectively highlighted in the opinion. The father of the deceased soldier sued the church and its pastor for damages in federal court recovering a verdict in the millions of dollars. The opinion reports the procedural itinerary finally bringing it to the Supreme Court of the United States. Even at this premature point before you have read a word of the opinion, you probably recognize the direction this case is likely going to take. You are certainly adequately equipped to do so having read cases which serve as a prelude of things to come pretty much across the legal landscape. Please pay close attention to the language of the majority opinion. Word choice is important, very telling, and whether there is any strength in the Court's justifications, rationale and suggestions, more so.

Most anyone reading about the events leading up to the litigation that ensued would be challenged to not find him or herself wrapped up to one degree or another in an emotion-provoking scenario. Most. There are others without sympathy. But that is not what this exercise is about. The facts in the case are important but not our present concern nor the concern of our work here. Here, we only want to focus on the way the Court went about crafting its opinion while at the same time thinking about what the Court did in other cases involving constitutional issues, like and similar, and otherwise. One might observe judicial inconsistency. If that is so, it might be a result of constitutional interpretation or absolutes being selectively injected into so many settings and used as tools employed in such a clumsy manner so as to result in cloudy legal equations invented piecemeal over time and place. Progeny with its broken genes, as it were, presents a problem. These rulings and rationale may be intended to be case specific, but they are not. In fact, they spill into realms not thought of let alone anticipated, laden with unintended consequences, confounding what could be the best of principles (if deployed with consistency and restraint) but with negative iatrogenic results in cases which follow. One might also witness intellectual gymnastics being practiced in a conceptual fog as they tumble through time into other unrelated cases, without any anticipation. That seems to be the status of constitutional law today. Claiming ineptitude, lack of foresight, or worse, picking a peg for a gibbet upon which to hang a case may not be an entirely fair assessment, but the cases translate into wobbly dogma, wild and infectious precedent with side effects of the most pernicious kind. Unfortunately, one might conclude, this is too often how the Court, wittingly or not, works. Its grasp for legitimacy, or authority, if you will, with no one, so far, seriously challenging or calling it into account for its conduct is bringing the Court to a precipice. That is about to change. When a court feels compelled to spend dozens and dozens of pages defending a simple position in its opinion, which it should be able to accomplish in but a few paragraphs, if not one, if it is sound, something is wrong. But, that is for you to decide. All that is asked here is that you take a look and think about it.

One might wonder, as the Court had done at an earlier time, and more recently by dissenting opinions, why it just cannot exercise its judgment and equity jurisdiction to generate sensible results relative to the case before it with a keen sensitivity to and placing limitations on its tangential effects? In other words, tailor the case to the facts at hand and limiting its holding to that case. Isn't that what it is really paid to do instead of manufacturing unrestrained contrivances and infectious dogma? Otherwise opinions are nothing more than blunt philosophies, and that should not be the law. In fact, it isn't unless it is allowed to be.

Blunders may be repaired. If the Court is convinced it has "erred" or that a previous case was "wrongly decided," the Court should candidly reverse itself and say why, which we have already seen with illustrations in cases regarding sodomy and segregation. More often, if you observe, it is the makeup of the Court which changes, and with that the interpretation of the Constitution changes, and hence the unfortunate politics of constitutional philosophy, the Constitution saying what some new appointee says it says. Good God. Then there is the metamorphosis of the *zeitgeist*. That could do it, too, if the crowd is large enough.

Think about these things, and we'll have a "chat" after Alito's dissent in the following case.

And now, *Snyder*.

SNYDER v. PHELPS ET AL.

562 U.S. 443

CERTIORARI TO THE UNITED STATES COURT OF APPEALS
FOR THE FOURTH CIRCUIT

Chief Justice ROBERTS delivered the opinion of the Court.

A jury held members of the Westboro Baptist Church liable for millions of dollars in damages for picketing near a soldier's funeral service. The picket signs reflected the church's view that the United States is overly tolerant of sin and that God kills American soldiers as punishment. The question presented is whether the First Amendment shields the church members from tort liability for their speech in this case.

I

A

Fred Phelps founded the Westboro Baptist Church in Topeka, Kansas, in 1955. The church's congregation believes that God hates and punishes the United States for its tolerance of homosexuality, particularly in America's military. The church frequently communicates its views by picketing, often at military funerals. In the more than 20 years that the members of Westboro Baptist have publicized their message, they have picketed nearly 600 funerals.

Marine Lance Corporal Matthew Snyder was killed in Iraq in the line of duty. Lance Corporal Snyder's father selected the Catholic church in the Snyders' hometown of Westminster, Maryland, as the site for his son's funeral. Local newspapers provided notice of the time and location of the service.

Phelps became aware of Matthew Snyder's funeral and decided to travel to Maryland with six other Westboro Baptist parishioners (two of his daughters and four of his grandchildren) to picket. On the day of the memorial service, the Westboro congregation members picketed on public land adjacent to public streets near the Maryland State House, the United States Naval Academy, and Matthew Snyder's funeral. The Westboro picketers carried signs that were largely the same at all three locations. They stated, for instance: "God Hates the USA/Thank God for 9/11," "America is Doomed," "Don't Pray for the USA," "Thank God for IEDs," "Thank God for Dead Soldiers," "Pope in Hell," "Priests Rape Boys," "God Hates Fags," "You're Going to Hell," and "God Hates You."

The church had notified the authorities in advance of its intent to picket at the time of the funeral, and the picketers complied with police instructions in staging their demonstration. The picketing took place within a 10-by-25-foot plot of public land adjacent to a public street, behind a temporary fence. That plot was approximately 1,000 feet from the church where the funeral was held. Several buildings separated the picket site from the church. The Westboro picketers displayed their signs for about 30 minutes before the funeral began and sang hymns and recited Bible verses. None of the picketers entered church property or went to the cemetery. They did not yell or use profanity, and there was no violence associated with the picketing.

The funeral procession passed within 200 to 300 feet of the picket site. Although Snyder testified that he could see the tops of the picket signs as he drove to the funeral, he did not see what was written on the signs until later that night, while watching a news broadcast covering the event.

B

Snyder filed suit against Phelps, Phelps's daughters, and the Westboro Baptist Church (collectively Westboro or the church) in the United States District Court for the District of Maryland under that court's diversity jurisdiction. Snyder alleged five state tort law claims: defamation, publicity given to private life, intentional infliction of emotional distress, intrusion upon seclusion, and civil conspiracy....

A jury found for Snyder on the intentional infliction of emotional distress, intrusion upon seclusion, and civil conspiracy claims, and held Westboro liable for $2.9 million in compensatory damages and $8 million in punitive damages.... The District Court remitted the punitive damages award to $2.1 million, but left the jury verdict otherwise intact.

In the Court of Appeals, Westboro's primary argument was that the church was entitled to judgment as a matter of law because the First Amendment fully protected Westboro's speech. The Court of Appeals agreed....

We granted certiorari.

II

Whether the First Amendment prohibits holding Westboro liable for its speech in this case turns largely on whether that speech is of public or private concern, as determined by all the circumstances of the case. "[S]peech on 'matters of public concern' is 'at the heart of the First Amendment's protection.'"

* * *

The First Amendment reflects "a profound national commitment to the principle that debate on public issues should be uninhibited, robust, and wide-open." *New York Times Co.* v. *Sullivan*.... That is because "speech concerning public affairs is more than self-expression; it is the essence of self-government." ...Accordingly, "speech on public issues occupies the highest rung of the hierarchy of First Amendment values, and is entitled to special protection."

* * *

"[N]ot all speech is of equal First Amendment importance," however, and where matters of purely private significance are at issue, First Amendment protections are often less rigorous.... That is because restricting speech on purely private matters does not implicate the same constitutional concerns as limiting speech on matters of public interest: "[T]here is no threat to the free and robust debate of public issues; there is no potential interference with a meaningful dialogue of ideas"; and the "threat of liability" does not pose the risk of "a reaction of self-censorship" on matters of public import.

* * *

Deciding whether speech is of public or private concern requires us to examine the "content, form, and context" of that speech, "as revealed by the whole record." ...In considering content, form, and context, no factor is dispositive, and it is necessary to evaluate all the circumstances of the speech, including what was said, where it was said and how it was said.

The "content" of Westboro's signs plainly relates to broad issues of interest to society at large, rather than matters of "purely private concern." ...While these messages may fall short of refined social or political commentary, the issues they highlight – the political and moral conduct of the United States and its citizens, the fate of our Nation, homosexuality in the military, and scandals involving the Catholic clergy – are matters of public import. The signs certainly convey Westboro's position on those issues, in a manner designed...to reach as broad a public audience as possible. And even if a few of the signs – such as "You're Going to Hell" and "God Hates You" – were viewed as containing messages related to Matthew Snyder or the Snyders specifically, that would not change the fact that the overall thrust and dominant theme of Westboro's demonstration spoke to broader public issues.

Apart from the content of Westboro's signs, Snyder contends that the "context" of the speech – its connection with his son's funeral – makes the speech a matter of private rather than public concern. The fact that Westboro spoke in connection with a funeral, however, cannot by itself transform the nature of Westboro's speech. Westboro's signs, displayed on public land next to a public street, reflect the fact that the church finds much to condemn in modern society. Its speech is "fairly characterized as constituting speech on a matter of public concern," and the funeral setting does not alter that conclusion.

Snyder argues that the church members in fact mounted a personal attack on Snyder and his family, and then attempted to "immunize their conduct by claiming that they were actually protesting the United States' tolerance of homosexuality or the supposed evils of the Catholic Church." We are not concerned in this case that Westboro's speech on public matters was in any way contrived to insulate speech on a private matter from liability. Westboro had been actively engaged in speaking on the subjects addressed in its picketing long before it became aware of Matthew Snyder, and there can be no serious claim that Westboro's picketing did not represent its "honestly believed" views on public issues.... There was no pre-existing relationship or conflict between Westboro and Snyder that might suggest Westboro's speech on public matters was intended to mask an attack on Snyder over a private matter.

* * *

Westboro's choice to convey its views in conjunction with Matthew Snyder's funeral made the expression of those views particularly hurtful to many, especially to Matthew's father. The record makes clear that the applicable legal term – "emotional distress" – fails to capture fully the anguish Westboro's choice added to Mr. Snyder's already incalculable grief. But Westboro conducted its picketing peacefully on matters of public concern at a public place adjacent to a public street. Such space occupies a "special position in terms of First Amendment protection."

* * *

Simply put, the church members had the right to be where they were. Westboro alerted local authorities to its funeral protest and fully complied with police guidance on where the picketing could be staged. The picketing was conducted under police supervision some 1,000 feet from the church, out of the sight of those at the church. The protest was not unruly; there was no shouting, profanity, or violence....

Given that Westboro's speech was at a public place on a matter of public concern, that speech is entitled to "special protection" under the First Amendment. Such speech cannot be restricted simply because it is upsetting or arouses contempt. "If there is a bedrock principle underlying the First Amendment, it is that the government may not prohibit the expression of an idea simply because society finds the idea itself offensive or disagreeable." ...Indeed, "the point of all speech protection...is to shield just those choices of content that in someone's eyes are misguided, or even hurtful."

* * *

The jury here was instructed that it could hold Westboro liable for intentional infliction of emotional distress based on a finding that Westboro's picketing was "outrageous." "Outrageousness," however, is a highly malleable standard with "an inherent subjectiveness about it which would allow a jury to impose liability on the basis of the jurors' tastes or views, or perhaps on the basis of their dislike of a particular expression."

. . .In a case such as this, a jury is "unlikely to be neutral with respect to the content of [the] speech," posing "a real danger of becoming an instrument for the suppression of...'vehement, caustic, and sometimes unpleasant[t]'" expression.... Such a risk is unacceptable, "in public debate [we] must tolerate insulting, and even outrageous, speech in order to provide adequate 'breathing space' to the freedoms protected by the First Amendment." ...What Westboro said, in the whole context of how and where it chose to say it, is entitled to "special protection" under the First Amendment, and that protection cannot be overcome by a jury finding that the picketing was outrageous.

For all these reasons, the jury verdict imposing tort liability on Westboro for intentional inflection of emotional distress must be set aside.

III

The jury also found Westboro liable for the state law torts of intrusion upon seclusion and civil conspiracy. The Court of Appeals did not examine these torts independently of the intentional infliction of emotional distress tort. Instead, the Court of Appeals reversed the District Court wholesale, holding that the judgment wrongly "attache[d] tort liability to constitutionally protected speech."

Snyder argues that even assuming Westboro's speech is entitled to First Amendment protection generally, the church is not immunized from liability for intrusion upon seclusion because Snyder was a member of a captive audience at his son's funeral. We do not agree. In most circumstances, "the Constitution does not permit the government to decide which types of otherwise protected speech are sufficiently offensive to require protection for the unwilling listener or viewer. Rather...the burden normally falls upon the viewer to avoid further bombardment of [his] sensibilities simply by averting [his] eyes."

* * *

IV

Our holding today is narrow. We are required in First Amendment cases to carefully review the record, and the reach of our opinion here is limited by the particular facts before us. As we have noted, "the sensitivity and significance of the interests presented in clashes between First Amendment and [state law] rights counsel relying on limited principles that sweep no more broadly than the appropriate context of the instant case."

* * *

Westboro believes that America is morally flawed; many Americans might feel the same about Westboro. Westboro's funeral picketing is certainly hurtful and its contribution to public discourse may be negligible. But Westboro addressed matters of public import on public property, in a peaceful manner, in full compliance with the guidance of local officials. The speech was indeed planned to coincide with Matthew Snyder's funeral, but did not itself disrupt that funeral, and Westboro's choice to conduct its picketing at that time and place did not alter the nature of its speech.

Speech is powerful. It can stir people to action, move them to tears of both joy and sorrow, and – as it did here – inflict great pain. On the facts before us, we cannot react to that pain by punishing the speaker. As a Nation we have chosen a different course – to protect even hurtful speech on public issues to ensure that we do not stifle public debate. That choice requires that we shield Westboro from tort liability for its picketing in this case.

The judgment of the United States Court of Appeals for the Fourth Circuit is affirmed.

* * *

Justice ALITO, dissenting.

Our profound national commitment to free and open debate is not a license for the vicious verbal assault that occurred in this case.

Petitioner Albert Snyder is not a public figure. He is simply a parent whose son, Marine Lance Corporal Matthew Snyder, was killed in Iraq. Mr. Snyder wanted what is surely the right of any parent who experiences such an incalculable loss: to bury his son in peace. But respondents, members of the Westboro Baptist Church, deprived him of that elementary right. They first issued a press release and thus turned Matthew's funeral into a tumultuous media event. They then appeared at the church, approached as closely as they could without trespassing, and launched a malevolent verbal attack on Matthew and his family at a time of acute emotional vulnerability. As a result, Albert Snyder suffered severe and lasting emotional injury. The Court now holds that the First Amendment protected respondents' right to brutalize Mr. Snyder. I cannot agree.

I

Respondents and other members of their church have strong opinions on certain moral, religious, and political issues, and the First Amendment ensures that they have almost limitless opportunities to express their views. They may write and distribute books, articles, and other texts; they may create and disseminate video and audio recordings; they may circulate petitions; they may speak to individuals and groups in public forums and in any private venue that wishes to accommodate them; they may picket peacefully in countless locations; they may appear on television and speak on the radio; they may post messages on the Internet and send out e-mails. And they may express their views in terms that are "uninhibited," "vehement," and "caustic."

* * *

It does not follow, however, that they may intentionally inflict severe emotional injury on private persons at a time of intense emotional sensitivity by launching vicious verbal attacks that make no contribution to public debate. To protect against such injury, "most if not all jurisdictions" permit recovery in tort for the intentional infliction of emotional distress (or IIED)....

This is a very narrow tort with requirements that "are rigorous, and difficult to satisfy." ...To recover, a plaintiff must show that the conduct at issue caused harm that was truly severe.... "[R]ecovery will be meted out sparingly, its balm reserved for those wounds that are truly severe and incapable of healing themselves."

* * *

A plaintiff must also establish that the defendant's conduct was "'so outrageous in character, and so extreme in degree, as to go beyond all possible bounds of decency, and to be regarded as atrocious, and utterly intolerable in a civilized community."

* * *

Although the elements of the IIED tort are difficult to meet, respondents long ago abandoned any effort to show that those tough standards were not satisfied here. On appeal, they chose not to contest the sufficiency of the evidence.... They did not dispute that Mr. Snyder suffered "wounds that are truly severe and incapable of healing themselves." ...Nor did they dispute that their speech was "so outrageous in character, and so extreme in degree, as to go beyond all possible bounds of decency, and to be regarded as atrocious, and utterly intolerable in a civilized community." ...Instead, they maintained that the

First Amendment gave them a license to engage in such conduct. They are wrong.

II

* * *

This Court has recognized that words may "by their very utterance inflict injury" and that the First Amendment does not shield utterances that form "no essential part of any exposition of ideas, and are of such slight social value as a step to truth that any benefit that may be derived from them is clearly outweighed by the social interest in order and morality."

* * *

III

In this case, respondents brutally attacked Matthew Snyder, and this attack, which was almost certain to inflict injury, was central to respondents' well-practiced strategy for attracting public attention.

* * *

This strategy works because it is expected that respondents' verbal assaults will wound the family and friends of the deceased and because the media is irresistibly drawn to the sight of persons who are visibly in grief. The more outrageous the funeral protest, the more publicity the Westboro Baptist Church is able to obtain. Thus, when the church recently announced its intention to picket the funeral of a 9-year-old girl killed in the shooting spree in Tucson – proclaiming that she was "better off dead" – their announcement was national news, and the church was able to obtain free air time on the radio in exchange for canceling its protest. Similarly, the church got air time on a talk radio show in exchange for canceling its threatened protest at the funeral of five Amish girls killed by a crazed gunman.

In this case, respondents implemented the Westboro Baptist Church's publicity-seeking strategy. Their press release stated that they were going "to picket the funeral of Lance Cpl. Matthew A. Snyder" because "God Almighty killed Lance Cpl. Snyder. He died in shame, not honor – for a fag nation cursed by God.... Now in Hell – sine die." ...This announcement guaranteed that Matthew's funeral would be transformed into a raucous media event and began the wounding process. It is well known that anticipation may heighten the effect of a painful event.

On the day of the funeral, respondents, true to their word, displayed placards that conveyed the message promised in their press release. Signs stating "God Hates You" and "Thank God for Dead Soldiers" reiterated the message that God had caused Matthew's death in retribution for his sins.... Others, stating "You're Going to Hell" and "Not Blessed Just Cursed," conveyed the message that Matthew was "in Hell – sine die."

Even if those who attended the funeral were not alerted in advance about respondents' intentions, the meaning of these signs would not have been missed. Since respondents chose to stage their protest at Matthew Snyder's funeral and not at any of the other countless available venues, a reasonable person would have assumed that there was a connection between the messages on the placards and the deceased. Moreover, since a church funeral is an event that naturally brings to mind thoughts about the afterlife, some of respondents' signs – *e.g.* "God Hates You," "Not Blessed Just Cursed," and "You're Going to Hell" – would have likely been interpreted as referring to God's judgment of the deceased.

* * *

In light of this evidence, it is abundantly clear that respondents, going far beyond commentary on matters of public concern, specifically attacked Matthew Snyder because (1) he was a Catholic and (2) he was a member of the United States military. Both Matthew and petitioner were private figures, and this attack was not speech on a matter of public concern. While commentary on the Catholic Church or the United States military constitutes speech on matters of public concern, speech regarding Matthew Snyder's purely private conduct does not.

* * *

IV

This Court concludes that respondents' speech was protected by the First Amendment for essentially three reasons, but none is sound.

First- and most important- the Court finds that "the overall thrust and dominant theme of [their] demonstration spoke to" broad public issues. As I have attempted to show, this portrayal is quite inaccurate; respondents' attack on Matthew was of central importance. But in any event, I fail to see why actionable speech should be immunized simply because it is interspersed with speech that is protected....

Second, the Court suggests that respondents' personal attack on Matthew Snyder is entitled to First Amendment protection because it was not motivated by a private grudge, but I see no basis for the strange distinction that the Court appears to draw. Respondents' motivation – "to increase publicity for its views," – did not transform their statements attacking the character of a private figure into statements that made a contribution to debate on matters of public concern....

Third, the Court finds it significant that respondents' protest occurred on a public street, but this fact alone should not be enough to preclude IIED liability. To be sure, statements made on a public street may be less likely to satisfy the elements of the IIED tort than statements made on private property, but there is no reason why a public street in close proximity to the scene of a funeral should be regarded as a free-fire zone in which otherwise actionable verbal attacks are shielded from liability. If the First Amendment permits the States to protect their residents from the harm inflicted by such attacks – and the Court does not hold otherwise – then the location of the tort should not be dispositive. A physical assault may occur without trespassing; it is no defense that the perpetrator had "the right to be where [he was]." And the same should be true with respect to unprotected speech. Neither classic "fighting words" nor defamatory statements are immunized when they occur in a public place, and there is no good reason to treat a verbal assault based on the conduct or character of a private figure like Matthew Snyder any differently.

* * *

VI

Respondents' outrageous conduct caused petitioner great injury, and the Court now compounds that injury by depriving petitioner of a judgment that acknowledges the wrong he suffered.

In order to have a society in which public issues can be openly and vigorously debated, it is not necessary to allow the brutalization of innocent victims like petitioner. I therefore respectfully dissent.

*

No matter what one might first be inclined to say at this point, some kind of a bias would be apt to shout its presence so loudly that a muting "on the other hand" expression in balance could never be a sufficient brake. In an attempt to maintain some equilibrium, carefully balanced, one might get through a reasonable analysis. Yet we see terms and phrases come and go, only to return, and then, poof! Gone again. Concepts. Doctrines. "Experience has shown," and the like. Make a list. Let's throw some up and see what happens. How about "the collective conscience of the American people" being possibly a good one with which to start; or, how about "traditions so deeply rooted that they are fundamental to our society;" maybe "rights so basic that they emanate from the totality of the Constitution" (that's a good one, and seems to have universal relevance, no?); or, "jurors are smart enough to do the right thing." Hell fire, we don't even have to get into penumbras here.

We have repeatedly seen these "intellectualizations" at work in our readings. Don't think for a second the Court brings them into play willy-nilly. They are horsed into the battle as if by a General placing field pieces. So too, they may be inappropriate or vary as to their efficiency from scene to scene, sealing victory here, but elsewhere so counterproductive as to be not just useless, but destructive of the ends desired and previously decided upon. Poof, they are gone! Ask the clerks. And the more these poetic bouquets are used, the less secure they are in their judgment. It's a psychiatric thing. They don't even know it. In fact, they can't know. Protestation, as is exaggeration, is a cover for prevarication. Unfortunately, they infect cases which follow, unless constrained, tailored, as it were, and even then there is unavoidable bleed-over. At least these are things worth thinking about.

There are some points raised in the opinion which might deserve a second look. Reasonable minds might differ as to whether or not there is trifling here, but if the Court chooses to make offerings, regardless of motive or intent, they would seem to be fair game for consideration, and I mean consideration beyond their face as we are here wont to do. Also, how can you pass up an opportunity to look into the subconscious? The Court gazes into penumbras; why can't we look into its subconscious? It's really much clearer than you might think, and you will see (have seen) it. Penumbras are without their own evidence. Rorschachs they are not. What is "seen" is completely contrived, constructs, as it were, to reach an end (and if there is any evidence to the contrary, admissible or not, let us see it). If this was done in other areas of life, one would have to consider the appropriateness of hospitalization. With the subconscious, however, there usually is evidence supporting rational inferences based on sources from which they are drawn: it is called behavior. All truth is spoken through behavior, another of the great principles ranking right up there with behavior being predictably consistent over time and place. From it, particularly where consistent, which typically it is, we may draw conclusions, make deductions, work to get at the truth, a veritable window into the soul, if you will.

One point most worthy of consideration (in fact it is key in the process of the examination of the Court's conscience, its essential being, the character of its own constitution collectively and as individuals, if you will) is the Court's aside that Snyder only saw the "tops" of the signs, adding that this was by way of his "own admission" (for whatever intended weight or diversion that was supposed to carry, but I certainly don't see this as the Court getting itself off the hook onto which it has put itself). Please allow a question: what does *that* have to do with the case *if* the speech in question is on the "highest rung" of the hierarchy of First Amendment freedoms and fully protected as commentary of public concern? What difference does it make if Snyder even saw them or not, in full or otherwise? Admitted or not?! Constitutionally, quite obviously, it doesn't. This is not a light point, and it is a very unhappy one. Why was it put in the opinion? Do they protesteth too much? To suggest someone needs to review their work would be too snide and crude a snipe for our mission. But someone ought to do a stand-back analysis of what is wrought, intentionally or unintentionally...unimpassioned, uninvolved critique, perhaps. Those without counsel tend to do foolish things. Apparently, the Court can't or simply won't do it. There has to be something at work here.

How about this: the content of Phelps' signs address, the Court contends, public rather than private issues. That's false. It's false by the Court's own words. It quotes a sign as saying, "Thank God for Dead Soldiers." Snyder's son is a dead soldier. Is there anything further to say? Is there anyone on the planet who wouldn't make that connection? Anyone but, professedly, some of the scriveners? Why did the Court say that? What need was there? Hollow justifications speak to a contrary truth.

Continuing, the Court says, and besides that, no profanity was used. Really! "God Hates Fags!" If that isn't profanity, what is it? If you were to hold up a sign to the bench that declared "God Hates Fags," let's say even from way in the back of the courtroom, without even directing the statement to any particular one of the members, in total silence, as the case said, a statement at large, what do you think would happen? Is the courtroom a more solemn place than a fallen soldier's family funeral? Well, is it? How about in the field or at sea? Is decorum more important in one place than the other? Or, what about a sign that said "Thank God for Dead Judges," following the death of one of the members who had historically voted for abortion? Or, against it for that matter? What would the Court declare this demonstration to be, a prayer session not allowed on publicly owned property because we all enjoy the protection of the establishment clause of the First Amendment? Or, would it go into its switch hit mode and silently cry out, "What we have here is freedom of speech." And so, it (the Court) would be obliged to avert its eyes, just as was suggested Mr. Snyder do with his eyes, audaciously supported by its citation to the case of *Erznoznik v. Jacksonville*, 422 U.S. 205 (1975), certainly worth reading. That is what the Court suggested in *Erznoznik* and *Snyder*. I wonder if that would be good enough for the gander? Would the Court smile having this wonderful warm, fuzzy feeling inside that this is America, with an American at work, exercising his freedom of speech, his conscience over-flowing and his sense of deep-rooted traditions in a state of tumescence, swelled chest and all? If you don't like it, avert your eyes, it is suggested. So, what about the verbal bully on the playground? We know words hit as hard as fists. For humans, with their indelible memories, probably harder. Yet it seems as though, according to the Court's reasoning, the children, who also have no other place to go, would not have to just avert their eyes, but also their ears. What do you think? Are you starting to get a feel for this, maybe in the sense of a new gestalt fashioned by the hand of the Court itself?

Snyder wasn't a public figure as was Sullivan in *New York Times v. Sullivan*, 376 U.S. 254 (1964), nor did Phelps' exhortations make him one, which might have otherwise protected him from civil liability. And to suggest that Snyder "avert his eyes" so as to eliminate the application of the face-to-face "fighting words" doctrine of *Chaplinsky v. New Hampshire*, 315 U.S. 568 (1942), could be seen as untoward by some who might wonder, where is he supposed to look, at the floor of the funeral car? Possibly some "breathing space" could be found there, citing *Boos v. Barry*, 485 U.S. 312 (1988). Where is he supposed to go? To where may he retreat, into the traditions and conscience of the American people deploying the shroud of his dropped countenance to ward off the assault upon his soul or spirit? Do you see these opinions starting to bleed together creating a new order?

One could ask if the ethos of a nation is of any value, and if it is, is it entitled to be protected, or at least spared from judicial assault? That is a fair question, is it not? Or, coming in the other way, for what should it be sacrificed? What seems to stand out in the opinions so far is the waiving bouquets and selected shibboleths of constitutional grace and beauty in the name of freedom, liberty, and unfettered expression representing the Court's view of the nation's ethos and being used, *inter alia,* in the defense of pornography under the guise of free expression, lying against public figures, and the Court's centerpiece of abortion as a matter of, *inter alia,* privacy (without any reference to equal protection)…but not protecting the family at the funeral of a fallen soldier and in its anguish struggling to recover and stand tall…, is somewhat of a challenge, is it not?

Laws of wise restraint? Traditions of a nation? The conscience of the people? Rights so deeply rooted as to be fundamental? If these concepts have any substance whatsoever, and not just used to dress a window when convenient, a kind of intellectual prostitution, would not the question fairly have to be asked, what would Washington say about this? What would Jefferson say? What would Franklin say? I'm just curious, what do you think Lincoln would say? Even Marshall? If we are talking about traditions, conscience of the people, deeply rooted fundamental rights, should not such questions be asked? Want to try on Grant, Sherman, Lee, or Patton? How about Puller? What would Chesty say? Or, would it be more truth getting to ask what would Puller do, putting it in the behaviorist setting? If we are going to allow the Court to reach back into the conscience, the deeply rooted rights and traditions of the people to decide a case, shouldn't it be required to do so in every Bill of Rights case? Just think about it; is there even one case where such concepts shouldn't play a vital part? Name one!

Here it's the First Amendment as also extended to the states by the Fourteenth. Like it or not, it is what makes America America. Remember the first pages we went through together? We aren't English or Irish or Italian or Slavic or Israeli or Mexican or African or Pacifican. We are Americans, as constitutionally defined, or we are supposed to be, and when we are not, our divided house will fall. If we revert to multicultural sects as our primary identifier, we will no longer be Americans. Is that for which the soldier died? If one were to be candid in death, in the giving of a life, one might shake his head and say, "I may not like it, but it is better than the other way around." If he were able, this is probably what the dead Marine would have said. But here the assault is upon a living person. The dead are dead and cannot be further harmed, something not without a difference. Phelps may have been free to do what he did, as a matter of public law, but privately it may have to come with a price. Just as there are some things money can't buy, there are also some things which carry a tariff—social, financial, or otherwise—which can't be shaken off by the stroke of a pen, or a fresh political view or egocentric bias on what is constitutional. Furthermore, it is the law that is supposed to provide a remedy for a wrong suffered. In this case, the people (as a jury) spoke, over which the Court ran roughshod, apparently allowing anger and hate to be elevated in the name of the Constitution above dignity, grace, and privacy, or one might so conclude. What happened to the laws of wise restraint which truly make us free?

Unfortunately, talk in the corridors reveals one of the more ghastly aspects of this opinion in terms of what it evokes among those who have served and read it, being that it was decided by people who have never served a day of active duty in harm's way, aren't serving, and never will, as noted. They have no way of knowing. It simply cannot be known to them. They would do well by attending an Arlington event…just one. At least some insight might be gained. It is a tribute paid and earned, something the Court can't take away. Sully it? Maybe. No more. It doesn't come in books or on screens. Seemingly, one would therefore be well advised to tread lightly, recognizing and honoring wise restraint. This will become more important as the future unfolds. It is a problem and will become more so as our future is cast upon us, make no mistake (see *infra*). They have taken a case that involves the kind of people who have allowed them to be there. No one has suggested that this is a good joke taken too far. It is worse. One could find the Court in contempt for failing to recognize this and act accordingly. It is this vantage point from which is contemplated the concept of the First Amendment, as did those who drafted it. We did not start with the First Amendment; we started with the concept of freedom—freedom from as well as freedom to.

These are not easy questions. Often, as the saying goes, hard cases make bad law, but that is not really true. Often coming down on one side at the expense of the other is justified in the overall scheme of things. Welcome to the law. But there is also the notion of temperance. The Court has referred to this on many occasions when taking some legislation to task as not being sufficiently narrowly tailored to meet the fine balance, nice and true, between the interests of government and the people. But when it comes to its own legislation, its own sweeping doctrines and declarations, tailoring somehow has been overlooked, and a mosh pit rule is cast upon the citizens it is supposed to serve. You have already seen it several times. You also witness the result by looking around at your new world.

Now, on to the next issue. What was good enough for *Clay* apparently was not good enough for *Bowles*.

XVII

BOWLES V. RUSSELL

L et us prepare ourselves for *Bowles v. Russell.* Legal philosophy, indeed even on its most mundane level, *viz.*, the practice, virtually universally holds that form should not prevail over function, or more particularly, legally speaking, procedural rules should not prime the substance of law (or justice in the premises as it is sometimes put). That is, methodology, the technical aspects of procedure, should not trump the substantive or the fundamental rights of the parties before the Court. Technique and its legal "niceties" should not trump justice, put simply. One's rights should not be denied for ministerial reasons or technical procedural rules that have nothing to do with the justice of the matter at hand. One's legal fate should not be the product of gamesmanship. It is certainly fair, nay necessary, to have rules cannot be gainsaid, but the dispensing of justice should not be governed by the gamesmanship of counsel and procedural gymnastics, let alone trickery or unexpected surprises in their deployment which have nothing to do with the merits of a given case particularly in light of the "no harm, no foul" concept. The same holds for the eventuality of a professional or procedural mistake. The art of the game should not be determinative of a party's rights. The law, as opposed to procedure, should control, or at least most would say, and historically the commentators have so held. The courts? Not so much.

Fair play and substantial justice is based on the facts of the case as found by the jury, if there is one, otherwise by the judge. Juries must be demanded in many civil cases or they are waived. Juries are provided in serious criminal cases unless they are waived. But as a procedural matter, a party litigant does not get a jury in a civil action unless it is demanded and typically a fee is paid. If counsel forgets it, the right to a jury trial is lost, or waived attendant to the procedural misstep. That's the usual rule. Seems fair enough, or is it? There is a reason.

Once the facts are found, the judge applies the law to the facts. In other words, at base, the facts and the substantive law seemingly ought to control the outcome of the case. This could be looked upon as reflective of the real aspect of the case or controversy at hand. In other words, the outcome doesn't, or at least shouldn't rise or fall on the basis of some technicality unrelated to the facts, law, and/or justice of the case; the case should be left to be decided upon its own merits.

Outcomes in this regard are generally good. But, there are cases where that is not true, and we have a justiciable miscarriage, or the purpose of the law is spontaneously aborted, as it were. However, even in such cases, the judge has some discretionary corrective devices employable to prevent such an event, e.g., mistrial, *remittitur, additur,* rehearing, a finding of non-culpability, or simply a grant of leave to appeal for consideration by a panel of judges in a higher court *pendente lite,* and even as startling as it may seem, a court-ordered judgment notwithstanding the verdict (*judgment non obstante veredicto*). Judges have enormous judicial powers.

This is a general picture of "practice" in the civil courts albeit simplified. In criminal courts, it can be and often is quite different, and for important reasons. Yet in many cases throughout the system, the aggrieved party is simply left to suffer the fate of incompetent counsel and often without a meaningful remedy as a result of a procedural misstep.

On the other hand, there are features of procedure, or the rules of procedure, technically and properly referred to as "adjective law," the gamesmanship, the chess-like aspect of the proceeding, which can, in effect, control the outcome of the case or controversy, particularly when artfully if not craftily employed. This is something that could be referred to as "form over substance," and is frowned upon by most, particularly losers, but quite real in the realm of "effective" representation. When such a procedural misstep occurs, i.e., filing a case too late resulting in its procedural dismissal—as opposed to an "on the merits" decision, a classic case of legal malpractice results. This would be akin to failing to timely diagnose an obviously curable disease which instead, through delay, became lethal. In the setting here, it would be typically illustrated by a fatuous omission or failure to act which could have been easily avoided. This is the stuff of procedure, or adjective law. There is more to it, but there is the "law of the case" concerned with the rights of the parties, and then there is the "law" of its presentation, or "adjective law," commonly referred to as "procedure," the Court Rules. Both are usually subject to stated time limitations. Relatively speaking, procedural time limits are exceptionally short when compared to statutes of limitations barring legal rights altogether, and measured in days rather than years.

At the same time, there needs to be announced and understood standards, regulations, that is, rules by which the "game" is played if there is ever to be fair play and substantial justice in the final analysis. Few would argue that a free-for-all would be an ideal method of conflict resolution. Anarchy has never fared well. Trial by ordeal, combat, wager of battle or duel, although popular in certain colonial areas of what later became the United States, along with settling matters by use of the saber and pistol, has by and large fallen into disuse here, at least for now. But one could argue that in all but the most extreme cases, procedure, like the unruly dog of Equity Practice, should be kept firmly chained to its kennel. Fair enough. Yet at the same time, all in the name of fairness, where the hardship is sufficiently great, the hand of Equity and the over-riding relief it can provide should not be stayed.

The major cause of legal malpractice in the U.S. is doing something late, or not at all. Starting a lawsuit after the Statute of Limitations on a claim that has run is often referred to as a case being time barred, or some procedural time limitation has been missed, as with a late or untimely answer to a filed and served summons and complaint leading to a default judgment. Or, possibly the late filing of an *interlocutory* claim, or notice of appeal, again, having nothing to do with the merits of the case, per se, that causes the case to fail. In fact, in many jurisdictions, if not all, these sorts of *delicts* exceed all other errors combined and are the source of the most common legal malpractice complaint. Hence, it seems natural to look at periods of limitation, sometimes simply referred to as "the statute," and a procedural rule that in result could have the same effect in the same light, being late to the game. Or, put otherwise, malpractice is what happens when counsel allows the "statute to run," or otherwise blew the Rule, words which will cause an offending attorney to precipitate.

The Statutes of Limitation are sometimes called "statutes of repose," that is, there is a point following the passage of a legislated pre-determined period of time where matters should be let lay where they are as no one has complained to date, at least formally or officially, for a variety of reasons. If one doesn't care enough to sue in five or ten years (there are all kinds of statutes [time limits] for all kinds of claims), there seems to be little good in letting them reach back into the distant past and dredge something up which may have been forgotten by most. The evidence on one side may have disappeared, witnesses may have moved or died, circumstances may have changed, memories may have faded, one of the possible parties has lived life and made plans on the basis that no suit would ever be filed, etc. The list of reasons goes on and on why there is a point when it would no longer be fair to let someone proceed after they had slept on their rights for an inordinate length of time. Many states say one has five or six years to sue on a contract, a promise, some may even say ten or even fifteen if it involves real estate. Many states say a claimant has two or three years to sue for a personal injury, or only one year if it was an intentional harm. Statutes of Limitation represent a pattern of variegated inconsistency, but every jurisdiction has them and they are numerous, each supposedly logically tailored to different kinds of claims. Court rules, not so much. They set time limits that seem to come and go in a relative instant. Three or four weeks to answer a filed and served summons and complaint are common.

At the same time, most states say that if a suit is filed beyond the statutory period, counsel for the defense must raise this issue as a defense in a timely fashion, (procedural rules usually requiring the defense of the Statute of Limitations [also known as an Affirmative Defense, procedurally speaking]) to be set forth in or along with the first responsive pleading to the Complaint filed, or a pleading to which a response is being filed for the first time, that first responsive pleading being typically denominated as an Answer (or possibly a Motion to Dismiss in some jurisdictions). If not done, many court rules say the protection of the "Statute" has been waived, or lost. Translated: Legal Malpractice. This time it is not just plaintiff's attorney who filed late, but the grief is instead cast and visited upon the defendant's lawyer (along with his client), who failed to raise it as a defense in a timely manner pursuant to the rules, with the delay here being measured, as indicated, in weeks (or days) instead of years in the case of statutory limitations (this is an illustration of a court rule barring a defense as a procedural matter [the statute typically bars claims altogether]). But it happens, perhaps as often as simply the late filing of claims (of all kinds). Again, the case is lost this time also on procedural grounds. This time the defendant suffers of procedural tardiness.

The aggrieved party, the one whom the lawyer failed to represent adequately, is not without a remedy as he can sue the attorney for malpractice, but now has two cases to prove. He has to prove the malpractice case against the offending counsel, which is often fairly cut and dried, as well as the case the attorney flubbed, having to show he would have prevailed in that case had it been permitted to proceed to trial, or so say most courts. At the same time, as an added problem, the aggrieved client would have to be blessed with a collectible or at least insured attorney. Surprisingly, that is not always the case.

If a prospective plaintiff stalls too long (past the statutory period to bring a claim), justice can be said to be served by having a law that simply says, at some point the claim is too late. There is a kind of justice in ultimate repose. Such statutes typically give plenty of time to act. In light of this, one might conclude time limits are fair and reasonable. It may be more than just unfortunate, causing one to argue why not let them proceed on the merits and not toss the case into the abyss just because a ministerial error had been committed, to which the careful, thorough practitioner would reply, where do you draw the line? Otherwise, where is the predictability and integrity of the law, and the orderly process before the courts? Why not permit judicial discretion one might ask? And should statutory limits on the substance of claims and procedural time limits be treated differently? As a practical matter, most courts have come down on the side of substantive and procedural time limits being upheld, with possibly somewhat more leniency procedurally, given possible lack of culpability.

Blowing the statute, usually measured in years, seems a reasonable defense, probably fair, in light of the typically long periods legislatively countenanced. Plaintiffs simply lose. But to blow a procedural rule by a day, or two, or three, seems to present another question. We have a case coming up which discusses the problem of a procedural error, if it may be called that, with three different courts up the appellate chain seeing it not only differently, but in three different ways, not surprisingly.

As just an aside, and maybe to put it into sharper focus, if a stale claim is brought, one barred by the Statute, but the defense fails to appropriately raise the defense, the case may proceed to judgment or verdict as if there were no time bar. In other words, the Statute doesn't vitiate the underlying cause, it doesn't take away its merit or rights to justice, it merely prevents it from proceeding in a court if properly asserted as a defense since it bars any remedy, again referred to as an Affirmative Defense. It may determine the practical outcome of the case, vice a substantive outcome of trial on the merits, but we say that the case rises or falls procedurally as being either ultimately brought in an untimely fashion, or not properly defended in a timely manner. It is a technical victory, one way or another, depending on your perspective; again, however, a clear case of malpractice on the part of counsel for the party who suffers.

Now, however, once the case has been filed and the procedural rules are in full force, the adjective law determines how the case is presented to the court and proceeds through the trial and appellate phases in accordance with a schedule of rules and procedural devices, all governed by time tables. The time frames are very short, as previously indicated, relative at least to time limits governed by the various Statutes of Limitation written by legislatures. Again, for example, one might have 21 or 28 days to answer a civil complaint after it has been personally served upon or in fact delivered to the defendant, typically with an announcement as to what it is at the time it is handed over or dropped at his feet (by post with a return receipt upon delivery is another method in some circumstances). Failure to file the answer within the time limits may or likely will result in a default if the plaintiff takes advantage of default procedures, which on occasion is consciously not done. Translated: defendant loses as to liability, with plaintiff proceeding to prove damages or crafting a proposed court-approved remedy, very broadly speaking. Similarly, short procedural time limits are imposed for such matters as Motions (a written request to the court coupled with an oral argument and/or a presentation by brief in support) requesting, for example, a court order to compel the production of evidence, the rehearing of a matter, or perhaps a new trial (commonly ten or fourteen days), or for the taking of an appeal to a higher court (commonly 30, 60, or 90 days). Failure to meet such procedural deadlines translates in the same manner, the right is lost, no rehearing, no new trial, no appeal. For being a day late!? Two or three? What if the judge told you, a prisoner *in propria persona* (representing yourself without a lawyer) that you had seventeen days in which to file your papers, but the court rule said fourteen, with the papers in question being filed on the sixteenth day? Should substantive rights be sacrificed, or at least the opportunity to be heard in open court, because something was done on Monday or Tuesday which should have been done on the previous Friday? Even if it were apropos for procedural time lines to be drawn, here the judge drew the line, albeit in error, but it was nevertheless drawn, and the prisoner relied upon it. Under the circumstances of *Bowles*, many courts would have said, let the man be heard. In *Bowles v. Russell*, 551 U.S. 205 (2007), *infra*, the highest court said no, five to four. This case involves a procedural time limit. You have enough adjective (procedural) law to analyze the Court's ruling. Read the opinion with a focus on rationale.

Now, *Bowles*.

*

BOWLES v. RUSSELL, WARDEN

551 U.S. 205

CERTIORARI TO THE UNITED STATES COURT OF APPEALS
FOR THE SIXTH CIRCUIT

JUSTICE THOMAS delivered the opinion of the Court.

In this case, a District Court purported to extend a party's time for filing an appeal beyond the period allowed by statute. We must decide whether the Court of Appeals had jurisdiction to entertain an appeal filed after the statutory period but within the period allowed by the District Court's order. We have long and repeatedly held that the time limits for filing a notice of appeal are jurisdictional in nature. Accordingly, we hold that petitioner's untimely notice – even though filed in reliance upon a District Court's order – deprived the Court of Appeals of jurisdiction.

I

In 1999, an Ohio jury convicted petitioner Keith Bowles of murder.... The jury sentenced Bowles to 15-years-to-life imprisonment.

Bowles then filed a federal habeas corpus application on September 5, 2002. On September 9, 2003, the District Court denied Bowles habeas relief. After the entry of final judgment, Bowles had 30 days to file a notice of appeal. He failed to do so. On December 12, 2003, Bowles moved to reopen the period during which he could file his notice of appeal pursuant to Rule 4(a)(6), which allows district courts to extend the filing period for 14 days from the day the district court grants the order to reopen, provided certain conditions are met.

On February 10, 2004, the District Court granted Bowles' motion. But rather than extending the time period by 14 days, as Rule 4(1)(6) and §2107(c) allow, the District Court inexplicably gave Bowles 17 days – until February 27 – to file his notice of appeal. Bowles filed his notice on February 26 – within the 17 days allowed by the District Court's order, but after the 14-day period allowed by Rule 4(a)(6) and §2107(c).

On appeal, respondent Russell argued that Bowles' notice was untimely and that the Court of Appeals therefore lacked jurisdiction to hear the case. The Court of Appeals agreed. It first recognized that this Court has consistently held the requirement of filing a timely notice of appeal is "mandatory and jurisdictional." The court also noted that Courts of Appeals have uniformly held that Rule 4(a)(6)'s 180-day period for filing a motion to reopen is also mandatory and not susceptible to equitable modification. Concluding that "the fourteen-day period in Rule 4(a)(6) should be treated as strictly as the 180-day period in that same Rule," the Court of Appeals held that it was without jurisdiction. We granted certiorari, and now affirm.

II

According to 28 U.S.C. § 2107(a), parties must file notices of appeal within 30 days of the entry of the judgment being appealed. District courts have limited authority to grant an extension of the 30-day time period. Relevant to this case, if certain conditions are met, district courts have the statutory authority to grant motions to reopen the time for filing an appeal for 14 additional days.

It is undisputed that the District Court's order in this case purported to reopen the filing period for more than 14 days. Thus, the question before us is whether the Court of Appeals lacked jurisdiction to entertain an appeal filed outside the 14-day window allowed by §2107(c) but within the longer period granted by the District Court.

A

This Court has long held that the taking of an appeal within the prescribed time is "mandatory and jurisdictional." ...Reflecting the consistency of this Court's holdings, the courts of appeals routinely and uniformly dismiss untimely appeals for lack of jurisdiction.

* * *

Jurisdictional treatment of statutory time limits makes good sense. Within constitutional bounds, Congress decides what cases the federal courts have jurisdiction to consider. Because Congress decides whether federal courts can hear cases at all, it can also determine when, and under what conditions, federal courts can hear them....

The resolution of this case follows naturally from this reasoning. As we have long held, when an "appeal has not been prosecuted in the manner directed, within the time limited by the acts of Congress, it must be dismissed for want of jurisdiction." Bowles' failure to file his notice of appeal in accordance with the statute therefore deprived the Court of Appeals of jurisdiction. And because Bowles' error is one of jurisdictional magnitude, he cannot rely on forfeiture or waiver to excuse his lack of compliance with the statute's time limitations.

B

Bowles contends that we should excuse his untimely filing because he satisfies the "unique circumstances" doctrine....

Today we make clear that the timely filing of a notice of appeal in a civil case is a jurisdictional requirement. Because this Court has no authority to create equitable exceptions to jurisdictional requirements, use of the "unique circumstances" doctrine is illegitimate. We see no compelling reason to resurrect the doctrine from its 40-year slumber. Accordingly, we reject Bowles' reliance on the doctrine[.]

* * *

C

If rigorous rules like the one applied today are thought to be inequitable, Congress may authorize courts to promulgate rules that excuse compliance with the statutory time limits.

III

The Court of Appeals correctly held that it lacked jurisdiction to consider Bowles' appeal. The judgment of the Court of Appeals is affirmed.

JUSTICE SOUTER, with whom JUSTICE STEVENS, JUSTICE GINSBURG, and JUSTICE BREYER join, dissenting.

The District Court told petitioner Keith Bowles that his notice of appeal was due on February 27, 2004. He filed a notice of appeal on February 26, only to be told that he was too late because his deadline had actually been February 24. It is intolerable for the judicial system to treat people this way, and there is not even a technical justification for condoning this bait and switch. I respectfully dissent.

I

"Jurisdiction," we have warned several times in the last decade, "is a word of many, too many, meanings." This variety of meaning has insidiously tempted courts, this one included, to engage in "less than meticulous," sometimes even "profligate...use of the term."

In recent years, however, we have tried to clean up our language, and until today we have been avoiding the erroneous jurisdictional conclusions that flow from indiscriminate use of the ambiguous word. Thus, although we used to call the sort of time limit at issue here "mandatory and jurisdictional," we have recently and repeatedly corrected that designation as a misuse of the "jurisdiction" label.

* * *

The stakes are high in treating time limits as jurisdictional. While a mandatory but nonjurisdictional limit is enforceable at the insistence of a party claiming its benefit or by a judge concerned with moving the docket, it may be waived or mitigated in exercising reasonable equitable discretion. But if a limit is taken to be jurisdictional, waiver becomes impossible, meritorious excuse irrelevant, and *sua sponte* consideration in the courts of appeals mandatory[.]

* * *

The time limit at issue here, far from defining the set of cases that may be adjudicated, is much more like a statute of limitations, which provides an affirmative defense, and is not jurisdictional. Statutes of limitations may thus be waived, or excused by rules, such as equitable tolling, that alleviate hardship and unfairness....

Consistent with the traditional view of statutes of limitations, and the carefully limited concept of jurisdiction, an exception to the time limit in 28 U.S.C. § 2107(c) should be available when there is a good justification for one for reasons we recognized three years ago. In *Harris Truck Lines, Inc.* v. *Cherry Meat Packers, Inc.*, 371 U.S. 215, 217 (1962).

* * *

In ruling that Bowles cannot depend on the word of a District Court Judge, the Court demonstrates that no one may depend on the recent, repeated, and unanimous statements of all participating Justices of this Court.

II

We have the authority to recognize an equitable exception to the 14-day limit, and we should do that here, as it certainly seems reasonable to rely on an order from a federal judge....

Thompson should control. In that case, and this one, the untimely filing of a notice of appeal resulted from reliance on an error by a District Court, an error that caused no evidence prejudice to the other party. Actually, there is one difference between *Thompson* and this case: Thompson filed his post-trial motions late, and the District Court was mistaken when it said they were timely; here, the District Court made the error out of the blue, not on top of any mistake by Bowles, who then filed his notice of appeal by the specific date the District Court had declared timely. If anything, this distinction ought to work in Bowles's favor. Why should we have rewarded Thompson, who introduced the error, but now punish Bowles, who merely trusted the District Court's statement?

* * *

I have to admit that Bowles's counsel probably did not think the order might have been entered on a different day from the day it was signed. He probably just trusted that the date given was correct, and there was nothing unreasonable in so trusting. The other side let the order pass without objection, either not caring enough to make a fuss or not even noticing the discrepancy; the mistake of a few days was probably not enough to ring the alarm bell to send either lawyer to his copy of the federal rules and then off to the courthouse to check the docket. This would be a different case if the year were wrong on the District Court's order, or if opposing counsel had flagged the error. But on the actual facts, it was reasonable to rely on a facially plausible date provided by a federal judge.

I would vacate the decision of the Court of Appeals and remand for consideration of the merits.

*

What do you think? You have observed what the Court thought, five to four. Not that we are concerned with whether the case was correctly decided, but what do you think? Or, was it wisely decided? Why was the time bar brushed aside in *Clay* with relief given, but not in *Bowles*? Why is it included here? What happened to the judge who wrongfully granted the extended time?

XVIII

WASHINGTON V. GLUCKSBERG

ashington, et al. v. Glucksberg, et al., presents a number of issues, substantive and procedural, along with conceptual challenges in the realms of morality, freedom (referred to as "personal choice" in some settings, which is a misnomer as virtually no choice of any significance is truly personal, but in one way or another involves or affects others), religion, compassion, even politics wending its way into the fray. Much of what is presented here as a prelude in preparation for our thinking about *Glucksberg* will reappear in the thoughts for consideration following the reading of the case. There are professional insiders, both legal and medical, who believe this was the wrong case to bring, and by the wrong parties. The subtleties and delicacies which permeate this area of jurisprudence called for the most thorough of planning and legal preparation. However, the case seems to have been a ham-handed frontal assault on a blunt force statute effectively outlawing the medical community from any attempt it might make in assisting one to bring a human life to an earlier conclusion under conditions of extremis than would have otherwise certainly occurred, as a matter of patient choice. In effect, the purpose of the statute was to prevent an escape from a life no longer worth living, or otherwise ending in relentless, protracted, unbearable, and often unmanageable pain. It could be said even the most pedestrian reader of the opinion might quickly conclude the Court had no idea, let alone an understanding, of the medical and psychic issues surrounding its conclusions attendant to the end-of-life drama, or any appreciation of who should control them whether based on deep-rooted traditions apart from or including the medical arts. This is not criticism, but rather a charge to you to think about what the opinion said and at the same time who said it.

The State of Washington passed a statute making it illegal to provide medical services to another who has made a conscious and competent choice to bring to a conclusion life as we know it to be under any circumstances. There are many in the medical profession who take the position that pain should not be a reason for any life-ending procedure as it can be "managed." Possibly true, at least in cases, but at the cost of not knowing for sure if the patient is at peace and the unpredictability of the sedation curve (the patient slipping in and out of consciousness or semi-consciousness, in and out of pain, in and out of purgatory—one has to have been there to understand). Administration of medication which keeps them consistently just below the threshold is nearly impossible to do, leaving the patient to repeatedly emerge into an unimaginable hell. Now the patient gets to experience a whole string of deaths. Lovely.

Then there is the cognitive side of the problem (which few caregivers will be willing to concede, or simply don't understand) which may be demonstrated through a simple test: a stroke patient (one having had a cerebrovascular accident of one sort or another) may appear to be comatose, or drugs may be administered so as to induce what appears to be a coma or coma-like state. Cases have been demonstrated where one can take the patient's hand and say, "If you can hear me, squeeze my hand," and they will. In other words, often, and possibly more often than not, they have an awareness of the world around them. Added to that, caregivers, not to mention relatives and visitors, may nonchalantly speak of the patient's impending death, or other horrific circumstances, in the patient's presence never realizing the patient may well be able to process what is being said, and yet have to suffer through it helplessly, all the time those in the room thinking the patient cannot hear or internally react as a result of an apparent comatose state, demonstrating the most crass of carelessness, ignorance or disregard. By being drugged into an apparent oblivion, the patient is effectively forced into a different hell, this one, albeit supposedly without pain, at least in the conventional sense (if that makes any difference) contrary to the patient's express and competent wishes, and now condemned to what they must feel to be, and utterly locked into, an even worse fate. But the Supreme Court says the patient must suffer as a constitutional matter. *Ne exeat causa mortis.* Marvelous!

Certainly fairness calls for another analytic perspective for your consideration: the Supreme Court simply concluded the State of Washington's legislation passed constitutional muster. The people's elected representatives said no physician assistance in the premises. As matters of health and welfare have traditionally been left to the states (as a constitutional matter), the law stands as written unless there is a frank invasion of federal constitutional rights outweighing the ends of the law under review all being quite in line with what many feel is the proper role of the (federal) Supreme Court.

The popular agenda driven media, needless to say, jumped on *Glucksberg* with its penchant to market its own labels, commonly political, and did so here referring to this as "assisted suicide" promulgated by another label for those who would help as "Dr. Death," with the resulting public opinion thusly being affected in a way which more ordered thought would not have otherwise countenanced, at least one could presuppose. With this, the high court seemed to cheerfully go along waiving the banners of deeply rooted traditions and the conscience of the nation.

Following the passage of the statute, a group of physicians retained counsel, postured themselves as plaintiffs, and filed what is known as a Declaratory Action in an appropriate United States District Court for a trial testing the constitutionality of the statute on grounds of violating a person's liberty as protected by, *inter alia*, the Fourteenth Amendment of the United States Constitution incorporating the Bill of Rights as to the states. The trial court had no trouble agreeing. The State of Washington appealed to a three-judge panel in the United States Court of Appeals for the Ninth Circuit which agreed with the appellants, but which was reversed, *en banc* (before all the judges of that court), ultimately affirming the trial court, and then petitioned the United States Supreme Court to take the matter up on *cert.*; it did, and again in one of its rare unanimous opinions, reversed the courts below. Why? Think about it as you read the opinion.

The first words SCOTUS printed in the opinion, following a statement of the issue in the case, were, "It has always been a crime to assist suicide in the State of Washington...." One would think somehow in a matter like this the Court could have started out a little differently, using at the least a different choice of words given the interests with which this case deals, issues of ultimate profundity, and the human beings affected in this entire scenario. In other words, deference to both sides, the simplest of decorum, recognized the free world over as a universal judicial standard of basic etiquette and good manners (not to mention the standard of practice among gentlemen) instead of launching an attack in the opening sentence casting the whole matter in criminal terms. Indeed, this Court, as have all others below it, has continually reminded itself and all those before it of the fact that just because a law has been the law for a long, long time is not necessarily good reason for its continuance. Regardless of how the Court may have ruled, or did rule, one might find such an impudent thumb in the eye of all those working for justice not only contemptuous, foolish from several perspectives, but an inaccurate standard upon which to ground a decision, an opinion (*viz.*, it has always been that way). Such a statement doesn't rise to even a sophomoric level of legal let alone philosophical analysis. At least some deference to judicial diplomacy, not to mention the parties before it, would seem to have been in order, led by a prelude of compassion at the very least (you might take note the court didn't start out in *Bowers* with the statement that it has always been a crime to commit sodomy in the State of Georgia).

A measured degree of restraint, delicacy, and respect could have been generated and used to set the scene for a deliberative analysis and explanation of its actions, recognizing that there are good and fair arguments and good and fair people on both sides of this case, rationally, religiously, and emotionally based, and honoring that fact. But, oh no. The chief, seizing the opportunity, lets his inner self blow right through in his first substantive opening line, and the other majority members never even caught it, or at least never made any attempt to put on the damper. If ever there was a case where the Court needed uninvolved counsel, this was it, although one member did seem to call for restraint and a deliberative analysis. And for the Court to say it had as many briefs of *amici curiae* as it could remember ever having been filed in a single case completely missed the point. If you look at those briefs, they are typically trenchant, entrenched in their own positions, narrow with rant so as to provide no counsel at all, just compressed argument. Not one brief, nor the basic opinion of the Court, ever adequately stepped back and asked what was truly before the Court, what has really happened over time, what with which we are now faced, what is it that may have changed, what may be coming down the road, why there has been some change of heart in some sectors…and not, "It has always been a crime…." No judicial statesmanship. None. Possibly a weak feint by one. No more. I suggest to you this opinion is not going to stand the test of time, a hallmark of good law. Follow-up is left to you.

To highlight for your observation and consideration, note Souter's concurrence where you may see a somewhat more considered, reflective, deliberative, even compassionate analysis not only keeping the issue alive in the premises, but to recognize that in another factual scenario, with a differently drawn statute, maybe at a later time, something new may emerge, and not this "It always has been…" business, which even the most mundane among us could find to be repulsive. The Court constantly complains that it finds statutes failing to meet constitutional muster as having been insufficiently "tailored" so as to "not infringe unnecessarily" upon "freedoms" beyond that in which the "State has a legitimate interest," and yet at the same time can't do that for itself, and in the work it crafts here for the people whose real lives are affected, is simply contemptuous. The Court has legislated and re-legislated widely in the area of criminal law, and likewise civilly, including free speech, religion, the area of abortion, so too with jurisdiction, patents, procedure…and the list goes on. But not here, not in the case of a dying person wishing to exercise some personal choice regarding what life has visited. Now they can't seem to find either the needles or the thread let alone any whole cloth! Why? Why is this case devoid of any creativity for which the Court has now become so infamous? Or, was it simply sending a message of ineptitude to the Washington state legislature?

The filing of a hundred briefs on one side and a hundred briefs on the other indicates the conversation is emotional, political, and/or religious, not legal. Think about what true professional work should look like. Briefs should recognize that there are meritorious arguments both ways (or the matter wouldn't be here in the first place) and they are as follows…etc., that the writer of this particular brief takes the following position based on the facts (honest, true, demonstrable facts), with reasonable assumptions (that don't border on effrontery to either the bench or bar), and the rationale which is then employed and presented.

Honest briefs on legitimate issues for the Court's consideration will reflect some common ground. From that point it is up to the Court to decide the questions within the premises of the case. Assuming the Court crafts something rational, thoughtful, and considerate of all concerned, all are happy. It might not have gone the way one would have chosen, but all are happy. It can be accepted. All have won in a very real sense. The Court has done its job. If a review is desired, an opportunity will present itself in the future, a new set of facts may emerge, as the *zeitgeist* is ever evolving. Or, the Court will "evolve." Or, as here, the legislature will respond. But only so long as the Court acts judiciously are any of us able to live comfortably with its decisions, or even whatever legislation it attempts to pass, so long as it is judicious, deliberative, and graceful, something which admits of lacking, much too often. What was it we heard in the halls at one time, in the words of Oliver Wendell Holmes: "A law should fall if there is no better reason for its existence than it was passed during the reign of King Henry the Eighth"? That can't be right, that couldn't be it, for if it were, the United States Supreme Court would have never opened this opinion as it did...never! Utterly foolish on many fronts might one not conclude? If it did so consciously, or other than through the offices of human inadvertence, there appears to be the revelation of a psychic underpinning of intellectual ill repute.

Let not the result blind our thinking. Leaving this matter to the legislature(s) and voters is probably better, and certainly lawful.

This area of government is a wonderful social laboratory, and with its unique and ubiquitous fact-finding resources a great crucible allowing wisdom arising from experience to flourish. If it goes awry constitutionally, the courts may step in, make a review, and perhaps the whole matter is simply started over. But that is all it should do. Its jurisdiction reaches no further, unless there has been general acceptance of a change in the architecture of government as a result of institutional inaction or professional malaise, being nothing new. *Dicta* and precatory language are not law. They are in fact oppressive and smothering of constitutionally protected legislative authority at all levels, toxic impudence to the genius of the separation of powers, notwithstanding their common use by the Court.

The problem to be observed is with the Court's behavior. To only say it protests too much would be an inadequate undercutting of its looking to sources which are irrelevant, and failing to look at sources of which it is impliedly aware (the members would have to have been in a forty-year sleep to claim they didn't know the more private side of practices in the premises), or worse, they knew, and never asked questions to raise the related issues, which is also concerning. Families, with and without physicians, have been in this business of life and death, from its inception, to its very end, for as long as anyone in this country, or others, can remember, doing exactly what the Washington statute purportedly prohibits. Not a word. It wouldn't take much inquiry to get confirmation.

Unimaginable, but it happened (or didn't happen). Then the Court goes on to say in its convenient choice of wonderful words such as "our Nation's history, legal traditions, and practices" this (the statute) just can't stand. "Our conscience, our medical integrity and ethics, the mystery of life itself concludes upon us a result we simply cannot avoid," is flatly disingenuous, at best. Frank effrontery to all those for whom the Court works—an insult to the intelligence of all concerned. It could have been handled differently in spite of the Court's arguably sound election to take a hands off position.

Make note of the authorities which the Court references in its opinion and upon which it builds its conclusions, with air-sickness bag in hand. On the one hand, the Court has allowed the "euthanasia" [*sans* the painlessness] employing a lance inserted up under the dorsal aspect of the skull of a partially born child without its permission while denying the same medical service to mentally competent individuals wishing to end their life painlessly due to intractable suffering in a terminal state and who believe they have a meaningless existence. In logic terms, the reasoning the Court employs is neither valid nor sound, and is materially and logically fallacious (a *non sequitur*). Will this Court ever see the big picture (the unintended consequences)?

Carefully scrutinize Souter's concurring opinion. It bodes of things to come.

Anyway, strap on your I.V., Keemosahbee, the State of Washington against Glucksberg, and its future progeny, is about to begin: we will meet again back on the other side. Now, *Glucksberg*.

*

WASHINGTON ET AL. V. GLUCKSBERG ET AL.

521 U.S. 702

CERTIORARI TO THE UNITED STATES COURT OF APPEALS
FOR THE NINTH CIRCUIT

CHIEF JUSTICE REHNQUIST delivered the opinion of the Court.

The question presented in this case is whether Washington's prohibition against "caus[ing]" or "aid[ing]" a suicide offends the Fourteenth Amendment to the United States Constitution. We hold that it does not.

It has always been a crime to assist a suicide in the State of Washington.

* * *

Petitioners in this case are the State of Washington and its Attorney General. Respondents Harold Glucksberg, M. D., Abigail Halperin, M. D., Thomas A. Preston, M. D., and Peter Shalit, M. D., are physicians who practice in Washington. These doctors occasionally treat terminally ill, suffering patients, and declare that they would assist these patients in ending their lives if not for Washington's assisted-suicide ban. In January 1994, respondents, along with three gravely ill, pseudonymous plaintiffs who have since died and Compassion in Dying, a nonprofit organization that counsels people considering physician-assisted suicide, sued in the United States District Court, seeking a declaration that Wash. Rev. Code § 9A.36.060(1) (1994) is, on its face, unconstitutional.

The plaintiffs asserted "the existence of a liberty interest protected by the Fourteenth Amendment which extends to a personal choice by a mentally competent, terminally ill adult to commit physician-assisted suicide." Relying primarily on *Planned Parenthood of*

Southeastern Pa. v. *Casey*, 505 U.S. 833 (1992), and *Cruzan* v. *Director, Mo. Dept. of Health*, 497 U.S. 261 (1990), the District Court agreed, 850 F. Supp., at 1459-1462, and concluded that Washington's assisted-suicide ban is unconstitutional because it "places an undue burden on the exercise of [that] constitutionally protected liberty interest."

* * *

A panel of the Court of Appeals for the Ninth Circuit reversed, emphasizing that "[i]n the two hundred and five years of our existence no constitutional right to aid in killing oneself has ever been asserted and upheld by a court of final jurisdiction." *Compassion in Dying* v. *Washington*, 49 F. 3d 586, 591 (1995). The Ninth Circuit reheard the case en banc, reversed the panel's decision, and affirmed the District Court. *Compassion in Dying* v. *Washington*, 79 F. 3d 790, 798 (1996). Like the District Court, the en banc Court of Appeals emphasized our *Casey* and *Cruzan* decisions. 79 F. 3d, at 813-816. The court also discussed what it described as "historical" and "current societal attitudes" toward suicide and assisted suicide, *id.*, at 806-812, and concluded that "the Constitution encompasses a due process liberty interest in controlling the time and manner of one's death – that there is, in short, a constitutionally-recognized 'right to die.'" After "[w]eighing and then balancing" this interest against Washington's various interests, the court held that the State's assisted-suicide ban was unconstitutional "as applied to terminally ill competent adults who wish to hasten their deaths with medication prescribed by their physicians." ...We granted certiorari, 518 U.S. 1057 (1996), and now reverse.

I

We begin, as we do in all due process cases, by examining our Nation's history, legal traditions, and practices.... In almost every State – indeed, in almost every western democracy – it is a crime to assist a suicide. The States' assisted-suicide bans are not innovations. Rather, they are longstanding expressions of the States' commitment to the protection and preservation of all human life. *Cruzan, supra,* at 280 ("[T]he States – indeed, all civilized nations – demonstrate their commitment to life by treating homicide as a serious crime. Moreover, the majority of States in this country have laws imposing criminal penalties on one who assists another to commit suicide"); see *Stanford* v. *Kentucky,* 492 U.S. 361, 373 (1989) ("[T]he primary and most reliable indication of [a national] consensus is...the pattern of enacted laws"). Indeed, opposition to and condemnation of suicide – and, therefore, of assisting suicide – are consistent and enduring themes of our philosophical, legal, and cultural heritages....

More specifically, for over 700 years, the Anglo-American common-law tradition has punished or otherwise disapproved of both suicide and assisting suicide. In the 13th century, Henry de Bracton, one of the first legal-treatise writers, observed that "[j]ust as a man may commit felony by slaying another so may he do so by slaying himself." ...The real and personal property of one who killed himself to avoid conviction and punishment for a crime were forfeit to the King; however, thought Bracton, "if a man slays himself in weariness of life or because he is unwilling to endure further bodily pain...[only] his movable goods [were] confiscated." Thus, "[t]he principle that suicide of a sane person, for whatever reason, was a punishable felony was...introduced into English common law." Centuries later, Sir William Blackstone, whose Commentaries on the Laws of England not only provided a definitive summary of the common law but was also a primary legal authority for 18th- and 19th-century American lawyers, referred to suicide as "self-murder" and "the pretended heroism, but real cowardice, of the Stoic philosophers, who destroyed themselves to avoid those ills which they had not the fortitude to endure...." Blackstone emphasized that "the law has...ranked [suicide] among the highest crimes," although, anticipating later developments, he conceded that the harsh and shameful punishments imposed for suicide "borde[r] a little upon severity."

For the most part, the early American Colonies adopted the common-law approach.

* * *

Over time, however, the American Colonies abolished these harsh common-law penalties. William Penn abandoned the criminal-forfeiture sanction in Pennsylvania in 1701, and the other Colonies (and later, the other States) eventually followed this example. Zephaniah Swift, who would later become Chief Justice of Connecticut, wrote in 1796:

> "There can be no act more contemptible, than to attempt to punish an offender for a crime, by exercising a mean act of revenge upon lifeless clay, that is insensible of the punishment. There can be no greater cruelty, than the inflicting [of] a punishment, as the forfeiture of goods, which must fall solely on the innocent offspring of the offender.... [Suicide] is so abhorrent to the feelings of mankind, and that strong love of life which is implanted in the human heart, that it cannot be so frequently committed, as to become dangerous to society. There can of course be no necessity of any punishment."

This statement makes it clear, however, that the movement away from the common law's harsh sanctions did not represent an acceptance of suicide; rather, as Chief Justice Swift observed, this change reflected the growing consensus that it was unfair to punish the suicide's family for his wrongdoing. Nonetheless, although States moved away from Blackstone's treatment of suicide, courts continued to condemn it as a grave public wrong.

* * *

Though deeply rooted, the States' assisted-suicide bans have in recent years been reexamined and, generally, reaffirmed. Because of advances in medicine and technology, Americans today are increasingly likely to die in institutions, from chronic illnesses.... Public concern and democratic action are therefore sharply focused on how best to protect dignity and independence at the end of life, with the result that there have been many significant changes in state laws and in the attitudes these laws reflect. Many States, for example, now permit "living wills," surrogate health-care decisionmaking, and the withdrawal or refusal of life-sustaining medical treatment. At the same time, however, voters and legislators continue for the most part to reaffirm their States' prohibitions on assisting suicide.

The Washington statute at issue in this case was enacted in 1975 as part of a revision of that State's criminal code. Four years later, Washington passed its Natural Death Act, which specifically stated that the "withholding or withdrawal of life-sustaining treatment...shall not, for any purpose, constitute a suicide" and that "[n]othing in this chapter shall be construed to condone, authorize, or approve mercy killing...." In 1991, Washington voters rejected a ballot initiative which, had it passed, would have permitted a form of physician-assisted suicide....

California voters rejected an assisted-suicide initiative similar to Washington's in 1993. On the other hand, in 1994, voters in Oregon enacted, also through ballot initiative, that State's "Death With Dignity Act," which legalized physician-assisted suicide for competent, terminally ill adults. Since the Oregon vote, many proposals to legalize assisted-suicide have been and continue to be introduced in the States' legislatures, but none has been enacted. And just last year, Iowa and Rhode Island joined the overwhelming majority of States explicitly prohibiting assisted suicide....

Thus, the States are currently engaged in serious, thoughtful examinations of physician-assisted suicide and other similar issues. For example, New York State's Task Force on Life and the Law – an ongoing, blue-ribbon commission composed of doctors, ethicists, lawyers, religious leaders, and interested laymen – was convened in 1984 and commissioned with "a broad mandate to recommend public policy on issues raised by medical advances." Over the past decade, the Task Force has recommended laws relating to end-of-life decisions, surrogate pregnancy, and organ donation. After studying physician-assisted suicide, however, the Task Force unanimously concluded that "[l]egalizing assisted suicide and euthanasia would pose profound risks to many individuals who are ill and vulnerable.... [T]he potential dangers of this dramatic change in public policy would outweigh any benefit that might be achieved."

Attitudes toward suicide itself have changed since Bracton, but our laws have consistently condemned, and continue to prohibit, assisting suicide. Despite changes in medical technology and notwithstanding an increased emphasis on the importance of end-of-life decisionmaking, we have not retreated from this prohibition. Against this backdrop of history, tradition, and practice, we now turn to respondents' constitutional claim.

II

The Due Process Clause guarantees more than fair process, and the "liberty" it protects includes more than the absence of physical restraint. *Collins* v. *Harker Heights*, 503 U.S. 115, 125 (1992) (Due Process Clause "protects individual liberty against 'certain government actions regardless of the fairness of the procedures used to implement them'") (quoting *Daniels* v. *Williams*, 474 U.S. 327, 331 (1986)). The Clause also provides heightened protection against government interference with certain fundamental rights and liberty interests. *Reno* v. *Flores*, 507 U.S. 292, 301-302 (1993); *Casey*, 505 U.S., at 851. In a long line of cases, we have held that, in addition to the specific freedoms protected by the Bill of Rights, the "liberty" specially protected by the Due Process Clause includes the rights to marry, *Loving* v. *Virginia*, 388 U.S. 1 (1967); to have children, *Skinner* v. *Oklahoma ex rel. Williamson*, 316 U.S. 535 (1942); to direct the education and upbringing of one's children, *Meyer* v. *Nebraska*, 262 U.S. 390 (1923); *Pierce* v. *Society of Sisters*, 268 U.S. 510 (1925); to marital privacy, *Griswold* v. *Connecticut*, 381 U.S. 479 (1965); to use contraception, *ibid.*; *Eisenstadt* v. *Baird*, 405 U.S. 438 (1972); to bodily integrity, *Rochin* v. *California*, 342 U.S. 165 (1952), and to abortion, *Casey, supra.* We have also assumed, and strongly suggested, that the Due Process Clause protects the traditional right to refuse unwanted lifesaving medical treatment. *Cruzan*, 497 U.S., at 278-279.

But we "ha[ve] always been reluctant to expand the concept of substantive due process because guideposts for responsible decisionmaking in this unchartered area are scarce and open-ended." *Collins*, 503 U.S., at 125. By extending constitutional protection to an asserted right or liberty interest, we, to a great extent, place the matter outside the arena of public debate and legislative action. We must therefore "exercise the utmost care whenever we are asked to break new ground in this field," lest the liberty protected by the Due Process Clause be subtly transformed into the policy preferences of the Members of this Court, *Moore*, 431 U.S. at 502 (plurality opinion).

Our established method of substantive-due-process analysis has two primary features: First, we have regularly observed that the Due Process Clause specially protects those fundamental rights and liberties which are, objectively, "deeply rooted in this Nation's history and tradition," *id.*, at 503 (plurality opinion); *Snyder* v. *Massachusetts*, 291 U.S. 97, 105 (1934) ("so rooted in the traditions and conscience of our people as to be ranked as fundamental"), and "implicit in the concept of ordered liberty," such that "neither liberty nor justice would exist if they were sacrificed," *Palko* v. *Connecticut*, 302 U.S. 319, 325, 326 (1937).

Second, we have required in substantive-due-process cases a "careful description" of the asserted fundamental liberty interest. *Flores, supra,* at 302; *Collins, supra,* at 125; *Cruzan, supra,* at 277-278. Our Nation's history, legal traditions, and practices thus provide the crucial "guideposts for responsible decisionmaking," *Collins, supra,* at 125, that direct and restrain our exposition of the Due Process Clause. As we stated recently in *Flores,* the Fourteenth Amendment "forbids the government to infringe...'fundamental' liberty interests *at all,* no matter what process is provided, unless the infringement is narrowly tailored to serve a compelling state interest." 507 U.S., at 302.

* * *

In our view, the development of this Court's substantive-due-process jurisprudence has been a process whereby the outlines of the "liberty" specially protected by the Fourteenth Amendment – never fully clarified, to be sure, and perhaps not capable of being fully clarified – have at least been carefully refined by concrete examples involving fundamental rights found to be deeply rooted in our legal tradition. This approach tends to rein in the subjective elements that are necessarily present in due process judicial review. In addition, by establishing a threshold requirement – that a challenged state action implicate a fundamental right – before requiring more than a reasonable relation to a legitimate state interest to justify the action, it avoids the need for complex balancing of competing interests in every case.

Turning to the claim at issue here, the Court of Appeals stated that "[p]roperly analyzed, the first issue to be resolved is whether there is a liberty interest in determining the time and manner of one's death," 79 F. 3d, at 801, or, in other words, "[i]s there a right to die?," *id.,* at 799.... [A]lthough *Cruzan* is often described as a "right to die" case, (Stevens, J., concurring in judgments) (*Cruzan* recognized "the more specific interest in making decisions about how to confront an imminent death"), we were, in fact, more precise: We assumed that the Constitution granted competent persons a "constitutionally protected right to refuse life-saving hydration and nutrition." The Washington statute at issue in this case prohibits "aid[ing] another person to attempt suicide," Wash. Rev. Code § 9A.36.060(1) (1994), and, thus, the question before us is whether the "liberty" specially protected by the Due Process Clause includes a right to commit suicide which itself includes a right to assistance in doing so.

We now inquire whether this asserted right has any place in our Nation's traditions.... [W]e are confronted with a consistent and almost universal tradition that has long rejected the asserted right, and continues explicitly to reject it today, even for terminally ill, mentally competent adults. To hold for respondents, we would have to reverse centuries of legal doctrine and practice, and strike down the considered policy choice of almost every State. See *Jackman* v. *Rosenbaum Co.*, 260 U.S. 22, 31 (1922) ("If a thing has been practiced for two hundred years by common consent, it will need a strong case for the Fourteenth Amendment to affect it"); *Flores*, 507 U.S., at 303 ("The mere novelty of such a claim is reason enough to doubt that 'substantive due process' sustains it").

Respondents contend, however, that the liberty interest they assert *is* consistent with this Court's substantive-due-process line of cases, if not with this Nation's history and practice. Pointing to *Casey* and *Cruzan*, respondents read our jurisprudence in this area as reflecting a general tradition of "self-sovereignty," and as teaching that the "liberty" protected by the Due Process Clause includes "basic and intimate exercises of personal autonomy." ...According to respondents, our liberty jurisprudence, and the broad, individualistic principles it reflects, protects the "liberty of competent, terminally ill adults to make end-of-life decisions free of undue government interference." The question presented in this case, however, is whether the protections of the Due Process Clause include a right to commit suicide with another's assistance. With this "careful description" of respondents' claim in mind, we turn to *Casey* and *Cruzan.*

In *Cruzan,* we considered whether Nancy Beth Cruzan, who had been severely injured in an automobile accident and was in a persistive vegetative state, "ha[d] a right under the United States Constitution which would require the hospital to withdraw life-sustaining treatment" at her parents' request. 497 U.S., at 269. We began with the observation that "[a]t common law, even the touching of one person by another without consent and without legal justification was a battery." We then discussed the related rule that "informed consent is generally required for medical treatment." After reviewing a long line of relevant state cases, we concluded that "the common-law doctrine of informed consent is viewed as generally encompassing the right of a competent individual to refuse medical treatment." Next, we reviewed our own cases on the subject, and stated that "[t]he principle that a competent person has a constitutionally protected liberty interest in refusing unwanted medical treatment may be inferred from our prior decisions." Therefore, "for purposes of [that] case, we assume[d] that the United States Constitution would grant a competent person a constitutionally protected right to refuse lifesaving hydration and nutrition." We concluded that, notwithstanding this right, the Constitution permitted Missouri to require clear and convincing evidence of an incompetent patient's wishes concerning the withdrawal of life-sustaining treatment.

Respondents contend that in *Cruzan* we "acknowledged that competent, dying persons have the right to direct the removal of life-sustaining medical treatment and thus hasten death," and that "the constitutional principle behind recognizing the patient's liberty to direct the withdrawal of artificial life support applies at least as strongly to the choice to hasten impending death by consuming lethal medication." Similarly, the Court of Appeals concluded that "*Cruzan,* by recognizing a liberty interest that includes the refusal of artificial provision of life-sustaining food and water, necessarily recognize[d] a liberty interest in hastening one's own death."

The right assumed in *Cruzan*, however, was not simply deduced from abstract concepts of personal autonomy. Given the common-law rule that forced medication was a battery, and the long legal tradition protecting the decision to refuse unwanted medical treatment, our assumption was entirely consistent with this Nation's history and constitutional traditions. The decision to commit suicide with the assistance of another may be just as personal and profound as the decision to refuse unwanted medical treatment, but it has never enjoyed similar legal protection. Indeed, the two acts are widely and reasonably regarded as quite distinct. In *Cruzan* itself, we recognized that most States outlawed assisted suicide – and even more do today – and we certainly gave no intimation that the right to refuse unwanted medical treatment could be somehow transmuted into a right to assistance in committing suicide.

Respondents also rely on *Casey*.

* * *

[T]he opinion discussed in some detail this Court's substantive-due-process tradition of interpreting the Due Process Clause to protect certain fundamental rights and "personal decisions relating to marriage, procreation, contraception, family relationships, child rearing, and education," and noted that many of those rights and liberties "involv[e] the most intimate and personal choices a person may make in a lifetime."

The Court of Appeals, like the District Court, found *Casey* "'highly instructive'" and "'almost prescriptive'" for determining "'what liberty interest may inhere in a terminally ill person's choice to commit suicide'":

> "Like the decision of whether or not to have an abortion, the decision how and when to die is one of 'the most intimate and personal choices a person may make in a lifetime,' a choice 'central to personal dignity and autonomy.'" 79 F. 3d, at 813-814.

Similarly, respondents emphasize the statement in *Casey* that:

> "At the heart of liberty is the right to define one's own concept of existence, of meaning, of the universe, and of the mystery of human life. Beliefs about these matters could not define the attributes of personhood were they formed under compulsion of the State." 505 U.S., at 851.

By choosing this language, the Court's opinion in *Casey* described, in a general way and in light of our prior cases, those personal activities and decisions that this Court has identified as so deeply rooted in our history and traditions, or so fundamental to our concept of constitutionally ordered liberty, that they are protected by the Fourteenth Amendment. The opinion moved from the recognition that liberty necessarily includes freedom of conscience and belief about ultimate considerations to the observation that "though the abortion decision may originate within the zone of conscience and belief, it is *more than a philosophic exercise.*" That many of the rights and liberties protected by the Due Process Clause found in personal autonomy does not warrant the sweeping conclusion that any and all important, intimate, and personal decisions are so protected, and *Casey* did not suggest otherwise.

The history of the law's treatment of assisted suicide in this country has been and continues to be one of the rejection of nearly all efforts to permit it. That being the case, our decisions lead us to conclude that the asserted "right" to assistance in committing suicide is not a fundamental liberty interest protected by the Due Process Clause.

* * *

First, Washington has an "unqualified interest in the preservation of human life."

* * *

Relatedly, all admit that suicide is a serious public-health problem....

Those who attempt suicide – terminally ill or not – often suffer from depression or other mental disorders....

The State also has an interest in protecting the integrity and ethics of the medical profession....

Next, the State has an interest in protecting vulnerable groups – including the poor, the elderly, and disabled persons – from abuse, neglect, and mistakes....

The State's interest here goes beyond protecting the vulnerable from coercion; it extends to protecting disabled and terminally ill people from prejudice, negative and inaccurate stereotypes, and "societal indifference"....

Finally, the State may fear that permitting assisted suicide will start it down the path to voluntary and perhaps even involuntary euthanasia.

* * *

We need not weigh exactingly the relative strengths of these various interests. They are unquestionably important and legitimate, and Washington's ban on assisted suicide is at least reasonably related to their promotion and protection. We therefore hold that Wash. Rev. Code § 9A.36.060(1) (1994) does not violate the Fourteenth Amendment, either on its face or "as applied to competent, terminally ill adults who wish to hasten their deaths by obtaining medication prescribed by their doctors."

* * *

Throughout the Nation, Americans are engaged in an earnest and profound debate about the morality, legality, and practicality of physician-assisted suicide. Our holding permits this debate to continue, as it should in a democratic society. The decision of the en banc Court of Appeals is reversed, and the case is remanded for further proceedings consistent with this opinion.

JUSTICE O'CONNOR, concurring.

* * *

The difficulty in defining terminal illness and the risk that a dying patient's request for assistance in ending his or her life might not be truly voluntary justifies the prohibitions on assisted suicide we uphold here.

JUSTICE STEVENS, concurring in the judgments.

The Court ends its opinion with the important observation that our holding today is fully consistent with a continuation of the vigorous debate about the "morality, legality, and practicality of physician-assisted suicide" in a democratic society. I write separately to make it clear that there is also room for further debate about the limits that the Constitution places on the power of the States to punish the practice.

I

* * *

History and tradition provide ample support for refusing to recognize an open-ended constitutional right to commit suicide. Much more than the State's paternalistic interest in protecting the individual from the irrevocable consequences of an ill-advised decision motivated by temporary concerns is at stake. There is truth in John Donne's observation that "No man is an island." The State has an interest in preserving and fostering the benefits that every human being may provide to the community – a community that thrives on the exchange of ideas, expressions of affection, shared memories, and humorous incidents, as well as on the material contributions that its members create and support. The value to others of a person's life is far too precious to allow the individual to claim a constitutional entitlement to complete autonomy in making a decision to end that life. Thus, I fully agree with the Court that the "liberty" protected by the Due Process Clause does not include a categorical "right to commit suicide which itself includes a right to assistance in doing so."

But just as our conclusion that capital punishment is not always unconstitutional did not preclude later decisions holding that it is sometimes impermissibly cruel, so is it equally clear that a decision upholding a general statutory prohibition of assisted suicide does not mean that every possible application of the statute would be valid. A State, like Washington, that has authorized the death penalty, and thereby has concluded that the sanctity of human life does not require that it always be preserved, must acknowledge that there are situations in which an interest in hastening death is legitimate. Indeed, not only is that interest sometimes legitimate, I am also convinced that there are times when it is entitled to constitutional protection.

* * *

IV

In New York, a doctor must respect a competent person's decision to refuse or to discontinue medical treatment even though death will thereby ensue, but the same doctor would be guilty of a felony if she provided her patient assistance in committing suicide. Today we hold that the Equal Protection Clause is not violated by the resulting disparate treatment of two classes of terminally ill people who may have the same interest in hastening death. I agree that the distinction between permitting death to ensue from an underlying fatal disease and causing it to occur by the administration of medication or other means provides a constitutionally sufficient basis for the State's classification. Unlike the Court, however, I am not persuaded that in all cases there will in fact be a significant difference between the intent of the physicians, the patients, or the families in the two situations.

There may be little distinction between the intent of a terminally ill patient who decides to remove her life support and one who seeks the assistance of a doctor in ending her life; in both situations, the patient is seeking to hasten a certain, impending death. The doctor's intent might also be the same in prescribing lethal medication as it is in terminating life support. A doctor who fails to administer medical treatment to one who is dying from a disease could be doing so with an intent to harm or kill that patient. Conversely, a doctor who prescribes lethal medication does not necessarily intend the patient's death – rather that doctor may seek simply to ease the patient's suffering and to comply with her wishes. The illusory character of any differences in intent or causation is confirmed by the fact that the American Medical Association unequivocally endorses the practice of terminal sedation – the administration of sufficient dosages of pain-killing medication to terminally ill patients to protect them from excruciating pain even when it is clear that the time of death will be advanced. The purpose of terminal sedation is to ease the suffering of the patient and comply with her wishes, and the actual cause of death is the administration of heavy doses of lethal sedatives. This same intent and causation may exist when a doctor complies with a patient's request for lethal medication to hasten her death.

Thus, although the differences the majority notes in causation and intent between terminating life support and assisting in suicide support the Court's rejection of the respondents' facial challenge, these distinctions may be inapplicable to particular terminally ill patients and their doctors. Our holding today in *Vacco* v. *Quill,* that the Equal Protection Clause is not violated by New York's classification, just like our holding in *Washington* v. *Glucksberg* that the Washington statute is not invalid on its face, does not foreclose the possibility that some applications of the New York statute may impose an intolerable intrusion on the patient's freedom.

There remains room for vigorous debate about the outcome of particular cases that are not necessarily resolved by the opinions announced today. How such cases may be decided will depend on their specific facts. In my judgment, however, it is clear that the so-called "unqualified interest in the preservation of human life," *Cruzan,* 497 U.S., at 282; *ante,* at 728, is not itself sufficient to outweigh the interest in liberty that may justify the only possible means of preserving a dying patient's dignity and alleviating her intolerable suffering.

JUSTICE SOUTER, concurring in the judgment.

Three terminally ill individuals and four physicians who sometimes treat terminally ill patients brought this challenge to the Washington statute making it a crime "knowingly...[to] ai[d] another person to attempt suicide," claiming on behalf of both patients and physicians that it would violate substantive due process to enforce the statute against a doctor who acceded to a dying patient's request for a drug to be taken by the patient to commit suicide. The question is whether the statute sets up one of those "arbitrary impositions" or "purposeless restraints" at odds with the Due Process Clause of the Fourteenth Amendment. I conclude that the statute's application to the doctors has not been shown to be unconstitutional, but I write separately to give my reasons for analyzing the substantive due process claims as I do, and for rejecting this one.

I

Although the terminally ill original parties have died during the pendency of this case, the four physicians who remain as respondents here continue to request declaratory and injunctive relief for their own benefit in discharging their obligations to other dying patients who request their help. The case reaches us on an order granting summary judgment, and we must take as true the undisputed allegations that each of the patients was mentally competent and terminally ill, and that each made a knowing and voluntary choice to ask a doctor to prescribe "medications...to be self-administered for the purpose of hastening...death." The State does not dispute that each faced a passage to death more agonizing both mentally and physically, and more protracted over time, than death by suicide with a physician's help, or that each would have chosen such a suicide for the sake of personal dignity, apart even from relief from pain. Each doctor in this case claims to encounter patients like the original plaintiffs who have died, that is, mentally competent, terminally ill, and seeking medical help in "the voluntary self-termination of life." While there may be no unanimity on the physician's professional obligation in such circumstances, I accept here respondents' representation that providing such patients with prescriptions for drugs that go beyond pain relief to hasten death would, in these circumstances, be consistent with standards of medical practice. Hence, I take it to be true, as respondents say, that the Washington statute prevents the exercise of a physician's "best professional judgment to prescribe medications to [such] patients in dosages that would enable them to act to hasten their own deaths."

In their brief to this Court, the doctors claim not that they ought to have a right generally to hasten patients' imminent deaths, but only to help patients who have made "personal decisions regarding their own bodies, medical care, and, fundamentally, the future course of their lives," and who have concluded responsibly and with substantial justification that the brief and anguished remainders of their lives have lost virtually all value to them....

In response, the State argues that the interest asserted by the doctors is beyond constitutional recognition because it has no deep roots in our history and traditions. But even aside from that, without disputing that the patients here were competent and terminally ill, the State insists that recognizing the legitimacy of doctors' assistance of their patients as contemplated here would entail a number of adverse consequences that the Washington Legislature was entitled to forestall. The nub of this part of the State's argument is not that such patients are constitutionally undeserving of relief on their own account, but that any attempt to confine a right of physician assistance to the circumstances presented by these doctors is likely to fail.

First, the State argues that the right could not be confined to the terminally ill. Even assuming a fixed definition of that term, the State observes that it is not always possible to say with certainty how long a person may live. . . . Second, the State argues that the right could not be confined to the mentally competent, observing that a person's competence cannot always be assessed with certainty, and suggesting further that no principled distinction is possible between a competent patient acting independently and a patient acting through a duly appointed and competent surrogate. Next, according to the State, such a right might entail a right to or at least merge in practice into "other forms of life-ending assistance," such as euthanasia. Finally, the State believes that a right to physician assistance could not easily be distinguished from a right to assistance from others, such as friends, family, and other health-care workers. The State thus argues that recognition of the substantive due process right at issue here would jeopardize the lives of others outside the class defined by the doctors' claim, creating risks of irresponsible suicides and euthanasia, whose dangers are concededly within the State's authority to address.

* * *

IV

A

Respondents claim that a patient facing imminent death, who anticipates physical suffering and indignity, and is capable of responsible and voluntary choice, should have a right to a physician's assistance in providing counsel and drugs to be administered by the patient to end life promptly. They accordingly claim that a physician must have the corresponding right to provide such aid, contrary to the provisions of Wash. Rev. Code § 9A.36.060 (1994). I do not understand the argument to rest on any assumption that rights either to suicide or to assistance in committing it are historically based as such. Respondents, rather, acknowledge the prohibition of each historically, but rely on the fact that to a substantial extent the State has repudiated that history. The result of this, respondents say, is to open the door to claims of such a patient to be accorded one of the options open to those with different, traditionally cognizable claims to autonomy in deciding how their bodies and minds should be treated. They seek the option to obtain the services of a physician to give them the benefit of advice and medical help, which is said to enjoy a tradition so strong and so devoid of specifically countervailing state concern that denial of a physician's help in these circumstances is arbitrary when physicians are generally free to advise and aid those who exercise other rights to bodily autonomy.

1

The dominant western legal codes long condemned suicide and treated either its attempt or successful accomplishment as a crime, the one subjecting the individual to penalties, the other penalizing his survivors by designating the suicide's property as forfeited to the government.... While suicide itself has generally not been considered a punishable crime in the United States, largely because the common-law punishment of forfeiture was rejected as improperly penalizing an innocent family, most States have consistently punished the act of assisting a suicide as either a common-law or statutory crime and some continue to view suicide as an unpunishable crime. Criminal prohibitions on such assistance remain widespread, as exemplified in the Washington statute in question here.

The principal significance of this history in the State of Washington, according to respondents, lies in its repudiation of the old tradition to the extent of eliminating the criminal suicide prohibitions. Respondents do not argue that the State's decision goes further, to imply that the State has repudiated any legitimate claim to discourage suicide or to limit its encouragement. The reasons for the decriminalization, after all, may have had more to do with difficulties of law enforcement than with a shift in the value ascribed to life in various circumstances or in the perceived legitimacy of taking one's own.... Thus it may indeed make sense for the State to take its hands off suicide as such, while continuing to prohibit the sort of assistance that would make its commission easier.... Decriminalization does not, then, imply the existence of a constitutional liberty interest in suicide as such; it simply opens the door to the assertion of a cognizable liberty interest in bodily integrity and associated medical care that would otherwise have been inapposite so long as suicide, as well as assisting a suicide, was a criminal offense.

This liberty interest in bodily integrity was phrased in a general way by then-Judge Cardozo when he said, "[e]very human being of adult years and sound mind has a right to determine what shall be done with his own body" in relation to his medical needs. *Schloendorff* v. *Society of New York Hospital*, 211 N. Y. 125, 129, 105 N. E. 92, 93 (1914). The familiar examples of this right derive from the common law of battery and include the right to be free from medical invasions into the body, *Cruzan* v. *Director, Mo. Dept. of Health*, 497 U.S., at 269-279.... Thus "[i]t is settled now...that the Constitution places limits on a State's right to interfere with a person's most basic decisions about . . . bodily integrity." *Casey*, 505 U.S., at 849.... Constitutional recognition of the right to bodily integrity underlies the assumed right, good against the State, to require physicians to terminate artificial life support,...and the affirmative right to obtain medical intervention to cause abortion....

It is, indeed, in the abortion cases that the most telling recognitions of the importance of bodily integrity and the concomitant tradition of medical assistance have occurred. In *Roe* v. *Wade*, the plaintiff contended that the Texas statute making it criminal for an person to "procure an abortion"...for a pregnant woman was unconstitutional insofar as it prevented her from "terminat[ing] her pregnancy by an abortion 'performed by a competent, licensed physician, under safe, clinical conditions'"...and in striking down the statute we stressed the importance of the relationship between patient and physician....

The analogies between the abortion cases and this one are several. Even though the State has a legitimate interest in discouraging abortion, the Court recognized a woman's right to a physician's counsel and care. Like the decision to commit suicide, the decision to abort potential life can be made irresponsibly and under the influence of others, and yet the Court has held in the abortion cases that physicians are fit assistants. Without physician assistance in abortion, the woman's right would have too often amounted to nothing more than a right to self-mutilation, and without a physician to assist in the suicide of the dying, the patient's right will often be confined to crude methods of causing death, most shocking and painful to the decedent's survivors.

There is, finally, one more reason for claiming that a physician's assistance here would fall within the accepted tradition of medical care in our society, and the abortion cases are only the most obvious illustration of the further point. While the Court has held that the performance of abortion procedures can be restricted to physicians, the Court's opinion in *Roe* recognized the doctors' role in yet another way. For, in the course of holding that the decision to perform an abortion called for a physician's assistance, the Court recognized the good physician is not just a mechanic of the human body whose services have no bearing on a person's moral choices, but one who does more than treat symptoms, one who ministers to the patient.... This idea of the physician as serving the whole person is a source of the high value traditionally placed on the medical relationship. Its value is surely as apparent here as in the abortion cases, for just as the decision about abortion is not directed to correcting some pathology, so the decision in which a dying patient seeks help is not so limited. The patients here sought not only an end to pain (which they might have had, although perhaps at the price of stupor) but an end to their short remaining lives with a dignity that they believed would be denied them by powerful pain medication, as well as by their consciousness of dependency and helplessness as they approached death. In that period when the end is imminent, they said, the decision to end life is closest to decisions that are generally accepted as proper instances of exercising autonomy over one's own body, instances recognized under the Constitution and the State's own law, instances in which the help of physicians is accepted as falling within the traditional norm.

Respondents argue that the State has in fact already recognized enough evolving examples of this tradition of patient care to demonstrate the strength of their claim. Washington, like other States, authorizes physicians to withdraw life-sustaining medical treatment and artificially delivered food and water from patients who request it, even though such actions will hasten death.... The State permits physicians to alleviate anxiety and discomfort when withdrawing artificial life-supporting devices by administering medication that will hasten death even further. And it generally permits physicians to administer medication to patients in terminal conditions when the primary intent is to alleviate pain, even when the medication is so powerful as to hasten death and the patient chooses to receive it with that understanding.

2

* * *

Respondents base their claim on the traditional right to medical care and counsel, subject to the limiting conditions of informed, responsible choice when death is imminent, conditions that support a strong analogy to rights of care in other situations in which medical counsel and assistance have been available as a matter of course. There can be no stronger claim to a physician's assistance than at the time when death is imminent, a moral judgment implied by the State's own recognition of the legitimacy of medical procedures necessarily hastening the moment of impending death.

In my judgment, the importance of the individual interest here, as within that class of "certain interests" demanding careful scrutiny of the State's contrary claim . . . cannot be gainsaid. Whether that interest might in some circumstances, or at some time, be seen as "fundamental" to the degree entitled to prevail is not, however, a conclusion that I need draw here, for I am satisfied that the State's interests described in the following section are sufficiently serious to defeat the present claim that its law is arbitrary or purposeless.

B

The State has put forward several interests to justify the Washington law as applied to physicians treating terminally ill patients, even those competent to make responsible choices: protecting life generally, discouraging suicide even if knowing and voluntary, and protecting terminally ill patients from involuntary suicide and euthanasia, both voluntary and nonvoluntary....

It is not necessary to discuss the exact strengths of the first two claims of justification in the present circumstances, for the third is dispositive for me. That third justification is different from the first two, for it addresses specific features of respondents' claim, and it opposes that claim not with a moral judgment contrary to respondents', but with a recognized state interest in the protection of nonresponsible individuals and those who do not stand in relation either to death or to their physicians as do the patients whom respondents describe. The State claims interests in protecting patients from mistakenly and involuntarily deciding to end their lives, and in guarding against both voluntary and involuntary euthanasia. Leaving aside any difficulties in coming to a clear concept of imminent death, mistaken decisions may result from inadequate palliative care or a terminal prognosis that turns out to be error; coercion and abuse may stem from the large medical bills that family members cannot bear or unreimbursed hospitals decline to shoulder. Voluntary and involuntary euthanasia may result once doctors are authorized to prescribe lethal medication in the first instance, for they might find it pointless to distinguish between patients who administer their own fatal drugs and those who wish not to, and their compassion for those who suffer may obscure the distinction between those who ask for death and those who may be unable to request it. The argument is that a progression would occur, obscuring the line between the ill and the dying, and between the responsible and the unduly influenced, until ultimately doctors and perhaps others would abuse a limited freedom to aid suicides by yielding to the impulse to end another's suffering under conditions going beyond the narrow limits the respondents propose. The State thus argues, essentially, that respondents' claim is not as narrow as it sounds, simply because no recognition of the interest they assert could be limited to vindicating those interests and affecting no others. The State says that the claim, in practical effect, would entail consequences that the State could, without doubt, legitimately act to prevent.

The mere assertion that the terminally sick might be pressured into suicide decisions by close friends and family members would not alone be very telling. Of course that is possible, not only because the costs of care might be more than family members could bear but simply because they might naturally wish to see an end of suffering for someone they love. But one of the points of restricting any right of assistance to physicians would be to condition the right on an exercise of judgment by someone qualified to assess the patient's responsible capacity and detect the influence of those outside the medical relationship.

The State, however, goes further, to argue that dependence on the vigilance of physicians will not be enough. First, the lines proposed here (particularly the requirement of a knowing and voluntary decision by the patient) would be more difficult to draw than the lines that have limited other recently recognized due process rights. . . . But the knowing and responsible mind is harder to assess. Second, this difficulty could become the greater by combining with another fact within the realm of plausibility, that physicians simply would not be assiduous to preserve the line. They have compassion, and those who would be willing to assist in suicide at all might be the most susceptible to the wishes of a patient, whether the patient was technically quite responsible or not. Physicians, and their hospitals, have their own financial incentives, too, in this new age of managed care. Whether acting from compassion or under some other influence, a physician who would provide a drug for a patient to administer might well go the further step of administering the drug himself; so, the barrier between assisted suicide and euthanasia could become porous, and the line between voluntary and involuntary euthanasia as well. The case for the slippery slope is fairly made out here, not because recognizing one due process right would leave a court with no principled basis to avoid recognizing another, but because there is a plausible case that the right claimed would not be readily containable by reference to facts about the mind that are matters of difficult judgment, or by gatekeepers who are subject to temptation, noble or not.

Respondents propose an answer to all this, the answer of state regulation with teeth. Legislation proposed in several States, for example, would authorize physician-assisted suicide but require two qualified physicians to confirm the patient's diagnosis, prognosis, and competence; and would mandate that the patient make repeated requests witnessed by at least two others over a specified timespan; and would impose reporting requirements and criminal penalties for various acts of coercion.

But at least at this moment there are reasons for caution in predicting the effectiveness of the teeth proposed.... The day may come when we can say with some assurance which side is right, but for now it is the substantiality of the factual disagreement, and the alternatives for resolving it, that matter. They are, for me, dispositive of the due process claim at this time.

I take it that the basic concept of judicial review with its possible displacement of legislative judgment bars any finding that a legislature has acted arbitrarily when the following conditions are met: there is a serious factual controversy over the feasibility of recognizing the claimed right without at the same time making it impossible for the State to engage in an undoubtedly legitimate exercise of power; facts necessary to resolve the controversy are not readily ascertainable through the judicial process; but they are more readily subject to discovery through legislative factfinding and experimentation. It is assumed in this case, and must be, that a State's interest in protecting those unable to make responsible decisions and those who make no decisions at all entitles the State to bar aid to any but a knowing and responsible person intending suicide, and to prohibit euthanasia. How, and how far, a State should act in that interest are judgments for the State, but the legitimacy of its action to deny a physician the option to aid any but the knowing and responsible is beyond question.

* * *

Legislatures...have superior opportunities to obtain the facts necessary for a judgment about the present controversy. Not only do they have more flexible mechanisms for factfinding than the Judiciary, but their mechanisms include the power to experiment, moving forward and pulling back as facts emerge within their own jurisdictions. There is, indeed, good reason to suppose that in the absence of a judgment for respondents here, just such experimentation will be attempted in some of the States.

...Now, it is enough to say that our examination of legislative reasonableness should consider the fact that the Legislature of the State of Washington is no more obviously at fault than this Court is in being uncertain about what would happen if respondents prevailed today. We therefore have a clear question about which institution, a legislature or a court, is relatively more competent to deal with an emerging issue as to which facts currently unknown could be dispositive. The answer has to be, for the reasons already stated, that the legislative process is to be preferred. There is a closely related further reason as well.

One must bear in mind that the nature of the right claimed, if recognized as one constitutionally required, would differ in no essential way from other constitutional rights guaranteed by enumeration or derived from some more definite textual source than "due process." An unenumerated right should not therefore be recognized, with the effect of displacing the legislative ordering of things, without the assurance that its recognition would prove as durable as the recognition of those other rights differently derived. To recognize a right of lesser promise would simply create a constitutional regime too uncertain to bring with it the expectation of finality that is one of this Court's central obligations in making constitutional decisions.

Legislatures, however, are not so constrained. The experimentation that should be out of the question in constitutional adjudication displacing legislative judgments is entirely proper, as well as highly desirable, when the legislative power addresses an emerging issue like assisted suicide. The Court should accordingly stay its hand to allow reasonable legislative consideration. While I do not decide for all time that respondents' claim should not be recognized, I acknowledge the legislative institutional competence as the better one to deal with that claim at this time.

JUSTICE GINSBURG, concurring in the judgments.

I concur in the Court's judgments in these cases substantially for the reasons stated by JUSTICE O'CONNOR in her concurring opinion.

JUSTICE BREYER, concurring in the judgments.

* * *

I agree with the Court...that the articulated state interests justify the distinction drawn between physician assisted suicide and withdrawal of life support. I also agree with the Court that the critical question in both of the cases before us is whether "the 'liberty' specially protected by the Due Process Clause includes a right" of the sort that the respondents assert. I do not agree, however, with the Court's formulation of that claimed "liberty" interest. The Court describes it as a "right to commit suicide with another's assistance." But I would not reject the respondents' claim without considering a different formulation, for which our legal tradition may provide greater support. That formulation would use words roughly like a "right to die with dignity." But irrespective of the exact words used, at its core would lie personal control over the manner of death, professional medical assistance, and the avoidance of unnecessary and severe physical suffering – combined.

*

Any thoughts about the excerpts from Souter's opinion? A surprise for many. Was he trying to pave the road ahead while still concurring with the majority, again, possibly the wrong case at the wrong time? If you think back to the introduction of this particular case and then observe coming through what he could finally muster, parenthetically speaking: "We have the wrong statute here, we weren't presented that with which we really needed to work, we have the wrong parties, and maybe it has reached us at the wrong time...." It would have been much more professional, much more jurisprudential, much more deliberative and balanced to open with such thoughts instead of the lead language of the majority opinion blathering "It has always been a crime..." which is tantamount to saying "it has always been that way," a pathetically foolish way to open any kind of intellectual discourse particularly in the realm of law, not to mention a setting so sensitive, and then to immediately follow at Roman numeral I with "We begin, as we do in all due process cases, by examining our nation's history, legal traditions and practices." Really? Think back.

Apparently it was never adequately brought to the Court's attention what goes on behind the scenes in the practice of medicine where truth dwells, nor was it observed *sua sponte*, as the Court is not reluctant to do when convenient to reach an end. One might see a hint of this reality in the "penumbra" of Souter's concurrence. But, for the majority to drown its position in a concrete encasement of rhetoric is not what one might see as robust and circumspect analysis, something reasonable men would not likely countenance, not that there aren't fans. However, whatever anyone's belief may be (and that is how this case was handled by its scrivener), this matter is still in its developmental stage in a world that's a-changing. Now, in the way of charity and mercy (recognized terms of equity practice), the Court may have been ham-handed because the plaintiffs/respondents as noted came into the courts ham-handed *ab initio*, with a ham-handed statute (but one cannot avoid taking notice plaintiffs won [including an *en banc* hearing before the United States Circuit Court of Appeals for the Ninth Circuit], then all the way up to SCOTUS where they were reversed).

Rehnquist was known from time to time to ride some fairly doctrinal rails given the right case. Maybe this was one. And at the same time, it can't be overlooked that he did assign himself to write the opinion in which he went, let us say, to great lengths to make and "bolster" his point. However, he never knew what was coming through. He couldn't have. That is why the subconscious is called the subconscious. His inner being boiling through or not, given all the givens of the case, the decision is viewed as correct by many who have the acumen to make an informed judgment. Surprised? My guess half of you see it that way and half of you don't. But remember, our job is not to take sides on these matters. Here we are looking at the Court and its work, specifically at the margins, and how it influences so many other things in the American fabric with this case being an interesting illustration of the horrific effect a wrong case or clumsy statute brought into the jurisprudential system as a test can have not only in terms of present justice, but for years, even decades to come (the State of Washington did fight back, but in a way which also might surprise you—not every sapless state does, not to mention Congress). Nevertheless, as a result of *Glucksberg*, there is now a SCOTUS opinion that has a chilling effect on the work of legislatures nationwide to craft something that makes sense relative to the times in which we live, and to strike a balance among all those who have concerns. An option was not even considered. No "choice" here (compare *Stenberg*). Physicians do not practice their craft, medicine, with hammers and tongs. Neither should lawyers. Both are human factors professions.

Whether or not you are pro-choice relative to end-of-life issues, one of the opinions does exude some integrity with a faint suggestion that the matter might best be left to legislatures, again which more closely answer to the will of the people as being elective institutions, having fact-gathering machinery and a cathedral for extensive hearings and research before acting.

Now, let us think about Souter's opinion for a moment. Maybe one may candidly say this: it lays out in fairly clear terms how the Court should go about testing for constitutionality of any particular state statute under the due process clause of the Fourteenth Amendment (Rehnquist does take a swing at it, but according to his own "views," which seemingly isn't what a "constitutionalist" is supposed to do), and then proceeds to do so in the case of the Washington statute. Looking at it from a little different perspective, even Souter is saying, nearly *sub silentio*, wrong case, at possibly the wrong time (see the last paragraph of his opinion). You also observed in another concurring opinion a similar palliative approach, not so *sub silentio*, of a call for a better set of facts where work may be needed.

Some believe *Casey* cited at the outset of *Stenberg, supra*—interesting that an abortion case(s) worked its way into this case dealing with end-of-life problems. Significant?—as an unintended consequence, may have invited the ill-timed and ill-conceived preemptive attack on the statute in question. The attack on the statute succeeded and survived its first two trimesters of nascent legal life, but the prior court opinions were aborted at the hands of the Supreme Court. All of this might not be fairly placed solely at the feet of SCOTUS (or for Tenth Amendment reasons) as it usually only deals with what it is presented ("usually" in the sense the Court has been known to haul in its own evidence and other "findings" when expedient to do so). Yet, professionals understand this is a matter ultimately with which the Court must and eventually will have to deal on not just a genuine and honest constitutional basis (even if the basic principle is simply left to the states in accordance with the Bill of Rights), but in the environment of reality, something we briefly take into consideration later. Stevens even says, in thinking somewhat parallel to that of Souter, that although *Glucksberg* suggests the mission of the Washington statute is not facially invalid as a constitutional matter, under precepts of due process (infirm because of the way it was drafted), the possibility is not foreclosed that the statute in its present form may pose an "intolerable intrusion" into a patient's end-of-life issues and freedoms (heavily paraphrased), or put otherwise, there seems to be a hint that a "properly" drafted statute could survive review although judicial developments along these lines have not yet come to fruition. For now, let us look at what is actually before us, accepting the fact there is much disagreement among the professional and academic ranks relative to what the case actually says. With that, we forge ahead.

The opinion goes on a *tour de force* in this sensitive arena involving legitimate diverging views, lay, legal, medical, and theological alike, being not just one of the difficult issues of our times, but a matter which will in time present future features that are all but unspeakable today. It is coming. Could it be the case's abundance of unnecessary dicta sounds a clarion signal, the siren of an attempted future judicial roadblock, or an awkward offer of suggested legislation, without the rules and specificity of details the abortion cases offered? Such an unrelenting, callous, hard line ("It has always been a crime…") raises questions and concerns regarding what to expect from the Court in the future as mankind proceeds with life, at least as it is presently known, and how the United States, presumably marching moral point for the world in the community of nations (or did) decides the course of life and death, generally, or who gets to be born and who gets to die, and when and how, at least insofar as the trajectory of recent judicial history would take us in telescoping out its logical conclusions. Will not the Court have to do some awkward back-peddling? Or, will it simply continue to legislate?

Some of the Associate Justices did mute their language somewhat, but what ultimately came out of the Court was more of a one-man show. Four joined the majority opinion. Four concurrences in result were filed. Or, put a little differently, what is this Court going to say ten or fifteen years from now, (taken up *infra*)? Taking apart an honorable lower court with parenthetical snippets seems less than unnecessary. For any court to go on and chide the authority below by claiming a "radical" reading of this high court's prior opinions, verbatim, seems to be an unnecessary assault and insult beneath the high calling of what is supposed to be a supreme court, supposedly the best we have to offer. More is expected here, as well as a respect for the solemnity of that with which we are dealing here, and with what it dealt with there. To quote an opinion doesn't make a reading radical…does it? And then to trot out *stare decisis* seems a little disingenuous, disingenuous in the sense you will discover the Court commonly employs the doctrine if it chooses to stand pat, but back in the closet it goes when a major, new, "groundbreaking opinion," a "watershed case," a "landmark" is about to be "handed down." Frankly, there are few knowledgeable attorneys in the country who will not candidly say such "jurisprudence" is a joke. Most judges would even say it is a joke. Take a poll. Go ahead, ask. Any court which attempts to create a lasting fortress hoisted on pillars of its own petards does not understand the self-defeating nature of this approach, nor does it do its duty by failing to leave self out of the equation, known as service above self.

It is true, there are "compelling state interests" at work here, and it is also true any impingement on constitutionally recognized freedoms by legislation must be "narrowly tailored" so as not to impinge any more than absolutely necessary on such freedoms while protecting legitimate "state interests" if the statute is to be saved. If one were to conclude the statute is over-broad, there is then a rational legal argument the majority opinion is, on that test, correct, at least constitutionally, but leave it at that. Send the case and its statute back to the State of Washington for a re-work, and save the spit-balls. One may like that result or not. However, liking or not liking is not relevant to our work here. It is a challenge to accept that perspective, but that is the premise of our approach to and analysis of the Court's work.

Yet, there are only three sentences, two of which recognize anything debatable here, in just one and the last paragraph of the majority opinion representing all the majority can bring itself to say deferentially. Might not the Court have simply said, "as to end of life measures, we are not pro-choice in the context of the matter before us." That would do it. No need to feel compulsion to castigate anyone or anything. No need to cast around for phantom constitutional makeweights. Needless to say, it would then also not have to deal with trimesters in the premises, or partial death procedures, and thus a nice, easily attainable cut and dried end result. A little crass? Maybe. But the statute said assistance could not be given. Petitioners argued that assistance should be available by way of the Supreme Court declaring the statute unconstitutional on a variety of grounds. This the Court refused to do. In effect, the Court said it was up to the people of the State of Washington via their legislature. After some reflection, maybe you have entertained the thought that possibly it was the Washington legislature which was the most ham-handed.

The State of Washington responded with RCW 70.245, titled "The Death With Dignity Act," which is the law of that state today. Three other states have like and similar legislation notwithstanding *Glucksberg*. One state permits the assistance of a physician by court decision. The new Washington statute never uses the term "suicide," not even once. Why? Possibly because it doesn't deal with suicide, at least as defined by the common law and history, or the event it covers isn't suicide today. Rehnquist, in his opinion and as supported by the concurring opinions, uses the term suicide along with other correlative terms such as "self-murder" over one hundred times. What a revelation. What does that tell us about the opinion? What does that tell us about SCOTUS? On what basis was the case actually decided? The Constitution? Was the Court candid? How many times was the term feticide used in the abortion opinions? Again, no position taking, but keeping in mind even word choice is behavior recalling the psychiatric principle. We look well past the fray.

Indeed, the people of the State of Washington responded.

*

Chapter 70.245 RCW

THE WASHINGTON DEATH WITH DIGNITY ACT

70.245.020

(1) An adult who is competent, is a resident of Washington state, and has been determined by the attending physician and consulting physician to be suffering from a terminal disease, and who has voluntarily expressed his or her wish to die, may make a written request for medication that the patient may self-administer to end his or her life in a humane and dignified manner in accordance with this chapter.

70.245.030

(1) A valid request for medication under this chapter shall be in substantially the form described in RCW 70.245.220, signed and dated by the patient and witnessed by at least two individuals who, in the presence of the patient, attest that to the best of their knowledge and belief the patient is competent, acting voluntarily, and is not being coerced to sign the request.

(2) One of the witnesses shall be a person who is not:

(a) A relative of the patient by blood, marriage, or adoption;

(b) A person who at the time the request is signed would be entitled to any portion of the estate of the qualified patient upon death under any will or by operation of law; or

(c) An owner, operator, or employee of a health care facility where the qualified patient is receiving medical treatment or is a resident.

(3) The patient's attending physician at the time the request is signed shall not be a witness.

(4) If the patient is a patient in a long-term care facility at the time the written request is made, one of the witnesses shall be an individual designated by the facility and having the qualifications specified by the department of health by rule.

70.245.040

(1) The attending physician shall:

(a) Make the initial determination of whether a patient has a terminal disease, is competent, and has made the request voluntarily;

(b) Request that the patient demonstrate Washington state residency under RCW 70.245.130;

(c) To ensure that the patient is making an informed decision, inform the patient of:

(i) His or her medical diagnosis;

(ii) His or her prognosis;

(iii) The potential risks associated with taking the medication to be prescribed;

(iv) The probable result of taking the medication to be prescribed; and

(v) The feasible alternatives including, but not limited to, comfort care, hospice care, and pain control;

(d) Refer the patient to a consulting physician for medical confirmation of the diagnosis, and for a determination that the patient is competent and acting voluntarily;

(e) Refer the patient for counseling if appropriate under RCW 70.245.060;

(f) Recommend that the patient notify next of kin;

(g) Counsel the patient about the importance of having another person present when the patient takes the medication prescribed under this chapter and of not taking the medication in a public place;

(h) Inform the patient that he or she has an opportunity to rescind the request at any time and in any manner, and offer the patient an opportunity to rescind at the end of the fifteen-day waiting period under RCW 70.245.090;

(i) Verify, immediately before writing the prescription for medication under this chapter, that the patient is making an informed decision;

(j) Fulfill the medical record documentation requirements of RCW 70.245.120;

(k) Ensure that all appropriate steps are carried out in accordance with this chapter before writing a prescription for medication to enable a qualified patient to end his or her life in a humane and dignified manner; and

(l)(i) Dispense medications directly, including ancillary medications intended to facilitate the desired effect to minimize the patient's discomfort, if the attending physician is authorized under statute and rule to dispense and has a current drug enforcement administration certificate; or

(ii) With the patient's written consent:

(A) Contact a pharmacist and inform the pharmacist of the prescription; and

(B) Deliver the written prescription personally, by mail or facsimile to the pharmacist, who will dispense the medications directly to either the patient, the attending physician, or an expressly identified agent of the patient. Medications dispensed pursuant to this subsection shall not be dispensed by mail or other form of courier.

(2) The attending physician may sign the patient's death certificate which shall list the underlying terminal disease as the cause of death.

*

A review of *Stenberg* would be instructive at this point, and would draw into sharper focus our thinking about *Glucksberg*.

XIX

POSTLUDE

The Caperton v. Massey cases

Citizens United v. Federal Election Commission

DeBoer v. Snyder

ow for your entertainment and reading pleasure, I direct your attention to the *Caperton v. Massey* cases where the Supreme Court of Appeals of West Virginia stuck its thumb in the eye of SCOTUS, followed by *Citizens United v. Federal Election Commission,* and *DeBoer v. Snyder* [which will be reported out as a consolidated case in *Obergefell v. Hodges,* ___U.S. ___], which are the final cases unfortunately, at least for now. As for these cases, I leave you on your own. You have all the ability, skill, and tools to make your own informed judgments.

*

Caperton v. Massey

556 U.S. 868

followed by

Caperton v. Massey

225 W. Va. 128

HUGH M. CAPERTON, ET AL., PETITIONERS v. A. T. MASSEY
COAL COMPANY, INC. ET AL

ON WRIT OF CERTIORARI TO THE SUPREME COURT OF
APPEALS OF WEST VIRGINIA

556 U.S. 868 (2009)

JUSTICE KENNEDY delivered the opinion of the Court.

In this case the Supreme Court of Appeals of West Virginia reversed a trial court judgment, which had entered a jury verdict of $50 million. Five justices heard the case, and the vote to reverse was 3 to 2. The question presented is whether the Due Process Clause of the Fourteenth Amendment was violated when one of the justices in the majority denied a recusal motion. The basis for the motion was that the justice had received campaign contributions in an extraordinary amount from, and through the efforts of, the board chairman and principal officer of the corporation found liable for the damages.

Under our precedents there are objective standards that require recusal when "the probability of actual bias on the part of the judge or decisionmaker is too high to be constitutionally tolerable." *Withrow* v. *Larkin*, 421 U.S. 35, 47 (1975). Applying those precedents, we find that, in all the circumstances of this case, due process requires recusal.

I.

In August 2002 a West Virginia jury returned a verdict that found respondents A. T. Massey Coal Co. and its affiliates (hereinafter Massey) liable for fraudulent misrepresentation, concealment, and tortious interference with existing contractual relations. The jury awarded petitioners Hugh Caperton, Harman Development Corp., Harman Mining Corp., and Sovereign Coal Sales (hereinafter Caperton) the sum of $50 million in compensatory and punitive damages.

In June 2004 the state trial court denied Massey's post-trial motions challenging the verdict and the damages award, finding that Massey "intentionally acted in utter disregard of [Caperton's] rights and ultimately destroyed [Caperton's] businesses because, after conducting cost-benefit analyses, [Massey] concluded it was in its financial interest to do so."

* * *

Don Blankenship is Massey's chairman, chief executive officer, and president. After the verdict but before the appeal, West Virginia held its 2004 judicial elections. Knowing the Supreme Court of Appeals of West Virginia would consider the appeal in the case, Blankenship decided to support an attorney who sought to replace Justice McGraw. Justice McGraw was a candidate for reelection to that court. The attorney who sought to replace him was Brent Benjamin.

In addition to contributing the $1,000 statutory maximum to Benjamin's campaign committee, Blankenship donated almost $2.5 million to "And For The Sake Of The Kids," a political organization formed under 26 U.S.C. §527. The §527 organization opposed McGraw and supported Benjamin. Blankenship's donations accounted for more than two-thirds of the total funds it raised. This was not all. Blankenship spent, in addition, just over $500,000 on independent expenditures – for direct mailings and letters soliciting donations as well as television and newspaper advertisements – "'to support...Brent Benjamin.'"

To provide some perspective, Blankenship's $3 million in contributions were more than the total amount spent by all other

Benjamin supporters and three times the amount spent by Benjamin's own committee....

Benjamin won....

In October 2005, before Massey filed its petition for appeal in West Virginia's highest court, Caperton moved to disqualify now-Justice Benjamin under the Due Process Clause and the West Virginia Code of Judicial Conduct, based on the conflict caused by Blankenship's campaign involvement. Justice Benjamin denied the motion in April 2006. He indicated that he "carefully considered the bases and accompanying exhibits proffered by the movants." But he found "no objective information...to show that this Justice has a bias for or against any litigant, that this Justice has prejudged the matters which comprise this litigation, or that this Justice will be anything but fair and impartial." In December 2006 Massey filed its petition for appeal to challenge the adverse jury verdict. The West Virginia Supreme Court of Appeals granted review.

In November 2007 that court reversed the $50 million verdict against Massey. The majority opinion, authored by then-Chief Justice Davis and joined by Justices Benjamin and Maynard, found that "Massey's conduct warranted the type of judgment rendered in this case." It reversed, nevertheless, based on two independent grounds – first, that a forum-selection clause contained in a contract to which Massey was not a party barred the suit in West Virginia, and, second, that res judicata barred the suit due to an out-of-state judgment to which Massey was not a party. Justice Starcher dissented, stating that the "majority's opinion is morally and legally wrong." Justice Albright also dissented, accusing the majority of "misapplying the law and introducing sweeping 'new law' into our jurisprudence that may well come back to haunt us."

Caperton sought rehearing, and the parties moved for disqualification of three of the five justices who decided the appeal.

Photos had surfaced of Justice Maynard vacationing with Blankenship in the French Riviera while the case was pending. Justice Maynard granted Caperton's recusal motion. On the other side Justice Starcher granted Massey's recusal motion, apparently based on his public criticism of Blankenship's role in the 2004 elections. In his recusal memorandum Justice Starcher urged Justice Benjamin to recuse himself as well. He noted that "Blankenship's bestowal of his personal wealth, political tactics, and 'friendship' have created a cancer in the affairs of this Court." Justice Benjamin declined Justice Starcher's suggestion and denied Caperton's recusal motion.

The court granted rehearing. Justice Benjamin, now in the capacity of acting chief justice, selected Judges Cookman and Fox to replace the recused justices. Caperton moved a third time for disqualification, arguing that Justice Benjamin had failed to apply the correct standard under West Virginia law – *i.e.* whether "a reasonable and prudent person, knowing these objective facts, would harbor doubts about Justice Benjamin's ability to be fair and impartial." Caperton also included the results of a public opinion poll, which indicated that over 67% of West Virginians doubted Justice Benjamin would be fair and impartial. Justice Benjamin again refused to withdraw, noting that the "push poll" was "neither credible nor sufficiently reliable to serve as the basis for an elected judge's disqualification."

In April 2008 a divided court again reversed the jury verdict, and again it was a 3-to-2 decision. Justice Davis filed a modified version of [her] prior opinion, repeating the two earlier holdings. She was joined by Justice Benjamin and Judge Fox. Justice Albright, joined by Judge Cookman, dissented: "Not only is the majority opinion unsupported by the facts and existing case law, but it is also fundamentally unfair. Sadly, justice was neither honored nor served by the majority." ...The dissent also noted "genuine due process implications arising under federal law" with respect to Justice Benjamin's failure to recuse himself.... ([C]iting

Aetna Life Ins. Co. v. *Lavoie,* 475 U.S. 813 (1986); *In re Murchison*, 349 U.S. 133, 1365 (1955)).

Four months later – a month after the petition for writ of certiorari was filed in this Court – Justice Benjamin filed a concurring opinion. He defended the merits of the majority opinion as well as his decision not to recuse. He rejected Caperton's challenge to his participation in the case under both the Due Process Clause and West Virginia law. Justice Benjamin reiterated that he had no "'direct, personal, substantial, pecuniary interest' in this case." ...Adopting "a standard merely of 'appearances,'" he concluded, "seems little more than an invitation to subject West Virginia's justice system to the vagaries of the day – a framework in which predictability and stability yield to supposition, innuendo, half-truths, and partisan manipulations."

* * *

We granted certiorari.

* * *

It is axiomatic that "[a] fair trial in a fair tribunal is a basic requirement of due process." *Murchison, supra,* at 136.... The early and leading case on the subject is *Tumey* v. *Ohio,* 273 U.S. 510 (1927).

* * *

As new problems have emerged that were not discussed at common law, however, the Court has identified additional instances which, as an objective matter, require recusal. These are circumstances "in which experience teaches that the probability of actual bias on the part of the judge or decisionmaker is too high to be constitutionally tolerable." *Withrow*, 421 U.S., at 47. To place the present case in proper context, two instances where the Court has required recusal merit further discussion.

A

The first involved the emergence of local tribunals where a judge had a financial interest in the outcome of a case, although the interest was less than what would have been considered personal or direct at common law.

This was the problem addressed in *Tumey*. There, the mayor of a village had the authority to sit as a judge (with no jury) to try those accused of violating a state law prohibiting the possession of alcoholic beverages. Inherent in this structure were two potential conflicts. First, the mayor received a salary supplement for performing judicial duties, and the funds for that compensation derived from the fines assessed in a case. No fines were assessed upon acquittal. The mayor-judge thus received a salary supplement only if he convicted the defendant.

* * *

The Court held that the Due Process Clause required disqualification "both because of [the mayor-judge's] direct pecuniary interest in the outcome, and because of his official motive to convict and to graduate the fine to help the financial needs of the village." ...The Court articulated the controlling principle:

> "Every procedure which would offer a possible temptation to the average man as a judge to forget the burden of proof required to convict the defendant, or which might lead him not to hold the balance nice, clear and true between the State and the accused, denies the latter due process of law."

The Court was thus concerned with more than the traditional common-law prohibition on direct pecuniary interest. It was also concerned with a more general concept of interests that tempt adjudicators to disregard neutrality.

* * *

III

Based on the principles . . . we turn to the issue before us. This problem arises in the context of judicial elections, a framework not presented in the precedents we have reviewed and discussed.

Caperton contends that Blankenship's pivotal role in getting Justice Benjamin elected created a constitutionally intolerable probability of actual bias. Though not a bribe or criminal influence, Justice Benjamin would nevertheless feel a debt of gratitude to Blankenship for his extraordinary efforts to get him elected. That temptation, Caperton claims, is as strong and inherent in human nature as was the conflict the Court confronted in Tumey and Monroeville when a mayor-judge (or the city) benefited financially from a defendant's conviction.

* * *

The difficulties of inquiring into actual bias, and the fact that the inquiry is often a private one, simply underscore the need for objective rules. Otherwise there may be no adequate protection against a judge who simply misreads or misapprehends the real motives at work in deciding the case. The judge's own inquiry into actual bias, then, is not one that the law can easily superintend or review.... In lieu of exclusive reliance on that personal inquiry, or on appellate review of the judge's determination respecting actual bias, the Due Process Clause has been implemented by objective standards that do not require proof of actual bias.... In defining these standards the Court has asked whether, "under a realistic appraisal of psychological tendencies and human weakness," the interest "poses such a risk of actual bias or prejudgment that the practice must be forbidden if the guarantee of due process is to be adequately implemented."

We turn to the influence at issue in this case. Not every campaign contribution by a litigant or attorney creates a probability of bias that requires a judge's recusal, but this is an exceptional case. ...We conclude that there is a serious risk of actual bias – based on objective and reasonable perceptions – when a person with a personal stake in a particular case had a significant and disproportionate influence in placing the judge on the case by raising funds or directing the judge's election campaign when the case was pending or imminent. The inquiry centers on the contribution's relative size in comparison to the total amount of money contributed to the campaign, the total amount spent in the election, and the apparent effect such contribution had on the outcome of the election.

Applying this principle, we conclude that Blankenship's campaign efforts had a significant and disproportionate influence in placing Justice Benjamin on the case. Blankenship contributed some $3 million to unseat the incumbent and replace him with Benjamin. His contributions eclipsed the total amount spent by all other Benjamin supporters and exceeded by 300% the amount spent by Benjamin's campaign committee.

* * *

Massey responds that Blankenship's support, while significant, did not cause Benjamin's victory. In the end the people of West Virginia elected him, and they did so based on many reasons other than Blankenship's efforts. Massey points out that every major state newspaper, but one, endorsed Benjamin.... It also contends that then-

Justice McGraw cost himself the election by giving a speech during the campaign, a speech the opposition seized upon for its own advantage.

* * *

Whether Blankenship's campaign contributions were a necessary and sufficient cause of Benjamin's victory is not the proper inquiry. Much like determining whether a judge is actually biased, proving what ultimately drives the electorate to choose a particular candidate is a difficult endeavor, not likely to lend itself to a certain conclusion. This is particularly true where, as here, there is no procedure for judicial factfinding and the sole trier of fact is the one accused of bias. Due process requires an objective inquiry into whether the contributor's influence on the election under all the circumstances "would offer a possible temptation to the average...judge to...lead him not to hold the balance nice, clear and true." *Tumey, supra,* at 532.

* * *

The temporal relationship between the campaign contributions, the justice's election, and the pendency of the case is also critical. It was reasonably foreseeable, when the campaign contributions were made, that the pending case would be before the newly elected justice. The $50 million adverse jury verdict had been entered before the election, and the Supreme Court of Appeals was the next step once the state trial court dealt with post-trial motions. So it became at once apparent that, absent recusal, Justice Benjamin would review a judgment that cost his biggest donor's company $50 million. Although there is no allegation of a quid pro quo agreement, the fact remains that Blankenship's extraordinary contributions were made at a time when he had a vested stake in the outcome. Just as no man is allowed to be a judge in his own cause, similar fears of bias can arise when – without the consent of the other parties – a man chooses the judge in his own cause. And applying this principle to the judicial election process, there was here a serious, objective risk of actual bias that required Justice Benjamin's recusal.

* * *

On these extreme facts the probability of actual bias rises to an unconstitutional level.

IV

Our decision today addresses an extraordinary situation where the Constitution requires recusal. Massey and its amici predict that various adverse consequences will follow from recognizing a constitutional violation here – ranging from a flood of recusal motions to unnecessary interference with judicial elections. We disagree. The facts now before us are extreme by any measure. The parties point to no other instance involving judicial campaign contributions that presents a potential for bias comparable to the circumstances in this case.

* * *

One must also take into account the judicial reforms the States have implemented to eliminate even the appearance of partiality. Almost every State – West Virginia included – has adopted the American Bar Association's objective standard: "A judge shall avoid impropriety and the appearance of impropriety." ...The ABA Model Code's test for appearance of impropriety is "whether the conduct would create in reasonable minds a perception that the judge's ability to carry out judicial responsibilities with integrity, impartiality and competence is impaired."

* * *

The judgment of the Supreme Court of Appeals of West Virginia is reversed, and the case is remanded for further proceedings not inconsistent with this opinion.

It is so ordered.

CHIEF JUSTICE ROBERTS, with whom JUSTICE SCALIA, JUSTICE THOMAS, and JUSTICE ALITO join, dissenting.

I, of course, share the majority's sincere concerns about the need to maintain a fair, independent, and impartial judiciary – and one that appears to be such. But I fear that the Court's decision will undermine rather than promote these values.

Until today, we have recognized exactly two situations in which the Federal Due Process Clause requires disqualification of a judge: when the judge has a financial interest in the outcome of the case, and when the judge is trying a defendant for certain criminal contempts. Vaguer notions of bias or the appearance of bias were never a basis for disqualification, either at common law or under our constitutional precedents. Those issues were instead addressed by legislation or court rules.

Today, however, the Court enlists the Due Process Clause to overturn a judge's failure to recuse because of a "probability of bias." Unlike the established grounds for disqualification, a "probability of bias" cannot be defined in any limited way. The Court's new "rule" provides no guidance to judges and litigants about when recusal will be constitutionally required. This will inevitably lead to an increase in allegations that judges are biased, however groundless those charges may be. The end result will do far more to erode public confidence in judicial impartiality than an isolated failure to recuse in a particular case.

I

There is a "presumption of honesty and integrity in those serving as adjudicators." *Withrow* v. *Larkin*, 421 U.S. 35, 47 (1975). All judges take an oath to uphold the Constitution and apply the law impartially, and we trust that they will live up to this promise.

* * *

It is well established that a judge may not preside over a case in which he has a "direct, personal, substantial pecuniary interest." *Tumey* v. *Ohio*, 273 U.S. 510, 523 (1927). This principle is relatively straightforward, and largely tracks the longstanding common-law rule regarding judicial recusal.

* * *

It may also violate due process when a judge presides over a criminal contempt case that resulted from the defendant's hostility towards the judge. In *Mayberry* v. *Pennsylvania*, 400 U.S. 455 (1971), the defendant directed a steady stream of expletives and *ad hominem* attacks at the judge throughout the trial. When that defendant was subsequently charged with criminal contempt, we concluded that he "should be given a public trial before a judge other than the one reviled by the contemnor." ...Subject to the two well-established exceptions described above, questions of judicial recusal are regulated by "common law, statute, or the professional standards of the bench and bar." *Bracy* v. *Gramley*, 520 U.S. 899, 904 (1997).

In any given case, there are a number of factors that could give rise to a "probability" or "appearance" of bias: friendship with a party or lawyer, prior employment experience, membership in clubs or associations, prior speeches and writings, religious affiliation, and countless other considerations. We have never held that the Due Process Clause requires recusal for any of these reasons, even though they could be viewed as presenting a "probability of bias." Many state *statutes* require recusal based on a probability or appearance of bias, but "that alone would not be sufficient basis for imposing a *constitutional* requirement under the Due Process Clause."

* * *

II

In departing from this clear line between when recusal is constitutionally required and when it is not, the majority repeatedly emphasizes the need for an "objective" standard. ...The majority's analysis is "objective" in that it does not inquire into Justice Benjamin's motives or decisionmaking process. But the standard the majority articulates – "probability of bias" – fails to provide clear, workable guidance for future cases. At the most basic level, it is unclear whether the new probability of bias standard is somehow limited to financial support in judicial elections, or applies to judicial recusal questions more generally.

But there are other fundamental questions as well. With little help from the majority, courts will now have to determine:

1.   How much money is too much money? What level of contribution or expenditure gives rise to a "probability of bias"?

2.   How do we determine whether a given expenditure is "disproportionate"? Disproportionate *to what*?

3.   Are independent, non-coordinated expenditures treated the same as direct contributions to a candidate's campaign? What about contributions to independent outside groups supporting a candidate?

4.   Does it matter whether the litigant has contributed to other candidates or made large expenditures in connection with other elections?

5.   Does the amount at issue in the case matter? What if this case were an employment dispute with only $10,000 at stake? What if the

plaintiffs only sought non-monetary relief such as an injunction or declaratory judgment?

6.   Does the analysis change depending on whether the judge whose disqualification is sought sits on a trial court, appeals court, or state supreme court?

7.   How long does the probability of bias last? Does the probability of bias diminish over time as the   election recedes? Does it matter whether the judge plans to run for reelection?

8.   What if the "disproportionately" large expenditure is made by an industry association, trade union, physicians' group, or the plaintiffs' bar? Must the judge recuse in all cases that affect the association's interests? Must the judge recuse in all cases in which a party or lawyer is a member of that group? Does it matter how much the litigant contributed to the association?

9.   What if the case involves a social or ideological issue rather than a financial one? Must a judge recuse from cases involving, say, abortion rights if he has received "disproportionate" support from individuals who feel strongly about either side of that issue? If the supporter wants to help elect judges who are "tough on crime," must the judge recuse in all criminal cases?

10.   What if the candidate draws "disproportionate" support from a particular racial, religious, ethnic, or other group, and the case involves an issue of particular importance to that group?

11.   What if the supporter is not a party to the pending or imminent case, but his interests will be affected by the decision? Does the Court's analysis apply if the supporter "chooses the judge" not in *his* case, but in someone else's?

12.   What if the case implicates a regulatory issue that is of great importance to the party making the expenditures, even though he has no direct financial interest in the outcome (*e.g.*, a facial challenge to an agency rulemaking or a suit seeking to limit an agency's jurisdiction)?

13.   Must the judge's vote be outcome determinative in order for his non-recusal to constitute a due process violation?

14.   Does the due process analysis consider the underlying merits of the suit? Does it matter whether the decision is clearly right (or wrong) as a matter of state law?

15.   What if a lower court decision in favor of the supporter is affirmed on the merits on appeal, by a panel with no "debt of gratitude" to the supporter? Does that "moot" the due process claim?

16.   What if the judge voted against the supporter in many other cases?

17.   What if the judge disagrees with the supporter's message or tactics? What if the judge expressly *disclaims* the support of this person?

18.   Should we assume that elected judges feel a "debt of hostility" towards major *opponents* of their candidacies? Must the judge recuse in cases involving individuals or groups who spent large amounts of money trying unsuccessfully to defeat him?

19.   If there is independent review of a judge's recusal decision, *e.g.*, by a panel of other judges, does this completely foreclose a due process claim?

20.   Does a debt of gratitude for endorsements by newspapers, interest groups, politicians, or celebrities also give rise to a constitutionally unacceptable probability of bias? How would we measure whether such support is disproportionate?

21.   Does close personal friendship between a judge and a party or lawyer now give rise to a probability of bias?

22.   Does it matter whether the campaign expenditures come from a party or the party's attorney? If from a lawyer, must the judge recuse in every case involving that attorney?

23.   Does what is unconstitutional vary from State to State? What if particular States have a history of expensive judicial elections?

24.   Under the majority's "objective" test, do we analyze the due process issue through the lens of a reasonable person, a reasonable lawyer, or a reasonable judge?

25.   What role does causation play in this analysis? The Court sends conflicting signals on this point. The majority asserts that "[w]hether Blankenship's campaign contributions were a necessary and sufficient cause of Benjamin's victory is not the proper inquiry." *Ante*, at 15. But elsewhere in the opinion, the majority considers "the apparent effect such contribution had on the outcome of the election," *ante*, at 14, and whether the litigant has been able to "choos[e] the judge in his own cause," *ante*, at 16. If causation is a pertinent factor, how do we know whether the contribution or expenditure had any effect on the outcome of the election? What if the judge won in a landslide? What if the judge won primarily because of his opponent's missteps?

26.   Is the due process analysis less probing for incumbent judges – who typically have a great advantage in elections – than for challengers?

27.   How final must the pending case be with respect to the contributor's interest? What if, for example, the only issue on appeal is whether the court should certify a class of plaintiffs? Is recusal required just as if the issue in the pending case were ultimate liability?

28.   Which cases are implicated by this doctrine? Must the case be pending at the time of the election? Reasonably likely to be brought? What about an important but unanticipated case filed shortly after the election?

29.   When do we impute a probability of bias from one party to another? Does a contribution from a corporation get imputed to its executives, and vice-versa? Does a contribution or expenditure by one family member get imputed to other family members?

30.   What if the election is nonpartisan? What if the election is just a yes-or-no vote about whether to retain an incumbent?

31.   What type of support is disqualifying? What if the supporter's expenditures are used to fund voter registration or get-out-the-vote efforts rather than television advertisements?

32.   Are contributions or expenditures in connection with a primary aggregated with those in the general election? What if the contributor supported a different candidate in the primary? Does that dilute the debt of gratitude?

33.   What procedures must be followed to challenge a state judge's failure to recuse? May *Caperton* claims only be raised on direct review? Or may such claims also be brought in federal district court under 42 U.S.C. §1983, which allows a person deprived of a federal right by a state official to sue for damages? If §1983 claims are available, who are the proper defendants? The judge? The whole court? The clerk of court?

34.   What about state-court cases that are already closed? Can the losing parties in those cases now seek collateral relief in federal district court under §1983? What statutes of limitation should be applied to such suits?

35.   What is the proper remedy? After a successful *Caperton* motion, must the parties start from scratch before the lower courts? Is any part of the lower court judgment retained?

36.   Does a litigant waive his due process claim if he waits until after decision to raise it? Or would the claim only be ripe after decision, when the judge's actions or vote suggest a probability of bias?

37.   Are the parties entitled to discovery with respect to the judge's recusal decision?

38.   If a judge erroneously fails to recuse, do we apply harmless-error review?

39.   Does the *judge* get to respond to the allegation that he is probably biased or is his reputation solely in the hands of the parties to the case?

40.   What if the parties settle a *Caperton* claim as part of a broader settlement of the case? Does that leave the judge with no way to salvage his reputation?

These are only a few uncertainties that quickly come to mind. Judges and litigants will surely encounter others when they are forced to, or wish to, apply the majority's decision in different circumstances. Today's opinion requires state and federal judges simultaneously to act as political scientists (why did candidate X win the election?), economists (was the financial support disproportionate?), and psychologists (is there likely to be a debt of gratitude?).

The Court's inability to formulate a "judicially discernible and manageable standard" strongly counsels against the recognition of a novel constitutional right. ...The need to consider these and countless other questions helps explain why the common law and this Court's constitutional jurisprudence have never required disqualification on such vague grounds as "probability" or "appearance" of bias.

III

A

To its credit, the Court seems to recognize that the inherently boundless nature of its new rule poses a problem. But the majority's only answer is that the present case is an "extreme" one, so there is no need to worry about other cases.

* * *

But this is just so much whistling past the graveyard. Claims that have little chance of success are nonetheless frequently filed. The success rate for certiorari petitions before this Court is approximately 1.1%, and yet the previous Term some 8,241 were filed. Every one of the "*Caperton* motions" or appeals or §1983 actions will claim that the judge is biased, or probably biased, bringing the judge and the judicial system into disrepute. And all future litigants will assert that their case is *really* the most extreme thus far.

Extreme cases often test the bounds of established legal principles. There is a cost to yielding to the desire to correct the extreme case, rather than adhering to the legal principle. That cost has been demonstrated so often that it is captured in a legal aphorism: "Hard cases make bad law."

* * *

B

And why is the Court so convinced that this is an extreme case? It is true that Don Blankenship spent a large amount of money in connection with this election. But this point cannot be emphasized strongly enough: Other than a $1,000 direct contribution from Blankenship, *Justice Benjamin and his campaign had no control over how this money was spent.*

* * *

Moreover, Blankenship's independent expenditures do not appear "grossly disproportionate" compared to other such expenditures in this very election. "And for the Sake of the Kids" – an independent group that received approximately two-thirds of its funding from Blankenship – spent $3,623,500 in connection with the election. ...But large independent expenditures were also made in support of Justice Benjamin's opponent. "Consumers for Justice" – an independent group that received large contributions from the plaintiffs' bar – spent approximately $2 million in this race. ...And Blankenship has made large expenditures in connection with several previous West Virginia elections, which undercuts any notion that his involvement in this election was "intended to influence the outcome" of particular pending litigation.

* * *

It is also far from clear that Blankenship's expenditures affected the outcome of this election. Justice Benjamin won by a comfortable 7-point margin (53.3% to 46.7%). Many observers believed that Justice Benjamin's opponent doomed his candidacy by giving a well-publicized speech that made several curious allegations; this speech was described in the local media as "deeply disturbing" and worse. ...Justice Benjamin's opponent also refused to give interviews or participate in debates. All but one of the major West Virginia newspapers endorsed Justice Benjamin. Justice Benjamin just might have won because the voters of West Virginia thought he would be a better judge than his opponent. Unlike the majority, I cannot say with any degree of certainty that Blankenship "cho[se] the judge in his own cause." ...I would give the voters of West Virginia more credit than that.

* * *

It is an old cliché, but sometimes the cure is worse than the disease. I am sure there are cases where a "probability of bias" should lead the prudent judge to step aside, but the judge fails to do so. Maybe this is one of them. But I believe that opening the door to recusal claims under the Due Process Clause, for an amorphous "probability of bias," will itself bring our judicial system into underserved disrepute, and diminish the confidence of the American people in the fairness and integrity of their courts. I hope I am wrong.

I respectfully dissent.

JUSTICE SCALIA, dissenting.

The principal purpose of this Court's exercise of its certiorari jurisdiction is to clarify the law. See this Court's Rule 10. As THE CHIEF JUSTICE's dissent makes painfully clear, the principal consequence of today's decision is to create vast uncertainty with respect to a point of law that can be raised in all litigated cases in (at least) those 39 States that elect their judges. This course was urged upon us on grounds that it would preserve the public's confidence in the judicial system.

* * *

The decision will have the opposite effect. What above all else is eroding public confidence in the Nation's judicial system is the perception that litigation is just a game, that the party with the most resourceful lawyer can play it to win, that our seemingly interminable legal proceedings are wonderfully self-perpetuating but incapable of delivering real-world justice. The Court's opinion will reinforce that perception, adding to the vast arsenal of lawyerly gambits what will come to be known as the Caperton claim. The facts relevant to adjudicating it will have to be litigated – and likewise the law governing it, which will be indeterminate for years to come, if not forever. Many billable hours will be spent in poring through volumes of campaign finance reports, and many more in contesting nonrecusal decisions through every available means.

A Talmudic maxim instructs with respect to the Scripture: "Turn it over, and turn it over, for all is therein." The Babylonian Talmud, Tractate Aboth, Ch. V, Mishnah 22 (I. Epstein ed. 1935). Divinely inspired text may contain the answers to all earthly questions, but the Due Process Clause most assuredly does not. The Court today continues its quixotic quest to right all wrongs and repair all imperfections through the Constitution. Alas, the quest cannot succeed – which is why some wrongs and imperfections have been called nonjusticiable. In the best of all possible worlds, should judges sometimes recuse even where the clear commands of our prior due process law do not require it? Undoubtedly. The relevant question, however, is whether we do more good than harm by seeking to correct this imperfection through expansion of our constitutional mandate in a manner ungoverned by any discernable rule. The answer is obvious.

*

HUGH M. CAPERTON, Harman Development Corporation, Harman Mining Corporation, and Sovereign Coal Sales, Inc., Plaintiffs Below, Appellees,

v.

A.T. MASSEY COAL COMPANY, INC., Elk Run Coal Company, Inc., Independence Coal Company, Inc., Marfork Coal Company, Inc., Performance Coal Company, and Massey Coal Sales Company, Inc., Defendants Below, Appellants.

225 W.Va. 128

Supreme Court of Appeals of West Virginia

Background: Coal mine lessees and lessee's principal brought action against corporate purchaser of coal buyer and purchaser's subsidiaries, alleging tortious interference, fraudulent misrepresentation, and fraudulent concealment in connection with purchaser's declaration of force majeure and subsequent refusal to purchase contractual coal allotment from lessees. The Circuit Court, Boone County, Jay M. Hoke, J., 2005 WL 5679073, entered judgment of more than $50 million on jury verdict for lessees, and denied purchaser's and subsidiaries' post-judgment motions for judgment as a matter of law, a new trial, or remittitur. Purchase and subsidiaries appealed. On rehearing, the Supreme Court of Appeals, 223 W.Va. 624...reversed and remanded with directions. Certiorari was granted. The United States Supreme Court, 556 U.S. 868...reversed and remanded.

DAVIS, Acting Chief Justice:

The Appellants herein and defendants below, A.T. Massey Coal Company, Inc., and various of its subsidiaries, appeal from a March 15, 2005, order entered in the Circuit Court of Boone County, which denied their post-judgment motions for judgment as a matter of law, a new trial, or remittitur, in response to the entry of a judgment of more than $50 million in favor of the appellees herein, and plaintiffs below, Hugh M. Caperton, Harman Development Corporation, Harman Mining Corporation, and Sovereign Coal Sales, Inc. In this appeal, A.T. Massey Coal Company and its subsidiaries allege numerous errors that purportedly occurred throughout the proceedings below.

This case is presently before this Court on remand from the United States Supreme Court.[1] Based upon our thorough consideration of the parties' arguments, the relevant case law, and the record on appeal, this Court concludes, based upon the existence of a forum-selection clause contained in a contract that directly related to the conflict giving rise to the instant lawsuit, that the circuit court erred in denying a motion to dismiss filed by A.T. Massey Coal Company and its subsidiaries. Accordingly, we reverse the judgment in this case and remand for the circuit court to enter an order dismissing, with prejudice, this case against A.T. Massey Coal Company and its subsidiaries.

I.

FACTUAL HISTORY

Central to the dispute underlying this appeal is the Harman Mine, an underground coal mine located in Buchanan County, Virginia, that produced very high quality metallurgical coal. Prior to 1993, the Harman Mine was owned by Inspiration Coal Corporation (hereinafter referred to as "inspiration") through three subsidiaries: Harman Mining Corporation (hereinafter referred to as "Harman Mining"), Sovereign

---

[1] The first opinion filed in connection with appeal was vacated based upon the subsequent voluntary disqualification of two of the justices who participated in the earlier proceedings in this Court. A second opinion entered on rehearing was reversed by the United States Supreme Court based upon that Court's determination that an additional justice should have been disqualified. See *Caperton v. A.T. Massey Coal Co., Inc.,* 550 U.S. 868, 129 S.Ct. 2252, 173 L.Ed.2d 1208 (2009) A detailed recitation of the complex procedural history is set out in the body of this opinion at Section II, *infra.*

Coal Sales, Inc. (hereinafter referred to as "Sovereign"), and Southern Kentucky energy Company (hereinafter referred to as "Southern"). For many years, all of the coal from the Harman Mine had been sold to Wellmore Coal Corporation (hereinafter referred to as "Wellmore"), a subsidiary of United Coal Corporation. In April 1992, Sovereign and Southern entered a coal supply agreement (hereinafter referred to as "the 1992 CSA") with Wellmore. Under the 1992 CSA, Wellmore was to purchase from Sovereign and Southern approximately 750,000 tons of coal per year for a period of ten years.

In 1993, Hugh M. Caperton (hereinafter referred to as "Mr. Caperton"), a plaintiff below and appellee herein, formed Harman Development Corporation (hereinafter referred to as "Harman Development"). In that same year, Harman Development purchased the three previously mentioned subsidiaries of Inspiration: Harman Mining, Sovereign and Southern, and thereby became the owner of the Harman Mine. Harman Development, Harman Mining, and Sovereign are all plaintiffs to this action below, and are appellees herein (hereinafter collectively referred to as "the Harman Companies"). In 1997, in order to fund improvements to the Harman Mine, the Harman Companies sold all the Harman Mine reserves to Penn Virginia Corporation, and then leased back those reserves that could be mined in a cost-effective manner.

From the time the Harman Companies became owners of the Harman Mine until 1997, coal form the Harman Mine was purchased by Wellmore in accordance with the 1992 CSA. Prior to the expiration of the 1992 CSA, in March 1\of 1997, a new CSA with a higher price per ton of coal (hereinafter referred to as "the 1997 CSA") was negotiated between Sovereign, Wellmore, and Harman Mining. The 1997 CSA was to be in effect for a period of five years, commencing retroactively on

January 1, 1997. It included, among other things, a *force majeure* clause,[1] and a forum-selection clause requiring that "[a]ll actions brought in connection with this Agreement shall be filed in and decided by the Circuit Court of Buchanan County, Virginia."[2]

During the course of the 1992 CSA, and at the time the 1997 CSA was executed, one of Wellmore's primary customers was LTV Steel

---

[1] [f.8 in original] The *force majeure* clause was nearly identical to one that had been included in the 1992 CSA, and stated, in relevant part,

[t]he term "force majeure" as used herein shall mean any and all causes reasonably beyond the control of SELLER or BUYER, as applicable, which cause SELLER or BUYER to fail to perform hereunder, such as, but not limited to, acts of God, acts of the public enemy, epidemics, insurrections, riots, labor disputes and strikes, government closures, boycotts, labor and material shortages, fires, explosions, floods, breakdowns or outages of or damage to coal preparation plants, equipment or facilities, interruptions or reduction to power supplies or coal transportation (including, but not limited to, railroad car shortages) embargoes, and acts of military or civil authorities, which wholly or partly prevent the mining, processing, loading, and/or delivering of the coal by SELLER, or which wholly or partly prevent the receiving, accepting storing, processing or shipment of the coal by BUYER.... Pertaining to BUYER, the term "force majeure" as used herein shall further include occurrence(s) of a force majeure event at any of BUYER's customer's plants and facilities, except that the effects of any such force majeure event shall not justify BUYER in reducing its purchase of coal hereunder in greater proportion than the coal to be purchased hereunder bears to all BUYER's sources of supply, including BUYER's own mines, for BUYER's metallurgical coal sold to domestic coke producers. SELLER and BUYER shall promptly notify the other following commencement of a force majeure. If because of a force majeure SELLER or BUYER, respectively, is unable to carry out its obligations under this Agreement and if such Party shall promptly give to the other Party written notice of such force majeure, then the obligations of the Party giving such notice and the corresponding obligations of the other Party shall be suspended to the extent made necessary by such force majeure and during its continuance; provided however, (i) that such obligations shall be suspended only to the extent made necessary by such force majeure and only during its continuance, and (ii) that the Party giving such notice shall act promptly in [*sic*] reasonable manner to eliminate such force majeure....

[2] [f.9 in original] This forum-selection clause is identical to one that had been included in the 1992 CSA.

(hereinafter referred to as "LTV"). Wellmore sold and shipped nearly two-thirds of the coal it purchased from the Harman Companies to LTV's coke plant located in Pittsburgh, Pennsylvania.[1] On July 19, 1997, LTV announced that it intended to close its Pittsburgh coke plant due to a change in emissions regulations promulgated by the Environmental Protection Agency.

A.T. Massey Coal Company (hereinafter referred to as "Massey"), a defendant below and appellant herein, had tried unsuccessfully for several years to sell its West Virginia minded coal directly to LTV.[2] Due to its lack of success in selling to LTV on its own, Massey determined to acquire LTV's supplier, Wellmore, and its parent corporation, United Coal Corporation (hereinafter referred to as "United").[3] Massey purchased Wellmore and United on July 31, 1997. Since there was no long-term agreement between LTV and Wellmore, Massey hoped to substitute its own coal for the Harman Mine coal that Wellmore had been supplying to LTV. An internal Massey memorandum admitted during trial revealed that Massey understood there were risks to its plan, most notably the possibility that the relationship between LTV and Wellmore might not continue under Massey ownership of Wellmore. The circuit court found that, in spite of this risk, and despite the knowledge that LTV was "extremely reluctant to change a long-

---

[1] [f.10 in original] LTV purchased from Wellmore a premium blend of coal from the Harman Mine mixed with other, lesser quality coals. The circuit court expressly found that "[c]oal from the Harman Mine is metallurgical coal with very favorable coking characteristics prized by steelmakers like LTV."

[2] [f.11 in original] This coal was inferior in quality to the coal obtained from the Harman Mine and sold to LTV through Wellmore.

[3] [f.12 in original] The Harman Companies and Mr. Caperton presented evidence at trial to establish that Massey had for some time desired to sell coal to LTV, and opined that it was this desire that motivated Massey's acquisition of Wellmore, and further motivated Massey to eliminate the Harman Companies as its competitors via the destruction of those companies.

established, successful coal blend" that included coal from the Harman Mine, Massey nevertheless "provided LTV with firm price quotes for coal mainly from Massey Mines, not Harman coal, and insisted that LTV make Massey its sole-source provider via a long-term coal contract."[1] As a consequence of Massey's actions, LTV ceased buying coal from Wellmore. Thereafter, on August 5, 1997, Wellmore, at the direction of Massey, gave notice to the Harman Companies by letter stating that if LTV did in fact close its Pittsburgh plant, then Wellmore anticipated a pro rata reduction in tonnage under the *force majeure* clause of the 1997 CSWA.

Subsequent to Wellmore's August 5th letter, Massey entered into negotiations with the Harman Companies for the purchase of the Harman Mine. During the course of these negotiations, confidential information regarding the Harman Mine's operations, including its desire to eventually mine adjoining Pittston reserves, as well as confidential information pertaining to the finances of the Harman Companies and of Mr. Caperton, personally, was shared with Massey. The Harman Companies also expressed to Massey their disagreement that the LTV closure of its Pittsburgh coke plant constituted a *force majeure* event.

Thereafter, on December 1, 1997, Wellmore, at Massey's direction, declared *force majeure* based on LTV's closure of its Pittsburgh coke plant, and advised the Harman Companies that it would purchase only 205,707 tons of the 573,000 minimum tons of coal required under the 1997 CSA. According to the express findings of the circuit court on this point,

---

[1] [f.13 in original] Massey made these demands notwithstanding its knowledge that LTV had historically demonstrated a preference for multiple suppliers and had not entered multi-year coal supply contracts. Additionally, the firm price for its coal that Massey quoted to LTV represented "a handsome improvement" over the prices at which Massey had been selling its coal.

[o]nly after Massey's marketing efforts caused the loss of LTV's business did Massey direct Wellmore to declare "force majeure" against Harman, a declaration which Massey knew would put Harman out of business. Massey acknowledged Wellmore was readily able to purchase and sell the Harman coal, but instead chose to have Wellmore declare "force majeure" based upon a cost benefit analysis Massey performed which indicated that it would increase its profits by doing so. Furthermore, before Massey directed the declaration of "force majeure," Massey concealed the fact that the LTV business was lost and Massey delayed Wellmore's termination of Harman's contract until late in the year, knowing it would be virtually impossible for Harman to find alternate buyers for its coal at that point in time. Once Wellmore suddenly stopped purchasing Harman's output, Harman had no ability to stay in business. In the meantime, Massey sold Wellmore.

Massey continued in negotiations with the Harman Companies and Mr. Caperton for Massey's purchase of the Harman Mine, and the parties agreed to close the transaction on January 31, 1998. However, Massey delayed and, as the circuit court found, "ultimately collapsed the transaction in such a manner so as to increase [the Harman Companies'] financial distress." In addition, Massey utilized the confidential information it had obtained from the Harman Companies to take further actions, such as purchasing a narrow band of the Pittston coal reserves surrounding the Harman Mine in order to make the Harman Mine unattractive to others and thereby decrease its value. During the negotiations for the sale of the Harman Mine to Massey, Massey had also learned that Mr. Caperton had personally guaranteed a number of the Harman Companies' obligations. Subsequently, the Harman Companies filed for bankruptcy.

Thereafter, in May 1998, Harman Mining and Sovereign sued Wellmore in the Circuit Court of Buchanan County, Virginia, alleging causes of action for breach of contract and for breach of the covenant of good faith and fair dealing arising from Wellmore's declaration of force majeure. However, Harman Mining and Sovereign voluntarily withdrew their tort claim prior to trial. Following trial on the contract claim, a jury found in favor of Harman Mining and Sovereign and awarded $6 million in damages. [Footnotes omitted.]

II

PROCEDURAL HISTORY

Shortly after the Virginia action was filed, on October 29, 1998, Harman Development, Harman Mining, Sovereign and Mr. Caperton, individually, filed the instant action in the Circuit Court of Boone County, West Virginia, against A.T. Massey Coal Company, Inc., Elk Run Coal Company, Inc., Independence Coal Company, Inc., Mar Fork Coal Company, Inc., Performance Coal Company, and Massey Coal Sales Company, Inc. (hereinafter collectively referred to as "the Massey Defendants"). The first amended complaint in this action was filed on December 10, 1998, and asserted claims of tortious interference with existing contractual relations, tortious interference with prospective contractual relations, fraudulent misrepresentation, civil conspiracy, negligent misrepresentation, and punitive damages. Though numerous pre-trial motions were filed in the underlying action, one in particular is relevant to our resolution of this matter: in December 1998, the Massey Defendants filed a motion to dismiss. In their memorandum in support of the motion, the Massey Defendants argued, *inter alia,* that the forum-selection clause of the 1997 CSA required this action to be filed in Buchanan County, Virginia. The circuit court denied the Massey Defendants' motion to dismiss.

Ultimately, only three of the theories of liability asserted in this action were presented to the jury for a verdict: tortious interference, fraudulent misrepresentation and fraudulent concealment. On August 1, 2002, the jury found in favor of all plaintiffs on all three grounds and returned a verdict, including punitive damages, of $50,038,406.00. On August 30, 2002, the Massey Defendants filed a motion seeking judgment as a matter of law, a new trial, or, in the alternative, remittitur. Following a lengthy delay, by order entered March 17, 2005, the circuit court denied the post-trial motions. An appeal to this Court followed.

On November 21, 2007, this Court handed down its written opinion reversing the judgment of the circuit court and remanding for entry of an order dismissing with prejudice the case against the Massey Defendants. Subsequently, two of the justices who had participated in deciding the appeal voluntarily disqualified themselves, two circuit court judges were designated to sit on this Court by temporary assignment for the purpose of deciding the case on rehearing, and the November 21, 2007, opinion of the Court was vacated. The case was submitted on rehearing on March 12, 2008, and the Court's opinion, again reversing the judgment of the circuit court and remanding for entry of an order dismissing with prejudice the case against the Massey Defendants, was filed on April 3, 2008.

Thereafter, Mr. Caperton and the Harman Companies filed a petition for writ of certiorari in the United States Supreme Court asserting that acting Chief Justice Benjamin's refusal to grant their motions seeking his disqualification amounted to a violation of the Due Process Clause of the Fourteenth Amendment to the United States Constitution. The Supreme Court granted the petition on November 14, 2008. Thereafter, by a five-four decision, the Supreme Court reversed and remanded the case concluding that Justice Benjamin's participation in the decision of this case created an "unconstitutional 'potential for bias.'"

* * *

IV

DISCUSSION

* * *

B. Forum-Selection Clause

Although numerous issues have been raised on appeal in this case, we find that the instant matter may be resolved on the issue of the forum-selection clause contained in the 1997 CSA between Sovereign Coal Sales, Inc., Wellmore Coal Corporation, and Harman Mining Corporation.

[5] The 1997 CSA between Sovereign, Wellmore, and Harman Mining provided that the "[a]greement, in all respects, shall be governed, construed and enforced in accordance with the substantive laws of the Commonwealth of Virginia. All actions brought in connection with this Agreement shall be filed in and decided by the Circuit Court of Buchanan County, Virginia...." In the proceeding below, the Massey Defendants filed a motion to dismiss alleging, in relevant part, that the forum-selection clause in the 1997 CSA required that any action related to that agreement be brought in the Circuit Court of Buchanan County, Virginia. Accordingly, the Massey Defendants argued that the action was improperly before the Circuit Court of Boone County, West Virginia, and that the instant action should therefore be dismissed. The circuit court denied the motion to dismiss.

[6] This case presents the first opportunity for this Court to address substantive issues involving forum-selection clauses. By way of definition, it has been recognized that "[a] 'forum selection' provision in a contract designates a particular state or court as the jurisdiction in which the parties will litigate disputes arising out of the contract and their

contractual relationship." ...While forum-selection clauses historically were disfavored, such is no longer the case, so long as the clause is fair and reasonable:

* * *

During the past two decades, the rules governing the validity of various "forum selection" clauses have been relaxed considerably, the courts following a pattern similar to that which has already been discussed in connection with arbitration clauses. Thus, while it remains true today that a clause or provision *unreasonably or improperly* attempting to deprive a court of its jurisdiction will not be enforced, the modern trend is to respect the enforceability of contracts containing clauses limiting judicial jurisdiction, if there is nothing unfair or unreasonable about them.

* * *

Having found no impediment to the enforcement of forum-selection clauses in general, we now must endeavor to specifically determine whether the forum-selection clause of the 1997 CSA should have been enforced in the instant case.

[8] In *Phillips* v. *Audio Active Limited,* 494 F.3d 378 (2d Cir. 2007), the United States Court of Appeals for the Second Circuit articulated a four-part test for determining whether a claim should be dismissed based upon a forum-selection clause. We find this test supported by reason and logic, and by the manner in which such cases have been resolved in other courts; therefore, we now hold that

[d]etermining whether to dismiss a claim based on a forum[-]selection clause involves a four-part analysis. The first inquiry

is whether the clause was reasonably communicated to the party resisting enforcement.... The second step requires [classification of] the clause as mandatory or permissive, *i.e.*,...whether the parties are *required* to bring any dispute to the designated forum or [are] simply *permitted* to do so. [The third query] asks whether the claims and parties involved in the suit are subject to the forum selection clause....

If the [forum-selection] clause was communicated to the resisting party, has mandatory force and covers the claims and parties involved in the dispute, it is presumptively enforceable.... The fourth, and final, step is to ascertain whether the resisting party has rebutted the presumption of enforceability by making a sufficiently strong showing that "enforcement would be unreasonable [and] unjust, or that the clause was invalid for such reasons as fraud or overreaching."

* * *

[16] Turning to the instant case, the forum-selection clause utilized mandatory language that identified the jurisdiction wherein disputes would be tried: "[a]ll actions brought in connection with this Agreement *shall* be filed in and decided by the Circuit Court of Buchanan County, Virginia" (Emphasis added). Accordingly, we are presented with a mandatory forum-selection clause. ...Having determined that the forum-selection clause at issue in this case is a mandatory clause, we must now determine whether the claims and parties involved in the suit are governed by said clause.

3. Claims and Parties.

The third part of our analysis is to determine whether the claims and parties involved in the suit are governed by the forum-selection clause. We address these questions separately.

a. Are the claims asserted in the instant suit subject to the forum-selection clause?[1]

Mr. Caperton and the Harman Companies have argued that the claims asserted in this action are not governed by the forum-selection clause because they are tort, as opposed to contract, claims. We disagree.

[17] It has been recognized that,

> [w]hen a party seeks to enforce a mandatory forum-selection clause, a court must determine whether the claims in question fall within the scope of that clause.... The court bases this determination on the language of the clause and the nature of the claims that are allegedly subject to the clause.

* * *

[18-21] Turning to the case at hand, we must first examine the language of the mandatory forum-selection clause at issue. Because the

---

[1] [f. 29 in original] At the outset of this issue, we point out that, because the forum-selection clause issue was addressed by the circuit court in the context of the Massey Defendants' motion to dismiss, this Court is constrained to address the claims as they were asserted in the amended complaint. This is because the amended complaint represents the record that was before the circuit court at the time of its ruling on the Massey Defendants' motion to dismiss. Although facts pertaining to the claims asserted in the amended complaint were further developed during the course of the trial, such facts are not proper for our consideration on review of this issue.

1997 CSA expressly states that it "shall be...construed...in accordance with the substantive laws of the Commonwealth of Virginia," we will scrutinize the language of the clause pursuant to Virginia law. Notably, under Virginia law, "[w]ritten contracts are construed as written, without adding terms that were not included by the parties. When the terms in a contract are plain and unambiguous, the contract is construed according to its plain meaning. The words that the parties used are normally given their usual, ordinary and popular meaning."

The forum-selection clause of the 1997 CSA states in plain language that it applies to "[a]ll actions brought in connection with this Agreement." Due to the inclusion of the phrase "all actions," we perceive no intent by the parties to this agreement to limit in any way the type of actions to which it applies. Thus, for example, it would apply equally to contract claims, tort claims, and statutory claims, so long as such claims are "brought in connection with" the 1997 CSA.

* * *

Accordingly, because none of the relevant claims asserted in the amended complaint would have existed in the absence of Wellmore's declaration of *force majeure* under the 1997 CSA, these claims are all "brought in connection with" the 1997 CSA and, as a consequence, are within the scope of the forum-selection clause contained therein.

b. Are the parties involved in the suit subject to the forum-selection clause?

The Harman Companies and Mr. Caperton have argued that, as strangers to the 1997 CSA, the Massey Defendants are precluded from enforcing its terms as they are not third-party beneficiaries of the contract. The Harman Companies and Mr. Caperton further argued that two of the plaintiffs to this action, Harman Development and Mr. Caperton (in his individual capacity), are not signatories to the 1997 CSA and, therefore, may not be bound by its terms. We disagree.

* * *

[22] Based upon the foregoing, we now hold that a range of transaction participants, signatories and non-signatories, may benefit from and be subject to a forum selection clause. In order for a non-signatory to benefit from or be subject to a forum selection clause, the non-signatory must be closely related to the dispute such that it becomes foreseeable that the non-signatory may benefit from or be subject to the forum selection clause.

[23] Applying the foregoing holding to the facts of the instant case, we first note that, as to the plaintiffs, Sovereign; Mr. Caperton, as president of Sovereign; and Harman Mining were signatories to the 1997 CSA; Harman Development and Mr. Caperton, in his individual capacity, were not. However, Sovereign and Harman are wholly-owned subsidiaries of Harman Development, and Mr. Caperton is the sole owner of Harman Development. Under these facts, Mr. Caperton and Harman Development were closely connected to the 1997 CSA such that it was foreseeable that they would be subject to the forum-selection clause contained therein. As we determined in the preceding section of this opinion, the three factually-supported claims asserted in the first amended complaint[1] all flowed from the wrongful declaration of *force*

---

[1] [f.35 in original] As we noted in the preceding section of this opinion, the forum-selection clause issue was addressed below in the context of a motion to dismiss; therefore, we consider the claims as they were asserted in the first amended complaint. Notably, though, only three of the claims asserted in the amended complaint were ultimately presented to the jury for a verdict, indicating that there was insufficient evidence to

(Footnote continued on next page)

majeure under the 1997 CSA, and were brought in connection with that contract. Accordingly, we find that Mr. Caperton and Harman Development are bound by the forum-selection clause of the 1997 CSA.

* * *

4. Rebuttal.

Because the forum-selection clause was communicated to the resisting party, has mandatory force and covers the claims and parties involved in this dispute, it is presumptively enforceable. Thus, the final step to our analysis is to ascertain whether the Harman Companies and Mr. Caperton have rebutted the presumption of enforceability by making a sufficiently strong showing that enforcement would be unreasonable or unjust, or that the clause was invalid for such reasons as fraud or overreaching.

* * *

In this case, the Harman Companies and Mr. Caperton have not argued, either below or before this Court, that enforcement of the forum-selection clause of the 1997 CSA, i.e. requiring that this case be litigated in Virginia, was unreasonable or unjust at the time of the Massey Defendants' motion to dismiss...or that the clause was invalid for such reasons as fraud or overreaching. Instead, on the initial rehearing of this case, and again on remand from the United States Supreme Court, the Harman Companies and Mr. Caperton have argued, in part, that it is unjust to apply the forum-selection clause to deprive them of the large jury verdict awarded below. However, this improperly frames the issue.

---

support the remaining claims. Therefore, we limit our consideration to only those three claims that ultimately went to the jury.

The proper question is whether enforcement of the forum-selection clause was unjust or unreasonable *at the time of the Massey Defendants' motion to dismiss based upon the forum-selection clause.* The Harman Companies and Mr. Caperton have not come forth with any facts or argument that enforcement of the forum-selection clause was unreasonable or unjust at that time. Accordingly, the forum-selection clause should have been enforced by the circuit court, and that court's failure to grant the Massey Defendants' motion to dismiss based upon the forum-selection clause was an abuse of discretion....

5. **Retroactivity of the New Forum-Selection Clause.** On remand from the United States Supreme Court, the Harman Companies and Mr. Caperton argue, as they did on the initial rehearing of this case, that the new forum-selection clause principles of law herein developed should not be applied retroactively to them.... They contend, among other things, that due process principles prohibit such application. We disagree.

* * *

[32] The Supreme Court of Appeals of West Virginia, like all courts in the country, adheres to the common law principle that, "[a]s a general rule, judicial decisions are retroactive in the sense that they apply both to the parties in the case before the court and to all other parties in pending cases." *Crowe* v. *Bolduc*, 365 F.3d 86, 93 (1st Cir. 2004).

* * *

Although the common law rule presumes that appellate judicial decisions apply retroactively, "[t]he courts of this country long have recognized exceptions to the rule of retroactivity[.]" *Ashland Oil, Inc.* v. *Rose,* 177 W.Va. 20, 23, 350 S.E.2d 531, 534 (1986). The seminal case by this Court addressing the issue of an exception to retroactivity is

Bradley v. *Appalachian Power Co.,* 163 W.Va. 332, 256 S.E.2d 879 (1979).

* * *

To resolve the issue of retroactivity, in the context of new law that overruled prior case law, *Bradley* looked for guidance from the United States Supreme Court's decision in *Chevron Oil Co.* v. *Huson,* 404 U.S. 97, 92 S.Ct. 349, 30 L.Ed.2d 296 (1971), *overruled by Harper* v. *Virginia Department of Taxation,* 509 U.S. 86, 113 S.Ct. 2510, 125 L.Ed.2d 74 (1993).[1] After examining relevant language from the opinion in *Chevron, Bradley* fashioned the following test:

> In determining whether to extend full retroactivity, the following factors are to be considered: First, the nature of the substantive issue overruled must be determined. If the issue involves a traditionally settled area of law, such as contracts or property as distinguished from torts, and the new rule was not clearly foreshadowed, then retroactivity is less justified. Second, where the overruled decision deals with procedural law rather than substantive, retroactivity ordinarily will be more readily accorded. Third, common law decisions, when overruled, may result in the overruling decision being given retroactive effect, since the substantive issue usually has a narrower impact and is

---

[1] [f.40 in original] The *Bradley* decision acknowledged a prior principle of law created by the Court that involved retroactivity, but found that prior principle was too narrow. *See* Syl. Pt. 2, *Falconer* v. *Simmons,* 51 W.Va. 172, 41 S.E. 193 (1902) ("An overruled decision is regarded not law, as never having been the law, but the law as given in the later case is regarded as having been the law, even at the date of the erroneous decision. To this rule there is one exception, — that where there is a statute, and a decision giving it a certain construction, and there is a contract valid under such construction, the later decision does not retroact so as to invalidate such contract.")

likely to involve fewer parties. Fourth, where, on the other hand, substantial public issues are involved, arising from statutory or constitutional interpretations that represent a clear departure from prior precedent, prospective application will ordinarily be favored. Fifth, the more radically the new decision departs from previous substantive law, the greater the need for limiting retroactivity. Finally, this Court will also look to the precedent of other courts which have determined the retroactive/ prospective question in the same area of the law in their overruling decisions.

The retroactivity test announced in *Bradley* has been relied upon by this Court whenever the issue of retroactivity has arisen in a civil case. However, the *Bradley* test is narrowly confined to deciding whether to retroactively apply a new principle of law that was created in a case that overruled prior precedent. The narrow constraints of *Bradley* have proved to be problematic whenever this Court has examined retroactivity in the context of a new principle of law created in a case that did not overrule prior precedent.

* * *

With the *Chevron* factors as a guide, we now hold that in determining whether to extend full retroactivity to a new principle of law established in a civil case that *does not overrule* any prior precedent, which is an issue that was not addressed in *Bradley* v. *Appalachian Power Co.,* 163 W.Va. 332, the following factors will be considered. First, we will determine whether the new principle of law was an issue of first impression whose resolution was clearly foreshadowed. Second, we must determine whether or not the purpose and effect of the new rule will be enhanced or retarded by applying the rule retroactively. Finally, we will determine whether full retroactivity of the new rule would produce substantial inequitable results.

In the instant proceeding, we are called upon to decide whether or not the principles of law developed in this opinion, involving forum-selection clauses, should be applied retroactively to the parties. Under the test set out above, we find no impediment to applying the new forum-selection clause principles to the parties in this case.

[34] a. The new forum-selection clause principles were clearly foreshadowed.

The Harman Companies and Mr. Caperton argue that the new forum-selection clause principles applied in this case were not foreshadowed by any prior decision of this Court. We disagree.

* * *

[W]e need not look to a national trend to find that the new forum-selection clause principles developed in this case were foreshadowed. As previously pointed out in this opinion, over twenty-five years ago in *General Electric Co.* v. *Keyser,* 166 W.Va. 456 (1981), this Court indicated that forum-selection clauses were not against the public policy of this State. Specifically, we stated in *Keyser,*

> We have had occasion, however, to discuss, indirectly, forum selection clauses. Although our law on this point is skeletal, it does indicate that contract clauses which affect matters such as jurisdiction and the like should be carefully analyzed. Unquestionably, forum selection clauses are not contrary to public policy in and of themselves for they are sanctioned in commercial sales agreements[.]

Keyser, 166 W.Va. at 461 n. 2, 275 S.E.2d at 291 n. 2. Clearly, *Keyser* placed the parties in this action on notice that, when presented with an opportunity, this Court would "carefully" analyze all matters relevant to the forum-selection clause presented on appeal. Contrary to the arguments of the Harman Companies and Mr. Caperton, there is no requirement that there must exist specific precedent that foreshadowed exactly how this Court would resolve new issues involving a forum-selection clause. If such a situation was the law in this State or any jurisdiction in the country, there would be very few cases decided on appeal that created new law which could be applied to the parties before the appellate court. This is not the law in the country nor in West Virginia. Consequently, we find that the new forum-selection clause principles created in this opinion were foreshadowed by *Keyser.*

* * *

Accordingly, we conclude that the forum-selection clause principles of law adopted by this opinion may properly be applied to the parties to the instant proceeding.

V.
CONCLUSION

For the reasons stated in the body of this opinion, we reverse the judgment in this case and remand for the circuit court to enter an order dismissing this case against A.T. Massey Coal Company and its subsidiaries with prejudice.

Reversed and remanded.

Chief Justice BENJAMIN, having been disqualified, did not participate in the decision of this case.

Senior Status Judge HOLLIDAY sitting by temporary assignment.

WORKMAN, Justice, dissenting.

Neither the sheer length of the majority's opinion, nor the large number of cases cited (but erroneously applied), nor even its expansive conclusory statements, can obfuscate its lack of sound legal reasoning and its result-driven approach.

In enunciating *eight* major new points of law and applying them retroactively (with no opportunity for the parties to make a record under the new law), scrapping mountains of prior precedent that give deference to the finders of fact below (and instead making new factual determinations at this level), rewarding the defendant (whose conduct is seemingly recognized by all as reprehensible) the spoils of its fraudulent acts, and then characterizing the result as "equitable," the majority has turned West Virginia jurisprudence on its ear.

Specifically, the majority holds that Massey, despite engaging in wide-ranging fraudulent conduct, both in connection with the 1997 Coal Supply Agreement ("the CSA"), as well as separate and apart from it, is entitled to benefit from the forum-selection clause not only with regard to matters relating to the CSA, but even with respect to actions completely unconnected to that contract. The majority reaches this conclusion despite the fact that the forum-selection clause is contained in a contract to which Massey was not a party, with which Massey tortiously interfered, and under which Massey never acted in good faith. In so doing, the majority not only deprives the plaintiffs of the substantial damages awarded to them by the rightful finders of fact, a Boone County jury, but also leaves them with no legal recourse by which to address Massey's extensive pattern of fraudulent conduct. It similarly eliminates any recovery for the plaintiffs' numerous creditors in the three pending bankruptcy cases, to whom most of the judgment would have gone. Not least among those creditors are the Harman Companies' union miners who lost their jobs as a result of Massey's fraudulent conduct, and the Harman Companies' hundreds of retirees, to whom the Harman Companies previously paid pensions and medical benefits.

Because the majority unjustly strips Massey's victims of their rightful verdict by creating extensive new law and manipulating the existing law to achieve the end result, I dissent.

* * *

I. Facts

The plaintiffs in the underlying case, Harman Development Corporation, Harman Mining Corporation, and Sovereign Coal Sales, Inc. (collectively "the Harman Companies"), and Hugh M. Caperton ("Mr. Caperton"), sued A.T. Massey Coal Company, Inc. and several of its subsidiaries (collectively "Massey") in the Circuit Court of Boone County, West Virginia. The Harman Companies alleged, among other things, that Massey engaged in tortious interference with several of the Harman Companies' and Mr. Caperton's existing contracts, and further that Massey engaged in fraudulent concealment and made fraudulent misrepresentations in its dealings with the plaintiffs. After a lengthy trial, during which the plaintiffs produced overwhelming evidence of Massey's intentional fraudulent acts, a jury in Boone County awarded the plaintiffs more than fifty million dollars in damages.

Early in the course of that litigation, Massey filed a motion to dismiss based on improper venue, arguing that a forum-selection clause contained in the CSA, a contract between two of the Harman Companies and Wellmore Coal Corporation ("Wellmore"), required that all actions brought in connection with the contract be litigated in Virginia. The Circuit Court of Boone County denied that motion. The majority now reverses, holding that because *one* of Massey's alleged fraudulent acts – its fraudulent declaration of *force majeure* – was performed "in connection with" the CSA, all of the plaintiffs' claims, even those completely unconnected to the CSA, should have been brought in Virginia. In reaching this conclusion, the majority ignores Massey's significant fraudulent acts that were unrelated to the CSA but that culminated in the financial destruction of the Harman Companies and Mr. Caperton. Instead the majority declares that the fraudulent declaration of *force majeure* was *the act* from which *all* of the plaintiffs' damages flowed. This is simply not true. As determined by the fact-finders and fully demonstrated by the record below, Massey engaged in a web of deceit replete with fraudulent acts, many of which were separate and apart from the declaration of *force majeure.*

Specifically, the evidence introduced at trial showed that Massey engaged in a wide-ranging scheme to expand the market for its own coal, obtain access to the Harman Companies' valuable coal reserves and eliminate the Harman Companies and Mr. Caperton as competitors from the metallurgical coal market. While aggressive competition and even sharp practice in business dealings is certainly not actionable in and of itself, it becomes actionable when a party engages in fraudulent misrepresentations and fraudulent concealment to achieve those goals. Here, Massey developed a scheme in which it simultaneously disrupted the Harman Companies' existing coal supply contract with Wellmore, thus eliminating the Harman Companies' primary source of revenue, while engaging in fraudulent, bad-faith negotiations with Mr. Caperton for the sale of his interest in the Harman Companies' assets. Through these fraudulent negotiations, Massey lured Mr. Caperton and the Harman Companies into a false sense of security, thereby deterring them from seeking other buyers for their coal. Moreover, Massey actively dissuaded other potential buyers and took steps to ensure that the Harman Companies' reserves would be unattractive to anyone else. Ultimately, after ensuring that Mr. Caperton would be unable to find any other willing buyers, Massey collapsed the sale negotiations altogether, thereby forcing the Harman Companies and Mr. Caperton into bankruptcy.

In furtherance of this fraudulent scheme, Massey engaged in actions that cannot reasonably be considered to have any "connection with" the CSA. For example:

(1) After Massey expressed a desire to purchase Mr. Caperton's interest in the Harman Companies, *Mr. Caperton, at Massey's request, shared confidential information with Massey relating to his business plans.* Specifically, beginning at a meeting in late November 1997, and continuing through January 1998, Mr. Caperton provided Massey with confidential business information including mine maps, reserve studies, drill information, and, importantly, the Harman Companies' plans to expand into adjoining reserves owned by Pittston Coal Company ("Pittston"). Mr. Caperton also advised Massey of the Harman Companies' debt obligations, including debts for which Mr. Caperton was personally obligated, and advised Massey of the terms of the Harman Companies' lease with Penn Virginia Coal Company ("Penn Virginia"), the owner and lessor of the Harman Companies' coal reserves;

(2) As the negotiations for proposed sale of Mr. Caperton's interest in the Harman Companies continued, Massey represented that it intended to take over the Harman Companies' lease with Penn Virginia "as is," and the parties agreed to close the deal on January 31, 1998. *At Massey's request, Mr. Caperton shut down the Harman Companies' operations on January 19, 1998, in preparation for that closing date.* An internal memo circulated between Massey officers, however, indicated that, unbeknownst to Mr. Caperton, Massey had no intention of closing on the agreed-upon date. Moreover, *Massey knowingly allowed the Harman Companies to continue to believe the January 31, 1998, date would be met,* and allowed Mr. Caperton to shut down operations as planned despite knowing, from the confidential information that it had previously obtained, that such action would have serious financial consequences for

both the Harman Companies and for Mr. Caperton, due to his personal guarantees of certain of the Harman Companies' loans;

(3) After refusing to close the deal by the original deadline, Massey continued to intentionally mislead the Harman Companies and Mr. Caperton into believing that an agreement would be reached. Among other things, Massey executed several "letters of intent" to Mr. Caperton and several creditors of the Harman Companies. For example, in a letter dated February 9, 1998, to Mr. Caperton, Massey promised to, among other things, "pursue good faith negotiations" to reach a deal permitting Massey to acquire Mr. Caperton's interest in the Harman Companies;

(4) Two days after this letter, on February 11, 1998, Massey announced that it had sold Wellmore to Black Diamond Company ("Black Diamond"). As part of that sale, *Massey directed Black Diamond not to pursue the acquisition of the Harman Companies, a possibility in which Black Diamond had previously expressed an interest;*

(5) With the plaintiffs still unaware of Massey's true intentions, the parties agreed to a new closing date of March 13, 1998. Hours before the transaction was set to close, and despite Massey's previous assertions that it would accept the Penn Virginia lease "as is," *Massey intentionally collapsed the deal by demanding unreasonable changes to the proposed lease with Penn Virginia.* Those demands included changing the term of the lease, the royalty rate, the mining provisions and the recoupment period. Although Penn Virginia agreed to certain further concessions, Massey refused to negotiate at all, and the deal crumbled;

(6) After collapsing the deal, *Massey, using the confidential information it had obtained through the sale negotiation process,* purchased a narrow band of coal surrounding the Harman Companies' reserves from Pittston, in order to create a barrier that would prevent any company other than Massey from being able to expand the Harman Companies' operations. Massey's own internal documents acknowledged that this purchase ensured that the Harman Companies' property would be unattractive to

any potential buyer other than Massey, thus ensuring that Massey would be able to acquire the Harman property "in the long run," obviously implying after bankruptcy.

None of these acts bore any connection to the CSA. Yet the majority sweeps them under the CSA in a conclusory manner, with no attempt to offer any reasoning or explanation for doing so. Indeed, rather than acknowledge the gravity of Massey's foregoing conduct, the majority, using tunnel vision, focuses solely on the declaration of *force majeure.*

As a result of this conduct, the Harman Companies defaulted on the terms of their lease with Penn Virginia, violated the terms of their contractual obligations to their miners and the UMWA, defaulted on loans to creditors, and ultimately declared bankruptcy. Because Mr. Caperton had personally guaranteed certain loans on behalf of the Harman Companies, he was forced into personal bankruptcy. As a further consequence of Massey's scheme, Mr. Caperton defaulted on land reclamation liabilities under Federal and State environmental laws and, as a result, was entered into the Office of Surface Mining's Applicant Violator System, which effectively prevents him from obtaining any future coal mining permits or otherwise working in a position of authority in that industry.

II. Enforceability of the Forum-Selection Clause

The majority announces that this case presents the first opportunity for this Court to address substantive issues relating to the enforcement of forum-selection clauses. In so stating, it broadly asserts that this Court has "previously indicated our general approval of forum-selection clauses," because this Court has noted, in dicta contained in a footnote, that such clauses are not contrary to public policy. Specifically, in *General Electric Company* v. *Keyser,* 166 W.Va. 456 (1981), this Court stated in footnote two:

We have had occasion, however, to discuss, indirectly, forum selection clauses. Although our law on this point is skeletal, it does indicate that contract clauses which affect matters such as jurisdiction and the like should be carefully analyzed....

As the Federal court observed, West Virginia appears not to subscribe to the rule that choice of forum clauses are void per se. "Rather the rule of most jurisdictions and the rule that this Court believes that West Virginia should and would adopt is that such clauses will be enforced only when found to be reasonable and just." *Leasewell, Ltd.* v. *Jake Shelton Ford Inc.,* 423 F.Supp. 1011, 1015 (S.D.W.Va. 1976).

* * *

Id. at 461 n. 2, 275 S.E.2d at 292 n. 2. An objective reading of this footnote does not support the majority's sweeping conclusion that this Court's prior law indicates "general approval" of forum-selection clauses. Rather, the footnote indicates skepticism of such clauses by requiring that they be "carefully analyzed," and further implies that such clauses should only be enforced where they are "reasonable and just."

Nevertheless, the majority misstates that forum-selection clauses are viewed with favor in West Virginia, and proceeds to adopt a test for determining the enforceability of a forum-selection clause.... Specifically, the majority sets forth the following four factors for consideration: (1) whether the clause was reasonably communicated to the party resisting enforcement, (2) whether the clause is mandatory or permissive, (3) whether the claims and parties involved in the suit are subject to the forum-selection clause, and (4) whether the resisting party has rebutted the presumption of enforceability by making a sufficiently strong showing that enforcement would be unreasonable and unjust, or that the clause was invalid for such reasons as fraud or overreaching. Although at least two of these four new factors obviously require fact-driven determinations, the majority not only adopts these new principles of law out of the blue, it then refuses to give the plaintiffs a chance to present evidence on them and, incredibly, proceeds to make *de novo* findings of fact themselves!

* * *

B. Scope of the Plaintiff's Claims

The broad language of the forum-selection clause in this case provides that it applies to "all actions brought *in connection with*" the CSA. The facts in this case, however, establish that it was Massey's actions relating to the sale of Mr. Caperton's interest in the Harman Companies – actions that were not related in any way to the CSA – that directly caused the Harman Companies' and Mr. Caperton's complete financial demise.

* * *

Like many of its other determinations, the majority simply makes conclusory statements without any support or reasoning.

Importantly, this case involves *fraud*, rather than an act of negligence or straightforward breach of contract. Courts in many other jurisdictions have refused to enforce forum-selection clauses where the plaintiff has asserted claims of wide-ranging *fraudulent* conduct. In such cases, the court considering the forum-selection clause concluded that the "gist" of the asserted claims exceeded the scope of the contract containing the forum-selection clause and, thus, the court refused to allow the defendant to benefit from the clause.

* * *

III. Retroactive Application of the New Principles of Law

Even if the majority was correct that, under its new law relating to the enforceability of forum-selection clauses, this suit should have been brought in Virginia, it is clearly unjust to enforce the new principles of law in this case, particularly by doing so without remanding the case for application of the new test by the circuit court. Indeed, I am at a complete loss to understand how the majority can allow Massey to benefit-to the tune of more than fifty million dollars plus interest-from a forum-selection clause contained in a contract that Massey actively sought to destroy. That the majority considers the application of the forum-selection clause in this case to be an "equitable result" is beyond comprehension.

A. Due Process Violation

As previously discussed, the majority adopts a brand new legal test for determining the validity and applicability of a forum-selection clause, a test which necessarily requires findings of fact. The majority, however, refuses to remand the case for application of the test by the circuit court. Instead, flying in the face of clear precedent, the majority makes its own findings of fact in applying the test, without providing the plaintiffs any opportunity to establish an appropriate evidentiary record. Accordingly, because the plaintiffs did not have a crystal ball during the early stages of this case, they are precluded from even attempting to comport with the new legal principles set forth by the majority.

* * *

The majority's application of its new retroactivity test to the instant case, however, is arbitrary and unjust. Indeed, when applied to this case, even the new test clearly weighs *against* retroactive application. Not only are the majority's new principles of law relating to forum-selection clauses not "clearly foreshadowed," enforcement of these new principles plainly produces a "substantially inequitable result."

* * *

In the case at hand, however, no prior decisions of this Court provide any foreshadowing whatsoever that this Court would be adopting any new legal principles relating to forum-selection clauses, much less those that have been adopted in this case. To say that the majority's new test was "clearly foreshadowed" requires great poetic license and a true stretch of the imagination.

2. Application Creates Substantially Inequitable Results

I vehemently disagree with the majority's conclusion that no "inequitable result" ensues from applying its new principles of law to the suit at issue. A jury, after considering all the evidence relating to the *merits* of the case, found Massey guilty of tortiously interfering with the plaintiffs' existing contracts, as well as making fraudulent misrepresentations and engaging in fraudulent concealment. It awarded the plaintiffs more than fifty million dollars in damages. As previously stated, much of that verdict would have gone to repaying the Harman Companies' creditors, who were also victims of Massey's conduct. To reverse such a verdict on the basis of a circuit court's decision on *venue - an issue wholly unrelated to the merits of the case* - cannot be fair or equitable, particularly without having given the plaintiffs an opportunity to prove, under the new principles of law, that the forum-selection clause in this case should not have been enforced. This injustice is further exacerbated by the fact that the applicable statutes of limitations prohibit the Harman Companies and Mr. Caperton from bringing their claims in Virginia, where the majority now holds they should have been brought.

Thus, the plaintiffs are left without *any* recourse against Massey's illegal behavior.

In support of its conclusion that retroactive application of the new legal principles is equitable in this case, the majority merely states that "there is no evidence in the record to show that the forum-selection clause involved in this case was not freely bargained for by the actual signatories to the agreement." This incredibly narrow and result-oriented view of what makes the retroactive application of a new point of law "inequitable" is very troubling. The majority once again refuses to consider the fact that Massey was being sued because of its *fraudulent course of conduct,* one important element of which was its breach of the very contract that contained the forum-selection clause. *To allow a party that engages in such fraudulent behavior to then benefit from the contract that it sought to destroy is the very definition of inequitable.* Accordingly, "substantial inequitable results" are produced by the retroactive application of the majority's new legal principles and the new law should not be retroactively enforced in this case.

*

Citizens United v. Federal Election Commission

558 U.S. 310

As you read this case, observe the interplay between the majority and dissenting opinions, and compare this to the suggested thoughts throughout the book for your own analysis. Also note the opinion refers to, *inter alia*, both the *New York Times* and *Caperton* cases.

You will like it. And yes, the final result comes down to Five to Four. Have a nice year.

*

SUPREME COURT OF THE UNITED STATES

CITIZENS UNITED, APPELLANT v. FEDERAL ELECTION COMMISSION

558 U.S. 310 (2010)

On Appeal From the United States District Court for the District of Columbia

JUSTICE KENNEDY delivered the opinion of the Court.

Federal law prohibits corporations and unions from using their general treasury funds to make independent expenditures for speech defined as an "electioneering communication" or for speech expressly advocating the election or defeat of a candidate. 2 U.S.C. §441b. Limits on electioneering communications were upheld in *McConnell* v. *Federal Election Comm'n*, 540 U.S. 93, 203-209 (2003). The holding of *McConnell* rested to a large extent on an earlier case, *Austin* v. *Michigan Chamber of Commerce*, 494 U.S. 652 (1990). *Austin* had held that political speech may be banned based on the speaker's corporate identity.

In this case we are asked to reconsider *Austin* and, in effect, *McConnell*. It has been noted that "*Austin* was a significant departure from ancient First Amendment principles," *Federal Election Comm'n* v. *Wisconsin Right to Life, Inc.*, 551 U.S. 449, 490 (2007) *(WRTL)* (SCALIA, J., concurring in part and concurring in judgment). We agree with that conclusion and hold that *stare decisis* does not compel the continued acceptance of *Austin*. The Government may regulate corporate political speech through disclaimer and disclosure requirements, but it may not suppress that speech altogether. We turn to the case now before us.

I

A

Citizens United is a nonprofit corporation. It brought this action in the United States District Court for the District of Columbia. A three-judge court later convened to hear the cause. The resulting judgment gives rise to this appeal.

Citizens United has an annual budget of about $12 million. Most of its funds are from donations by individuals; but, in addition, it accepts a small portion of its funds from for-profit corporations.

In January 2008, Citizens United released a film entitled *Hillary: The Movie.* We refer to the film as *Hillary.* It is a 90-minute documentary about then-Senator Hillary Clinton, who was a candidate in the Democratic Party's 2008 Presidential primary elections. *Hillary* mentions Senator Clinton by name and depicts interviews with political commentators and other persons, most of them quite critical of Senator Clinton. *Hillary* was released in theaters and on DVD, but Citizens United wanted to increase distribution by making it available through video-on-demand.

Video-on-demand allows digital cable subscribers to select programming from various menus, including movies, television shows, sports, news, and music. The viewer can watch the program at any time and can elect to rewind or pause the program. In December 2007, a cable company offered, for a payment of $1.2 million, to make *Hillary* available on a video-on-demand channel called "Elections '08." Some video-on-demand services require viewers to pay a small fee to view a selected program, but here the proposal was to make *Hillary* available to viewers free of charge.

To implement the proposal, Citizens United was prepared to pay for the video-on-demand; and to promote the film, it produced two 10-second ads and one 30-second ad for *Hillary.* Each ad includes a short (and, in our view, pejorative) statement about Senator Clinton, followed by the name of the movie and the movie's Website address. Citizens United desired to promote the video-on-demand offering by running advertisements on broadcast and cable television.

B

Before the Bipartisan Campaign Reform Act of 2002 (BCRA), federal law prohibited—and still does prohibit— corporations and unions from using general treasury funds to make direct contributions to candidates or independent expenditures that expressly advocate the election or defeat of a candidate, through any form of media, in connection with certain qualified federal elections. BCRA §203 amended §441b to prohibit any "electioneering communication" as well. ...An electioneering communication is defined as "any broadcast, cable, or satellite communication" that "refers to a clearly identified candidate for Federal office" and is made within 30 days of a primary or 60 days of a general election. The Federal Election Commission's (FEC) regulations further define an electioneering communication as a communication that is "publicly distributed." 11 CFR §100.29(a)(2) (2009). "In the case of a candidate for nomination for President...*publicly distributed* means" that the communication "[c]an be received by 50,000 or more persons in a State where a primary election...is being held within 30 days." Corporations and unions are barred from using their general treasury funds for express advocacy or electioneering communications. They may establish, however, a "separate segregated fund" (known as a political action committee, or PAC) for these purposes. 2 U.S.C. §441b(b)(2). The moneys received by the segregated fund are limited to donations from stockholders and employees of the corporation or, in the case of unions, members of the union.

C

Citizens United wanted to make *Hillary* available through video-on-demand within 30 days of the 2008 primary elections. It feared, however, that both the film and the ads would be covered by §441b's ban on corporate-funded independent expenditures, thus subjecting the corporation to civil and criminal penalties under §437g. In December 2007, Citizens United sought declaratory and injunctive relief against the FEC. It argued that (1) §441b is unconstitutional as applied to *Hillary;*

and (2) BCRA's disclaimer and disclosure requirements, BCRA §§201 and 311, 116 Stat. 88, 105, are unconstitutional as applied to *Hillary* and to the three ads for the movie.

The District Court denied Citizens United's motion for a preliminary injunction, 530 F.Supp.2d 274 (D.D.C. 2008) *(per curiam)*, and then granted the FEC's motion for summary judgment[.] ...The court held that §441b was facially constitutional under *McConnell*, and that §441b was constitutional as applied to *Hillary* because it was "susceptible of no other interpretation than to inform the electorate that Senator Clinton is unfit for office, that the United States would be a dangerous place in a President Hillary Clinton world, and that viewers should vote against her." 530 F.Supp.2d, at 279. The court also rejected Citizens United's challenge to BCRA's disclaimer and disclosure requirements. It noted that "the Supreme Court has written approvingly [175 L.Ed.2d 771] of disclosure provisions triggered by political speech even though the speech itself was constitutionally protected under the First Amendment."

* * *

II

Before considering whether *Austin* should be overruled, we first address whether Citizens United's claim that §441b cannot be applied to *Hillary* may be resolved on other, narrower grounds.

A

Citizens United contends that §441b does not cover *Hillary*, as a matter of statutory interpretation, because the film does not qualify as an "electioneering communication."

* * *

In our view the statute cannot be saved by limiting the reach of 2 U.S.C. §441b through this suggested interpretation. In addition to the costs and burdens of litigation, this result would require a calculation as to the number of people a particular communication is likely to reach, with an inaccurate estimate potentially subjecting the speaker to criminal sanctions. The First Amendment does not permit laws that force speakers to retain a campaign finance attorney, conduct demographic marketing research, or seek declaratory rulings before discussing the most salient political issues of our day. Prolix laws chill speech for the same reason that vague laws chill speech: People "of common intelligence must necessarily guess at [the law's] meaning and differ as to its application." The Government may not render a ban on political speech constitutional by carving out a limited exemption through an amorphous regulatory interpretation. We must reject the approach suggested by the *amici*.

* * *

C

Citizens United further contends that §441b should be invalidated as applied to movies shown through video-on-demand, arguing that this delivery system has a lower risk of distorting the political process than do television ads....

While some means of communication may be less effective than others at influencing the public in different contexts, any effort by the Judiciary to decide which means of communications are to be preferred for the particular type of message and speaker would raise questions as to the courts' own lawful authority. Substantial questions would arise if courts were to begin saying what means of speech should be preferred or disfavored. And in all events, those differentiations might soon prove to be irrelevant or outdated by technologies that are in rapid flux.

* * *

Courts, too, are bound by the First Amendment. We must decline to draw, and then redraw, constitutional lines based on the particular media or technology used to disseminate political speech from a particular speaker. It must be noted, moreover, that this undertaking would require substantial litigation over an extended time, all to interpret a law that beyond doubt discloses serious First Amendment flaws. The interpretive process itself would create an inevitable, pervasive, and serious risk of chilling protected speech pending the drawing of fine distinctions that, in the end, would themselves be questionable. First Amendment standards, however, "must give the benefit of any doubt to protecting rather than stifling speech." *WRTL, supra*, 551 U.S., at 469 (opinion of ROBERTS, C. J.) (citing *New York Times Co.* v. *Sullivan*, 376 U.S. 254, 269-270 (1964)).

* * *

E

As the foregoing analysis confirms, the Court cannot resolve this case on a narrower ground without chilling political speech, speech that is central to the meaning and purpose of the First Amendment. See *Morse* v. *Frederick*, 551 U.S. 393, 403 (2007). It is not judicial restraint to accept an unsound, narrow argument just so the Court can avoid another argument with broader implications. Indeed, a court would be remiss in performing its duties were it to accept an unsound principle merely to avoid the necessity of making a broader ruling. Here, the lack of a valid basis for an alternative ruling requires full consideration of the continuing effect of the speech suppression upheld in *Austin*.

* * *

This regulatory scheme may not be a prior restraint on speech in the strict sense of that term, for prospective speakers are not compelled by law to seek an advisory opinion from the FEC before the speech takes place... As a practical matter, however, given the complexity of the regulations and the deference courts show to administrative determinations, a speaker who wants to avoid threats of criminal liability and the heavy costs of defending against FEC enforcement must ask a governmental agency for prior permission to speak.... These onerous restrictions thus function as the equivalent of prior restraint by giving the FEC power analogous to licensing laws implemented in 16th- and 17th-century England, laws and governmental practices of the sort that the First Amendment was drawn to prohibit.... Because the FEC's "business is to censor, there inheres the danger that [it] may well be less responsive than a court—part of an independent branch of government—to the constitutionally protected interests in free expression." . . .When the FEC issues advisory opinions that prohibit speech, "[m]any persons, rather than undertake the considerable burden (and sometimes risk) of vindicating their rights through case-by-case litigation, will choose simply to abstain from protected speech—harming not only themselves but society as a whole, which is deprived of an uninhibited marketplace of ideas." ...Consequently, "the censor's determination may in practice be final."

This is precisely what *WRTL* sought to avoid. *WRTL* said that First Amendment standards "must eschew 'the open-ended rough-and-tumble of factors,' which 'invit[es] complex argument in a trial court and a virtually inevitable appeal.'" ...Yet, the FEC has created a regime that allows it to select what political speech is safe for public consumption by applying ambiguous tests. If parties want to avoid litigation and the possibility of civil and criminal penalties, they must either refrain from speaking or ask the FEC to issue an advisory opinion approving of the political speech in question. Government officials pore over each word of a text to see if, in their judgment, it accords with the 11-factor test they have promulgated. This is an unprecedented governmental intervention into the realm of speech.

The ongoing chill upon speech that is beyond all doubt protected makes it necessary in this case to invoke the [175 L.Ed.2d 780] earlier precedents that a statute which chills speech can and must be invalidated where its facial invalidity has been demonstrated. ...For these reasons we find it necessary to reconsider *Austin*.

III

The First Amendment provides that "Congress shall make no law...abridging the freedom of speech." Laws enacted to control or suppress speech may operate at different points in the speech process.

* * *

The law before us is an outright ban, backed by criminal sanctions. Section 441b makes it a felony for all corporations—including nonprofit advocacy corporations—either to expressly advocate the election or defeat of candidates or to broadcast electioneering communications within 30 days of a primary election and 60 days of a general election.

* * *

Section 441b is a ban on corporate speech notwithstanding the fact that a PAC created by a corporation can still speak.

* * *

Section 441b's prohibition on corporate independent expenditures is thus a ban on speech. As a "restriction on the amount of money a person or group can spend on political communication during a campaign," that statute "necessarily reduces the quantity of expression by restricting the number of issues discussed, the depth of their exploration, and the size of the audience reached." *Buckley* v. *Valeo*, 424 U.S. 1, 19 (1976) (*per curiam*). Were the Court to uphold these restrictions, the Government could repress speech by silencing certain voices at any of the various points in the speech process. ...If §441b applied to individuals, no one would believe that it is merely a time, place, or manner restriction on speech. Its purpose and effect are to silence entities whose voices the Government deems to be suspect.

Speech is an essential mechanism of democracy, for it is the means to hold officials accountable to the people.... The right of citizens to inquire, to hear, to speak, and to use information to reach consensus is a precondition to enlightened self-government and a necessary means to protect it. The First Amendment "'has its fullest and most urgent application' to speech uttered during a campaign for political office." *Eu* v. *San Francisco County Democratic Central Comm.*, 489 U.S. 214, 223 (1989).

* * *

Premised on mistrust of governmental power, the First Amendment stands against attempts to disfavor certain subjects or viewpoints. ...Prohibited, too, are restrictions distinguishing among different speakers, allowing speech by some but not others. ...As instruments to censor, these categories are interrelated: Speech restrictions based on the identity of the speaker are all too often simply a means to control content.

Quite apart from the purpose or effect of regulating content, moreover, the Government may commit a constitutional wrong when by law it identifies certain preferred speakers. By taking the right to speak from some and giving it to others, the Government deprives the disadvantaged person or class of the right to use speech to strive to establish worth, standing, and respect for the speaker's voice. The Government may not by these means deprive the public of the right and privilege to determine for itself what speech and speakers are worthy of consideration. The First Amendment protects speech and speaker, and the ideas that flow from each.

The Court has upheld a narrow class of speech restrictions that operate to the disadvantage of certain persons, but these rulings were based on an interest in allowing governmental entities to perform their functions. ...The corporate independent expenditures at issue in this case, however, would not interfere with governmental functions[.] ...[I]t is inherent in the nature of the political process that voters must be free to obtain information from diverse sources in order to determine how to cast their votes. At least before *Austin*, the Court had not allowed the exclusion of a class of speakers from the general public dialogue.

We find no basis for the proposition that, in the context of political speech, the Government may impose restrictions on certain disfavored speakers. Both history and logic lead us to this conclusion.

A

1

The Court has recognized that First Amendment protection extends to corporations. ...*New York Times Co.* v. *Sullivan*, 376 U.S. 254....

This protection has been extended by explicit holdings to the context of political speech. ...Under the rationale of these precedents, political speech does not lose First Amendment protection "simply because its source is a corporation."...

At least since the latter part of the 19th century, the laws of some States and of the United States imposed a ban on corporate direct contributions to candidates. ...Yet not until 1947 did Congress first prohibit independent expenditures by corporations and labor unions in §304 of the Labor Management Relations Act 1947. ...In passing this Act Congress overrode the veto of President Truman, who warned that the expenditure ban was a "dangerous intrusion on free speech."

* * *

3

Thus the law stood until *Austin*. *Austin* "uph[eld] a direct restriction on the independent expenditure of funds for political speech for the first time in [this Court's] history." 494 U.S., at 695 (Kennedy, J., dissenting). There, the Michigan Chamber of Commerce sought to use general treasury funds to run a newspaper ad supporting a specific candidate. Michigan law, however, prohibited corporate independent expenditures that supported or opposed any candidate for state office. A violation of the law was punishable as a felony. The Court sustained the speech prohibition.

...The *Austin* Court identified a new governmental interest in limiting political speech: an antidistortion interest. *Austin* found a compelling governmental interest in preventing "the corrosive and distorting effects of immense aggregations of wealth that are accumulated with the help of the corporate form and that have little or no correlation to the public's support for the corporation's political ideas."...

B

The Court is thus confronted with conflicting lines of precedent: a pre-*Austin* line that forbids restrictions on political speech based on the speaker's corporate identity and a post-*Austin* line that permits them.

* * *

There is simply no support for the view that the First Amendment, as originally understood, would permit the suppression of political speech by media corporations. The Framers may not have anticipated modern business and media corporations. ...Yet television networks and major newspapers owned by media corporations have become the most important means of mass communication in modern times. The First Amendment was certainly not understood to condone the suppression of political speech in society's most salient media. It was understood as a response to the repression of speech and the press that had existed in England and the heavy taxes on the press that were imposed in the colonies. ...The great debates between the Federalists and the Anti-Federalists over our founding document were published and expressed in the most important means of mass communication of that era—newspapers owned by individuals. ...At the founding, speech was open, comprehensive, and vital to society's definition of itself; there were no limits on the sources of speech and knowledge.... G. Wood, Creation of the American Republic 1776–1787, p. 6 (1969) ("[I]t is not surprising that the intellectual sources of [the Americans'] Revolutionary thought were profuse and various"). The Framers may have been unaware of certain types of speakers or forms of communication, but that does not mean that those speakers and media are entitled to less First Amendment protection than those types of speakers and media that provided the means of communicating political ideas when the Bill of Rights was adopted.

Austin interferes with the "open marketplace" of ideas protected by the First Amendment. ...It permits the Government to ban the political speech of millions of associations of citizens.... Most of these are small corporations without large amounts of wealth. ...This fact belies the Government's argument that the statute is justified on the ground that it prevents the "distorting effects of immense aggregations of wealth." ...It is not even aimed at amassed wealth.

The censorship we now confront is vast in its reach. The Government has "muffle[d] the voices that best represent the most significant segments of the economy." And "the electorate [has been] deprived of information, knowledge and opinion vital to its function." ...By suppressing the speech of manifold corporations, both for-profit and nonprofit, the Government prevents their voices and viewpoints from reaching the public and advising voters on which persons or entities are hostile to their interests. Factions will necessarily form in our Republic, but the remedy of "destroying the liberty" of some factions is "worse than the disease." The Federalist No. 10, p. 130. Factions should be checked by permitting them all to speak,...and by entrusting the people to judge what is true and what is false.

The purpose and effect of this law is to prevent corporations, including small and nonprofit corporations, from presenting both facts and opinions to the public. This makes *Austin*'s antidistortion rationale all the more an aberration.... Corporate executives and employees counsel Members of Congress and Presidential administrations on many issues, as a matter of routine and often in private. An *amici* brief filed on behalf of Montana and 25 other States notes that lobbying and corporate communications with elected officials occur on a regular basis. ...When that phenomenon is coupled with §441b, the result is that smaller or nonprofit corporations cannot raise a voice to object when other corporations, including those with vast wealth, are cooperating with the Government. That cooperation may sometimes be voluntary, or it may be at the demand of a Government official who uses his or her authority, influence, and power to threaten corporations to support the Government's policies. Those kinds of interactions are often unknown and unseen. The speech that §441b forbids, though, is public, and all can judge its content and purpose. References to massive corporate treasuries should not mask the real operation of this law. Rhetoric ought not obscure reality.

* * *

When Government seeks to use its full power, including the criminal law, to command where a person may get his or her information or what distrusted source he or she may not hear, it uses censorship to control thought. This is unlawful. The First Amendment confirms the freedom to think for ourselves.

2

What we have said also shows the invalidity of other arguments made by the Government. For the most part relinquishing the antidistortion rationale, the Government falls back on the argument that corporate political speech can be banned in order to prevent corruption or its appearance. In *Buckley*, the Court found this interest "sufficiently important" to allow limits on contributions but did not extend that reasoning to expenditure limits. When *Buckley* examined an expenditure ban, it found "that the governmental interest in preventing corruption and the appearance of corruption [was] inadequate to justify [the ban] on independent expenditures."

* * *

When *Buckley* identified a sufficiently important governmental interest in preventing corruption or the appearance of corruption, that interest was limited to *quid pro quo* corruption. ...The fact that speakers may have influence over or access to elected officials does not mean that these officials are corrupt:

> "Favoritism and influence are not...avoidable in representative politics. It is in the nature of an elected representative to favor certain policies, and, by necessary corollary, to favor the voters and contributors who support those policies. It is well understood that a substantial and legitimate reason, if not the

only reason, to cast a vote for, or to make a contribution to, one candidate over another is that the candidate will respond by producing those political outcomes the supporter favors. Democracy is premised on responsiveness. *McConnell*, 540 U.S., at 297, (opinion of Kennedy, J.).

Reliance on a "generic favoritism or influence theory...is at odds with standard First Amendment analyses because it is unbounded and susceptible to no limiting principle."

* * *

The appearance of influence or access, furthermore, will not cause the electorate to lose faith in our democracy. By definition, an independent expenditure is political speech presented to the electorate that is not coordinated with a candidate.... The fact that a corporation, or any other speaker, is willing to spend money to try to persuade voters presupposes that the people have the ultimate influence over elected officials. This is inconsistent with any suggestion that the electorate will refuse "'to take part in democratic governance'" because of additional political speech made by a corporation or any other speaker....

Caperton v. *A. T. Massey Coal Co.*, 556 U.S. 868 (2009), is not to the contrary. *Caperton* held that a judge was required to recuse himself "when a person with a personal stake in a particular case had a significant and disproportionate influence in placing the judge on the case by raising funds or directing the judge's election campaign when the case was pending or imminent." ...The remedy of recusal was based on a litigant's due process right to a fair trial before an unbiased judge. See *Withrow* v. *Larkin*, 421 U.S. 35, 46 (1975). *Caperton*'s holding was limited to the rule that the judge must be recused, not that the litigant's political speech could be banned.

* * *

4

We need not reach the question whether the Government has a compelling interest in preventing foreign individuals or associations from influencing our Nation's political process.... Section 441b is not limited to corporations or associations that were created in foreign countries or funded predominantly by foreign shareholders. Section 441b therefore would be overbroad even if we assumed, *arguendo,* that the Government has a compelling interest in limiting foreign influence over our political process....

C

Our precedent is to be respected unless the most convincing of reasons demonstrates that adherence to it puts us [130 S.Ct. 912] on a course that is sure error. "Beyond workability, the relevant factors in deciding whether to adhere to the principle of *stare decisis* include the antiquity of the precedent, the reliance interests at stake, and of course whether the decision was well reasoned."...

These considerations counsel in favor of rejecting *Austin*, which itself contravened this Court's earlier precedents in *Buckley* and *Bellotti.* "This Court has not hesitated to overrule decisions offensive to the First Amendment." ..."*[S]tare decisis* is a principle of policy and not a mechanical formula of adherence to the latest decision."...

For the reasons above, it must be concluded that *Austin* was not well reasoned....

* * *

Rapid changes in technology—and the creative dynamic inherent in the concept of free expression—counsel against upholding a law that restricts political speech in certain media or by certain speakers.

...Today, 30-second television ads may be the most effective way to convey a political message. ...Soon, however, it may be that Internet sources, such as blogs and social networking Web sites, will provide citizens with significant information about political candidates and issues. Yet, §441b would seem to ban a blog post expressly advocating the election or defeat of a candidate if that blog were created with corporate funds.... The First Amendment does not permit Congress to make these categorical distinctions based on the corporate identity of the speaker and the content of the political speech.

* * *

Due consideration leads to this conclusion: *Austin*, 494 U.S. 652, should be and now is overruled. We return to the principle established in *Buckley* and *Bellotti* that the Government may not suppress political speech on the basis of the speaker's corporate identity. No sufficient governmental interest justifies limits on the political speech of nonprofit or for-profit corporations.

D

* * *

Given our conclusion we are further required to overrule the part of McConnell that upheld BCRA §203's extension of §441b's restrictions on corporate independent expenditures. See 540 U.S., at 203-209. The *McConnell* Court relied on the antidistortion interest recognized in *Austin* to uphold a greater restriction on speech than the restriction upheld in *Austin,* see 540 U.S., at 205, and we have found this interest unconvincing and insufficient. This *part of McConnell* is now overruled.

IV

A

Citizens United next challenges BCRA's disclaimer and disclosure provisions as applied to *Hillary* and the three advertisements for the movie. Under BCRA §311, televised electioneering communications funded by anyone other than a candidate must include a disclaimer that [130 S.Ct. 914] "'____ is responsible for the content of this advertising.'" 2 U.S.C. §441d(d)(2). The required statement must be made in a "clearly spoken manner," and displayed on the screen in a "clearly readable manner" for at least four seconds. It must state that the communication "is not authorized by any candidate or candidate's committee"; it must also display the name and address (or Web site address) of the person or group that funded the advertisement. §441d(a)(3). Under BCRA §201, any person who spends more than $10,000 on electioneering communications within a calendar year must file a disclosure statement with the FEC....

Disclaimer and disclosure requirements may burden the ability to speak, but they "impose no ceiling on campaign-related activities," *Buckley,* 424 U.S., at 64, and "do not prevent anyone from speaking," *McConnell, supra,* at 201 (internal quotation marks and brackets omitted)....

In *Buckley*, the Court explained that disclosure could be justified [175 L.Ed.2d 800] based on a governmental interest in "provid[ing] the electorate with information" about the sources of election-related spending.... There was evidence in the record that independent groups were running election-related advertisements " 'while hiding behind dubious and misleading names.'" ...The Court therefore upheld BCRA §§201 and 311 on the ground that they would help citizens "'make informed choices in the political marketplace.'"

* * *

For the reasons stated below, we find the statute valid as applied to the ads for the movie and to the movie itself.

* * *

C

For the same reasons we uphold the application of BCRA §§201 and 311 to the ads, we affirm their application to *Hillary*. We find no constitutional impediment to the application of BCRA's disclaimer and disclosure requirements to a movie broadcast via video-on-demand. And there has been no showing that, as applied in this case, these requirements would impose a chill on speech or expression.

V

When word concerning the plot of the movie *Mr. Smith Goes to Washington* reached the circles of Government, some officials sought, by persuasion, to discourage its distribution. See Smoodin, "Compulsory" Viewing for Every Citizen: *Mr. Smith* and the Rhetoric of Reception, 35 Cinema Journal 3, 19, and n. 52 (Winter 1996) (citing Mr. Smith Riles Washington, Time, Oct. 30, 1939, p. 49); Nugent, Capra's Capitol Offense, N. Y. Times, Oct. 29, 1939, p. X5. Under *Austin*, though, officials could have done more than discourage its distribution—they could have banned the film. After all, it, like *Hillary,* was speech funded by a corporation that was critical of Members of Congress. *Mr. Smith Goes to Washington* may be fiction and caricature; but fiction and caricature can be a powerful force.

Modern day movies, television comedies, or skits on Youtube.com might portray public officials or public policies in unflattering ways. Yet if a covered transmission during the blackout period creates the background for candidate endorsement or opposition, a felony occurs solely because a corporation, other than an exempt media corporation, has made the "purchase, payment, distribution, loan, advance, deposit, or gift of money or anything of value" in order to engage in political speech. 2 U.S.C. §431(9)(A)(i). Speech would be suppressed in the realm where its necessity is most evident: in the public dialogue preceding a real election. Governments are often hostile to speech, but under our law and our tradition it seems stranger than fiction for our Government to make this political speech a crime. Yet this is the statute's purpose and design.

Some members of the public might consider *Hillary* to be insightful and instructive; some might find it to be neither high art nor a fair discussion on how to set the Nation's course; still others simply might suspend judgment on these points but decide to think more about issues and candidates. Those choices and assessments, however, are not for the Government to make. "The First Amendment underwrites the freedom to experiment and to create in the realm of thought and speech. Citizens must be free to use new forms, and new forums, for the expression of ideas. The civic discourse belongs to the people, and the Government may not prescribe the means used to conduct it." *McConnell, supra*, at 341, 124 S.Ct. 619, 157 L.Ed.2d 491 (opinion of KENNEDY, J.).

The judgment of the District Court is reversed with respect to the constitutionality of 2 U.S.C. §441b's restrictions on corporate independent expenditures. The judgment is affirmed with respect to BCRA's disclaimer and disclosure requirements. The case is remanded for further proceedings consistent with this opinion.

It is so ordered.

Justice SCALIA, with whom Justice ALITO joins, and with whom Justice THOMAS joins in part, concurring.

I join the opinion of the Court. [1]

I write separately to address Justice STEVENS' discussion of "*Original Understandings*[.]" ...This section of the dissent purports to show that today's decision is not supported by the original understanding of the First Amendment. The dissent attempts this demonstration, however, in splendid isolation from the text of the First Amendment. It never shows why "the freedom of speech" that was the right of Englishmen did not include the freedom to speak in association with other individuals, including association in the corporate form. To be sure, in 1791 (as now) corporations could pursue only the objectives set forth in their charters; but the dissent provides no evidence that their speech in the pursuit of those objectives could be censored.

Instead of taking this straightforward approach to determining the Amendment's meaning, the dissent embarks on a detailed exploration of the Framers' views about the "role of corporations in society." The Framers didn't like corporations, the dissent concludes, and therefore it follows (as night the day) that corporations had no rights of free speech. Of course the Framers' personal affection or disaffection for corporations is relevant only insofar as it can be thought to be reflected in the understood meaning of the text they enacted—not, as the dissent suggests, as a freestanding substitute for that text. But the dissent's distortion of proper analysis is even worse than that. Though faced with a constitutional text that makes no distinction between types of speakers, the dissent feels no necessity to provide even an isolated statement from the founding era to the effect that corporations are *not* covered, but places the burden on petitioners to bring forward statements showing that they *are* ("there is not a scintilla of evidence to support the notion that anyone believed [the First Amendment] would preclude regulatory distinctions based on the corporate form[.]"...

Despite the corporation-hating quotations the dissent has dredged up, it is far from clear that by the end of the 18th century corporations were despised. If so, how came there to be so many of them? The dissent's statement that there were few business corporations during the eighteenth century—"only a few hundred during all of the

18th century"—is misleading.... There were approximately 335 charters issued to business corporations in the United States by the end of the 18th century.[1] ...This was a "considerable extension of corporate enterprise in the field of business," and represented "unprecedented growth,".... Moreover, what seems like a small number by today's standards surely does not indicate the relative importance of corporations when the Nation was considerably smaller. As I have previously noted, "[b]y the end of the eighteenth century the corporation was a familiar figure in American economic life." ...Even if we thought it proper to apply the dissent's approach of excluding from First Amendment coverage what the Founders disliked, and even if we agreed that the Founders disliked founding-era corporations; modern corporations might not qualify for exclusion. Most of the Founders' resentment towards corporations was directed at the state-granted monopoly privileges that individually chartered corporations enjoyed. Modern corporations do not have such privileges, and would probably have been favored by most of our enterprising Founders—excluding, perhaps, Thomas Jefferson and others favoring perpetuation of an agrarian society. Moreover, if the Founders' specific intent with respect to corporations is what matters, why does the dissent ignore the Founders' views about other legal entities that have more in common with modern business corporations than the founding-era corporations? At the time of the founding, religious, educational, and literary corporations were incorporated under general incorporation statutes, much as business corporations are today. ...There were also small unincorporated business associations, which

---

[1] [f.2 in original] The dissent protests that 1791 rather than 1800 should be the relevant date, and that "[m]ore than half of the century's total business charters were issued between 1796 and 1800." Post, at 35, n. 53. I used 1800 only because the dissent did. But in any case, it is surely fanciful to think that a consensus of hostility towards corporations was transformed into general favor at some magical moment between 1791 and 1796.

some have argued were the "'true progenitors'" of today's business corporations. ...Were all of these silently excluded from the protections of the First Amendment?

* * *

Historical evidence relating to the textually similar clause "the freedom of...the press" also provides no support for the proposition that the First Amendment excludes conduct of artificial legal entities from the scope of its protection. The freedom of "the press" was widely understood to protect the publishing activities of individual editors and printers.... But these individuals often acted through newspapers, which (much like corporations) had their own names, outlived the individuals who had founded them, could be bought and sold, were sometimes owned by more than one person, and were operated for profit.... Their activities were not stripped of First Amendment protection simply because they were carried out under the banner of an artificial legal entity. And the notion which follows from the dissent's view, that modern newspapers, since they are incorporated, have free-speech rights only at the sufferance of Congress, boggles the mind.

The dissent says that when the Framers "constitutionalized the right to free speech in the First Amendment, it was the free speech of individual Americans that they had in mind." ...That is no doubt true. All the provisions of the Bill of Rights set forth the rights of individual men and women—not, for example, of trees or polar bears. But the individual person's right to speak includes the right to speak *in association with other individual persons.* Surely the dissent does not believe that speech by the Republican Party or the Democratic Party can be censored because it is not the speech of "an individual American." It is the speech of many individual Americans, who have associated in a common cause, giving the leadership of the party the right to speak on their behalf. The association of individuals in a business corporation is no different—or at least it cannot be denied the right to speak on the simplistic ground that it is not "an individual American."

But to return to, and summarize, my principal point, which is the conformity of today's opinion with the original meaning of the First Amendment. The Amendment is written in terms of "speech," not speakers. Its text offers no foothold for excluding any category of speaker, from single individuals to partnerships of individuals, to unincorporated associations of individuals, to incorporated associations of individuals—and the dissent offers no evidence about the original meaning of the text to support any such exclusion. We are therefore simply left with the question whether the speech at issue in this case is "speech" covered by the First Amendment. No one says otherwise. A documentary film critical of a potential Presidential candidate is core political speech, and its nature as such does not change simply because it was funded by a corporation. Nor does the character of that funding produce any reduction whatever in the "inherent worth of the speech" and "its capacity for informing the public[.]" ...Indeed, to exclude or impede corporate speech is to muzzle the principal agents of the modern free economy. We should celebrate rather than condemn the addition of this speech to the public debate.

Justice STEVENS, with whom Justice GINSBURG, Justice BREYER, and Justice SOTOMAYOR join, concurring in part and dissenting in part.

The real issue in this case concerns how, not if, the appellant may finance its electioneering. Citizens United is a wealthy nonprofit corporation that runs a political action committee (PAC) with millions of dollars in assets. Under the Bipartisan Campaign Reform Act of 2002 (BCRA), it could have used those assets to televise and promote *Hillary: The Movie* wherever and whenever it wanted to. It also could have spent unrestricted sums to broadcast *Hillary* at any time other than the 30 days before the last primary election. Neither Citizens United's nor any other corporation's speech has been "banned[.]" ...All that the parties dispute is whether Citizens United had a right to use the funds in its general treasury to pay for broadcasts during the 30-day period. The notion that the First Amendment dictates an affirmative answer to that question is, in my judgment, profoundly misguided. Even more misguided is the notion that the Court must rewrite the law relating to campaign expenditures by *for-profit* corporations and unions to decide this case.

The basic premise underlying the Court's ruling is its iteration, and constant reiteration, of the proposition that the First Amendment bars regulatory distinctions based on a speaker's identity, including its "identity" as a corporation. While that glittering generality has rhetorical appeal, it is not a correct statement of the law. Nor does it tell us when a corporation may engage in electioneering that some of its shareholders oppose. It does not even resolve the specific question whether Citizens United may be required to finance some of its messages with the money in its PAC. The conceit that corporations must be treated identically to natural persons in the political sphere is not only inaccurate but also inadequate to justify the Court's disposition of this case.

In the context of election to public office, the distinction between corporate and human speakers is significant. Although they make enormous contributions to our society, corporations are not actually members of it. They cannot vote or run for office. Because they may be managed and controlled by nonresidents, their interests may conflict in fundamental respects with the interests of eligible voters. The financial resources, legal structure, and instrumental orientation of corporations raise legitimate concerns about their role in the electoral process. Our lawmakers have a compelling constitutional basis, if not also a democratic duty, to take measures designed to guard against the potentially deleterious effects of corporate spending in local and national races.

The majority's approach to corporate electioneering marks a dramatic break from our past. Congress has placed special limitations on campaign spending by corporations ever since the passage of the Tillman Act in 1907, ch. 420, 34 Stat. 864. We have unanimously concluded that this "reflects a 558 U.S. 395 permissible assessment of the dangers posed by those entities to the electoral process," *FEC* v. *National Right to Work Comm.*, 459 U.S. 197, 209 (1982) *(NRWC)*, and have accepted the "legislative judgment that the special characteristics of the corporate structure require particularly careful regulation," *id.*, at 209-210. The Court today rejects a century of history when it treats the distinction between corporate and individual campaign spending as an invidious novelty born of *Austin* v. *Michigan Chamber of Commerce*, 494 U.S. 652 (1990). Relying largely on individual dissenting opinions, the majority blazes through our precedents, overruling or disavowing a body of case law including *FEC* v. *Wisconsin Right to Life, Inc.,* 551 U.S. 449 (2007) *(WRTL)*, *McConnell* v. *FEC*, 540 U.S. 93 (2003), *FEC* v. *Beaumont*, 539 U.S. 146 (2003), *FEC* v. *Massachusetts Citizens for Life, Inc.,* 479 U.S. 238 (1986) *(MCFL)*, *NRWC*, 459 U.S. 197, and *California Medical Assn.* v. *FEC*, 453 U.S. 182 (1981).

* * *

I

The Court's ruling threatens to undermine the integrity of elected institutions across the Nation. The path it has taken to reach its outcome will, I fear, do damage to this institution. Before turning to the question whether to overrule *Austin* and part of *McConnell*, it is important to explain why the Court should not be deciding that question.

Scope of the Case

The first reason is that the question was not properly brought before us. In declaring §203 of BCRA facially unconstitutional on the ground that corporations' electoral expenditures may not be regulated any more stringently than those of individuals, the majority decides this case on a basis relinquished below, not included in the questions presented to us by the litigants, and argued here only in response to the Court's invitation. This procedure is unusual and inadvisable for a court. Our colleagues' suggestion that "we are asked to reconsider *Austin* and, in effect, *McConnell*," *ante*, at 886, 175 L.Ed.2d, at 769, would be more accurate if rephrased to state that "we have asked ourselves" to reconsider those cases.

In the District Court, Citizens United initially raised a facial challenge to the constitutionality of §203.... In its motion for summary judgment, however, Citizens United expressly abandoned its facial challenge[.]

* * *

"'It is only in exceptional cases coming here from the federal courts that questions not pressed or passed upon below are reviewed[.]'"...

Setting the case for reargument was a constructive step, but it did not cure this fundamental problem. Essentially, five Justices were unhappy with the limited nature of the case before us, so they changed the case to give themselves an opportunity to change the law.

* * *

This is not merely a technical defect in the Court's decision. The unnecessary resort to a facial inquiry "run[s] contrary to the fundamental principle of judicial restraint that courts should neither anticipate a question of constitutional law in advance of the necessity of deciding it nor formulate a rule of constitutional law broader than is required by the precise facts to which it is to be applied."

* * *

The majority suggests that, even though it expressly dismissed its facial challenge, Citizens United nevertheless preserved it – not as a freestanding "claim," but as a potential argument in support of "a claim that the FEC has violated its First Amendment right to free speech." ...By this novel logic, virtually any submission could be reconceptualized as "a claim that the Government has violated my rights," and it would then be available to the Court to entertain any conceivable issue that might be relevant to that claim's disposition. Not only the as-applied/facial distinction, but the basic relationship between litigants and courts, would be upended if the latter had free rein to construe the former's claims at such high levels of generality. There would be no need for plaintiffs to argue their case; they could just cite the constitutional provisions they think relevant, and leave the rest to us.

Finally, the majority suggests that though the scope of Citizens United's claim may be narrow, a facial ruling is necessary as a matter of remedy. Relying on a law review article, it asserts that Citizens United's dismissal of the facial challenge does not prevent us "'from making broader pronouncements of invalidity in properly 'as-applied' cases.'" *Ante*, at 14 (quoting Fallon, As-Applied and Facial Challenges and Third-Party Standing, 113 Harv. L. Rev. 1321, 1339 (2000) (hereinafter Fallon)); accord, *ante*, at 5, (opinion of ROBERTS, C. J.) ("Regardless whether we label Citizens United's claim a 'facial' or 'as-applied' challenge, the consequences of the Court's decision are the same"). The majority is on firmer conceptual ground here. Yet even if one accepts this part of Professor Fallon's thesis, one must proceed to ask *which* as-applied challenges, if successful, will "properly" invite or entail invalidation of the underlying statute.

* * *

Narrower Grounds

It is all the more distressing that our colleagues have manufactured a facial challenge, because the parties have advanced numerous ways to resolve the case that would facilitate electioneering by nonprofit advocacy corporations such as Citizens United, without toppling statutes and precedents. Which is to say, the majority has transgressed yet another "cardinal" principle of the judicial process: "[I]f it is not necessary to decide more, it is necessary not to decide more[.]"...

Consider just three of the narrower grounds of decision that the majority has bypassed. First, the Court could have ruled, on statutory grounds, that a feature-length film distributed through video-on-demand does not qualify as an "electioneering communication" under §203 of BCRA, 2 U.S.C. §441b....

Second, the Court could have expanded the *MCFL* exemption to cover §501(c)(4) nonprofits that accept only a *de minimis* amount of money from for-profit corporations. Citizens United professes to be such a group: Its brief says it "is funded predominantly by donations from individuals who support [its] ideological message."...

Finally, let us not forget Citizens United's as-applied constitutional challenge. Precisely because Citizens United looks so much like the *MCFL* organizations we have exempted from regulation, while a feature-length video-on-demand film looks so unlike the types of electoral advocacy Congress has found deserving of regulation, this challenge is a substantial one. As the appellant's own arguments show, the Court could have easily limited the breadth of its constitutional holding had it declined to adopt the novel notion that speakers and speech acts must always be treated identically—and always spared expenditures restrictions—in the political realm. Yet the Court nonetheless turns its back on the as-applied review process that has been a staple of campaign finance litigation....

This brief tour of alternative grounds on which the case could have been decided is not meant to show that any of these grounds is ideal, though each is perfectly "valid," *ante*, at 892, 175 L.Ed.2d, at 775 (majority opinion). It is meant to show that there were principled, narrower paths that a Court that was serious about [175 L.Ed.2d 826] judicial restraint could have taken. There was also the straightforward path: applying *Austin* and *McConnell*, just as the District Court did in holding that the funding of Citizens United's film can be regulated under them. The only thing preventing the majority from affirming the District Court, or adopting a narrower ground that would retain *Austin*, is its disdain for *Austin*.

II

The final principle of judicial process that the majority violates is the most transparent: *stare decisis*. I am not an absolutist when it comes to *stare decisis*, in the campaign finance area or in any other. No one is. But if this principle is to do any meaningful work in supporting the rule of law, it must at least demand a significant justification, beyond the preferences of five Justices, for overturning settled doctrine. "[A] decision to overrule should rest on some special reason over and above the belief that a prior case was wrongly decided." *Planned Parenthood of Southeastern Pa.* v. *Casey*, 505 U.S. 833, 864 (1992). No such justification exists in this case, and to the contrary there are powerful prudential reasons to keep faith with our precedents.

* * *

Perhaps in recognition of this point, the Court supplements its merits case with a smattering of assertions. The Court proclaims that "*Austin* is undermined by experience since its announcement." *Ante*, at 48. This is a curious claim to make in a case that lacks a developed record. The majority has no empirical evidence with which to substantiate the claim; we just have its *ipse dixit* that the real world has not been kind to *Austin*. Nor does the majority bother to specify in what sense *Austin* has been "undermined." Instead it treats the reader to a string of non sequiturs: "Our Nation's speech dynamic is changing," *ante*, "[s]peakers have become adept at presenting citizens with sound bites, talking points, and scripted messages," "[c]orporations...do not have monolithic views[.]" ...How any of these ruminations weakens the force of *stare decisis*, escapes my comprehension.

* * *

Although the majority opinion spends several pages making these surprising arguments, it says almost nothing about the standard considerations we have used to determine *stare decisis* value, such as the antiquity of the precedent, the workability of its legal rule, and the reliance interests at stake....

We have recognized that "[s]tare decisis has special force when legislators or citizens 'have acted in reliance on a previous decision, for in this instance overruling the decision would dislodge settled rights and expectations or require an extensive legislative response.'" ...*Stare decisis* protects not only personal rights involving property or contract but also the ability of the elected branches to shape their laws in an effective and coherent fashion. Today's decision takes away a power that we have long permitted these branches to exercise. State legislatures have relied on their authority to regulate corporate electioneering, confirmed in *Austin*, for more than a century. The Federal Congress has relied on this authority for a comparable stretch of time, and it specifically relied on *Austin* throughout the years it spent developing and debating BCRA. The total record it compiled was *100,000 pages* long. Pulling out the rug beneath Congress after affirming the constitutionality of §203 six years ago shows great disrespect for a coequal branch.

By removing one of its central components, today's ruling makes a hash out of BCRA's "delicate and interconnected regulatory scheme." ...Consider just one example of the distortions that will follow: Political parties are barred under BCRA from soliciting or spending "soft money," funds that are not subject to the statute's disclosure requirements or its source and amount limitations. ...Going forward, corporations and unions will be free to spend as much general treasury money as they wish on ads that support or attack specific candidates, whereas national parties will not be able to spend a dime of soft money on ads of any kind. The Court's ruling thus dramatically enhances the role of corporations and unions—and the narrow interests they represent—vis-à-vis the role of political parties—and the broad coalitions they represent—in determining who will hold public office.

* * *

In the end, the Court's rejection of *Austin* and *McConnell* comes down to nothing more than its disagreement with their results. Virtually every one of its arguments was made and rejected in those cases, and the majority opinion is essentially an amalgamation of resuscitated dissents. The only relevant thing that has changed since *Austin* and *McConnell* is the composition of this Court. Today's ruling thus strikes at the vitals of *stare decisis*, "the means by which we ensure that the law will not merely change erratically, but will develop in a principled and intelligible fashion" that "permits society to presume that bedrock principles are founded in the law rather than in the proclivities of individuals."

* * *

V

Today's decision is backwards in many senses. It elevates the majority's agenda over the litigants' submissions, facial attacks over as-applied claims, broad constitutional theories over narrow statutory grounds, individual dissenting opinions over precedential holdings, assertion over tradition, absolutism over empiricism, [175 L.Ed.2d 871] rhetoric over reality. Our colleagues have arrived at the conclusion that *Austin* must be overruled and that §203 is facially unconstitutional only after mischaracterizing both the reach and rationale of those authorities, and after bypassing or ignoring rules of judicial restraint used to cabin the Court's lawmaking power. Their conclusion that the societal interest in avoiding corruption and the appearance of corruption does not provide an adequate justification for regulating corporate expenditures on candidate elections relies on an incorrect description of that interest, along with a failure to acknowledge the relevance of established facts and the considered judgments of state and federal legislatures over many decades.

In a democratic society, the longstanding consensus on the need to limit corporate campaign spending should outweigh the wooden application of judge-made rules. The majority's rejection of this principle "elevate[s] corporations to a level of deference which has not been seen at least since the days when substantive due process was regularly used to invalidate regulatory legislation thought to unfairly impinge upon established economic interests." ...At bottom, the Court's opinion is thus a rejection of the common sense of the American people, who have recognized a need to prevent corporations from undermining self-government since the founding, and who have fought against the distinctive corrupting potential of corporate electioneering since the days of Theodore Roosevelt. It is a strange time to repudiate that common sense. While American democracy is imperfect, few outside the majority of this Court would have thought its flaws included a dearth of corporate money in politics.

I would affirm the judgment of the District Court.

Justice Thomas, concurring in part and dissenting in part.

I join all but Part IV of the Court's opinion.

Political speech is entitled to robust protection under the First Amendment. I dissent from Part IV of the Court's opinion, however, because the Court's constitutional analysis does not go far enough. . . .

Congress may not abridge the "right to anonymous speech" based on the "'simple interest in providing voters with additional relevant information[.]'" . . .In continuing to hold otherwise, the Court misapprehends the import of "recent events" that some *amici* describe "in which donors to certain causes were blacklisted, threatened, or otherwise targeted for retaliation." ...The Court properly recognizes these events as "cause for concern,"...but fails to acknowledge their constitutional significance....

Amici's examples relate principally to Proposition 8, a state ballot proposition that California voters narrowly passed in the 2008 general election. Proposition 8 amended California's Constitution to provide that "[o]nly marriage between a man and a woman is valid or recognized in California." ...Any donor who gave more than $100 to any committee supporting or opposing Proposition 8 was required to disclose his full name, street address, occupation, employer's name (or business name, if self-employed), and the total amount of his contributions.[1] ...The

---

[1] BCRA imposes similar disclosure requirements. See, e.g., 2 U.S.C. §434(f)(2)(F) ("Every person who makes a disbursement for the direct costs of producing and airing electioneering communications in an aggregate amount in excess of $10,000 during any calendar year" must disclose "the names and addresses of all contributors who contributed an

(Footnote continued on next page)

California Secretary of State was then required to post this information on the Internet....

Some opponents of Proposition 8 compiled this information and created Web sites with maps showing the locations of homes or businesses of Proposition 8 supporters. Many supporters (or their customers) suffered property damage, or threats of physical violence or death, as a result. They cited these incidents in a complaint they filed after the 2008 election, seeking to invalidate California's mandatory disclosure laws. Supporters recounted being told: "Consider yourself lucky. If I had a gun I would have gunned you down along with each and every other supporter," or, "we have plans for you and your friends." ...Proposition 8 opponents also allegedly harassed the measure's supporters by defacing or damaging their property. Two religious organizations supporting Proposition 8 reportedly received through the mail envelopes containing a white powdery substance.

Those accounts are consistent with media reports describing Proposition 8-related retaliation. The director of the nonprofit California Musical Theater gave $1,000 to support the initiative; he was forced to resign after artists complained to his employer.... The director of the Los Angeles Film Festival was forced to resign after giving $1,500 because opponents threatened to boycott and picket the next festival. And a woman who had managed her popular, family-owned restaurant for 26 years was forced to resign after she gave $100, because "throngs of [angry] [175 L.Ed.2d 873] protesters" repeatedly arrived at the restaurant and "shout[ed] 'shame on you' at customers." ...The police even had to "arriv[e] in riot gear one night to quell the angry mob" at the restaurant. . . .Some supporters of Proposition 8 engaged in similar tactics; one real estate businessman in San Diego who had donated to a group opposing

---

aggregate amount of $1,000 or more to the person making the disbursement").

Proposition 8 "received a letter from the Prop. 8 Executive Committee threatening to publish his company's name if he didn't also donate to the 'Yes on 8' campaign.'"...

The success of such intimidation tactics has apparently spawned a cottage industry that uses forcibly disclosed donor information to *pre-empt* citizens' exercise of their First Amendment rights. Before the 2008 Presidential election, a "newly formed nonprofit group...plann[ed] to confront donors to conservative groups, hoping to create a chilling effect that will dry up contributions." ...Its leader, "who described his effort as 'going for the jugular,'" detailed the group's plan to send a "warning letter...alerting donors who might be considering giving to right-wing groups to a variety of potential dangers, including legal trouble, public exposure and watchdog groups digging through their lives.'"...

These instances of retaliation sufficiently demonstrate why this Court should invalidate mandatory disclosure and reporting requirements. But *amici* present evidence of yet another reason to do so—the threat of retaliation from *elected officials*. As *amici's* submissions make clear, this threat extends far beyond a single ballot proposition in California. For example, a candidate challenging an incumbent state attorney general reported that some members of the State's business community feared donating to his campaign because they did not want to cross the incumbent; in his words, "'I go to so many people and hear the same thing: "I sure hope you beat [the incumbent], but I can't afford to have my name on your records. He might come after me next.'" ...The incumbent won reelection in 2008.

My point is not to express any view on the merits of the political controversies I describe. Rather, it is to demonstrate using real-world, recent examples—the fallacy in the Court's conclusion that "[d]isclaimer and disclosure requirements...impose no ceiling on campaign-related activities, and do not prevent anyone from speaking." ...Of course they do. Disclaimer and disclosure requirements enable private citizens and elected officials to implement political strategies *specifically calculated* to curtail campaign-related activity and prevent the lawful, peaceful exercise of First Amendment rights.

* * *

[T]he Court's promise that as-applied challenges will adequately protect speech is a hollow assurance. Now more than ever, §§201 and 311 will chill protected speech because—as California voters can attest—"the advent of the Internet" enables "prompt disclosure of expenditures," which "provide[s]" political opponents "with the information needed" to intimidate and retaliate against their foes. Thus, "disclosure permits citizens...to react to the speech of [their political opponents] in a proper"—or undeniably *improper*—"way" long before a plaintiff could prevail on an as-applied challenge.

I cannot endorse a view of the First Amendment that subjects citizens of this Nation to death threats, ruined careers, damaged or defaced property, or preemptive and threatening warning letters as the price for engaging in "core political speech, the 'primary object of First Amendment protection.'" ...Accordingly, I respectfully dissent from the Court's judgment upholding BCRA §§201 and 311.

*

On 6 November 2014, the United States Court of Appeals for the Sixth Circuit upheld a Michigan statute banning same sex marriage reversing the opinion below squarely setting up the issue for review by SCOTUS. The arguments will be impassioned. History, both past and recent, will be trotted out in an effort to influence the Court.

Will the Court find gays and lesbians in the penumbras? Will long-standing and deep-rooted American traditions come into play? Do we have the conscience of the nation at stake here? On the other hand, what part will freedom of choice, or liberty, or privacy play, all being formidable and legitimate constitutional concerns? This will be interesting. And, you will now read the Court's ruling with a new-found understanding. Remember, you will be looking for not just the Court's perspicacity, but its prescience as well. This is exciting stuff.

It is presently before the Court as a collection of consolidated cases titled on *cert.* as *DeBoer v. Snyder* [*Certiorari* No. 14-571]. The proceedings may be followed on-line at: <scotusblog.com/case-file/cases/deboer-v-snyder/>. As of this writing, it apparently will be reported out as *Obergefell v. Hodges,* ___U.S. ___.

XX

REPRISE

ow that we have reached the final stages of our work, let us reflect on and continue to think about some issues in our lives and life in the country today. Where would you like to start? How about the debasement of mankind in general, particularly women, but men, too? What is it that makes so many people unhappy with their lives, and who they are, simply as a matter per se. What has happened to personal commitment, responsibility, the sanctity of contract? On an ever-growing and now large scale, why is it we treat one another as chattels, without any sense of respect, awash in vulgarity? What is it that raped our order, and the value and dignity of simply being human, be it man or woman, whoever and whatever they may be? Why the ubiquitous dishonesty? What happened to self-reliance? Why is the country soft? What happens when the government manages its citizens instead of the citizens managing themselves, or the citizens managing their government, for that matter? Of what possible relevance could these things have here?

*

What about a time-tested code, a cultural-national ethic if you will, fundamental and seemingly universal standards of behavior by which civilized and well-ordered and successful people have lived, those things which our fellow travelers on this plane of existence at one time simply figured into life's equation and standard of conduct over the years? Is this not within the realm of education, public or otherwise, being among the most basic of human social cornerstones? Consider fundamental basic education, the kind which develops the mind, teaching it to think, providing it with abilities and techniques which later can be generalized to other problem-solving settings of whatever kind, and the ability to generate solutions to life's challenges and difficulties, the sort of education which was required as the nation was developing, *ab initio*. Where is the inculcation of an understanding and respect for the country and its form of government, the price which had to be paid with rivers of men's blood to bring it to life, and the responsibility of all to protect and preserve it if we wish to remain free and enjoy its fruits ("Ask not what your country can do for you…")?

To get an idea, take another look at the eighth grade final examination from one hundred years ago (that is approximately three generations). Go ahead. It's on the web. You'll quickly get the idea. Why all of those "difficult" subjects? Math, physics, literature, language, history, logic, the arts. To what possible use could they ever be put? The modern educator must not think much of them anymore. Curriculums have been gutted. Or, maybe there simply aren't the necessary teachers who can manage what is challenging and developmental? Maybe the concept of educating the public has changed, or administrators simply see it differently now. Have politics or preferences found their way into public education? It has changed, however. Why is that?

Education, to be education, provides more than just information. It should develop the mind so as to be able to think abstractly, to anticipate and recognize problems, to be able to proceed through a regime of testability, and process constructs through one's own mental equations and formulas of conceptual or formal thought whether it is acquired in accordance with the Ausubelian school or the Brunerian school, or based on any other theory of learning for that matter. It makes no difference, ultimately. The ends and abstract abilities are much the same. Anything less isn't education. Education today seems to be more of a linear string of bits of information selected by agents of the government, and that is how it is tested. It doesn't even rise to the level of training. It doesn't teach how to think, it teaches what to think. Do not fool yourselves, a national disaster is in the making…. A national disaster is in the making, and less than a generation away. We can no longer function without outside help…at any level.

There may be a solution: bigger schools, smaller classes, more money for the teachers, and double the size and pay of the administration to get the very best, add lots of new diversified courses, real world hands-on subjects which might lead to a job. Possibly teaching how to do something is the answer. That makes sense. Parents will buy it. This will lead to a paying job. The student's education is now valuable to him or her, and it is also of value to the state. If this new approach to regulated education, matching training with the job market, becomes too expensive, eliminate the arts (both performing and aesthetic) and athletics. Eliminate the intellectual subjects. What do they have to do with our culture, our national integrity, our ability to fulfill our civic responsibility as citizens? Isn't it the jobs, stupid?! Or are jobs (training) and education mutually exclusive while standing on some balance of equal footing? Oh, why bother? It is now all hand-holding anyway. Every kid gets a trophy.

Is it anywhere taught the price of gaining and preserving freedom along with the resultant benefits of opportunity are high, and they can be easily lost? Is it anywhere taught that discipline, commitment, and restraint are required for our preservation? What about the value and importance of an educated voter, one that has a basic sense of economics and history. Are they not the pillars of a democratic society? Do citizens today know what it takes to succeed? Do they even know what success is? Are we to find our new-order freedoms in pornography, abortion, no-fault, falsehoods, and lack of restraint...politics by advertisement...painted faces and network airheads extolling the virtues of those up for election who have alluring messages seeking to attract the support of the most vulnerable and helpless among us, then throw them a fish as the nation goes over a cliff? What has brought the nation here?

Are you able to imagine where the nation would be today if its people were disciplined, the social order well-structured and loyally supportive ("Ask what *you* can do for your country...."), with resources developed, and productive citizens and businesses fostered? Are you able to imagine where the nation would be today if politicians put the interests of the nation ahead of their own? Well, are you? Does this have any relevance here? Stop now, and think back through the cases you have read.

*

Has SCOTUS legislated away all personal responsibility and initiative, or has Atlas shrugged? Morbid obesity, the great antecedent to diabetes, as well as hypertension, cerebral accidents, joint disease, a bouquet of cancers, and galloping (as it were) depression, are causative of premature death and lingering pathologies, not to mention the overwhelming effect they have on families and the health care system. Obesity is just now tipping over the fifty percent point nationally, and with it is coming another financial crisis, there being enough of the population eating itself into the nation's crematoriums, and the health care system into bankruptcy. One might presume early exits will lessen the burden on the welfare and disability rolls, except possibly in Chicago also famous for its celebrated cemetery turnout at the polls.

As half the population (and growing) bellies up for medical services for self-inflicted pathologies of every kind imaginable, what is to be done? Being a formidable voting bloc, what will Congress do? Someone has to pay for it. Taxes for better programs, you say? Where does that money come from? Let us legislate some discipline, you say? What happened to that? Are these the people who are going to develop and defend the nation? Maybe the nation can regulate itself to health and victory.

Work feeds the psyche and social side of life as much as it does the wallet. It is far more than an economic event. Take it away and you get what we have. Outsourcing work may have a profit incentive, but for whom and at what cost to others? The government played a role in these international trade agreements, but with what in mind? All truth is spoken through behavior.

Relevant here?

In the world of crime, where does one start? Cause, data, societal reaction, political response, the economy both before and after the fact? Maybe start with the fact the United States is the most imprisoned culture and country on earth? In fact, there are sub-groups within the society where over half of its members are convicted felons (not just felons by deed), having been incarcerated, presently serving sentences, many more than once, or are otherwise "in the system." Added to this is the fact most criminals are not even apprehended. Most reported crimes are not solved, indeed most crimes are not even reported (read as one in ten, or fewer).

Crime must be a viable alternative lifestyle, it must pay, or perhaps there are no other alternatives. It is a way to make a living, and as commented on comes with paid vacations and a guaranteed retirement if things don't work out. Difficult to imagine, is it not? Totally incomprehensible, you say, as incomprehensible as 9/11, simply not being within the bank of reason. But, it is happening, more is coming, and the curve will be exponential. Do not disillusion yourself, we are devolving into war in our towns and cities, this one from within. Who is it that swore to uphold the Constitution (that *is* the United States – review the Introduction) against all enemies, foreign and domestic? What has destroyed the fundamental structures of the culture, the glue of a society and nation?

Crime costs us more than education. Both are simply different forms of waste of our own making (Financial Tertiary Instances, see *infra*). Most do not like crime, most like education and we perennially spend more on both and perennially have less to show for it. Both groups, the ex-cons and the uneducated, are unemployable and can't perform up to any acceptable par even on standard tests we have ourselves developed, if one could call them that, "…tailored to be relevant, fair, sensitive to needs and feelings, and respectful to those in today's world." But wait, obesity and its clinical sequelae will likely win the race to the deficit pit. Just think, a new world populated by felons, ignoramuses, and the morbidly obese. The solution? Legalize gambling and marijuana. Simple enough. The new "America," the "Transformed America," all a product of a stifled economy, a failing education system, keeping its citizens dependent, enjoying broken services, and taking refuge in drugs, all based on measures put in place. Sorry, but let us not be pessimistic as change will surely come. It will….

*

Medical technology today is indeed a marvel: the sophisticated, minimally invasive surgical tools, the diagnostic equipment, the scanning devices, the prosthetics, the list is long…absolutely amazing. Much of it is beyond the imagination of even a professional one generation ago. But the treatment costs of this upward arc are as dramatic as the science itself, following, unfortunately, a more accelerating geometric curve. And so far as research and costs going into new therapies and medicines...the same thing. Staggering. Worse. The cost of research, testing, and development keeps some of the drug industry teetered on the financial brink. The costs are genuine, no doubt, little question (why would manufacturers of medicines price themselves out of business when their success is dependent on not only past successes, but future successes as well—in other words, rationally priced contrary to hysteria and as politicized by a few—there are exceptions). High science comes with a high price tag. There is no way around it. Stop blaming the hospitals or the health care providers or the companies who bring these life-saving (extending) devices and medications to market. It is not only expensive, but costs will continue to rise on the trigonometric function of the tangent as they have in the past, at a rate beyond that of the rise of the national economy (which today doesn't pose much of a race), not to mention individual incomes as well, needless to say. That is the way it is. It is the technological tangential cost curve, the modern-day Tower of Babel. If it is bad now, it will be worse tomorrow, and more so the tomorrow after that.

There is an endpoint where for everyone it simply cannot be afforded by even the government. Get used to it, and get ready. There is an end, or shall we say a solution. The Court will have to "rethink" its position, will it not? Ultimately, the issue will come down to technology versus some value set, the ethics and values of the great and long-standing traditions of mankind versus, say, economic reality. It will effectively be a colossal battle of institutions, corporeal and incorporeal. But, the question is coming and it will have to be dealt with, as is the usual case, on the brink of disaster, maybe in the crucible of collapse or at least great ferment. Where do such matters end up? Congress? Question: who will decide who gets what treatment, or any treatment, who lives, and according to what tenets? That should be an easy one. A two or three or five word essay should do the job. Elected officials will never touch it.

*

The population is exploding, but even that no longer garners any attention. But it is, with the poor, the uneducated, the morbid, the incarcerated, the formerly incarcerated, the anti-social being more and more over-represented in the general populace, with the attendant growing separation of social classes. From time to time, the press will get a gnat in its pants and cry out that another ice age is coming, watch out, or the planet is about to catch fire, or "Methuselah is on the front porch and ringing the bell." When that wears out, it becomes "this is just healthy growth" until the next election cycle. How fast we forget, and politicians know it, invention after invention.

We need the labor. Right? At least labor which will work, and those who do and are serious move up. True, even today. Opportunity may never have been greater for those who are ready, willing and able to join in. We have a whole new class which apparently will ride right up over any underclass. The fact is the population was half its present size only two generations ago. The problem is many members of the American population tend to be undereducated and unhealthy, detached and unconcerned. Are they going to be our financial saviors? Are their taxes (and presently most are not taxed at all) going to be passed through the government to pay for Social Security, Medicare and, as displaced by the ACA, Medicaid (and subsequent programs which do not as of yet even have names), government employee and politicians' retirement and health programs? Will the one hundred to one, then fifty to one, then ten to one, now three to one, soon to be a one to one ratio in terms of those who are working and paying taxes (to support those who are not) and who will have loaded on their backs these costs, not to mention everything else the government does, pays, and gives away, or otherwise writing hot checks creating the illusion of prosperity, eventually lose all incentive? Who are these people? You may be surprised what is in the offing. The emerging class willing to work may ultimately tell the government to go to hell and refuse to pay for governmental boondoggles, or let us say, start privatizing their own income streams.

In other words, the morbidly obese in the waiting room…you are paying for them, you are supporting them, and if the economics are allowed to play out in accordance with its present trajectory, you will be working less for yourself than for your ignorant, malnourished, helpless neighbors who forgot to use their government issued condoms, or so say the numbers. It is happening. Certainly any politician worth his salt is going to say that isn't so, or, it can be made up, it can be worked out, do a little more deficit spending here and there (which also costs citizens even though it is nearly invisible as it shrinks whatever you happen to be paid in terms of real spending power leaving the citizen with the same dollar count but now worth less—but who among your neighbors understands that?), or otherwise just make some changes, there are happy days just ahead, we just need to keep up our spirits, and hope fiercely. Not just fools, but damnable fools…. Where did they come from?!

As an aside, there is a provision in the Constitution (Amendment XIV, Section 4) which says, "The validity of the public debt of the United States, authorized by law…shall not be questioned." At first blush, it sounds like SCOTUS cannot do anything about deficit spending, a profligate Congress or executive branch. On the other hand, SCOTUS has been known to be, shall we say, creative when it comes to problem solving, so why not here? The elected politicians are not going to do anything. So, how does the high court find any jurisdiction? "Lawful." Is it lawful for anyone or any institution to spend money it doesn't have? Is it lawful to spend a nation into economic collapse, then political collapse, then defeat? Could it be heard from any quarter that our elected officials are not carrying out their sworn duty to defend the nation and protect its Constitution? Where are the public service lawyers on this one?

*

Do Americans generally have even the foggiest idea let alone the wisp of a concern as to what wealth is all about? What is required for a nation to successfully compete among nations? What is it that permits a nation to economically thrive and flourish? Is it generally known?

A nation has two and only two sources of wealth: natural resources and competitive human resources (labor combined with knowledge) willing to participate in production. At base, nothing else. Everything is built from there up. Economic success comes down to these two points of origin. This paradigm is the First Principle of Economics, and encompasses the three Doctrines of Financial Instances. Without access to at least one of these resources (human and naturally occurring), a nation in a world economy cannot successfully participate let alone compete [mere traders have never done very well and have little leverage]. Both, I suppose, may be imported, or dealt with on a business basis from abroad, but the nation which thrives in the long run has both, domestically. There are nations which have one and import the other, but take note, they are unstable, and at the mercy of their logistics. Economists are going to go into apoplexy over this, but it is the simple truth. A prosperous economy simply does not arise out of selling insurance to one another, which the U.S. does, only we charge it.

The inherent wealth of natural resources is self-defining. When resources are used by humans who are engaged in the intellectual and physical production of something of greater value than the material with which they started, and placed into the stream of commerce, commercial wealth is then created, the paradigm of First Financial Instances. Everyone else, no matter what they do, are along for the ride and soak up whatever portion of that wealth which may come their way as "pay" in the chain and process of, *inter alia,* planning and delivery [Financial Secondary Instances – Tertiary being waste (excessive Secondary Instances) and crime]. Financial Secondary Instances are non-productive services associated with the commercial stream of commerce being those which are undeniably necessary to make the economic engine run, a *sine qua non* of the end result, but they in fact take from the fundamental wealth produced for markets and therefore in effect share in the fruits of its creation, the revenue it ultimately generates. Included are other necessary logistical, administrative, marketing, and supportive participants not productive in nature. Also from First Financial Instances is taken, *inter alia,* profits to the owners and equity holders, returns on investment and speculators' bounty, hence,

Secondary Financial Instances. "Economists" would like to hold it to be more complicated than that. It isn't, at least in terms of fundamental wealth. Fundamental wealth is the combining of resources and labor. From there the economic strata starts and is accordingly diluted with the economic service side simply superimposed. Efficiency then becomes the challenge played out in the crucible of competition and competitive markets. Any economy which stands on other than this basic wealth stratagem has feet of clay. Whether this would survive the scrutiny of a dissertation committee as being devoid of the expected bovine scatology is.... Running for cover is always an amusing and entertaining spectacle. Intellectual prevarication is not.

Look around the world. Wealthy nations either have resources, or acquire resources and apply the effects of labor to them, and the most successful have both, and husband both as a matter of national policy. A few countries are endowed with resources and simply market them to the world, and because they participate in this specialized stream of commerce their governments pretty much take care of their citizens and all their needs (often with America's help), at least until the ruling class can no longer pay its bills, and/or America's help is put in doubt. This makes for some, shall we say, complicated geopolitics in view of a potential interruption of the supply of their commodities. Their fate is not far off, and it, too, will be interesting. Energy independence, for example, is more vital to your safety and economic stability than the government would like to have you believe, the very safety of your streets and neighborhoods.

This country husbands neither resources nor the necessary human factors (read, *inter alia*, jobs), indeed, it hampers both for political reasons. Comprehensible given the leadership, but completely incomprehensible given the needs of the nation, national security, and the constitutional oath taken for every office. Non-productive labor and unnecessary services dilute fundamental wealth, and must be administered judiciously just as basic natural and human resources must be managed judiciously.

Administrators are among the biggest soakers, with their numbers and efficiencies being difficult to rein in, as they seem to self-procreate. Insurance, taxes, packaging, transportation, etc., and the list is long, are all important, all necessary within practical limits in a successful economic machine, but in excess [Tertiary] they unnecessarily subtract from fundamental wealth and the health of the economy, and weaken competitive strength. An economist will say, without them we would have nothing. True enough, up to a point. But true wealth is the capital of resources and labor in combination. As overhead goes up (non-productive labor and acquired resources), realistic wealth goes down, being just as inflationary as deficit spending. A real estate broker sells a piece of property and takes a commission. No wealth is created. There may be a profit realized, or a taxable event may have occurred, there may have been income generated in the periphery which in turn is spent, money moves, but that is not wealth as much as the generic economist would have you believe. Part of the overall engine? Yes. Is the system complex? Yes, it is. But, it is a relative thing not only internally, but externally as well in what we now call the global markets. However, it is all based on human and/or natural resources. If competition is stifled, if labor is not focused, if resources are not fostered, the system begins to fail and starts in a downward spiral of inefficiencies, with an upward spiral of expenditures and losses, recovery coming at a very high cost if ever at all, and in more than economic ways.

Nations are not created equal, at least in the sense of being equally endowed. Whether economic systems plod or race along, governments often step in (for political reasons, or otherwise [to prevent "civil" unrest]) to do, as it is claimed, equity. Some people need help. Others not so much. Many a lot. But now, most get something, and virtually everyone gets a check at some time in their lives. Supporting those who have retired, same thing. Cash is spent. Profits are made. Taxes are collected. The economy chugs along. True enough. But no substantive fundamental wealth results, nothing to develop the stability and strength of a nation. Competition in world markets is polluted. Apart from substantive wealth, it's all a house of cards and a fragile, unstable economy results, and engendered dependency ultimately roils into collapse. Yet, not so much as a wisp of ferly even as the face of bankruptcy sneers down upon the nation. We shall surely get that for which we collectively hoped.

Added to this is the problem that promises to pay incomes to people no longer in the workforce, or about to leave it, or were never in it, often with other benefits attached, payable to those who will never again or maybe never did contribute to even the shadow economy (those who do not participate in the creation of fundamental wealth), are staggering. It ought to be well-nigh advisable to observe that this cannot continue to be done. It cannot be practiced *ad infinitum*. Why cannot Americans see this? Or can they, and a different sociological pathology or responsibility set is at work? Or were they blinded? How did that happen? Think about the cases…think about what you have read so far.

And what about taxes to pay state and local legacies far beyond present services for years to come, paid out of earnings and property *ad valorem*? One is effectively being forced to buy property again and again. Property values are being soaked up via dilution by governments to pay over to people who don't, never did, or are no longer making a contribution to the nation's wealth. It is happening and it is accelerating. Isn't that a "taking"? Is it a necessary taking? Isn't there something in the Constitution about the taking of property without compensation? Isn't money property? Isn't deflating the value of one's money by government fiat a taking? Is that lawful? Are there not at least some constitutional limits? Note and think about the last clause of Amendment V, its penumbras, its emanations, its radiations all laden with implications.

Looking at it again, might not an argument be made that Congress's destruction of the economy could be against the law of the land? That is, the public (lawful) debt might not be questioned (as to its integrity) as a constitutional matter, but what about making legislation which itself violates due process (in terms of a taking) according to the traditional terms of the subject (takings) so carefully laid out in majority opinions, dissents, and concurrences handed down for as long as the Court has been sitting? Why may not the Court say there is a point where further debt cast upon the citizens is a denial of due process and does not serve to protect the Union as members of the government are sworn to do? Seems clear enough. If the government came in and seized money (hasn't happened anywhere else…, has it?), that would be a violation of due process…, wouldn't it? In specie and *per valorem* as well. Are there not some parametric restraints, some constitutional limits in this regard? We have all heard the complaint that the government recklessly taxes and spends. It is actually the opposite: the government recklessly spends, and then taxes. Here is how it happens: taxes are either directly levied or the value of the dollar is reduced via deficit spending. The upshot is the same: the government spending money it does not have. Is that "lawful"? It seems some creative lawyer ought to be able to come up with a constitutional theory. Would SCOTUS find this effrontery, or would it recognize the omnibus *Cardozian* maxim of equity, "[l]et the hardship be strong enough and equity will find a way"? Are not officials sworn to uphold the Constitution and protect the nation from enemies, both foreign and domestic? Might not SCOTUS stretch far enough to recognize that what the drafters intended encompasses this issue? This is just something to think about as novel constitutional issues are surely to be presented to the Court in the future.

For another pleasant thought, contemplate this: at base, what is it that undergirds every war? The question is, will the Court be equipped to deal with such matters?

*

And then there is the issue of intra-gender differences or variances capable of being as remarkably varied as inter-gender differences raising the issue of degree of genderness in the context of everything from athletics to personal relationships, and, needless to say, that ubiquitous constitutional quagmire, choices. Any constitutional jurisdiction here? Athletics, perhaps to probably. Personal relationships? Not so much, at least for now.

So, what about LGBT issues and the oncoming myriad of related gender questions? We now have several genders, some mixed according to many authorities, or do we? Scientifically, as well as socially, it is not as simple as that. Recognition and incipient acceptance? It's here, but still veiled. Facilities and accommodations, separate or combined? They are coming. A separate classification, legal status, and a new *corpus juris*, so to speak? Well, yes. Who will ultimately decide? The Supreme Court, unless of course, it finally dawns on Congress that a measurable segment of the population (possibly three to four percent, more or less depending on the authority upon which one chooses to rely, and far more as recognized on the curve analysis, *infra*) is represented here, and legislative responses to the issues would be politically advisable (is not that how Congress acts?).

However, before going there, examine what is actually before us in that regard. It may be looked upon as a frank medical matter, or to put it less pejoratively, a biological matter. There are also those who would say, or at least pitch it as being an environmental matter, or socially and experientially based. But does that make a difference, constitutionally speaking?

Check your sensitivities at the door. Think about it. Regardless as to how one feels, what is before us is an affectable matter calling for delicate balances, not "It has always been a crime…." It is a fact of life unbound by time or place. It impacts citizens' rights. It is therefore a constitutional matter. So, let us think about it for a moment as the matter heads "upstairs." The door has begun to open. See *DeBoer* (now *Obergefell*) and its progeny to come.

Instead of succumbing to "statistics," as commonly as the unenlightened are wont to do, and as we are able to perform mental abstractions, unfettered by notions of the perennial right or wrong polemics since we dwell above such tauromachy, let us visualize two circles of equal size, side by side on the blackboards of our minds. Let us label the one on the left "male" and the one on the right "female." This is traditionally how the world sees gender. The fact is it's not even close to what actually exists, clinically or socially. What we are going to do now is to slide those two circles over and partially upon one another until they overlap by about fifty percent so that the outer circumference of one passes through the center point of the other circle leaving somewhat more than fifty percent of each circle exposed as uncovered on each side, and somewhat less than fifty percent of the area of two circles in the overlapped position, sort of an eclipse (in reality, the overlap would actually be more—clinicians might not be in agreement as to percentages—but for purposes of discussion, the fifty-fifty relationship is sufficient here—sufficient at least to convey the concept, visualization, and message). Now place the center of these two partially overlapped circles over the axis of the horizontal coordinate (the x-axis or abscissa), half above and half below, and the geographic center of the overlapped circles over the vertical coordinate (the y-axis or ordinate), half to the left and half to the right. The x-axis will represent "degree of genderness" (a biological construct), and the y-axis "behavioral expressions" (a psychological construct). As can be readily seen, the possibilities, for practical purposes, are infinite. Now we have started to demonstrate a better or more complete (if not perfect) conception of gender. In other words, gender is far from being an absolute in any sense of degree or manifestation, and is in fact very much on what will turn out to be a multivariate curve. This paradigm will be referred to as the Biobehavioral Genderesque Matrix representing a constellation of infinite variables. Let us disabuse ourselves now of the idea there are only two genders, or at least discrete genders, or even three if that brings comfort to some, which of course is not the point here. To say there are many, with their margins and parameters still unknown, or at least untracked, is an understatement. In other words, gender is on a continuum, referred to by us as a curve. Let's take a look....

We can say this about the overlapped circles: there are those who would find themselves in the un-eclipsed portion of their respective areas, male or female. That is to say, one in the unmasked portion of either the male or female constellation would be viewed as being fully or substantially biologically ingendered, while still recognizing degrees of prominence, yet, at the extremes, left and right, one might observe another as being representative of masculinity or femininity personified, political correctness aside.

In the middle reposes a blend. Notice, however, that it shades from one side to the other with women becoming less feminine as we move to the left of their orbit and men becoming less masculine as we move to the right of their orbit. Or put otherwise, as we move from left of center to the western most limits of the eclipsed portion of the diagram, the more masculinized our female is. And, likewise, the reciprocal for the male who finds himself on the eastern most parts of the overlap being a more feminized male. Know that this has nothing to do with who as human beings, per se, they may be. Masculinized women tend to be…. Feminized men tend to be…. The reciprocals and blends are myriad. The possibilities are veritably infinite. Is there a constitutional question here far beyond *DeBoer*? Far beyond *DeBoer*! Will the bench ever contemplate this let alone take it into consideration, even giving it recognition, or foresee the issues as it crafts its opinion? Well, will it?

In the central area of this diagrammatic representation the most "gender confusion" (see DSM, Gender Identity Disorder) is likely to be observed, if at all. Or to reduce it to a simple explanatory sentence, regardless of our anatomy (which itself is not always manifested in a frank physiological expression gender-wise, sufficient data on which is presently insufficient), the human species ranges from males being very masculine to being very effeminate, and females who are very feminine to very masculine, with many of the males on this curve (in the penumbra of the overlap, if you will) being more feminine than many females, and females who are more masculine than many males, a readily observable fact. Anatomically they usually, but not always, seem to fall into a fairly clear biological classification or gender assignment (behaviorally less so), but the fact is, there are many men far more feminine than many women, and vice versa. It is the near preponderance of the overlap which may be startling to some. No one seems to want to look. Our social inclination has been to turn a blind eye (the political thing to do). It seems to have become an unmentionable. The observant will recognize, however, it is emerging.

It was once fashionable for some to refer to people who tended to cluster in the center, be they male or female by assignment or biological qualification, as "androgynous," and it was all good. It had a sort of fashionable complimentary character, for a while. Descriptive terms for those within their gender category but featuring enduring traits from across the gender lines, however, were often not as complimentary. Androgynous? OK. Much of anything else, not so good. Following a brief episode, even the moniker "androgynous" was not received pleasantly by most, particularly men, many of whom seemed not to have a proclivity to be either female or reflect femaleness, while it seemed palliative to the other party, the oftentimes speaker, usually because it was perceived to be, if not self-elevating, at least a leveling term. The why of this proclivity has apparently escaped most scientists, or so the paucity of reported studies (read that politically selected for publication) would suggest. Maybe it is was a political anathema, and simply avoided, ignored, a common tactic also among the elected. At one time it was often seen by many as a hermaphroditic-like slur or a put-down to ease one's own assignment inadequacies or concerns, perceived or otherwise. The fact is androgyny was ultimately lighted upon for political reasons, and a new era of gender politics began. A new description of "equality" began to emerge, the embryonic struggle for sameness, as it were. It opened the door to a new status which was going to be politically acceptable for some, leading to the opening of doors to other thematic variables which in time would also become politically acceptable for others. In other words (fast forward to today, or tomorrow), to think there is only the male, female, or even homosexual as categories is simply not the case. These are the facts biologically, and now emerging legally.

As stated, there are multivariate expressions both physiologically resting along the abscissa as well as behaviorally resting along the ordinate, constituting florid variations within the paradigm of the Biobehavioral Genderesque Matrix, far beyond the male/female dichotomy. In this abscissa-ordinate display, one will witness a multi-dimensional presentation from the biologically hermaphroditical to colorfully different constellations of transsexual behaviors to ambiguous genitalia to orientation confusion, a myriad of sexual preferences (far outside "today's" male, female, homosexual "triad," as it were), and beyond, *ad infinitum*. We are not a society, or species, of just male and female, nor so far as the world order is concerned for that matter. Quite to the contrary, unlike much if not virtually all of the rest of the animal kingdom, or life forms of any kind, we are indeed a panoply of *gendre differentia* with variations far beyond the brief outline presented here. This is but a scratch.

Social forces may impact the outward expression of these biological variations, provoking some to exhibit behavioral traits, suppressing others, but with the underlying systemics remaining intact. They are effectively uneffected. Affectively is another matter. Reliable observable indications are that this is a frankly biological phenomenon in etiology, at least according to the scientific test of being present *ab initio,* incipient developmentally, refractory to change and stable over time, in fact through all recorded time, in character, prevalence, incidence, and persistence. That seals the issue for scientists. Or put this way, such markers as indicated suggest all of this is inherited and therefore biological, or genetic if you prefer. This, of course, is a matter of rabid debate far from resolution. Although prevalence rates have been debated, different positions taken tend to reflect points of politics apart from points of science. The "why" side of this is of course one of the imponderables to which we do not yet have conclusive evidence beyond the possibility of the fracture of an allele in the chromosomal array, or a random or accidental paring through the scientific optic, or along the same lines and possibly more compelling, simple familial history. Add to all of this the notion that gender is on a curve, and the whole matter becomes a challenge to even ponder let alone organize and isolate for scientific study, but studies are coming. The perpetual problem is, of course, which ones will get published. So far as the law is concerned—hold your breath.

The endocrinologists also have some words to say about this, but their observations are retrospective and looking for biochemical attributional causes (backward science, which much is). Forward testability is not possible in this realm, at least not now, but it is coming. At this time we can only speculate about systemic features which may stimulate and influence any display, manifestation, or expression, even including the characteristic gender expressions, as potentially seated in the genetic map, regulatory tissue at the cellular level, the brain, and/or the body's biochemistry, reflecting not only physical manifestation but attendant emotional components as well. What can only be said is the "equation" is what it is for now, which is a long step away from where the conceptualization was on the subject less than a professional generation ago (see the first DSM), and certainly in terms of where it is going. What does that have to do with what we are doing here? Full integration? Implausible for now. What about equal protection? Any due process lurking here? Think about it. Some answers may be emerging. Questions: why would we be concerned with such matters here? And, will these notions ever be considered by the Supreme Court in the case of *DeBoer v. Snyder* and its companions dealing with homosexual, same sex or "same gender" marriage? This should be interesting. Indeed, will the Court even peer beyond the case(s) before it? It has had a history of not doing so. I wonder why?

*

De novo, e una ventra mas, divorce at one time was a criminal, or a quasi-criminal proceeding, and virtually unavailable to the crowd. Even the aristocracy had to resort to other measures to obtain relief. The right to a decree was often based on criminal behavior of one sort or another. To the parents or at least the grandparents of the reader of this book, it was an unmentionable. Like abortion, one couldn't use the word in polite company.

Today, prior to marriage, especially in cases where one or both of the parties to the planned wedding have substantial assets, or are accustomed to seeking legal consultation in the ordinary course of their lives before doing anything financially significant, preplanning for divorce is not only common, but advisable. Couples actually make preparations for divorce well before the marriage ever takes place, the now celebrated "prenuptial agreement," sometimes confirmed in a postnuptial contract with titles to assets being adjusted by agreement, antebellum. May the farce be with you. In almost every circuit, city, commonwealth, parish, or state court, divorce cases outnumber all other civil cases combined. In all jurisdictions, mentioned earlier, they exceed all other kinds of civil cases. As a result, sometimes separate divorce courts have even been set up to handle just matrimonial matters, splitting property and the associated issues concerning the affected children. They are called "Family Courts" to go along with Juvenile Courts, Drug Courts, and what not. Charming! The next court is left to your imagination, but it's coming. The guv-a-ment's gonna take care of it. How comforting.

More is lost in the divorce courts than from all other sources and causes of loss in the country, directly and indirectly, financially (with the possible exception of deficit spending), emotionally, in terms of stability, deep-rooted traditions and otherwise. A few decades ago, state legislatures in most jurisdictions passed what were dubbed "no-fault divorce laws" where one party to a marriage could file with a court and obtain a divorce commonly only having to tell the court that the objects of matrimony have broken down and there is no reasonable likelihood the marriage can be preserved. Many courts do not even require the testimony on oath. Simply say it in open court, *pro confesso,* upon the defendant's default or following the withdrawal of its answer to the suit. *Presto*! Divorced! Generally the court would require matters of property and children be resolved before the divorce was finalized, although there could be exceptions under "exigent" circumstances. There even cases where the court has entered judgment *nunc pro tunc* making its effective date at a prior time. Nevertheless, the three-way contract of matrimony between the two partners of the marriage (at least in accordance with today's standards) and the State could be broken at the will of one of the partners, and for no reason other than the testimony just quoted, true or not.

Half of marriages end in divorce, and the marriage failure rate for those who remarry is worse according to several studies, not surprisingly. The effect upon children is devastating, usually forever life scarring, the human glue of trust forever destroyed. It catapults through their lives forever changing structures of not only stability and trust, but contaminating future relationships by blood as well as by law, and the failure which is cast upon them tumbles on. There are exceptions, but few. The family and all that is good which comes from it is gone. A sequela to all of this is that many, heading to most, simply never will get married. Why bother? (Fifty years ago, illegitimacy rates were approaching ten percent and considered a national crisis. Today they are exceeding fifty percent, and it's hardly discussed, inappropriate to do so. Telescoped out, children will become wards [property] of the state. Nah! That's never happened.) The net result is the "family" in effect is becoming an institution of running dogs. Simple observation tells the tale. Question: what brought this about, and, why is this even possibly relevant here?

*

A cure for cancer has been found! Yes, I know you know the reality of the matter is there is no cure for cancer for there is no one disease of "cancer." Rather it is a broad spectrum of diseases profoundly different in nature, and how they respond differently to a myriad of therapies, if at all, as well as what their suspected etiologies may be, at least for the time being. Several pathologies are included under the rubric of cancer, which aren't technically cancers at all. But, it's good for business. They may be subsumed under the heading of cancer, but to think of it as "a" disease is inaccurate.

Failures of the immune system (and the general health of the organism) and the body's ability to heal itself or repair diseased tissue account for more "cancers" than do the ocean of "carcinogens" in which we all live, and this is likely an understatement. It may be the carcinogens overwhelm whatever immune response is or was present. Propensity is inherited, no doubt. In most cases we have weakened ourselves. Diet and lack of activity, as is the environment, are among the culprits. In other words, in large measure we are essentially responsible for, and/or on occasion hereditarily predisposed to, most of our own cancers. Trillions, not billions, of dollars have been thrown at the quest for a "cure." On balance and overall save some remarkable but specific breakthroughs, little can be shown for the effort. No one has demonstrated the efficacy for which this money was or is being spent as compared to other areas of science. It is a black hole. "Cure rates" measured in normal life extensions and remissions have been overall relatively nil. A case of early detection where the patient lives five years with aggressive and expensive treatment is often no different than a lately discovered cancer where death comes quickly, but the past years were happy and not filled with anxiety or an avalanche of wasted money and nauseating "treatments" is just as common a scenario. Those who advertise to the contrary are capitalizing on the desperate. Very sad, but merely further commentary as to what has happened to us as a culture. On the other hand, as to some pathologies, early detection is the *sine qua non* to a road back to health. Unfortunately, the fact is, therapies extend life in many cases on the average of months in some cases, if at all, taking a terrible toll on the patient physically, mentally, and financially, while some have had, but only a few, miraculous effects. It is true, instances of remarkable progress have been made, even spectacular. But relatively few diagnoses have such an outcome. And many, if not most, of those which might be cured are detected too late. The fact is, we will look back on our present-day therapies and find them as barbaric and foolish as bloodletting or trephining.

At the same time, the failure rate is certainly no reason to stop trying. Yet overall, the cost-benefit ratios in many cases look something like more than a million dollars a patient, if not a patient year, in a setting where unfortunately most die anyway. Exceptions abound, which of course puts into place the powerful effect of the variable (or random) ratio of reinforcement paradigm, and the quest resultantly continues. Overall, progress is disappointing (at least when considering the government's declaration of war on cancer a half century ago even being a plank in a presidential platform), often dismal, and frustrating to those working to get these pathologies under control both at the point of etiology or their first manifestation. The biochemistry behind the constellation of diseases is unimaginably complex. The keys rests in the immune system.

However, there are bright spots which wouldn't exist without the effort. The recent event of opening the genetic code is the one major break-through which has been and will significantly continue to be a road map to cures, finding ways in helping the body to repair itself at the cellular level. We are now on the brink. In other words, life is going to change because of all of this. But with cures, a seismic economic impact will be felt. An unimaginable financial crisis is in store, totally apart from the cost of therapies. The entire Social Security system and its counterparts will suffer an actuarial default in anticipation of being unable to fund itself in the very short term. Private and public pensions will snap under the weight of life expectancy being extended another ten years, just to guess a number. Everything in this realm of health care will have to be rationed. The nation will become top heavy with oldsters. What's Congress going to do?! Nothing. Or maybe use all of its might to figure out a way to make it worse. There will just not be enough necessary resources of all kinds to go around. Every single human service will be overwhelmed, many unable to adequately function, ultimately none at all. Next step? Triage. By whom? A panel of appointees? And we thought the Third Reich and its state-owned children was abhorrent, if anyone remembers (we do not honestly teach history any more…and so we are destined….)!

Then, someone is going to file a federal lawsuit. Penumbras? Deep-seated traditions? The conscience of the people? Fair play and substantial justice, be he prince or pauper? So, what is the Court to do…that which Congress refused or failed to do? Why do we ask this? Because there is precedent. Question: what will be the Court's solution? Surely that is where it will end up, will it not? Or will it be up to the fifth branch (the people)? Congress will not touch it….

*

Here is how the final scenario will unfold: The President is faced with eminent nuclear strikes against the United States; harbors will be lost, cities will be lost, the seat of government will be lost, possibly all could be lost. The citizenry will be cast into sheer panic. Animal behaviors will emerge. First responders will not appear, or remain. They will be overwhelmed and have other matters which to attend.

Intelligence has made it clear not only are the plans of attack complete with the means available, but the process of delivery exists (until recently the missing link—the "cold war" posed less of a threat than was publically believed) and is about to be initiated. There is little if any doubt. The President, not wanting to be hung by the heels from a light-post on the Mall, orders the Attorney General to file an original action with SCOTUS for a declaratory judgment as to the legality of the classified intended response to this imminent and real threat, first and pre-emptive nuclear strikes of overwhelming proportions expected to effectively reduce the would-be aggressors' nations to deserts of glass. The enemies' positions, personnel, and weaponry have been pre-targeted into ballistic and cruise missiles ready for delivery along with other guided ordnance. The enemies will essentially be annihilated. If struck first, the United States will unequivocally suffer the same fate. Notice the use of the term "will."

What if our leader is gutless and not willing to fight using whatever it takes to win? What if our leader thinks we have it coming? If the United States is defeated (seems inconceivable, doesn't it?), the nation's leaders will surely be executed in the most unceremonious way for war crimes attendant to tardy last ditch (probably nuclear) efforts to save themselves, no question, as would have been the case at the end of the Second World War had it turned out differently, which it almost did. Few realize how close it was.

Let us try to see their point of view. Maybe we should negotiate. Maybe we can change their minds. Shall we not try it first? My God, the world is on fire! But the nation is asleep, or no one sees it or is willing to act. Cowardice and geopolitical indifference historically have always ended in defeat.

Note that lawyers on battlefields accompanying U.S. forces is now not just commonplace, rather it is the operational standard. Rule of engagement are politicized. That's how we do it now. But, under the circumstances here, time is of the essence. Without clearance from the Court, the President has informed the Joint Chiefs there will be no pre-emptive strike. Backwater contacts with key members of Congress have indicated there will be no help there, a not surprising revelation. Additionally, confidentiality would be out of the question. Twit City has members with their own personal agenda; shallow, feckless, spineless political parasites. You have seen it. A few are self-absorbed, narcissistic, born leakers putting self ahead of country. Foot soldiers of the Constitution they are not, and will never be.

The Chairman of the fourth branch of government has quietly but clearly indicated personally to the President if no orders are immediately forthcoming from her, she would be taken into protective custody (the Secret Service will pose no barrier), removed to a safe haven, and he will personally lead the launch of a pre-emptive strike. It is known as duty, a concept understood by few...a concept no longer taught.

Filing suit is nevertheless elected. How will the Court rule? SCOTUS deciding a military matter?! How could that be? How could it know? A body politic, again, made up of members who have never served, aren't serving, and never will serve so much as a day in harm's way, most frankly incapable of service, and as with most other members of government, totally devoid of any military knowledge or how the military functions operationally, strategically, and tactically, what it can, and cannot do and how quickly, now to decide a military question let alone a question of war relative to not just the security, but the very existence of the nation and the survival of its inhabitants? Are you serious?! Is there even jurisdiction here? Why were such matters constitutionally put in the hands of a Commander-in-Chief in the first place? Question: will this happen, and when it does...what results? And if the Four Star holds to his word...a nation to which he has pledged his life and sacred honor...?

XXI

EPILOGUE

hy all of these extraneous subjects, these seemingly wild scenarios (which they are not – they are real)? What do these things have to do with our examination of the work of the Court here, or its politicized nature, its seemingly contemptuous behavior, or legerdemain? If you haven't figured it out by now, one of us has failed. How does all of this fit with or among *Roth* and *Snyder,* or *Griswold* and *Lawrence*, or *Sullivan* and *Citizens United,* or *Stenberg* and *Glucksberg,* etc.? These scenarios are on the way. They represent but a few of the calamities with which you will be faced. Your work here is only a start. I do not envy you. I do not envy your generation. These issues will ultimately fall into the hands of the Supreme Court, save possibly one.

*

The President cannot help. Congress will not help. If the nation falls, it will be from within. A bankruptcy in statesmanship, *viz.*, politics, will be the end. America will be defeated because of internal abuses and lack of leadership at all levels. Somehow, the framers didn't take this into consideration. The founding fathers probably saw no need to do so. Character. Re-read the last sentence of the Declaration, and then read it again. Do you know what ultimately happened to the signers (I urge you to research this)? The behaviors we see today were unthinkable then. Why is that so? What has taken away from us all that was possessed then? Just think where we would be if it were otherwise, a disciplined people and nation....

These are just some of the unimaginable problems on the horizon. The clarion call was sounded years ago (see *inter alia*: Plato's *The Republic*), but has gone unheeded. Possibly the best hope is if the members of the Supreme Court can maintain their present self-appointed authority (beyond *Marbury*) and ability to carry out orders over time (*viz.*, avoid rebellion), it is the only body which can act quickly enough in the setting of a politically paralyzed, self-serving, elected, irresponsible government, feckless and functionless in its characterological vacuum to deal with such otherwise overwhelming problems, given the nation's present state of affairs, and make the needed decisions possibly saving the nation, even if it is five to four.

*

Congratulations, you have a new perspective. Please know I did not set out in this work to offend anyone but to encourage the reader to consider the issues discussed herein and to form his or her own opinions.

Oh, and by the way, it did make a difference to that star fish. But, who was the fisherman?

I invite you to continue this journey with me....

APPENDIX I

In C O N G R E S S, JULY 4, 1776.

The unanimous Declaration of the thirteen united States of America,

When in the Course of human events, it becomes necessary for one people to dissolve the political bands which have connected them with another, and to assume among the powers of the earth, the separate and equal station to which the Laws of Nature and of Nature's God entitle them, a decent respect to the opinions of mankind requires that they should declare the causes which impel them to the separation.————We hold these truths to be self-evident, that all men are created equal, that they are endowed by their Creator with certain unalienable Rights, that among these are Life, Liberty and the pursuit of Happiness.————That to secure these rights, Governments are instituted among Men, deriving their just powers from the consent of the governed, ————That whenever any Form of Government becomes destructive of these ends, it is the Right of the People to alter or to abolish it, and to institute new Government, laying its foundation on such principles and organizing its powers in such form, as to them shall seem most likely to effect their Safety and Happiness. Prudence, indeed, will dictate that Governments long established should not be changed for light and transient causes; and accordingly all experience hath shewn, that mankind are more disposed to suffer, while evils are sufferable, than to right themselves by abolishing the forms to which they are accustomed. But when a long train of abuses and usurpations, pursuing invariably the same Object evinces a design to reduce them under absolute Despotism, it is their right, it is their duty, to throw off such Government, and to provide new Guards for their future security.——Such has been the patient sufferance of these Colonies; and such is now the necessity which constrains them to alter their former Systems of Government. The history of the present King of Great Britain is a history of repeated injuries and usurpations, all having in direct object the establishment of an absolute Tyranny over these States. To prove this, let Facts be submitted to a candid world.——He has refused his Assent to Laws, the most wholesome and necessary for the public good.——He has forbidden his Governors to pass Laws of immediate and pressing importance, unless suspended in their operation till his Assent should be obtained; and when so suspended, he has utterly neglected to attend to them.——He has refused to pass other Laws for the accommodation of large districts of people, unless those people would relinquish the right of Representation in the Legislature, a right inestimable to them and formidable to tyrants only.—He has called together legislative bodies at places unusual, uncomfortable, and distant from the depository of their public Records, for the sole purpose of fatiguing them into compliance with his measures.—He has dissolved Representative Houses repeatedly, for opposing with manly firmness his invasions on the rights of the people.——He has refused for a long time, after such dissolutions, to cause others to be elected; whereby the Legislative powers, incapable of Annihilation, have returned to the People at large for their exercise; the State remaining in the mean time exposed to all the dangers of invasion from without, and convulsions within.——He has endeavoured to prevent the population of these States; for that purpose obstructing the Laws for Naturalization of Foreigners; refusing to pass others to encourage their migrations hither, and raising the conditions of new Appropriations of Lands. ——He has obstructed the Administration of Justice, by refusing his Assent to Laws for establishing Judiciary powers.——He has made Judges dependent on his Will alone, for the tenure of their offices, and the amount and payment of their salaries.——He has erected a multitude of New Offices, and sent hither swarms of Officers to harrass our people, and eat out their substance.——He has kept among us, in times of peace, Standing Armies without the Consent of our legislatures.——He has affected to render the Military independent of and superior to the Civil power.——He has combined with others to subject us to a jurisdiction foreign to our constitution, and unacknowledged by our laws; giving his Assent to their Acts of pretended Legislation: —For Quartering large bodies of armed troops among us: ——For protecting them, by a mock Trial, from punishment for any Murders which they should commit on the Inhabitants of these States: —For cutting off our Trade with all parts of the world: ——For imposing Taxes on us without our Consent: ——For depriving us in many cases, of the benefits of Trial by Jury: ——For transporting us beyond Seas to be tried for pretended offences.—For abolishing the free System of English Laws in a neighbouring

Province, establishing therein an Arbitrary government, and enlarging its Boundaries so as to render it at once an example and fit instrument for introducing the same absolute rule into these Colonies: ——For taking away our Charters, abolishing our most valuable Laws, and altering fundamentally the Forms of our Governments: ——For suspending our own Legislatures, and declaring themselves invested with power to legislate for us in all cases whatsoever.——He has abdicated Government here, by declaring us out of his Protection and waging War against us.—He has plundered our seas, ravaged our Coasts, burnt our towns, and destroyed the lives of our people.——He is at this time transporting large Armies of foreign Mercenaries to compleat the works of death, desolation and tyranny, already begun with circumstances of Cruelty & perfidy scarcely paralleled in the most barbarous ages, and totally unworthy the Head of a civilized nation.——He has constrained our fellow Citizens taken Captive on the high Seas to bear Arms against their Country, to become the executioners of their friends and Brethren, or to fall themselves by their Hands.——He has excited domestic insurrections amongst us, and has endeavoured to bring on the inhabitants of our frontiers, the merciless Indian Savages, whose known rule of warfare, is an undistinguished destruction of all ages, sexes and conditions.——In every stage of these Oppressions We have Petitioned for Redress in the most humble terms: Our repeated Petitions have been answered only by repeated injury. A Prince whose character is thus marked by every act which may define a Tyrant, is unfit to be the ruler of a free people.——Nor have We been wanting in attentions to our Brittish brethren. We have warned them from time to time of attempts by their legislature to extend an unwarrantable jurisdiction over us. We have reminded them of the circumstances of our emigration and settlement here. We have appealed to their native justice and magnanimity, and we have conjured them by the ties of our common kindred to disavow these usurpations, which, would inevitably interrupt our connections and correspondence. They too have been deaf to the voice of justice and of consanguinity. We must, therefore, acquiesce in the necessity, which denounces our Separation, and hold them, as we hold the rest of mankind, Enemies in War, in Peace Friends.

We, therefore, the Representatives of the united States of America, in General Congress, Assembled, appealing to the Supreme Judge of the world for the rectitude of our intentions, do, in the Name, and by Authority of the good People of these Colonies, solemnly publish and declare, That these United Colonies are, and of Right ought to be Free and Independent States; that they are Absolved from all Allegiance to the British Crown, and that all political connection between them and the State of Great Britain, is and ought to be totally dissolved; and that as Free and Independent States, they have full Power to levy War, conclude Peace, contract Alliances, establish Commerce, and to do all other Acts and Things which Independent States may of right do. And for the support of this Declaration, with a firm reliance on the protection of divine Providence, we mutually pledge to each other our Lives, our Fortunes and our sacred Honor.

APPENDIX II

THE BILL OF RIGHTS AND 14TH AMENDMENT

Amendment I

Congress shall make no law respecting an establishment of religion, or prohibiting the free exercise thereof, or abridging the freedom of speech, or of the press; or the right of the people peaceably to assemble, and to petition the Government for a redress of grievances.

Amendment II

A well regulated Militia, being necessary to the security of a free State, the right of the people to keep and bear Arms, shall not be infringed.

Amendment III

No Soldier shall, in time of peace be quartered in any house, without the consent of the Owner, nor in time of war, but in a manner to be prescribed by law.

Amendment IV

The right of the people to be secure in their persons, houses, papers, and effects, against unreasonable searches and seizures, shall not be violated, and no Warrants shall issue, but upon probable cause, supported by Oath or affirmation, and particularly describing the place to be searched, and the persons or things to be seized.

Amendment V

No person shall be held to answer for a capital, or otherwise infamous crime, unless on a presentment or indictment of a Grand Jury, except in cases arising in the land or naval forces, or in the Militia, when in actual service in time of War or public danger; nor shall any person be subject for the same offence to be twice put in jeopardy of life or limb; nor shall be compelled in any criminal case to be a witness against himself, nor be deprived of life, liberty, or property, without due process of law; nor shall private property be taken for public use, without just compensation.

Amendment VI

In all criminal prosecutions, the accused shall enjoy the right to a speedy and public trial, by an impartial jury of the State and district wherein the crime shall have been committed, which district shall have been previously ascertained by law, and to be informed of the nature and cause of the accusation; to be confronted with the witnesses against him; to have compulsory process for obtaining witnesses in his favor, and to have the Assistance of Counsel for his defence.

Amendment VII

In Suits at common law, where the value in controversy shall exceed twenty dollars, the right of trial by jury shall be preserved, and no fact tried by a jury, shall be otherwise re-examined in any Court of the United States, than according to the rules of the common law.

Amendment VIII

Excessive bail shall not be required, nor excessive fines imposed, nor cruel and unusual punishments inflicted.

Amendment IX

The enumeration in the Constitution, of certain rights, shall not be construed to deny or disparage others retained by the people.

Amendment X

The powers not delegated to the United States by the Constitution, nor prohibited by it to the States, are reserved to the States respectively, or to the people.

————

Amendment XIV

Section 1.

All persons born or naturalized in the United States, and subject to the jurisdiction thereof, are citizens of the United States and of the state wherein they reside. No state shall make or enforce any law which shall abridge the privileges or immunities of citizens of the United States; nor shall any state deprive any person of life, liberty, or property, without due process of law; nor deny to any person within its jurisdiction the equal protection of the laws.

Section 2.

Representatives shall be apportioned among the several states according to their respective numbers, counting the whole number of persons in each state, excluding Indians not taxed. But when the right to vote at any election for the choice of electors for President and Vice President of the United States, Representatives in Congress, the executive and judicial officers of a state, or the members of the legislature thereof, is denied to any of the male inhabitants of such state, being twenty-one years of age, and citizens of the United States, or in any way abridged, except for participation in rebellion, or other crime, the basis of representation therein shall be reduced in the proportion which the number of such male citizens shall bear to the whole number of male citizens twenty-one years of age in such state.

Section 3.

No person shall be a Senator or Representative in Congress, or elector of President and Vice President, or hold any office, civil or military, under the United States, or under any state, who, having previously taken an oath, as a member of Congress, or as an officer of the United States, or as a member of any state legislature, or as an executive or judicial officer of any state, to support the Constitution of the United States, shall have engaged in insurrection or rebellion against the same, or given aid or comfort to the enemies thereof. But Congress may by a vote of two-thirds of each House, remove such disability.

Section 4.

The validity of the public debt of the United States, authorized by law, including debts incurred for payment of pensions and bounties for services in suppressing insurrection or rebellion, shall not be questioned. But neither the United States nor any state shall assume or pay any debt or obligation incurred in aid of insurrection or rebellion against the United States, or any claim for the loss or emancipation of any slave; but all such debts, obligations and claims shall be held illegal and void.

Section 5.

The Congress shall have power to enforce, by appropriate legislation, the provisions of this article.

TABLE OF AUTHORITIES

www.ingramcontent.com/pod-product-compliance
Lightning Source LLC
Chambersburg PA
CBHW060112200326
41518CB00008B/805